Clojure in Action

Clojure in Action

AMIT RATHORE

MANNING

SHELTER ISLAND

To my parents, my son, and my wonderful wife

For online information and ordering of this and other Manning books, please visit
www.manning.com. The publisher offers discounts on this book when ordered in quantity.
For more information, please contact

> Special Sales Department
> Manning Publications Co.
> 20 Baldwin Road
> PO Box 261
> Shelter Island, NY 11964
> Email: orders@manning.com

Manning Publications Co. 20 Baldwin Road PO Box 261 Shelter Island, NY 11964	Development editor: Susan Harkins Copyeditors: Linda Recktenwald Typesetter: Dennis Dalinnik Cover designer: Marija Tudor

ISBN: 9781935182597
Printed in the United States of America
1 2 3 4 5 6 7 8 9 10 – MAL – 17 16 15 14 13 12 11

brief contents

v

contents

13 More on functional programming 307

14 Protocols, records, and types 339

15 More macros and DSLs 367

preface

I can tell you how much I enjoy being a geek. I can tell you how fascinated I was with the punch-cards my dad showed me back in 1985. I can tell you how I got my first computer when I was seven. And I can tell you that I've loved programming since 1989. I can tell you a great many things about all that, but I'm not sure how interesting they'd be.

Instead, let me tell you about my quest for an answer of sorts. There's been one issue about our industry that has continued to puzzle me over the years: why is it that no software project is ever as simple as it seems? Why is it that no project ever comes out on time and on budget? Why are there always bugs? Why doesn't it ever quite do what was intended? And why is it always so hard to make changes to the software? No matter how clean the slate is when a project starts, why does it always become a big ball of mud?

Almost everyone acknowledges the problem, and they seem to accept the status quo. Most of our industry deals with it by adding buffers to schedules and budgets, and by accepting mediocre software. Isn't there a better way?

This book is not the answer, not by a long shot. But it is part of my exploration of the way forward. It is my notion that better tools can help us create better software.

This raises the obvious question: what is a better tool? Better at what? I believe the answer is that a better tool is one that helps manage complexity better. After all, complexity is one of the root causes for the state of things in our world. Indeed, Fred Brooks wrote about complexity in a paper as early as 1986. He drew a distinction between essential complexity and accidental complexity. Essential complexity is inherent in the problem domain, whereas accidental complexity is introduced by things external to the problem domain. For example, in a software project that deals with filing taxes, complexity that arises from convoluted tax-codes is part of the domain, and hence essential. Any complexity that arises from, say, employing the rather intricate visitor pattern, is accidental.

So let me rephrase my statement: a better tool helps us minimize accidental complexity. It lets us do our job as best as we can, while getting out of the way. And great tools go beyond that; they give us leverage. They let us amplify our effectiveness as designers and programmers, without introducing problems of their own. The Lisp programming language was designed to be just such a tool. And Clojure is an amazingly well designed Lisp.

Every programmer who stumbles onto Lisp has a story, and mine is similar to many. I started my professional career with Java, and eventually ran into a wall with what I could create with it. I started exploring dynamic languages and they felt more expressive and malleable. Mostly, I enjoyed using Python and Ruby, and wrote several nontrivial applications with them. I was working at a company called ThoughtWorks at the time, and I had a lot of like-minded colleagues to work with. Eventually, one of them turned me onto Common Lisp. The more I read about the language, the more I began to realize how primitive other languages were. I used Common Lisp on a few personal projects, but never did anything major with it; it did however have a profound effect on my code in all the other languages I was using, and I kept looking for an opportunity to use a Lisp on a real-world project.

I finally got my chance in 2008. I had moved to the Bay Area in California, and ended up joining the founding team of a startup named Runa. In true Silicon Valley tradition, our first office was in the founder's garage. We wanted to disrupt the world of eCommerce with Runa. The idea was to collect lots of data, use machine-learning techniques to make sense of it all, and then present personal deals to select shoppers in real-time. And in order to do all that, we had to overcome serious technological challenges. The system needed to handle thousands of requests a second. It needed to handle several terabytes of data a day. It needed to be scriptable via a set of high-level, declarative DSLs. It needed to support hot code-swaps so it could be updated on the fly. It needed to run on the cloud, and it needed to be entirely API-driven. And we had to build it without much in the way of resources; we were an engineering team of three.

With these kinds of constraints, we needed a language that gave us leverage. So we turned to this new language called Clojure. It was a modern, functional language that ran on the JVM. It also promised to solve the problems inherent in concurrent, multi-threaded code. And it was a Lisp!

I was the architect at this startup, and am now the VP of Engineering. I staked the success of our future on this new (pre-release at the time) programming language created by someone who I had never heard of before. But everything I read about it resonated with me; all the pieces fit. We've been using Clojure ever since with incredible success. Our team has grown over the past three years, but it's still about an order of magnitude smaller than other teams at similar companies. I suspect they're using plain old Java. If nothing else, the past three years have upheld my belief that tools matter, and that some are far superior to others.

When we started out, I used to think of our usage of Clojure as our secret weapon—but the Clojure community is so strong and supportive that making it an open secret seemed like a much better idea. I started the Bay Area Clojure User Group, and we've now got hundreds of members. I like to think there are dozens of people who have come to our meetings, liked what they heard, and decided to use Clojure on their own projects.

In that same spirit, I wrote this book to share my experience with Clojure with you. It's my hope that I can convince some of you to look beyond the parentheses to what is possible with a Lisp in general, and with Clojure specifically. I hope you find this book useful and enjoyable.

acknowledgments

The past two years have been quite an intense experience. Writing a book while working on a startup (and having your first child) is definitely not a recipe for relaxation! I would never have managed to get through it without the support of my incredibly patient wife, Deepthi. There were times when I just hit a blank wall and her encouragement is all that kept me going. Thanks, sweetheart, I could never have done this without you!

I would also like to thank my parents who started me down this path all those years ago. I grew up in India at a time when computers were these fantastical things, out of reach for most people. They took a loan to buy me a computer, instead of buying their first car, and without that I wouldn't be here today. So thanks a million, Mom and Dad!

I also want to acknowledge Ravi Mohan, who in 2001 pointed me to Lisp and to Paul Graham's essays. Thanks for showing me the way! And, I guess, thanks also to Paul Graham, who is an inspiration to many of us.

Thanks to the folks at Runa, for letting me work on this book. Ashok Narasimhan, the founder, was extremely supportive of the whole effort. The rest of my colleagues were also very supportive. Specifically, I'd like to thank Robert Berge, Kyle Oba, and George Jahad for their feedback and encouragement. Finally, I'd like to give special thanks to Siva Jagadeesan who has supported me throughout this effort in so many ways.

At Manning, I'd like to thank Michael Stephens who provided guidance, feedback, and support during the many months it took to get the book done, and my development editor Susan Harkins for her help and patience and for sticking with the project from beginning to end. The production team of Linda Recktenwald, Dennis Dalinnik, Janet Vail, and Mary Piergies also deserves my thanks for turning my manuscript into the book you are reading today.

Finally, thanks to the following reviewers who read my manuscript during development and provided invaluable feedback: Doug Warren, Deepak Vohra, Jeroen Benckhuijsen, Sivakumar Thyagarajan, Kevin Butler, Jason Rogers, Craig Smith, Stuart Caborn, Robby O'Connor, Tim Moore, Peter Pavlovich, Federico Tomassetti, Steve Freeman, Dave Pawson, Joshua Heyer, Keith Kim, Christopher David Stevenson, Ramnivas Laddad, Andrew Oswald, Pratik Patel, Baishampayan Ghose, Anton Mazkovoi, Christopher Bailey, and Tom Flaherty.

Special thanks to Tom Flaherty who also served as technical proofreader for the book, checking the code and reading the final manuscript one more time, during production.

about this book

Programming languages vary a great deal on the productivity spectrum. On the one extreme, we have machine code and assembly language. Then come languages like C, eventually giving way to C++, Java, Scala, and others. On the other side of the spectrum are the functional and dynamic languages. Some of the favorites here include Ruby, Python, Perl, Erlang, Haskell, ML, and others. And these are just a tiny fraction of the landscape—there are dozens of other popular languages, and hundreds more that aren't in as much use.

With this dizzying alphabet soup of options, how does one choose the right language? Quite rightly, a lot of folks realize that there is no single correct choice, and that it depends on the job at hand. Even so, most people have one general purpose language that they use for most tasks. This book is about a new language called Clojure—one that is a compelling choice for general purpose programming.

The Clojure programming language has been influenced by dozens of languages and has taken the best of many worlds to become what it is today. Clojure is a modern Lisp, and it embraces the functional paradigm. It also runs on the JVM. This makes for a very potent combination. In today's world, where programmer productivity is paramount, Clojure shines. All else being equal, a good Clojure team can run circles around significantly larger teams using other languages. I've seen this in my own startup over the past three years.

How to use this book

Learning Clojure can be quite a leap for a lot of programmers. The drastically different syntax, the move from imperative to functional programming, immutability, the macro system ... these can be daunting. This book takes a slow and steady approach to learning the language and the various pieces. It assumes no prior experience with Lisp or with any functional programming language. It starts out with the absolute basics, and slowly layers on the different features of the language in a way to make it all fit together in an intuitive manner. It takes a first-principles approach to all the topics, first explaining why something needs to be done a certain way, and only then talking about the Clojure way.

Once you get past the basics, the book moves onto real-world usage of Clojure. You'll see how to write test-driven Clojure, access data-stores of various kinds (both relational and the NoSQL variety), create web services, use messaging to scale your applications to handle large volumes of traffic, use map/reduce to process data, understand distributed computing, and build up your business logic through domain-specific languages (DSLs).

To get the most out of the book, I've assumed you're familiar with an OO language like Java, C#, or C++, but no background in Lisp or Clojure is required.

Roadmap

Chapter 1 whets your appetite by giving a high-level description of the language, and what to expect from the remainder of the book

Chapter 2 goes over the the basics of installing and getting started with Clojure. It then dives into the most fundamental concept in Clojure—that of a first-class function. It completes the introduction by addressing program flow and the core data-structures.

Chapter 3 is about going deeper: it addresses functions in more depth, and then describes the scoping rules of the language. You'll discover that in addition to lexical scoping, Clojure supports dynamic scope, which behaves very differently. This chapter also addresses another unique feature of the language: destructuring. This lets you disintegrate data-structures to get at just those parts that you care about. Finally, it looks at Clojure's support of meta-data, that is data that can be used to annotate other data. A lot of this will be different from what you may be used to, but at the end of this chapter, you'll be able to read and write most simple Clojure programs.

Chapter 4 discusses Clojure's approach to polymorphism. If you're coming from the Java/C++ world, this is going to be quite different. Clojure's multimethods are an extremely open-ended way to implement polymorphic behavior, and they give the control of method dispatch directly to the programmer.

Chapter 5 covers how Clojure embraces the JVM. No programming language can succeed without a strong set of libraries, and Clojure neatly sidesteps this problem. It makes it trivial to use any Java library in your programs, giving you instant access to the thousands of battle-tested frameworks and libraries available. It also lets you continue to benefit from your previous investment in the Java stack.

Chapter 6 addresses Clojure's approach to state-management and concurrency. Again, this is a fresh take on the problem of mutable state. Clojure sports extremely performant immutable data-structures and implements an efficient STM system (software transactional memory). This combination lets the language offer built-in support for correct, safe, and lock-free concurrency. This is a big deal! Your programs can take advantage of multiple cores without any of the problems associated with traditional multi-threaded code.

Chapter 7 looks at yet another feature of Clojure that is different from most other programming languages. This is the macro system (not to be confused with C macros and the like). Clojure essentially provides language-level support for code-generation. It has a hook in its runtime that allows programmers to transform and generate code any way they like. This is an incredibly powerful feature that blurs the line between the language designer and an application programmer. It allows anyone to add features to the language.

Chapter 8 shows how you can raise your productivity level significantly by combining the process of writing test-driven code with the Clojure REPL (read-eval-print-loop, which is Clojure's command prompt shell). It also addresses mocking and stubbing functions to enable better unit-testing tactics.

Chapter 9 is about data storage. It not only talks about traditional relational databases such as MySQL, but also newer NoSQL ones such as HBase and Redis. With this information, you'll be able to pick the right one for your project, and know how to access them from Clojure in an idiomatic manner.

Chapter 10 looks at Clojure and the web. In this chapter, you'll build a simple web-service framework on your own. You'll also explore a few open-source projects that make it trivial to talk HTTP in your own projects—whether it is an API server or a dynamic website.

Chapter 11 shows how to use messaging systems to communicate between multiple Clojure processes. Specifically, you'll use RabbitMQ to build a distributed computing framework that can form the basis of your own little Clojure compute cluster.

Chapter 12 is about data processing with Clojure. It explains the map/reduce paradigm using the Clojure functions of the same name. You'll build a little map/reduce library that can be used as the basis for your own data-processing programs. Finally, you'll create a distributed master/slave data-processing framework that will allow you to process large volumes of data by harnessing Clojure worker processes running on multiple computers.

Chapter 13 dives deep into the functional programming paradigm. You'll create your own versions of the core higher-order functions: map, reduce, and filter. You'll also get a thorough understanding of partial application and currying of functions. Finally, you'll build your own OOP system on top of Clojure, and will lay to rest the concern about how Clojure relates to the OO paradigm. In fact, you'll not think of OO in the same way again.

Chapter 14 deals with the expression problem. You'll first review what this age-old problem is, and then you'll use Clojure multimethods to solve it in an elegant fashion. Then, you'll look at Clojure's own high-performance solution to it.

Chapter 15 is the last chapter and focuses on advanced macros and DSLs. This will bring you full circle: we started out in search of a tool that minimizes accidental complexity. Clojure allows you to bend the programming language to your will through the macro system, and this chapter takes a deeper dive into this feature. You'll design an internal DSL that will serve as an example of how you can use DSLs to drive core business logic in your Clojure applications.

Code conventions and downloads

All code in the book is presented in a `fixed-width font like this` to separate it from ordinary text. Code annotations accompany many of the listings, highlighting important concepts. In some cases, numbered bullets link to explanations that follow the listing.

Please see chapter 2 for instructions on how to download and install Clojure. You will find the full code for all the examples in the book available for download from the publisher's website at http://www.manning.com/ClojureinAction.

Author Online

The purchase of *Clojure in Action* includes free access to a private forum run by Manning Publications where you can make comments about the book, ask technical questions, and receive help from the author and other users. You can access and subscribe to the forum at http://www.manning.com/ClojureinAction. This page provides information on how to get on the forum once you're registered, what kind of help is available, and the rules of conduct in the forum.

Manning's commitment to our readers is to provide a venue where a meaningful dialogue between individual readers and between readers and the author can take place. It isn't a commitment to any specific amount of participation on the part of the author, whose contributions to the book's forum remain voluntary (and unpaid). We suggest you try asking the author some challenging questions, lest his interest stray!

The Author Online forum and the archives of previous discussions will be accessible from the publisher's website as long as the book is in print.

About the cover illustration

On the cover of *Clojure in Action* is "A woman from Sinj," a town in Croatia about 30 kilometers north of Split. The illustration is taken from a reproduction of an album of Croatian traditional costumes from the mid-nineteenth century by Nikola Arsenovic, published by the Ethnographic Museum in Split, Croatia, in 2003. The illustrations were obtained from a helpful librarian at the Ethnographic Museum in Split, itself situated in the Roman core of the medieval center of the town: the ruins of Emperor Diocletian's retirement palace from around AD 304. The book includes finely colored illustrations of figures from different regions of Croatia, accompanied by descriptions of the costumes and of everyday life.

Sinj is located in the Dalmatian region of Croatia and women's costumes in Dalmatia consist of layers of clothing worn over more clothing: a white blouse, skirt, or tunic is most common, with a colorful, embroidered apron decorated with complicated geometric patterns and fringes worn on top, as well as a red vest and black coat with colorful stitching added to stand out from the white blouse underneath. Jewelry consists mainly of beads worn around the neck or silver coins added as adornments to the costume. Both men and women wear a red or white pillbox cap (called a bareta or crvenkapa), with a white veil attached to the women's cap, like in the illustration on this cover.

Dress codes and lifestyles have changed over the last 200 years, and the diversity by region, so rich at the time, has faded away. It is now hard to tell apart the inhabitants of different continents, let alone of different hamlets or towns separated by only a few miles. Perhaps we have traded cultural diversity for a more varied personal life—certainly for a more varied and fast-paced technological life.

Manning celebrates the inventiveness and initiative of the computer business with book covers based on the rich diversity of regional life of two centuries ago, brought back to life by illustrations from old books and collections like this one.

Part 1

Getting started

Learning a new programming language is difficult for several reasons: there's a new syntax to learn, some potentially new concepts, and maybe a new paradigm. Most of all, it's difficult because a new language makes you feel like a novice again. Unless you stick with it and gain some experience, even a simple task will seem like a chore. Your incentive to stick with it, is knowing that the reward at the end of your labor will be worth the work.

Clojure is such a language. It may appear daunting at first, especially given the different syntax. State changes work differently in Clojure, so that's an adjustment. It's a functional programming language, so you need to get used to thinking in terms of functions. If you're coming from an OO background, then you have to structure your application code in a somewhat different way. These are only a few of the new things you have to deal with as you learn Clojure.

The reward at the end of all this effort is worth it. Learning Clojure, as is the case with any Lisp, is worth the effort for the profound enlightenment you'll have when you finally "get it." It will change the way you think about programming, no matter which language you use.

This part of the book will guide you through an introduction to the language. When you finish these seven chapters, you'll be ready to tackle some non-trivial programs of your own. So take a deep breath, and dive in!

Introduction to Clojure

This chapter covers

- Clojure basics
- What makes Clojure special
- Clojure as a Lisp
- Clojure as a functional programming language
- Clojure as a JVM-based language

The greatest single programming language ever designed.

Alan Kay on Lisp

Lisp is worth learning for the profound enlightenment experience you will have when you finally get it; that experience will make you a better programmer for the rest of your days, even if you never use Lisp itself a lot.

Eric Raymond

Any sufficiently complicated C or Fortran program contains an ad hoc, informally specified, bug-ridden, slow implementation of half of Common Lisp.

Philip Greenspun

1.1   *What is Clojure?*

Clojure is a new programming language, designed as a fresh take on Lisp, one of the oldest programming languages still in active use (it's the second oldest; only Fortran is older). Why would anyone want to learn something associated with such old technology? It turns out that although the answer is obvious to someone who already knows Lisp, it can't be explained without some background. This chapter attempts to provide that background.

We'll begin with the motivation for the language, in order to gain an understanding of why Lisp was created. After that, we'll address the seemingly strange syntax of the language. This unfamiliarity with Lisp syntax often causes people to be turned off the language; hence, it's important to understand the reasoning behind its choice. Once we get that out of the way, we'll address three main topics. The first will deal with what makes Lisp special and how Clojure benefits from being a Lisp. The second will explain what it means for Clojure to be a functional programming language. Finally, we'll discuss the advantage of Clojure being hosted on the Java Virtual Machine (JVM).

By the end of this chapter, you should have an understanding of what's possible with a language like Clojure. There is some code in this chapter that serves as examples of the topics being discussed. Because Clojure code looks so different from other languages you might be working with, you can choose to gloss over the code samples. Rest assured that the next few chapters take a more detailed look at each concept. The aim of this chapter is to arm you for what lies ahead in the remainder of the book: a deep dive into an incredible language that's both new and old.

1.1.1   *Clojure—the reincarnation of Lisp*

When someone says that Lisp is the world's most powerful programming language, many folks agree (even if they refer to the speaker as a smug Lisp weenie.) What other programming language can lay claim to something similar and get away with it? C++? Java? Ruby?

Many people think of Lisp as a dead language, one that no one uses anymore. At the same time, people hear of Lisp being used for some cutting-edge software systems in various domains: NASA's Pathfinder mission-planning software, algorithmic trading of hedge funds, airline reservations, data mining, natural language processing, expert systems, bio-informatics, robotics, electronic design automation, and so on.

Lisp has the reputation of being a dark art; indeed, it has been referred to as a secret weapon by several successful startups. All this is for good reason, and this chapter attempts to explain this mysticism by talking about a new Lisp called Clojure. This new computer programming language is not only a practical Lisp, but it has added to its effectiveness by embracing the functional paradigm, by incorporating concurrency semantics into its core, and by being hosted on the Java Virtual Machine.

At the end of this discussion, you won't be surprised to learn that Clojure is being used in an equally wide set of domains to solve an equally challenging set of problems:

in large-scale text-archiving and data-mining systems, software implementing semantic web technologies to understand the deep web, statistics and modeling packages, AI-driven price-optimization systems for e-commerce, flight-delay prediction, weather-based event forecasting for insurance purposes, robotics, drive worlds in the Second-Life environment, and so on.

We'll now explore each strength of the Clojure programming language in some depth.

1.1.2 How we got here

LISt Processing (Lisp) is a programming language, originally designed in 1958 by John McCarthy, who lists the Turing award among his many achievements. Its design arose from requirements in the field of artificial intelligence, specifically from a need to operate on symbolic expressions (instead of numbers) and to represent these expressions as lists of symbols. Lisp was also designed with functional abstraction as a means of managing complexity, which means that functions are first-class citizens of the language and can be passed around like values and can be composed of each other. This is different from languages like Java and Ruby. Finally, Lisp was created with a "code as data" ideology, which meant that code could be manipulated as easily as regular data. This combination of features, as you shall see, results in a tremendous level of expressiveness.

But over the next few years, circumstances conspired against Lisp. A lot of money was invested in AI research during the 70s and 80s, but AI ultimately delivered little of all it had promised. Because Lisp had become associated with the field of artificial intelligence, when the AI boom ended, so did the popularity of the language. Many blamed the failure of AI on Lisp, and the stigma has been difficult to lose.

Many Lisps have been born since those early days, and many Lisps have passed into oblivion. Some are still being used today, especially certain Common Lisps like SBCL, CMUCL, and Allegro CL. Several computer science schools use Scheme as a teaching language, a role that it's admirably suited for.

There have been several attempts at a Lisp hosted on the JVM: JScheme, Kawa, ABCL, and others. For a variety of reasons, these never became particularly popular. Clojure is the latest attempt at reviving Lisp on the JVM, and Rich Hickey, its creator, has done an incredible job. Clojure, finally, could be the Lisp that survives. Indeed, it could be the future of Lisp and of dynamic programming languages.

We'll wrap up this section with an overview of the approach this book will take in order to teach Clojure. We'll then dive right into the first thing most people talk about when starting to learn a Lisp-like language—the syntax.

1.1.3 How this book teaches Clojure

The philosophy of this book rests on two main pillars: emphasizing Clojure's first principles and taking a hands-on approach to understanding those principles. You'll see plenty of code examples that illustrate these concepts. Programming in Clojure requires a new way of thinking, one that's probably different from what you might be used to, depending on your programming background. We'll address this by focusing on the basics of Lisp, on functional programming, and on understanding the new facilities provided by Clojure.

As you work through the book, we'll write a lot of code that will be applicable to a variety of systems developed today. Once we get past the features of the language itself, we'll address real-world topics such as test-driven development, data storage, web services, and more. We'll look at scaling our Clojure applications through the use of messaging systems, and we'll even create a little distributed computing framework. We'll address using Clojure to process big data by leveraging technologies such as Hadoop and HBase. We'll also look at creating domain-specific languages in Clojure.

With this background, we're ready to explore Clojure. Our first stop is going to address a question nearly everyone asks the first time they see code written in the language: why does Clojure code look the way it does?

1.2 *Understanding Clojure syntax*

When most people think of learning a new programming language, they first think of syntax. Syntax is what makes languages look different from each other; indeed, it's often a reason why some people like (or dislike!) certain languages.

Syntax, however, is only skin-deep. Concrete syntax, which is the rules that the language imposes on the programmer in terms of what each construct looks like, isn't that important. Compilers generate a data structure called an abstract syntax tree after parsing the code written in the concrete syntax of the language. The source code of the program is discarded once the AST (abstract syntax tree) is generated. For all other phases of compilation (for example, semantic analysis), only the AST is required. You might say, therefore, that concrete syntax is fundamentally for humans. That's not to say that human convenience isn't important, but syntax shouldn't get in the way of what's possible with a computer language. (We'll revisit this issue in section 1.3.1.)

Clojure is an extremely simple language to learn; from a syntax point of view, there's nearly nothing to it. Take a look at the following line of Clojure code:

```
(add 3 5 7)
```

This expression is a call to the add function with three numbers as arguments. A function is always called this way, with the function name appearing first followed by any number of arguments. Let's examine the general rules of Clojure syntax.

A Clojure expression is either a symbol or a sequence. For example, in the one-liner just shown, the expression is a list containing four symbols (add, 3, 5, and 7). An example of an expression that contains only a symbol is 13 or +.

If an expression is a sequence, it's either empty or contains other symbols or sequences. A symbol is anything that appears in the program text. That's all there is to it! Note the recursive nature of these rules. By allowing a Clojure list to contain other lists (in essence allowing expressions to be nested), arbitrarily complex expressions can be represented. Further, because of this regularity, all Clojure expressions look the same. The same evaluation rule applies to nearly all Clojure expressions, with only a few special cases. The evaluation rule states that the first symbol in a list represents a function and is evaluated by treating the remaining expressions in the list as parameters. You saw this in the call to the add function previously.

This simplicity is also its strength and is what makes Lisp's famous macro system possible. Macros are tiny, inline code generators that any programmer can use to modify program code or even generate arbitrary code on the fly. This language-level construct that allows code generation and transformation at runtime (the compile phase of the runtime, to be specific) is one of the reasons why Clojure is so different from other languages and why it's so powerful. You'll learn a lot about macros in this book.

The remainder of this section talks about Clojure's syntax. The comparison with XML will help you realize that the unfamiliar parentheses have familiar cousins. By the time you're finished reading this section, you'll at least understand the reasoning behind all those parentheses. You'll certainly be more comfortable reading Clojure code. You may even begin to see the possibilities that representing code this way provides.

1.2.1 *XML and parentheses*

Many people get turned off at the sight of Clojure code; they complain about too many parentheses. Let's see why they're no big deal, and in fact, they're a large source of Clojure's capabilities. Few other programming languages have the sort of metaprogramming capabilities that Clojure has, and this is in large part due to the way code is represented in the language. First, however, you'll see that the unfamiliar syntax is similar to something most programmers are already familiar with.

XML has been used for many purposes, including as a programming language. XSLT is one such example. As a thought experiment, let's use XML to create our own programming language. It might look something like the following listing.

Listing 1.1 A small program written in our fictitious XML-based language

```
<program>
  <function name=addToStock>
    <param name=counter></param>
    <callFunction name=increment>
      <argument value=counter></argument>
    </callFunction>
  </function>
  <function name=removeFromStock>
    <param name=item></param>
    <callFunction name=decrementFromStockFile>
      <argument value=item></argument>
    </callFunction>
  </function>
</program>
```

This program should be understandable by anyone who has used any kind of XML-based programming tool. For example, Ant build files look similar in some respects. With a little imagination, you could envision a system that can read this file and execute the code described within it.

These days, however, everyone likes to criticize XML for being kludgy and verbose. So let's try to clean it up by removing nonessential things from this example. First, if we assume that these are source code files, we don't need the root `program` tag. Also, let's get rid of all closing tags, because we can still write a parser that understands the program structure without named closing tags. The resulting code might look like the next listing.

Listing 1.2   A slightly less verbose version of the same program

```
<function name=addToStock>
   <param name=counter></>
   <callFunction name=increment>
     <argument value=counter></>
   </>
 </>

  <function name=removeFromStock>
    <param name=item></>
    <callFunction name=decrementFromStockFile>
      <argument value=item></>
    </>
  </>
```

Let's make another couple of improvements: let's use starting angle brackets to denote the start of statements (no closing angle brackets until the end of the statement), and let's use a simple closing angle bracket to denote the ends. The code might now look like the following:

```
<function name=addToStock
   <param name=counter >
   <callFunction name=increment
     <argument value=counter >
   >
 >

  <function name=removeFromStock
    <param name=item >
    <callFunction name=decrementFromStockFile
      <argument value=item >
    >
  >
```

For our final set of changes, let's cook up a couple of rules. When defining a function, we'll use the special `define` construct, which is always followed by a set of symbols between brackets. These symbols begin with the name of the function being defined and are followed by its parameters. The `define` construct doesn't need an extra closing bracket because it ends with the body of the function definition.

Also, the first symbol in any non-special statement is always the name of a function, so we don't need to call out that fact. The following symbols are always parameters, so we don't need to call out that fact either. The resulting code looks like the following:

```
<define < addToStock counter >
    <increment counter > >
  <define < removeFromStock item >
    <decrementFromStockFile item > > >
```

This is still quite readable and still follows rules that a parser can use to decode. For a bit of flourish, let's switch to using the nicer, curvier parentheses instead of the pointy angle brackets. Take a look:

```
(define (addToStock counter)
    (increment counter))
  (define (removeFromStock item)
    (decrementFromStockFile item))
```

Believe it or not, this is Scheme (a Lisp dialect) syntax. Most Lisps look similar, with minor differences about how many parentheses are used and where they go.

The reason the parentheses exist is the same reason tags exist in XML, and that's to define a tree structure, which contains (in this case) the source code of the program. Just as XML can be manipulated (or generated) with ease, so can Lisp programs. This is because they get converted to simple data structures themselves. As mentioned earlier, this code manipulation and generation is done using the macro system. We'll explore the macro system a little bit in section 1.3.1 and then again in chapter 7. Thanks to this language-level code generation facility, some expressive abstractions can be created rather easily in Clojure.

Before completing this section, we'll address one more aspect of Clojure syntax. Clojure has syntactic sugar that makes it easy to work with all its core data structures, namely lists, vectors, and hashes. This convenience makes Clojure code more readable as well.

1.2.2 *Lists, vectors, and hashes*

Okay, so I lied a little bit. Clojure does have a little more syntax than other Lisps, but happily, this extra syntax improves readability.

In order to make it easier to read and write Clojure code, it uses two other types of brackets, square brackets and braces, in addition to the parentheses. As usual, simple lists are denoted using parentheses, and most of your Clojure code will use lists. Here's a typical example:

```
(do
    (process-element (first all-the-xs))
    (process-element (last all-the-ys))
    (find-max all-the-numbers))
```

Vectors are denoted using square brackets. Vectors are like lists and can be used like them, except that they can be indexed by integers. Clojure uses vectors to denote function arguments or binding forms.

```
(defn do-something [an-argument another-argument]
  (do-something-with-both an-argument another-argument)
  (return-answer an-argument another-argument))
```

Hash maps are denoted using braces. Hash maps behave as you'd expect; they're collections of key-value pairs where values can be indexed by their keys. Here's what that looks like:

```
(def a-map
  {:first-key "first-value"
   :second-key "second-value"
   "third-key" :third-value
   "fourth-key" 4})
```

The combination of these three notations—parentheses, square brackets, and braces—makes Clojure easy to read when compared to other Common Lisp or Scheme.

You should now have an idea of what Clojure code looks like and even why it looks like it does. With the question of the strange syntax out of the way, we can start talking about the other features that Clojure offers.

1.3   *The sources of Clojure's power*

Computers understand only one language, binary code. All other programming languages, including assembly (symbolic representation of the computer's instruction set), are at a higher level than native machine code. The reason these other languages exist is so that programmers don't have to deal with cryptic sequences of ones and zeroes. High-level languages increase the programmer's productivity.

Programming languages vary greatly in expressiveness. Low-level languages, such as assembly language and the C programming language, are useful for certain tasks, such as writing operating systems and device drivers. For most other programming tasks, software engineers favor high-level languages, such as C++, Java, Ruby, or Python. Each programming language has a different philosophy, for instance, static or dynamic, strongly or weakly typed. It's these differences in design that result in different levels of programmer productivity.

Clojure has three broad sources of power: the ideology of Lisp, the functional paradigm, and the JVM. The rest of this section explores each of these topics in some detail. The rest of this book illustrates these as well and makes the reasoning behind these choices quite apparent.

1.3.1   *Clojure and Lisp*

Lisp is different from most other programming languages. This is immediately apparent to anyone who looks at a fragment of Lisp code. In section 1.2, we talked about why the syntax looks as it does and how it relates to being able to generate code on the fly. Languages that represent code using their own data structures are said to follow the code-as-data philosophy.

This idea of code as data is why the Lisp family of languages can offer the ultimate in programmer productivity for such a large class of problems. Specifically, it allows program code to be manipulated or generated at runtime (at compile time to be specific), through a facility called the macro system. In section 1.3.4, we'll explore in more detail what it means for a language to be a Lisp.

1.3.2 Clojure and functional programming

A computer language is said to be functional if it treats computation as the application of mathematical functions. As in mathematics, functional programs have no state that arbitrarily mutates. In this sense, functional programming languages are different from other popular languages such as Ruby and Java. In essence, the difference is that these other languages are imperative in nature, which emphasizes modifying state as a means of representing computations.

Programming in functional languages is different from programming in imperative languages, and it can take a little getting used to. It's different from procedural languages (such as C), despite the superficial similarity of procedures and functions. The prime difference is that procedures aren't first class, which means that procedures are subroutines, whereas functions are real objects that can be passed around and created dynamically.

Being a functional language, however, Clojure is able to provide some rather unique features. These include immutability, higher-order functions, laziness, and the excellent concurrency semantics that allow Clojure programs to use all available CPU cores in a thread-safe manner. A combination of these features packs quite a punch. When combined with the fact that Clojure is a Lisp, magical things can be made to happen.

Code written in Clojure is a great deal shorter and less error prone when compared to that written in other languages. We'll examine why this is so next.

1.3.3 Clojure and the JVM

For a programming language to be productive, it needs to come packaged with a large set of libraries. Indeed, libraries often define a language as much as its syntax. Think of C++ with its standard library and the STL. As a corollary, the lack of a comprehensive set of libraries can cause a language to be neglected by the developer community. Indeed, in many ways, Lisp itself is an example of this problem.

Clojure sidesteps this problem neatly. By being hosted on the JVM, programmers have instant access to thousands of libraries and frameworks that serve a wide variety of purposes. The Clojure runtime benefits from the high-performance characteristics of the HotSpot VM, which can optimize programs at runtime to make them run faster. You'll see how to exploit this synergy with Java in your programs.

1.3.4 Clojure as a Lisp

As described earlier, having been designed back in 1958, Lisp is one of the oldest computer languages. It had originally been created as a notation to aid in the advancement of the theory of computation. Specifically, it was being used to develop a model of computation based on lambda calculus. Further, because it was born during a period of intense interest in artificial intelligence, there was a specific need to represent symbolic expressions as data. This combination of the functional basis and the idea of code as data made it suitable for the complex applications being developed at the time. In fact, the original Lisp spawned several dialects, and they all shared the same basic tenets. These languages formed the Lisp family of languages. Clojure shares these advantages because it too belongs to this family.

Over the past few pages, we've talked a little about the relationship of some of the features of Clojure to its syntax. The parentheses serve an important purpose (similar to tags in an XML document) by marking the beginning and the end of each unit of code. In order to understand what being a Lisp means for Clojure, you need to first understand a couple of terms: *s-expressions* and *forms*.

A line of Clojure code can be made up of a symbol that evaluates to something such as `account-balance` (a variable) or `calculate-total` (a function). It can be a literal such as the string `"Enter password"` or the number `124.95`. It can be a list (denoted by a pair of parentheses), which could in turn contain symbols, vectors, hash maps, sets, or other nested lists. When the program runs, these lines of code are first converted into Clojure objects called s-expressions. An example of an s-expression is `println`. Another is `(+ 1 2)`. Here's another example of a larger s-expression:

```
(defn print-all-things [a-list-of-things]
  (let [total (count a-list-of-things)]
    (println "Total things: " total)
    (dorun (map println a-list-of-things))))
```

Not all s-expressions are valid. An example of an invalid s-expression is `("me" "and" "you")`,because the first element of a Clojure s-expression must be a function, a macro, or a special form. You'll learn what these are soon. For now, suffice it to say that the string `"me"` is not one of these. A valid s-expression is one that follows all the rules of Clojure and is called a *form*. Valid Clojure programs are composed of one or more Clojure forms.

It's useful to have a basic understanding of how computer languages work. Figure 1.1 illustrates the three phases of processing before a file containing source code can execute as a program.

The lexical analyzer tokenizes the incoming character stream of the source code into symbols and words. The parser parses the tokens into an AST (abstract syntax tree, as was mentioned earlier). This AST is a syntax-free representation of the source code; it represents each line of code in a tree structure, as XML does. A simple example is shown in figure 1.2. From this point onward, the source code is no longer needed. The AST is checked for validity. If it follows the rules of the language, it's

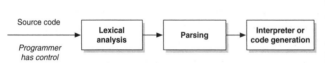

Figure 1.1   Shows the stages of a typical language processor and where the developer has programmatic control. Clojure doesn't follow this model, as you'll see.

deemed ready for the final stage. This third phase depends on whether the language is interpreted or compiled. If it's an interpreted language, each form is evaluated and executed in sequence. If it's compiled, machine code is generated, which can then be executed later.

With this background out of the way, we can talk about more interesting things. In computer languages that work as described previously, as far as the programmer is concerned, the source code is what gets executed (minus runtime optimizations). The whole AST thing is an internal detail well below the required level of abstraction when writing a program. In fact, the programmer has no control of what happens during the various stages of transformation and processing of the code.

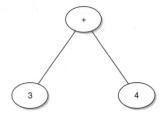

Figure 1.2 An example AST. This shows a tree structure representation of code that might be written as 1 + 2, in a language such as Java or Ruby. There's no notion of concrete syntax here.

You may well wonder why such a thing would even be desirable. What possible use could there be of being able to programmatically manipulate an AST of a program? It turns out that having such control allows for great flexibility, and it comes in the form of the macro system. We'll explore macros in the next section.

The Clojure language runtime, on the other hand, works differently from other languages. It features a just in time (JIT) compiler, and thanks to the JVM, it compiles and executes code extremely fast. Internally though, it can be thought of as having two separate phases, as illustrated in figure 1.3.

The first phase, as the name implies, concerns itself with reading the source code and converting it into s-expressions. Invalid s-expressions cause read errors, and the program will abort with an appropriate error message. The second phase is to evaluate valid s-expressions (forms) to produce a return value. If code needs to be compiled, it happens here and is then executed. As alluded to, the power of Lisp kicks in here, because the programmer has full control between the read and evaluate phases.

We're now going to examine the first phase in a little more detail. The Clojure reader is quite a marvel of innovation. Along with the syntax, It's what makes this whole macro thing possible.

THE READER

To understand this better, it's useful to know what the Clojure reader is and what it does. The reader is the entity that reads source code, from a program source file, for instance, and converts it into s-expressions. These s-expressions are composed of ordinary

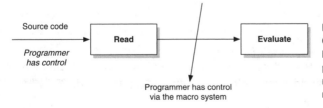

Figure 1.3 Shows the stages of the Clojure runtime. Unlike typical languages, the developer has programmatic control in between the read and evaluate stages, via the macro system.

Clojure data structures such as symbols, lists, vectors, sets, and hash maps. These data structures are then evaluated by the evaluator to produce a result. To make this more concrete, let's consider a contrived example. Here's a function definition in Clojure:

```
(defn my-own-function [an-argument another-argument]
  (println "The arguments were:" an-argument another-argument)
  (process-these an-argument another-argument))
```

Think of this as a list. The first symbol is `defn`, and it's followed by a symbol that's the name to which the function will be bound. Next, is a vector of two symbols, an-argument and another-argument. They're followed by yet another list that begins with `println`, and so on. This form represents a function definition, and when it's evaluated, the symbol `my-own-function` gets associated with the newly created function object.

To summarize, the reader converts source code into an AST implemented using Clojure's own data structures. The reader does this by using parentheses (and other brackets) as delimiters of each s-expression. In essence, the combination of the brackets and the reader allows code to be written in the AST directly. This is the reason why it's sometimes said that Lisp has no syntax. It's probably more accurate to say that Lisp has no concrete syntax. After all, as described earlier, language processors discard concrete syntax once the AST is created.

Programming languages that exhibit this property are called homoiconic (*homo* means same, *iconic* means representation). Code is written in the language's own data structures. This homoiconicity is also what makes Clojure's macro system possible, and you'll see this in the next section. Further, the reader invalidates the need to write language parsers because the reader does that already, and along with `eval` everything needed to write an internal DSL is already present. This is why most DSLs in Lisp look structurally similar to Lisp (as opposed to the English-like syntax favored by programmers of other languages). We'll explore this in some depth in chapter 15, and we'll write several DSLs that illustrate this point throughout the second part of this book. Meanwhile, let's get back to our discussion of the macro system.

THE MACRO SYSTEM

Having seen the s-expression for the definition of `my-own-function`, let's consider another data structure. This s-expression is structurally similar to the form that defined `my-own-function` previously:

```
(1 [2 3] (4 5 6 7) (8 9 10))
```

This is a nested list containing symbols that represent numbers. It contains a leading number, 1, a vector, [2 3], and two lists, (4 5 6 7) and (8 9 10). It's easy to imagine writing code that transformed this data structure into something else. The s-expressions representing the definition of `my-own-function` can also be manipulated the same way. For instance, let's add logic to log the fact that it was called. We'd like the new definition to be

```
(defn my-own-function [an-argument another-argument]
  (log-function-call "my-own-function")
  (println "The arguments were:" an-argument another-argument)
  (process-these an-argument another-argument))
```

Doing this programmatically is as simple as inserting another list into the original s-expression. The list that should be inserted is (log-function-call "my-own-function"). This list has log-function-call as its first symbol, followed by a string containing the name of the function being logged. This ability to programmatically manipulate code is what it means to have access to the AST as a simple data structure. It can be manipulated and transformed as desired. To make this useful, however, there needs to be a way for the transformed data structure to be evaluated instead of the original form. To be specific, it would need a hook between the read and evaluate phases of the Clojure runtime.

Clojure's macro system is exactly that hook. Macros are Clojure functions, but they accept s-expressions as their arguments. Because s-expressions are data structures, they can be transformed and returned, and the return values are used in place of the original forms. These code-transforming macros are used to create mini-languages on top of Clojure, or domain-specific languages (DSLs) as they're called these days.

Let's now look at how macros can be used to write code that manipulates code. Specifically, you'll see how the macro system can be used to eliminate duplication and to increase the expressiveness of the language by adding domain-specific constructs.

METAPROGRAMMING WITH MACROS

The introduction of Clojure's macro system poses a question: "What could such programmatic manipulation of code be used for?" The answer is "a lot" and has to do with metaprogramming, which is the idea of programs generating or manipulating other programs (or themselves). Such metaprogramming is used for several purposes, for instance, to reduce boilerplate code or to build syntactic abstractions (DSLs) on top of the core language. Clojure's macro system takes such metaprogramming to a whole new level when compared to metaprogramming facilities provided by languages such as Python or Ruby.

Another reason metaprogramming is easier in Clojure is because of its strange syntax. All Clojure forms have the same structure, which makes code generation easy compared to languages that have non-regular syntax. To generate Clojure code, you create Clojure data structures containing symbols and other data structures! This absence of formal syntax and the existence of the macro system make Clojure well suited to creating DSLs. In Clojure, creating mini-languages on top of the core language is a common approach to programming. It's the whole reason why Lisp is considered a *programmable* programming language.

To wrap up this section, let's look at a couple of examples of using macros.

EXAMPLE OF A MACRO—REMOVING BOILERPLATE

Certain kinds of boilerplate code can't be eliminated in languages like Java. Consider the following Java methods.

Listing 1.3   Typical duplication in Java code

```java
public List getExpenses(long userId, Date start_date, Date end_date) {
    AuditLogger.logLookup(userId, AuditCode.GET_EXPENSES);
    ExpensesConnection connection = new ExpensesConnection(userId);
    List expenses = connection.findAllBetween(start_date, end_date);
    connection.close();
    connection.flush();
    return expenses;
}

public void addExpense(long userId, Date date, BigDecimal amount) {
    AuditLogger.logLookup(userId, AuditCode.ADD_EXPENSES);
    ExpensesConnection connection = new ExpensesConnection(userId);
    connection.saveNewExpense(date, amount);
    connection.flush();
    connection.close();
}
```

In both these methods, the first thing that happens is that an audit log entry is created to record the fact that the method was called. Then, an `ExpensesConnection` object is created, which is used for different purposes in each method. The first two lines of code in each method are repeated. There's little we can do in Java to eliminate this duplication. We could try using the template method pattern, but it would still not be elegant enough, without gaining much in return.

Let's examine the same situation in Clojure. First, equivalent code in Clojure might look like that in the following listing.

Listing 1.4   The same code in Clojure, written as is

```clojure
(defn get-expenses [user-id start-date end-date]
  (create-audit-log user-id GET-EXPENSES)
  (let [connection (connect-to-expenses-db user-id)
        expenses (find-all-between connection start-date end-date)]
    (close-connection connection)
    (flush-connection connection)
    expenses))

(defn add-expense [user-id date amount]
  (create-audit-log user-id ADD-EXPENSE)
  (let [connection (connect-to-expenses-db user-id)]
    (save-new-expense connection date amount)
    (flush-connection connection)
    (close-connection connection)))
```

In Clojure, we could write a macro that we might name `with-audited-connection` that would handle this duplication. The resulting code would look like the following listing.

Listing 1.5   Removing duplication via a domain-specific macro

```clojure
(defn get-expenses [user-id start-date end-date]
  (with-audited-connection [user-id connection]
    (find-all-between connection start-date end-date)))
```

```
(defn add-expense [user-id date amount]
  (with-audited-connection [user-id connection]
    (save-new-expense connection date amount)))
```

The implementation of the with-audited-connection isn't shown here because chapter 7 focuses exclusively on macros, but the two functions in listing 1.5 are much cleaner than what would be possible with most languages. The domain-specific with-audited-connection macro is now available to use anywhere you need to connect to the expenses data store in an audited way. It also takes care of flushing and closing the connection, so you never have to remember to do this. This is another happy advantage, and it would be difficult to implement the same way in a language like Java. In fact, with-audited-connection can set things up so that any function called within its scope will be audited appropriately, without having to be explicit about it.

If this were a more dynamic language such as Ruby, you could get rid of some duplication by creating a third method that did the audit logging and accepted a block that did the remaining work. To see what macros can do that blocks and functions can't, let's look at another example that illustrates an even more powerful feature of macros—manipulating raw source code.

EXAMPLE OF A MACRO—SYNTACTIC ABSTRACTION

We discussed the advantages that a homoiconic language has in being able to make a macro system possible. Prefix notation goes along with it, because it adds uniformity to all function calls; the function object appears first, followed by arguments. This works fine for most functions, but it causes mathematical operators to look a bit strange, until you get used to them. Let's write a somewhat frivolous macro to support in-fix notation for math operators. First, a quick recap of what happens if we try to evaluate (1 + 2) at the REPL:

```
user=> (1 + 2)
; Evaluation aborted.
java.lang.Integer cannot be cast to clojure.lang.IFn
  [Thrown class java.lang.ClassCastException]
```

Our infix macro will allow us to write addition in this manner:

```
user=> (infix (1 + 2))
3
```

Experienced Lispers will question the advantage of creating such a macro, because prefix notation has significant advantages (that we'll explore shortly). The point is that it's easy to write such a macro in Clojure, and you'll see the implementation of this macro in chapter 7. As a hint, it literally manipulates the s-expression (1 + 2) into (+ 1 2). This is a trivial example of macros, but it would be rather hard to do this in most other languages.

Clojure macros can do much more. For now, it's worth noting that they are one of the crucial features of Clojure that distinguishes it from most other languages. Macros are the ultimate form of metaprogramming.

1.3.5 *More advantages of Clojure*

As you saw, the macro system is powerful indeed. There are, still more advantages that come from Clojure being a Lisp. We'll discuss a few of them now.

DYNAMIC LANGUAGE

Clojure, like Lisp, is a dynamic language. This means that many more things are determined at a program's runtime rather than when a compiler looks at the source code. This allows programs to be written in ways that wouldn't be possible in static languages. For example, many static languages require type declarations when using variables or defining functions, whereas Clojure doesn't.

As another example, Clojure has an `eval` function that allows code to be loaded up and executed at runtime. This feature is absent in nearly all static languages.

THE REPL

Clojure includes an interactive environment that allows code to be typed in and executed. It gives quick feedback and is helpful in incrementally writing code to solve the problem at hand. This interactive environment is called the REPL, which stands for read-eval-print loop.

Many Clojure editors integrate with the REPL. This allows programmers to use the IDEs' text-editing features to write the code the way they're used to. The integration provides a convenient way to evaluate code written in the editor inside of the REPL. Because the REPL is a long-running process, the edit-evaluate-test-edit cycle can keep going as long as the programmer wants. The workflow becomes an uninterrupted flow of feedback-driven editing and REPL interaction. In fact, in chapter 8, we'll illustrate this by using the REPL along with creating unit tests for a few functions, in a step-by-step manner. The ability to work this way makes REPL an important contributor to the increased productivity of working in Clojure.

This section talked about the advantages that Clojure gains from belonging to the Lisp family. There's another reason why Clojure code is often shorter than code in other languages, and it has to do with its primary means of representing computation: function evaluation. We'll explain why this is so in the next section.

1.3.6 *Clojure as a functional language*

Clojure deviates from many Lisps in that it exhibits far more functional purity. An example of this is in its choice of treating all Clojure data structures as immutable. Along with this aspect of functional programming, Clojure encourages the use of higher-order functions such as `map` and `reduce`. Core data structures are lazy, which means things get executed only as needed, thereby enabling some rather efficient programming constructs. An example of the use of laziness is the ability to define and use infinite sequences. Finally, Clojure takes advantage of its immutability and provides language-level support for safe, lock-free concurrency (using a software transactional memory model). We'll examine these features in this section.

HIGHER-ORDER FUNCTIONS

Clojure functions are first class, which means that functions can be passed as parameters to other functions, can be created dynamically, and can be returned from functions. They can be stored inside other data structures like regular data. Clojure also provides lexical closures, which is a powerful construct that allows for expressive code. You'll learn about closures, along with other aspects of functional programming, in the upcoming chapters of this book.

This functional aspect of Clojure makes it easy to write code using higher-level constructs like map, reduce, and filter, which apply arbitrary functions to lists of data. Given that all core data structures are immutable, this results in tight code that has fewer bugs than equivalent code in imperative languages such as Java or C++, because the code is far more declarative in nature. After all, lesser code leaves less scope for programming error. Look at the following listing for a slightly larger example.

> **Listing 1.6 Typical usage of higher-order functions**

```
(def post-headers [{:title "first one ever" :length 430}
                    {:title "second baby step" :length 650}
                    {:title "three is company" :length 720}
                    {:title "fourth for the road" :length 190}
                    {:title "five again" :length 280}]])

(defn long-post-headers [threshold-length headers]
  (let [is-long? (fn [header]
                    (> (header :length) threshold-length))]
    (filter is-long? headers)))

(defn long-post-titles [threshold-length headers]
  (map :title (long-post-headers threshold-length headers)))

(long-post-titles 300 post-headers)
```

The output of the last function call is

```
("first one ever" "second baby step" "three is company")
```

This is how a lot of functional code looks: mapping over sequences to collect things, filtering from sequences using predicate functions, and so on. Notice how you can define local functions like is-long? and how it functions as a closure around the threshold-length parameter.

All this leads to shorter code with fewer defects. Given how fundamental this is to Clojure, you'll be seeing a lot more about higher-order functions. For now, we'll look at another important aspect of functional languages: the absence of mutating state.

IMMUTABILITY

Clojure supports another aspect of functional programming, that of immutability. What this means is that all of Clojure's core data structures are immutable—once created they can't change. When something needs to change, a new object is created that includes the change and is returned. (Clojure's implementation of immutability performs extremely well and doesn't slow down programs). What this means in practice is that an entire class of bugs related to mutating state is eliminated from your code. To imagine how this might be so, consider an imperative for loop with a loop variable counter. If the programmer inadvertently modifies the value of counter in the body of the for loop, the code won't work properly. Similar bugs can happen with any mutable variable.

In languages that support immutability, the only way a function can do something is to return a new data structure and in this way each function is independent and can be written, debugged, and tested independently.

```
(def expenses [{:amount 12.99 :merchant "amazon"}])

(def updated-expenses (conj expenses {:amount 199.95 :merchant "frys"}))
```

That last function call returns a *new* sequence with the two expenses in it and is assigned to updated-expenses. The old sequence expenses remains unchanged. As you'll see, this immutability greatly aids Clojure's support of concurrency-safe multi-threaded programs.

By the way, in case you're wondering how you can possibly write real-world code with everything being immutable, relax! Clojure has fantastic support for explicit state management, and you'll see this soon.

LAZY AND INFINITE SEQUENCES

Most programming languages like Ruby and Java are eager. This means that when a method or constructor is called, it's executed immediately, and the result is returned. But sometimes it's desirable to defer such evaluation. An example where such a behavior is useful is to avoid unnecessary computation (say an expensive calculation returns a value that's never used).

Clojure solves this problem inside its core data structures. Clojure sequences can be *lazy*; this means that elements are not computed until the values are needed for something else. Most core functions produce lazy data structures that aren't realized until needed. Examples of such commonly used functions are map, reduce, and filter. Further, this implies that a chain of such function calls returns a value that's also lazy! This laziness is a source of great convenience, and you'll see more of it in action later.

As an example of laziness, Clojure allows the programmer to create infinite lists of data. These infinite data structures are called *streams* and are a different way to model the world. For instance, objects can be modeled as a series of events, as opposed to a snapshot of the world.

Here's a classic example of an infinite sequence; it's trivial but simple to understand. We'll create a sequence of all Fibonacci numbers. Yes, *all*, and because this sequence is lazy, elements will be calculated only as needed:

```
(defn next-terms [term-1 term-2]
  (let [term-3 (+ term-1 term-2)]
    (lazy-seq
      (cons term-3
            (next-terms term-2 term-3)))))
```

```
(defn fibonacci [t1 t2]
  (concat [t1 t2]
          (next-terms t1 t2)))

(take 15 (fibonacci 0 1))
```

This last function call is what realizes the lazy sequence of Fibonacci numbers. The result is

```
(0 1 1 2 3 5 8 13 21 34 55 89 144 233 377)
```

First, let's talk about the magic ingredient here, `lazy-seq`. It's a macro that doesn't evaluate its body immediately but returns a sequence-like object. This object will evaluate the body only when needed (and will also cache the result for subsequent uses, saving CPU cycles).

The important thing to realize about this code is that without `lazy-seq`, there'd be no useful way of using `next-terms`. You can see this by directly calling `next-terms` at the REPL; it will run in an infinite loop until the program runs out of memory. This happens because the REPL tries to print the sequence, and being infinite, the realization fails. By using certain functions like `take`, you can intelligently produce the required number of elements from such infinite sequences.

Languages like Java and Ruby need lots of boilerplate code that implements something like the lazy-load pattern to do something similar. Much of Clojure is already lazy, making code written in it automatically lazy. Such code then transparently benefits from this behavior. We'll visit this in more detail in the next chapter and in part 2 of the book, where we'll create an infinite sequence of messages read off a messaging system.

Now, you'll see another incredible benefit that results from a language being functional and immutable: the possibility of safe concurrency.

CONCURRENCY AND THE MULTICORE FUTURE

Moore's law states that the number of transistors that can be placed on a single integrated circuit doubles every 18–24 months. This is what has been happening to CPUs over the past two to three decades, and this gave us an exponential increase in processor speed. Advances in CPU speed can't proceed in this manner forever. Indeed Moore's law has pretty much already reached its limit in providing performance enhancements.

Over the past few years, instead of increasing the speed of individual processor cores, companies like Intel have started to increase the number of processor cores that go into a single CPU. This has caused software performance to become tied to Amdahl's law, which relates the possible performance of a running computation to the number of parallel processing units available. As the number of cores available on a CPU grows, software will need to make use of them; this will soon become a crucial way to make programs run faster.

Multithreaded programming means trouble, as anyone who has written multithreaded code knows. At least two things are related to this issue: getting multithreaded programs to behave correctly and using all available cores to speed up the program. Clojure helps with both.

SOFTWARE TRANSACTIONAL MEMORY

Clojure's state management system addresses the issue of correctness of multi-threaded programs. Not only does the language provide simple ways to handle mutation, but it also provides constructs that allow and enforce safe mutation.

Clojure implements a multiversion concurrency control (MVCC)–based software transactional memory (STM) model. What this means in simpler terms is that mutating the value of an object can only be done inside a transaction (think database transaction).

This has two advantages. The first is that code becomes self-documenting. When the value of something needs to change in a thread-safe manner, the programmer must be explicit and use a special Clojure construct for it: the ref. The other advantage is that if you attempt to modify the value inside a ref without an STM transaction, the Clojure runtime will throw an exception. This is how Clojure enforces the use of the transaction semantics and helps keep code thread-safe.

When a transaction needs to commit, and another thread has already committed a change to a shared ref, the later transaction is rolled back. Clojure's STM system even retries the failed transaction several times, and as far as the programmer is concerned, all this happens transparently (this behavior depends on the function used to effect the mutation; more on this in chapter 6). Here's an example of this in action.

Listing 1.7 Clojure's STM in action

```
(def total-expenditure (ref 0))

;; The following will throw a "No transaction running"
;; IllegalStateException exception
 (defn add-amount [amount]
   (ref-set total-expenditure (+ amount @total-expenditure)))

;; The following will work fine because it will do the update inside a
;; transaction

(defn add-amount [amount]
   (dosync
     (ref-set total-expenditure (+ amount @total-expenditure)))))
```

The @total-expenditure is a reader macro in action. It expands to (deref total-expenditure) and it gets the value out of the object that the ref is pointing to. Clojure provides several reader macros to make certain things convenient, and we'll visit them in the next chapter.

This language-level support for concurrency-safe state management is what makes Clojure extremely well suited for multithreaded applications. This is true whether code runs on a single core or on a multicore CPU. By using a ref and by making sure that updates are always performed inside a dosync block, access to the variable protected by the ref becomes thread safe.

Over the past couple of sections, you've seen how Clojure benefits from being a Lisp and from being a functional language. The macro system helps in creating powerful abstractions such as domain-specific languages. The functional features allow for

> **Writing Clojure-like code in an other languages**
>
> There's nothing to stop someone from writing code that treats variables as immutable (for example, by declaring them `final` in a language like Java, or through convention and discipline). Indeed, a large part of Clojure is written in Java, and you could imagine a program written with great care and careful consideration of all we've seen so far: immutability, an STM system for safe concurrency, and so on.
>
> There's a vast difference between such an approach and writing a similar program in Clojure. The first is that the Java code (say) would look alien to even fluent Java programmers, because it would be far from idiomatic. More importantly, the difference is that although the Java code would rely on convention and discipline, the Clojure runtime would enforce it. That means the Clojure program wouldn't work (and would complain loudly when an attempt was made to run it) if, for example, some part of the code violated either immutability or STM transactions.
>
> This support from the language makes programs written in Clojure less error prone and forms part of the reason why functional languages are a big deal.

higher-quality code thanks to higher-order functions and immutability. Finally, thanks to Clojure's built-in support for concurrency, programs can take advantage of multiple CPU cores without any effort from the programmer. These things all make Clojure a capable language. But it doesn't end there; by running on top of the Java runtime (the JVM), Clojure manages to solve a critical piece of the puzzle for any new language: the availability of libraries and interoperability with existing systems.

1.3.7 *Clojure as a JVM-based language*

Clojure is hosted on the Java Virtual Machine. This means that it's ultimately a Java program and runs as JVM byte code. The design of Clojure embraces interoperability with other Java libraries as one of its central goals. Indeed, when Rich Hickey designed Clojure, one of the goals was extreme practicality. In today's world, a practical programming language almost demands interoperability with Java. Clojure achieves this goal remarkably well, and in practice, this means several things.

The obvious advantage is that the Clojure programmer has instant access to the thousands of existing Java libraries. This substantially boosts productivity when compared with other Lisps (and indeed other programming languages) because there's probably a Java library for most systems and frameworks.

Another advantage that comes from running on the JVM is that Clojure can be embedded into Java programs, thereby providing an incredibly flexible scripting capability to the end user.

Often a combination of these two ideas leads to a system design where parts of the code are written in Java and other parts are written in Clojure. Clojure itself can be used as a glue language to bring the whole system together. This may be especially useful when legacy applications are involved.

One final advantage of being a JVM language is that of the JVM itself. Sun Microsystems (now Oracle) and the open-source community have together invested thousands of person-years into improving the JVM, and today it's one of the most efficient virtual machines. The HotSpot optimizer does amazing things to speed up code running on top of it, and Clojure benefits from all this innovation. Despite being incredibly dynamic, Clojure code gets compiled to Java byte code and runs as fast or nearly as fast as Java code itself. This gives programmers all of Clojure's benefits without any major performance costs.

CALLING JAVA FROM CLOJURE

It's trivial to use Java libraries from Clojure. For instance, here's an example of using a method on the string class to do some simple text manipulation:

```
user=> (.toUpperCase "clojure")
"CLOJURE"
```

This is especially convenient, because Clojure strings are Java strings. Further, once you import required classes using the `import` form, you can then use them like other Clojure code. For instance, Selenium is an open-source functional testing automation tool for web applications. You can find it at http://seleniumhq.org, and you'll need the Java Selenium client driver JAR on your classpath to try this example of using it to drive a browser:

```
(import '(com.thoughtworks.selenium DefaultSelenium))

(defn start-new-selenium []
  (let [s (DefaultSelenium. "localhost" 4444 "chrome*" "http://
    localhost:3000")]
    (.start s)
    s))
```

Clojure provides a few syntactic conveniences to help use Java classes. The `Default-Selenium.` (notice the period at the end) invokes the constructor of the class. Similarly, `.start` calls the instance method `start` on the newly constructed Selenium object.

There's syntactic sugar for creating new instances of Java classes, accessing static members of Java classes, and calling methods on Java objects. There are also helper macros that make using Java classes and objects from within Clojure easy. You can even implement interfaces using pure Clojure code. You'll see all this and more in chapter 5, which is dedicated to exploring Java-interop facilities of the Clojure language.

CALLING CLOJURE FROM JAVA

Calling a Clojure script from inside a Java program is easy too. Clojure is itself a Java program, so it's as simple as using any other Java library and knowing the API.

Here's an example:

```
import clojure.lang.RT;
import clojure.lang.Var;

// some code here
```

```
RT.loadResourceScript("clojure/file/from/classpath/clojure_script.clj");
Var aClojureFunction = RT.var("a-clojure-name-space",
                              "a-clojure-function");
aClojureFunction.invoke("an argument" "another one");
```

There's a lot more you can do here, including compiling all your Clojure code into Java byte code and then using it like any other library. This is called AOT (ahead of time) compilation, and you'll see all this and more in a future chapter.

TYPE HINTS

Clojure is an extremely dynamic language, but it strives to be so without the typical cost associated with doing everything at runtime. You can help run Clojure programs faster by giving the evaluator type hints about any Java class you're using. That way, Clojure will know how to call methods on objects of such classes without reflection.

Using type hints is easy; here's an example:

```
(import '(com.thoughtworks.selenium DefaultSelenium))

;; blah blah blah

(defn start-this-selenium [^DefaultSelenium selenium]
  (.start s)
  s)
```

The type hint is the ^ followed by the name of the class. When the start method is called, Clojure will do so without any reflection. This is much faster than without the type hint.

Typical programming workflow is to write the Clojure code, test it, and debug until you're satisfied. Then, if performance is a concern, add type hints to your code. It's easy and quick.

EXTENSIBILITY

It's worth mentioning one final point about Clojure being hosted on the JVM. Thanks to the internal design of the language, Clojure is easily extensible. This means that programmers can add to the core of Clojure in a natural manner. As an example, consider that Clojure's internal data structures like lists, vectors, and hash maps all behave in the same way: as sequences. Operations like map, reduce, and filter all work, no matter what kind of sequence is passed to them. Internally, they all do this because they all implement the ISeq interface.

The great thing about such a clean design is that anyone can add new data structure that implements the same ISeq interface. If your problem domain involves dealing with a stream of financial charges, for instance, you can imagine creating a new kind of sequence that would then work seamlessly with the core Clojure functions. Or, as another example, the Clojure-based Incanter project provides matrices that implement the ISeq interface. A matrix consists of a sequence of rows, and each row is a one-dimensional row matrix.

This extensibility pays off when existing (or even new) Java code needs to work with Clojure. By implementing the ISeq interface, the new data structure becomes native to Clojure and behaves the same as core Clojure data structures. This makes for easy extensibility of Clojure and allows programmers to use all core Clojure functions for free with their custom data structures.

So far, you've seen where Clojure derives its power—and this comes primarily from it being a JVM-based functional Lisp. Thinking in the functional way often takes some time, especially for those coming from imperative backgrounds (such as Java and Ruby). One of the first questions people ask is whether Clojure is object oriented. Although OO has been all the rage over the past couple of decades, it isn't the perfect way of solving all problems. In fact, it's only one of the many approaches that might apply in any situation. Clojure, as a language, doesn't limit the programmer by imposing a specific paradigm. Instead, it allows programmers to move beyond objects.

1.4   *Clojure—beyond object orientation*

People new to Lisp and Clojure often ask where the object-oriented (OO) paradigm fits into the picture. They're disappointed to find that such languages have no obvious support for objects. The truth is more nuanced. Clojure is more general than any specific paradigm. First, let's examine the landscape of programming language paradigms. Figure 1.4 shows that both functional and OO paradigms are only a couple from the wide array that exist in the field today.

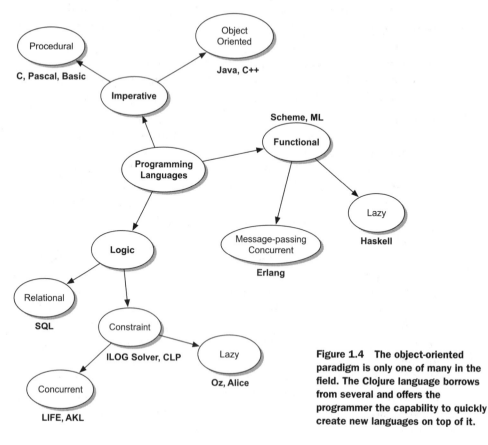

Figure 1.4   The object-oriented paradigm is only one of many in the field. The Clojure language borrows from several and offers the programmer the capability to quickly create new languages on top of it.

Because most concerns in this area are about Clojure's lack of object-oriented constructs, we'll talk about that a little. Consider, for example, that Clojure provides something called generic functions. In OO languages like Java or Ruby, method polymorphism is achieved by dispatching calls on the type of object the method is called on, and this is decided at runtime. Generic functions, also called multimethods, let the programmer decide how to dispatch functions at runtime. This is a far more capable approach to polymorphism, and you'll learn about this in a chapter on multimethods.

As you've seen, Clojure already sports various bits of different paradigms: functional, aspects of laziness, various options for concurrent programming, and so on. But as a language, it's much broader in its support for all kinds of other paradigms. You can write procedural code if you want, or you can write your program in a functional style. If you desire, Clojure programs can be written with an OO approach; indeed, you can build your own object-oriented language on top of the core language. You could build an Erlang-style process-oriented language on top of Clojure if you wanted to. The idea of building custom languages on top of a Lisp foundation isn't new. Before the term *domain-specific languages* (DSL) became popular, people were using Lisp to create such little languages. Clojure is well suited for this style of programming. The macro system built into Clojure plays a large role in this.

Clojure is also well suited for bottom-up design. Bottom-up design is an approach where higher-level components are built up from a collection of lower-level ones. A problem domain is analyzed, and several low-level components are created where each represents a single concept. These pieces are then combined to create the higher-level components as demanded by the problem at hand. Bottom-up design is often used to solve a whole class of problems in a specific domain rather than a specific instance of a problem. Systems built this way are more flexible and are more resilient to changing requirements.

Thanks to Clojure's functional paradigm (higher-order functions and closures) and the associated possibility of using function combination, it's a great language for designing systems in a bottom-up manner. In fact, Clojure programs are often "grown up" from the ground, by using this bottom-up decomposition of the domain, and are then combined with one or more little languages built on top of it. It's common to see Clojure programs that first create a mini-language that allows concepts in the problem domain to be expressed at a high level and then the problem solved in this language instead. This is a powerful style of programming that results in systems that are more flexible and code that's more readable and ultimately more maintainable. It's why Lisp is called a programmable programming language and is why Clojure benefits from being a Lisp.

The bottom line is that Clojure doesn't limit you by imposing a particular paradigm. It's general enough to support any paradigm that might suit the problem domain. Perhaps more important, it's capable of evolving into a language that works well for that paradigm and problem domain.

1.5   Summary

As you saw, Lisp is a special language, and Clojure is a special Lisp. It's homoiconic with almost no syntax and has a full macro system. It's a functional language with first-class functions and immutable data structures, and it has concurrency semantics built into its core. It's hosted on the extremely mature and performant Java VM, which allows it to offer seamless interoperability with Java code. Being as fast, or nearly as fast as Java, adds another gratifying advantage to Clojure: raw speed.

This combination packs a tremendous productivity punch. The dynamic programming style that Clojure makes possible is well suited to bottom-up design and results in programs that can do a lot more with a lot fewer lines of code. Indeed, when compared with equivalent lines of Ruby code, Clojure code can be two to three times smaller; when compared with Java, it can be nearly five to ten times smaller. Less code means fewer bugs. Clojure code comes close to satisfying the claim of being better, faster, smaller, and cheaper.

> **When is Clojure not applicable?**
>
> Although Clojure brings together the best ideas from a variety of programming languages, it's no panacea. There can be times when it isn't quite the language of choice for a project. The first issue is that despite the fact that the syntax is a key part of its strength, it can be alien and confusing to some programmers. If your team is unable to look past the unfamiliarity of the syntax, it can be difficult to embrace the language.
>
> Further, the macro system can be used for good or bad. We've explored some of its power in this chapter, and there's more throughout this book. But it's important to realize that macros aren't functions and that specifically, they don't compose well. It takes experience to know when a macro is the right tool for the job, and indeed, if you can do without a macro, you should. The misuse of macros results in suboptimal code, and a team without an experienced developer or two may suffer from this problem.
>
> The functional programming paradigm is also oftentimes a major shift for most developers. Because OOP is the most commonly used approach to writing software today, functional programming languages can leave developers at a loss as to how to design systems. It can be expeditious to have a developer or two on hand who has experience with functional programming. Without these, it can be difficult to get started.
>
> Having said that, every tool has its pros and cons. If you can mitigate these issues, then Clojure is often the best choice, especially for new projects.

Compared to several other dynamic languages, Clojure supports better rapid prototyping and incremental development of code. By combining the dynamism of the language and the hyperproductivity of the REPL, you can develop code quickly and in a more exploratory fashion. When a bottom-up approach to code is combined with a functional approach to domain modeling and the macro system, a powerful design pattern emerges—that of creating little languages on top of Clojure. This kind of metalinguistic programming is extremely expressive, and you'll learn a lot more about this throughout the rest of this book.

Further, the functional paradigm, along with immutable data structures, removes a whole class of bugs associated with imperative, state-based code design. And the concurrency support built into Clojure makes the complicated task of writing multi-threaded programs that work correctly downright easy. All this means that Clojure programs more often work right the first time and have fewer problems during their life spans.

Overall, using Clojure on a project can mean higher-quality software that runs faster and that can use multicore CPUs efficiently and correctly. The resulting code base will be smaller, which also means it will be cheaper to develop and maintain. It's possible that Clojure (or a variant of it) will be the Lisp that survives, indeed, as the language of the future.

The remaining chapters of the first part of the book will give you a thorough understanding of Clojure the language. They'll address practical issues of using it and advanced topics that show Clojure use in the real world. To get the most of the rest of this part, however, we'll need to get some more fundamentals out of the way. The next chapter is a quick breeze through most of the basic features of the language. With that background, the details in the following chapters will be easier to understand.

A whirlwind tour

This chapter covers

- Getting started with Clojure programming
- Clojure functions
- Program flow with Clojure
- Clojure's core data structures

In the previous chapter, you read about some powerful features of the Clojure language. You saw some code, but it probably looked a little alien. It's now time to set that right. This chapter and the next address the basics of writing code in Clojure. This one will walk you through the fundamentals of the structure and flow of Clojure programs. It will also give an overview of the various data structures that make up the core of the language. By the end of the next chapter, you'll be able to read most Clojure code and write your own programs.

2.1 Getting started

The best way to learn a programming language is to write some code. Before you can do that, you need a working installation of Clojure and some familiarity with the REPL. In this section, we'll download and install the language runtime and use the REPL to communicate with Clojure. Once you're comfortable with the basics of using the REPL, we'll try a slightly larger program. Finally, we'll close this section with a few more notes about Clojure syntax as it relates to comments, whitespace, case sensitivity, and so on.

2.1.1 *Installing Clojure*

Clojure is an open-source project hosted at github.com. Git is a distributed source code version-control system, and github.com is a popular Git hosting service. You can find Clojure at this web address: http://clojure.org/downloads. To download the source code, you'll need to have Git installed on your computer. Once you install it, go to your workspace directory and clone the Git repository with the following command:

```
git clone https://github.com/clojure/clojure.git
```

This will download the code from the master branch into the clojure directory in your workspace. Clojure is a Java project, and it uses the Ant build system. It comes with an Ant build file, which makes it easy to build the complete project. Assuming you have Ant installed, run the following command:

```
ant
```

Running this command will leave you with an appropriate Clojure JAR file. Running Clojure is as simple as starting any other Java program:

```
java -jar /path/to/clojure.jar
```

This will drop you into the Clojure REPL. The REPL is where most Clojure programs are born and developed.

2.1.2 *The Clojure REPL*

Clojure programs are usually not all typed out in one go. In fact, these days, programs in most languages are written using test-driven design (TDD). This technique allows the programmer to build up a larger program from smaller units of tested code. Doing this keeps programmer productivity high because the focus is always on one piece of the program at any given time. You write the test for something, write just enough code to make the test pass, and repeat the process. This style of development also has the added benefit of leaving behind a set of regression tests that can be used later. It ensures that as the program is modified and enhanced, nothing breaks existing functionality.

Clojure code can also be written with a TDD approach; indeed, it most often is. The Clojure REPL adds a fantastic tool that allows the programmer to be even more productive than when using plain TDD. This combination of using the REPL alongside the typical TDD style results in far shorter code-test-debug cycles.

As mentioned in chapter 1, the REPL stands for the read-eval-print loop. It's an interactive shell similar to those provided by languages such as Ruby and Python. The REPL prompt (the text behind the cursor that waits for keyboard input) is the name of the active namespace followed by the => symbol. When you first start the REPL, you will see the following prompt:

```
user=>
```

As this prompt shows, Clojure puts you into the default namespace of user. You can type Clojure code at this prompt, and it will be evaluated and the return value printed at the REPL. Here's an example:

```
user=> (+ 1 2)
3

user=> (defn my-addition [operand1 operand2] (+ operand1 operand2))
#'user/my-addition

user=> (my-addition 1 2)
3

user=> (my-addition 1000000000000000000 300000000000000000000)
301000000000000000000
```

Functions like my-addition are usually created first in the REPL, and then tested with various inputs. Once you're satisfied that the function works, you copy the test cases into an appropriate test file. You also copy the function definition into an appropriate source file and run the tests. At any time, you can modify the definition of the function in the REPL by redefining it, and your tests will run using the new definition. This is because the REPL is a long-running process with the various definitions in its memory. That means that functions using any such redefined functions will exhibit the new behavior.

Various editors can integrate with the REPL and provide convenient ways to evaluate code inside open editors. This kind of integration further increases the productivity of the REPL-based TDD cycle. Chapter 8 has much more detail on testing and TDD using Clojure.

A final note about the REPL: the Clojure reader accepts the stream of characters from the prompt (or any other source) and converts it into Clojure data structures. The data structures are evaluated to produce the result of the program. The Clojure printer attempts to print Clojure data structures in a format that can be read back by the reader. The reader is an almost magical entity, and we'll use it to do some powerful things. We'll also exploit the synergy between the reader and the printer.

Now that you've installed Clojure and are somewhat comfortable interacting with it via the REPL, let's write some more code. We'll begin with the traditional "Hello, world" program, and before ending the section, we'll address a few more points about Clojure syntax.

2.1.3 *Hello, world*

Let's get started with a simple program. To keep with tradition, we'll examine a program that prints "Hello, world," as shown here:

```
(println "Hello, world ")
```

OK, that was too simple. Let's write something a little more challenging. Let's imagine that we're creating a website for people to share pictures of their pets. The first task we might handle is a way to let users log into the site. The function we're going to write will check a user's credentials. For the sake of this example, we'll store our users in a Clojure hash map (you'll learn about hash maps later in this chapter). We'll use the usernames as keys, and each user's data will itself be stored as a hash map:

```
(def users {"kyle" {:password "secretk" :number-pets 2}
            "siva" {:password "secrets" :number-pets 4}
            "rob" {:password "secretr" :number-pets 6}
            "george" {:password "secretg" :number-pets 8}})
```

Now we can write a function that will decide if credentials are correct. It will accept a username and a password and then check to see if the associated user is valid:

```
(defn check-login [username password]
  (let [actual-password ((users username) :password)]
    (= actual-password password)))
```

The function is called check-login, and it takes two arguments, username and password. It does a simple check against our database of user information. You can ignore the let form for now; it's used to introduce the local name actual-password; we'll visit it again in the next section on program structure. We'll also show how to use maps and symbols toward the latter part of this chapter. Let's try check-login at the REPL:

```
user=> (check-login "siva" "secrets")
true

user=> (check-login "amit" "blah")
false
```

So it works. Before moving on to the various topics we have planned for this chapter, let's look at a couple of facilities provided by Clojure that can help with the learning process itself.

2.1.4 *doc and find-doc*

Clojure provides a useful macro called doc, which allows you to look up the documentation associated with any other function or macro. It accepts the name of the entity you're trying to learn about. Here's an example:

```
user=> (doc +)
-------------------------
clojure.core/+
([] [x] [x y] [x y & more])
  Returns the sum of nums. (+) returns 0.
```

Note that it prints not only the documentation string but also what arguments can be passed to the function or macro. Here's another example:

```
user> (doc doc)
-------------------------
clojure.core/doc
([name])
Macro
  Prints documentation for a var or special form given its name
```

Here, note that if the symbol refers to a macro, it informs you of that. Although doc is useful for when you know the name of the function or macro you want to look up, find-doc is useful if you aren't sure of the name.

FIND-DOC

The find-doc function accepts a string, which can be a regex pattern. It then finds the documentation for all functions or macros whose names or associated documentation match the supplied pattern. Here's an example:

```
user> (find-doc "lazy")
-----------------------
clojure.core/concat
([] [x] [x y] [x y & zs])
  Returns a lazy seq representing the concatenation of...
-----------------------
clojure.core/cycle
([coll])
  Returns a lazy (infinite!) sequence of repetitions of...

... more results
```

These two forms – doc and find-doc are quite useful at the REPL when you want to quickly look up what a function does or you want to find the right options.

We're now ready to start examining the various constructs of the Clojure language. Before we do, let's get a few administrative points about the syntax out of the way.

2.1.5 *A few more points on Clojure syntax*

In chapter 1, we discussed the unique, brackets-heavy syntax that Clojure employs. We examined why it exists and what power it bestows. Before moving on to the rest of this chapter, let's address a few more things that will come in handy when writing code.

PREFIX NOTATION

Clojure code uses *prefix notation* (also called polish notation) to represent function calls. For those who are new to Lisp, this definitely takes a little getting used to, especially when it comes to using math functions such +, /, *, and so on. Instead of writing 1 + 2, Clojure represents this evaluation as (+ 1 2). Prefix notation is less familiar than the mathematical form we all learned at school.

Regular functions, on the other hand, don't have this problem. In a language such as Ruby, you'd call an add function as follows:

```
add(1, 2)
```

If you look closely, this is also prefix notation because the name of the function appears first, followed by arguments. The advantage of prefix notation for functions is that the function appears as the first symbol, everything else that follows can be treated as arguments to it. The Clojure version moves the parentheses around (and drops the unnecessary comma, because whitespace is sufficient to delimit the arguments):

```
(add 1 2)
```

In most languages, mathematical functions like addition and subtraction are special cases built into the language as operators, in order to make it possible to represent math in the more familiar in-fix notation. Clojure avoids this special case by not having any operators at all. Instead, math functions are implemented using Clojure functions. All functions work the same way, whether they're math related or not.

By avoiding special cases and relying on the same prefix notation for all functions, Clojure maintains its regularity and gives us all the advantages that come from having no syntax. We discussed this aspect of the language in some detail in chapter 1. The main advantage we talked about was that it makes it easy to generate and manipulate code. For example, consider the regular way in which Clojure structures the conditional cond form (similar to case statements in other languages):

```
(cond
  (> x 0) (println "greater!")
  (= x 0) (println "zero! ")
  :default (println "neither!"))
```

This is a nested list, and it contains an even number of expressions that appear in pairs. The first element of each pair is a test expression, and the second is the respective value that's returned if the test expression succeeds. Generating such a simple list is easy, especially when compared to a case statement in a language like Java.

This is the reason Clojure uses prefix notation, and I can say from experience that programmers new to this way of calling functions get used to it in no time. Now, let's discuss another couple of aspects of writing Clojure code: whitespace and comments.

WHITESPACE AND COMMENTS

As you've seen, Clojure uses parentheses (and braces and square brackets) to delimit fragments of code. Unlike languages such as Ruby and Java, it doesn't need commas to delimit elements of a list (such as a vector or arguments passed to a function). You can use commas if you like, because Clojure treats them as whitespace and ignores them. So the following two function calls are equivalent:

```
(+ 1 2 3 4 5)
```

```
(+ 1, 2, 3, 4, 5)
```

Although Clojure ignores commas, it sometimes uses them to make things easier for the programmer to read. For instance, if you have a hash map like the following

```
(def a-map {:a 1 :b 2 :c 3})
```

and ask for its value at the REPL, the Clojure printer echoes it with commas:

```
{:a 1, :b 2, :c 3}
```

The results are easier to read, especially if you're looking at a large amount of data. Now let's look at comments.

Like most Lisps, single-line comments in Clojure are denoted using semicolons. To comment out a line of text, put one or more semicolons at the beginning. Here's an example:

```
;;this function does addition
(defn add [x y]
  (+ x y))
```

As an aside, some folks use the following convention relating to comment markers. Single semicolons are used when the comment appears after some program text. Double semicolons are used, as shown previously, to comment out an entire line of text. And finally, triple semicolons are used for block comments.

Clojure provides a rather convenient macro that can be used for multiline comments. The macro is called `comment`, and here's an example:

```
(comment
(defn this-is-not-working [x y]
  (+ x y)))
```

This causes the whole s-expression to be treated as a comment. Specifically, the `comment` macro ignores forms passed in and returns `nil`.

As a final note on syntax, let's address case sensitivity of Clojure.

CASE SENSITIVITY

Most Lisps are not case sensitive. Clojure, on the other hand, *is* case sensitive. Most modern programming languages are case sensitive today, so this should be easy for almost everyone to get used to.

Now that we've covered Clojure syntax, you're ready to learn about writing programs in the language. We'll begin by explaining the various constructs that influence the structure of Clojure code, such as `defn`, `let`, `do`, `loop`, and so on. The next couple of sections will cover program flow control and core data structures.

2.2   *Program structure*

In this section, we'll examine several constructs that are part of the Clojure language. Most of those that we discuss here are categorized as structural forms because they lend structure to the code; they set up local names, allow for looping and recursion, and the like. We'll begin with the most fundamental aspect of structuring Clojure code, namely the function.

2.2.1   *Functions*

Clojure is a functional language, which means that functions are first-class citizens of the language. In other words, functions can be created dynamically, be passed as arguments to other functions, can be returned from other functions, and can be stored as values inside other data structures. Clojure functions comply with all of the above.

Programming in a language that has first-class functions is a different experience compared with programming in a language that doesn't. This latter category includes languages such as Ruby and Java. To get started with Clojure functions, let's see how to define functions.

FUNCTION DEFINITION

Clojure offers the convenient `defn` macro, which allows traditional-looking function definitions, such as the following:

```
(defn addition-function [x y]
  (+ x y))
```

In reality, the `defn` macro expands to a combination of calls to `def` and `fn`, both of which are special forms. Here, `def` creates a var with the specified name, and is bound to a new function object. This function has a body as specified in the `defn` form. Here's what the equivalent expanded form looks like:

```
(def addition-function (fn [x y]
                           (+ x y)))
```

The `fn` special form accepts a sequence of arguments in square brackets, followed by the body of the function. The `fn` form can be used directly to define anonymous functions. The `def` form shown here assigns the function created using `fn` to the var `addition-function`.

VARIABLE ARITY

In order to define functions of variable arity, parameter lists can use the `&` symbol. An example is the addition function from Clojure core:

```
[+ x y & more]
```

This allows `+` to handle any number of arguments. Functions are explained in more detail in chapter 3. Now you'll learn about a form that helps in structuring the innards of functions themselves.

2.2.2 *The let form*

Consider the following function:

```
(defn average-pets []
  (/ (apply + (map :number-pets (vals users))) (count users)))
```

Don't worry yet about all that's going on here. Observe that the body of the function is quite a long, complex-looking line of code. Such code can take several seconds to read. It would be nice if we could break it down into pieces, in order to make the intent of the code clearer. The `let` form allows us to introduce locally named things into our code. Consider the following alternate implementation:

```
(defn average-pets []
  (let [user-data (vals users)
        number-pets (map :number-pets user-data)
        total (apply + number-pets)]
    (/ total (count users))))
```

Here, `user-data`, `number-pets`, and `total` are locally named values (they're similar to variables, but they can't vary because Clojure's data structures are immutable). Now the computation is much clearer, and it's easy to read and maintain this code.

Although this is a trivial example, you can imagine more complex use cases. Further, the let form can be used to name things that might be needed more than once in a piece of code. Indeed, you can introduce a local value computed from previously named values, within the same form, for instance:

```
(let [x 1
      y 2
      z (+ x y)]
  (println z))
```

More specifically, the let form accepts as its first argument a vector containing an even number of forms, followed by zero or more forms that get evaluated when the let is evaluated. The value of the last expression is returned.

THE UNDERSCORE IDENTIFIER

Before moving on, it's worth discussing the situation where you might not care about the return value of an expression. Typically, such an expression is called purely for its side effect. A trivial example is calling println. If you do this inside a let form for any reason, you'd need to specify an identifier in which to hold the return value. The code might look like this:

```
(defn average-pets []
  (let [user-data (vals users)
        number-pets (map :number-pets user-data)
        value-from-println (println "total  pets:" number-pets)
        total (apply + number-pets)]
    (/ total (count users)))))
```

In this code, the only reason you create value-from-println is because the let form needs a name to bind the value of each expression. In such cases where you don't care about the value, it's idiomatic to use a single underscore as the identifier name. Take a look at the following:

```
(defn average-pets []
  (let [user-data (vals users)
        number-pets (map :number-pets user-data)
        _ (println "total  pets:" number-pets)
        total (apply + number-pets)]
    (/ total (count users)))))
```

The underscore identifier can be used in any situation where you don't care about the value of something. This will be even more useful when we explore Clojure's destructuring support in the next chapter.

We've pretty much covered the let form. One important thing to note here is that although we've liberally used the term *variable* to mean the things we're naming inside let forms, most of Clojure is immutable. This means they're not true variables. We're going to explore immutability and mutation a lot more, starting with chapter 3. For now, let's continue with learning about the do form.

2.2.3 *Side effects with do*

In a pure functional language, programs are free of side effects. The only way to "do something" is for a function to compute a value and return it. Calling a function doesn't alter the state of the world in any way. Consider the following snippet of code:

```
(defn do-many-things []
  (do-first-thing)
  (do-another-thing)
  (return-final-value))
```

In a world without state and side effects, the do-many-things function would be equivalent to this one:

```
(defn do-many-things-equivalent []
  (return-final-value))
```

The calls to do-first-thing and do-another-thing can be eliminated without change in behavior, even without knowing what they do. This is because in a stateless world without side effects, the only thing that "does something" in do-many-things is the last function call to return-final-value, which presumably computes and returns a value. In such a world, there'd be no reason to ever call a series of functions (as shown in the first example), because only the last one would ever do anything useful.

The real world is full of state, and side effects are a necessity. For example, printing something to the console or to a log file is a side effect that changes the state of the world. Storing something in a database alters the state of the world and is another example of a side effect.

In order to combine multiple s-expressions into a single form, Clojure provides the do form. It can be used for any situation as described previously where some side effect is desired and the higher-order form accepts only a single s-expression. As an example, consider the if block:

```
(if (is-something-true?)
  (do
    (log-message "in true branch")
    (store-something-in-db)
    (return-useful-value)))
```

Normally, because the consequent part of the if form accepts only a single s-expression, without the do as shown here, it would be difficult to get the true case to call all three functions (log-message, store-something-in-db, and return-useful-value).

The do form is a convenient way to combine multiple s-expressions into one. This is a common idiom in macros, and plenty of core Clojure forms are macros that accept multiple forms as parameters and combine them into one using a do. Examples are when, binding, dosync, and locking.

Now that you know how to create blocks of code using do, we'll move on to learning about other structural constructs in the remainder of this section. First, though, let's look at exception handling in Clojure.

2.2.4   *try/catch/finally and throw*

A significant part of Clojure is written in Java, and the language runtime itself runs on the JVM. This is the reason why it was a natural choice to continue to use Java exceptions as the error notification system in Clojure. It's an aspect of transparent interoperability with existing Java code, as you'll see in chapter 5. Meanwhile, let's take a quick look at how to handle and also throw exceptions in Clojure code.

If an expression has the potential to throw an exception, a `try/catch/finally` block can be used to catch it and decide what to do with it. This is optional because Clojure doesn't expect you to handle checked exceptions as Java does. Here's an example, a modification of our previous function that calculates the average number of pets our users own:

```
(defn average-pets [users]
  (let [user-data (vals users)
        number-pets (map :number-pets user-data)
        total (apply + number-pets)]
    (/ total (count users))))
```

Now imagine that we had no users in our system yet:

```
(def no-users {})
```

If we try calling `average-pets` with `no-users`, we'll get an exception:

```
user> (average-pets no-users)
; Evaluation aborted.
Divide by zero
  [Thrown class java.lang.ArithmeticException]
```

Normally, we'd check for the empty list, but for illustration purposes, let's add a try/catch block:

```
(defn average-pets [users]
  (try
    (let [user-data (vals users)
          number-pets (map :number-pets user-data)
          total (apply + number-pets)]
      (/ total (count users)))
    (catch Exception e
      (println "Error!")
      0)))
```

When we now attempt the same thing as before, we get this:

```
user=> (average-pets no-users)
Error!
0
```

The general form of using `try/catch/finally` is straightforward:

```
(try expr* catch-clause* finally-clause?)
```

The form accepts multiple expressions as part of the `try` clause and multiple `catch` clauses. The `finally` clause is optional. The expressions passed to the try clause are evaluated one by one, and the value of the last is returned. If any of them generate an exception, the appropriate catch clause is executed based on the type (class) of the exception, and the value of that is then returned. The optional finally clause is always executed for any side effects that need to be guaranteed.

Exceptions can be thrown as easily using the throw form. In any place where you wish to throw an exception, you can do something like the following:

```
(throw (Exception. "this is an error!"))
```

throw accepts a Java exception object, so any kind of exception can be thrown using it.

That covers the basics of using the try/catch/finally form as well as throwing exceptions. This isn't a commonly used feature of the Clojure language, because it doesn't force you to handle or declare checked exceptions as Java does. There are several helper macros that take care of many situations where you might need to use this form. You'll see this more in chapter 5. In the meantime, our last stop in this section will be a brief exploration of reader macros.

2.2.5 *Reader macros*

We discussed the Clojure reader in chapter 1, and you saw that it converts program text into Clojure data structures. It does this by recognizing that characters such as parentheses, braces, and the like are special and that they form the beginning (and ending) of lists, hash maps, and so on. These rules are built into the reader.

Other characters are special also, because they signal to the reader that the form that follows them should be treated in a special way. In a sense, these characters extend the capability of the reader, and they're called reader macros. The simplest (and most traditional) example of a reader macro is the comment character (;). When the reader encounters a semicolon, it treats the rest of that line of code as a comment and ignores it.

The quotation reader macro is another simple example. Consider the following line of code:

```
(add 1 2 3 4 5)
```

This is a call to the add function, with the remaining symbols (numbers) as the parameters. Any list like this is treated the same way; the first element should resolve to a function and the remaining elements are treated as arguments to that function. If you want to avoid this, you can quote it using the quote form:

```
(quote (add 1 2 3 4 5))
```

This causes the whole list (including the first add symbol) to be treated as is (a list of symbols) and be returned. The reader macro (' is equivalent to using the quote form:

```
'(add 1 2 3 4 5)
```

Table 2.1 shows the available reader macros in Clojure.

You'll learn about each of these reader macros in the relevant section in the book. For instance, we'll use the last three quite heavily in the chapter about macros.

Table 2.1   Clojure's reader macros and their descriptions

Reader macro character	Description of reader macro
Quote (')	Quotes the form following it
Character (\)	Yields a character literal
Comment (;)	Single-line comment
Meta (^)	Associates metadata for the form that follows
Deref (@)	Dereferences the agent or ref that follows
Dispatch (#)	#{ } Constructs a set #″ Constructs a regex pattern #^ Associates metadata for the next form (deprecated) #'var quote—resolves the var that follows #() Constructs an anonymous function #_ Skips the following form
Syntax quote (`)	Syntax quote, used in macros to render s-expressions
Unquote (~)	Unquotes forms inside syntax-quoted forms
Unquote splice (~@)	Unquotes a list inside a syntax form, but inserts the elements of the list without the surrounding brackets

Reader macros are implemented as entries in a read table. An entry in this table is essentially a reader macro character associated with the macro function that describes how the form that follows is to be treated. Most Lisps expose this read table to the programmer, allowing them to manipulate it or add new reader macros. Clojure doesn't do this, and so you can't define your own reader macros.

In this section, you saw various structural constructs provided by Clojure. In the next section, you'll see forms that control the execution flow of Clojure programs.

2.3   *Program flow*

Clojure is a simple language to learn, with few special forms, and indeed few constructs that control the flow of execution. In this section, we'll begin with conditional program execution with the `if` special form and other macros built on the `if` form, and then we'll look at various functional constructs that allow for looping and working on sequences of data. Specifically, we'll consider `loop/recur`, followed by a few macros that use `loop/recur` internally to make it convenient to process sequences. We'll close this chapter with a few higher-order functions that apply other functions to sequences of data.

2.3.1 Conditionals

A conditional form is one that causes Clojure to either execute or not execute associated code. The most basic example of this is the `if` form. In Clojure, the general form of `if` looks like this:

```
(if test consequent alternative)
```

This shows that the `if` form accepts a test expression, which is evaluated to determine what to do next. If the test is true, the consequent is evaluated. If the test is false, and if an alternative form is provided, then it is evaluated instead (else `nil` is returned). Because the consequent and alternative clauses of the `if` form can only be a single s-expression, you can use the `do` form to have it do multiple things.

    `if` is a special form, which means that the Clojure language implements it internally as a special case. In a language that provides the `if` special form and a macro system, all other conditional forms can be implemented as macros, which is what Clojure does. Let's visit a few such macros.

IF-NOT

The `if-not` macro does the inverse of what the `if` special form does. The general structure of this macro is

```
(if-not test consequent alternative)
```

Here, if the test is `false`, the consequent is evaluated, else if it is `true` and the alternative is provided, it is evaluated instead.

COND

`cond` is like the case statement of Clojure. The general form looks like the following:

```
(cond & clauses)
```

Here's a trivial example of using `cond`:

```
(defn range-info [x]
  (cond
    (< x 0) (println "Negative!")
    (= x 0) (println "Zero!")
    :default (println "Positive!")))
```

As you can see, the clauses are pairs of expressions, each of the form `test consequent`. Each test expression is evaluated in sequence, and when one returns `true`, the associated consequent is evaluated and returned. If none returns `true`, we can pass in something that works as a true value (for example, the `:default` symbol as shown below), the associated consequent is evaluated and returned instead.

WHEN

Here's the general form of the `when` macro:

```
(when test & body)
```

This convenient macro is an `if` (without the alternative clause), along with an implicit `do`. This allows multiple s-expressions to be passed in as the body. Here's how it might be used:

```
(when (some-condition?)
  (do-this-first)
  (then-that)
  (and-return-this))
```

Note that there's no need to wrap the three functions in the body inside a do, because the when macro takes care of this. You'll find this a common pattern, and it's a convenience that most macros provide to their callers.

WHEN-NOT

when-not is the opposite of when, in that it evaluates its body if the test returns false (or nil). The general form looks similar to that of when:

```
(when-not test & body)
```

These are some of the many forms that allow programs to handle different kinds of conditional situations. Except for the if special form, they're all implemented as macros, which also implies that the programmer is free to implement new ones, suited to the domain of the program. In the next section, you'll see a little more detail about writing test expressions using logical functions.

LOGICAL FUNCTIONS

Any expression that evaluates to true or false can be used for the test expression in all the previously mentioned conditional forms. In order to write compound test expressions, Clojure provides some logical functions. Let's examine the logical and first. Here's the general form:

```
(and x & next)
```

It implies that and accepts one or more forms (zero or more; calling and without any arguments returns true). It evaluates each in turn, and if any returns nil or false, and returns that value. If none of the forms return false or nil, then and returns the value of the last form. and short circuits the arguments by not evaluating the remaining if any one returns false. Here's an example:

```
(if (and (is-member? user)
         (has-special-status? user))
  (welcome-warmly user))
```

or works in the opposite way. It also accepts one or more forms (zero or more, calling or without any arguments returns nil) and evaluates them one by one. If any returns a logical true, it returns it as the value of the or. If none return a logical true, then the value of the last one is returned. or also short-circuits its arguments. Here's an example:

```
(if (or (never-logged-in? user) (has-no-expenses? user))
  (email-encouragement user))
```

Another point of interest is that both and and or are also macros. This means that the Clojure language doesn't provide these as part of its core, but instead they're part of the standard library. It also means that we can write our own macros that behave like and or or and they would be indistinguishable from the language. I know we keep saying this, but you'll see what this means in chapter 7.

Finally, Clojure provides a not function that inverts the logical value of whatever is passed in as an argument. Here's an example:

```
(if (not (thrifty? user))
  (email-savings user))
```

As a relevant side note, Clojure provides all the usual comparison and equality functions. Examples are <, <=, >, >=, and =. They all work the way you'd expect them to, with an additional feature: they take any number of arguments. The < function, for instance, checks to see if the arguments are in increasing order. The = function is the same as Java's equals, but it works for a wider range of objects including nil, numbers, and sequences. Note that it's a single = symbol and not ==, which is commonly used in many programming languages.

These logical functions are sufficient in order to create compound logical expressions from simple ones. Our next stop in this section is going to be iterations—not strictly the kind supported by imperative languages such as C++ and Java, but the functional kind.

2.3.2 *Functional iteration*

Most functional languages don't have traditional iteration constructs like for because typical implementations of for require mutation of the loop counter. Instead, they use recursion and function application to process lists of things. We'll start this section by looking at the familiar while form, followed by examining Clojure's looping construct of loop/recur. Then we'll examine a few convenient macros such as doseq and dotimes, which are built on top of loop/recur.

WHILE

Clojure's while macro works in a similar fashion to those seen in imperative languages such as Ruby and Java. The general form is as follows:

```
(while test & body)
```

An example is

```
(while (request-on-queue?)
  (handle-request (pop-request-queue)))
```

Here, requests will continue to be processed as long as they keep appearing on the request queue. The while loop will end if request-on-queue? returns a value either false or nil, presumably because something else happened elsewhere in the system. Note that the only way for a while loop to end is for a side effect to cause the test expression to return false.

Now, let's move on to another looping construct, one that's somewhat different from imperative languages, because it relies on what appears to be recursion.

LOOP/RECUR

Clojure doesn't have traditional for loops for iteration; instead, programs can achieve similar behavior through the use of higher-level functions such as map and other functions in the sequence library. The Clojure version of iterative flow control is `loop` and the associated `recur`. Here's an example of calculating the factorial of a number n using `loop`/`recur`:

```
(defn fact-loop [n]
  (loop [current n fact 1]
    (if (= current 1)
      fact
      (recur (dec current) (* fact current)))))
```

Here's the general form of the `loop` form:

```
(loop bindings & body)
```

`loop` sets up bindings that work exactly like the `let` form does. In this example, [current n fact 1] works the same way if used with a `let` form: current gets bound to the value of n, and fact gets bound to a value of 1. Then it executes the supplied body inside the lexical scope of the bindings. In this case, the body is the `if` form.

Now let's talk about recur. It has similar semantics as the `let` form bindings:

```
(recur bindings)
```

The bindings are computed, and each value is bound to the respective name as described in the `loop` form. Execution then returns to the start of the `loop` body. In this example, recur has two binding values, (dec current) and (* fact current), which are computed and rebound to current and fact. The `if` form then executes again. This continues until the `if` condition causes the looping to end by not calling recur anymore.

recur is a special form in Clojure, and despite looking recursive, it doesn't consume the stack. It's the preferred way of doing self-recursion, as opposed to a function calling itself by name. The reason for this is that Clojure currently doesn't have tail-call optimization, though it's possible that this will be added at some point in the future if the JVM were to support it. recur can be used only from tail positions of code, and if an attempt is made to use it from any other position, the compiler will complain. For instance, this will cause Clojure to complain:

```
(defn fact-loop-invalid [n]
  (loop [current n fact 1]
    (if (= current 1)
      fact
      (recur (dec current) (* fact current)))
    (println "Done, current value:" current)))
```

The specific error you will see is

```
Can only recur from tail position
  [Thrown class java.lang.UnsupportedOperationException]
```

This will tip you off that you have a recur being used from a non-tail position of `loop`, and such errors in code are easy to fix.

As you've seen, loop/recur is easy to use. recur is more powerful and can cause execution to return to any recursion point. Recursion points can be set up, as you saw in the example, by a loop form or by a function form (enabling you to create self-recursive functions). You'll see the latter in action in the next chapter. Now let's look at a few macros that Clojure provides that make it easy to work with sequences without having to directly use loop/recur.

DOSEQ, DOTIMES

Imagine that you have a list of users and you wish to generate expense reports for each user. You could use the looping construct from the previous section, but instead there's a convenient way to achieve the same effect in the following dispatch-reporting-jobs function:

```
(defn run-report [user]
  (println "Running report for" user))

(defn dispatch-reporting-jobs [all-users]
  (doseq [user all-users]
    (run-reports user)))
```

Here, the form of interest is doseq. The simplest form accepts a vector containing two terms, where the first term is a new symbol, which will be sequentially bound to each element in the second term (which must be a sequence). The body will be executed for each element in the sequence. In this case, dispatch-reporting-jobs will call run-reports for each user present in the sequence all-users.

dotimes is similar. It's a convenience macro that accepts a vector containing a symbol and a number n, followed by the body. The symbol is set to numbers from 0 to (n – 1), and the body is evaluated for each number. Here's an example:

```
(dotimes [x 5]
    (println "Factorial of " x "is =" (factorial x)))
```

This will calculate and print the factorials of the numbers 0 through 4.

Despite the convenience of these macros, they're not used as much as you'd imagine, especially if you're coming from an imperative background. In Clojure, the most common pattern of computing things from lists of data is using higher-level functions such as map, filter, and reduce. We'll look at these briefly in the remainder of this section.

MAP

The simplest use of map accepts a unary function and a sequence of data elements. A *unary function* is a function that accepts only one argument. map applies this function to each element of the sequence and returns a new sequence that contains all the returned values. Here's an example:

```
(defn find-daily-totals [start-date end-date]
  (let [all-dates (dates-between start-date end-date)]
    (map find-total-expenses all-dates)))
```

Here, the last line is where map collects the values received from calling find-total-expenses on each date in all-dates. In other languages, this would have required much more code: an iteration block, a list that collects the return values, and a condition that checks to see if the list is exhausted. A single call to map does all this. Even though this is a common way of using map, it's even more general than this. map accepts a function that can take any number of arguments, along with the same number of sequences. It collects the result of applying the function to corresponding elements from each sequence. If the sequences are of varying lengths, map will only work through the shortest one.

FILTER

filter does something similar to map—it collects values. But it accepts a predicate function and a sequence and returns only those elements of the sequence that return a logically true value when the predicate function is called on them. Here's an example:

```
(defn non-zero-expenses [expenses]
  (let [non-zero? (fn [e] (not (zero? e)))]
    (filter non-zero? expenses)))
```

Or here's a more succinct alternative:

```
(defn non-zero-expenses [expenses]
  (filter pos? expenses))
```

pos? is a function that checks to see if the supplied argument is greater than zero.

For several kinds of calculations, you'll need to operate on only those expenses that aren't zero. non-zero-expenses is a function that removes all but such values, and it does so in one line of code (three words!).

REDUCE

The simplest form of reduce is a high-level function that accepts a function of arity 2 and a sequence of data elements. The function is applied to the first two elements of the sequence, producing the first result. The same function is then called again with this result and the next element of the sequence. This then repeats with the following element, and so on.

Let's write the factorial function using reduce:

```
(defn factorial [n]
  (let [numbers (range 1 (+ n 1))]
    (reduce * numbers)))
```

range is a Clojure function that returns a list of numbers starting from the first argument (inclusive) to the second argument (exclusive). This is why numbers is computed by calling range with 1 and (+ n 1). The rest is easy; you reduce the sequence using the multiply (*) function.

Let's examine how this works when factorial is called with 5. numbers is set to the result of calling range on 1 and 6, which is the sequence of the numbers 1, 2, 3, 4, and 5. This sequence is what reduce operates on, along with the multiplication function. The result of multiplying 1 and 2 (which is 2) is multiplied by 3 (resulting in 6). That is then multiplied by 4 (resulting in 24), which is finally multiplied by 5, resulting in 120.

reduce is a powerful function, and as shown here, it accomplishes in a single line of code what might require several lines in other languages.

FOR

What book can be complete without mentioning `for` in the context of iteration? We said earlier that few functional languages have a traditional `for` construct. Clojure does have `for`, but it isn't quite like what you might be used to. Similar to `doseq`, `for` is used for list comprehensions, which is a syntactic feature that allows sequences to be constructed out of existing ones. The general form of the `for` construct follows:

```
(for seq-exprs body-expr)
```

`seq-exprs` is a vector specifying one or more binding-form/collection-expr pairs. `body-expr` can use the bindings set up in `seq-exprs` to construct each element of the list. Consider the following example that generates a list of labels for each square on a chessboard:

```
(defn chessboard-labels []
  (for [alpha "abcdefgh"
        num (range 1 9)]
    (str alpha num)))
```

When called, this returns a list with all 64 labels:

```
user=> (chessboard-labels)
("a1" "a2" "a3" "a4" "a5"  …  "h6" "h7" "h8")
```

The `for` seq-exprs can take modifiers `:let`, `:when`, and `:while`. To see an example of `:when` in use, let's first consider a function that checks to see if a number is prime:

```
(defn prime? [x]
  (let [divisors (range 2 (inc (int (Math/sqrt x))))
        remainders (map #(rem x %) divisors)]
    (not (some zero? remainders))))
```

Although there are more efficient ways to test for a prime number, this implementation will suffice for our example. Now let's use `for` to write a function `primes-less-than`, which returns a list of all primes between 2 and the number passed in:

```
(defn primes-less-than [n]
  (for [x (range 2 (inc n))
        :when (prime? x)]
    x))
```

Notice how we specify a condition in the `for` form using the `:when` option. Let's test this function:

```
user=> (primes-less-than 50)
(2 3 5 7 11 13 17 19 23 29 31 37 41 43 47)
```

Let's look at another, slightly more complex example. Let's use the `prime?` function to find all pairs of numbers under, say, a number like 5, such that the sum of each is prime. Here it is:

```
(defn pairs-for-primes [n]
  (let [z (range 2 (inc n))]
    (for [x z y z :when (prime? (+ x y))]
      (list x y))))
```

Let's test it out:

```
user=> (pairs-for-primes 5)
((2 3) (2 5) (3 2) (3 4) (4 3) (5 2))
```

As you can see, Clojure's for is a powerful construct, and it can be used to create arbitrary lists. A great advantage of this feature is that it's almost declarative. For instance, the code in pairs-for-primes reads almost like a restatement of the problem itself.

Our next stop isn't strictly about program flow but about a couple of macros that are useful in writing other functions and macros.

2.3.3   *The threading macros*

You're going to learn a lot about macros in this book, starting with an introduction to them in chapter 7. From a developer point of view, there are several macros that are extremely useful. You've seen several already, and in this section you'll see two more, which make writing code a lot more convenient and result in more readable code as well. They're called threading macros.

THREAD-FIRST

Imagine that you need to calculate the savings that would be available to a user several years from now based on some amount they invest today. You can use the formula for compound interest to calculate this:

```
final-amount = principle * (1 + rate/100) ^ time-periods
```

You can write a function to calculate this:

```
(defn final-amount [principle rate time-periods]
  (* (Math/pow (+ 1 (/ rate 100)) time-periods) principle))
```

You can test that it works by calling it at the REPL:

```
user> (final-amount 100 20 1)
120.0

user> (final-amount 100 20 2)
144.0
```

This is fine, but the function definition is difficult to read, because it's written inside out, thanks to the prefix nature of Clojure's syntax. This is where the thread-first macro (called ->) helps, as shown in the following code:

```
(defn final-amount-> [principle rate time-periods]
  (-> rate
      (/ 100)
      (+ 1)
      (Math/pow time-periods)
      (* principle)))
```

It works the same, and you can confirm this on the REPL:

```
user> (final-amount-> 100 20 1)
120.0

user> (final-amount-> 100 20 2)
144.0
```

What the thread-first macro does is to take the first argument supplied and place it in the second position of the next expression. It's called thread-first because it moves code into the position of the first argument of the following form. It then takes the entire resulting expression and moves it into the second position of the following expression, and so on, until all expressions are exhausted. So when the macro expands in the case of our `final-amount->` function, the form looks like this:

```
(* (Math/pow (+ 1 (/ rate 100)) time-periods) principle)
```

To be more accurate, the call to Java's `Math/pow` is also expanded, but we'll explore that in chapter 5. For now, it's enough to see that the expanded form is exactly like the one we manually defined in `final-amount` earlier. The advantage is that `final-amount->` is much easier to write and to read.

In the next section, we'll examine a related macro, called thread-last.

THREAD-LAST

The thread-last macro (named `->>`) is a cousin of the thread-first macro. Instead of taking the first expression and moving it into the second position of the next expression, it moves it into the last place. It then repeats the process for all the expressions provided to it. Let's examine a version of the `factorial` function again:

```
(defn factorial [n]
  (apply *
         (range 1
                (+ 1
                   n))))
```

This is also written in the inside-out syntax, and it isn't immediately obvious what the sequence of operations is. Here's the same function rewritten using the `->>` macro:

```
(defn factorial->> [n]
  (->> n
       (+ 1)
       (range 1)
       (apply *)))
```

You can check that it works by testing it at the REPL:

```
user=> (factorial->> 5)
120
```

This macro expands our `factorial->>` function to

```
(apply * (range 1 (+ 1 n)))
```

This ensures that it works the same way as `factorial` defined previously. The main advantage of this macro (similar to the `->` macro) is that it lets developers focus on the sequence of operations, rather than ensuring they're writing the nested expressions correctly. It's also easy to read and maintain the resulting function.

In this section, you saw various ways to control the execution flow of Clojure programs. We started off with conditionals and explored the associated logical functions. We then addressed the idea of looping—not directly as imperative for loops do in other languages, but through a recursive form and through higher-order functions. Armed with this knowledge, you could write a lot of code without ever missing imperative constructs.

2.4   *Clojure data structures*

In this section, we're going to quickly explore the various built-in data types and data structures of Clojure. We'll start with the basic characters, strings, and so on and end with Clojure sequences.

2.4.1   *nil, truth, and falsehood*

You've seen these in action in the last several pages, so let's run a quick recap. Clojure's nil is equivalent to null in Java and nil in Ruby. It means "nothing." Calling a function on nil may lead to a NullPointerException, although core Clojure functions try to do something reasonable when operating on nil.

Boolean values are simple. Everything other than false and nil is considered true. There's an explicit true value, which can be used when needed.

2.4.2   *Chars, strings, and numbers*

Clojure characters are Java characters. Clojure has a reader macro, the backslash, which can be used to denote characters, like \a or \g.

Clojure strings are Java strings. They're denoted using double quotes (because single quote is a reader macro, which as you saw earlier, means something else entirely). For this reason, it's useful to know the API provided by the Java String class. Some examples are

```
(.split "clojure-in-action" "-")
```

and

```
(.endsWith "program.clj" ".clj")
```

both of which return what you'd expect. Note the leading periods in .split and .endsWith. This is Clojure syntax for calling a Java method, and chapter 5 focuses entirely on Java interop.

Clojure numbers are implemented in a rather elegant fashion. They're Java-boxed numbers that ultimately derive from the java.lang.Number class. BigInteger, BigDecimal, Double, Float, and the like are all part of that hierarchy.

Clojure does define one more type of number: the ratio. Ratios are created when two integers are divided such that they can't be reduced any further. Here's an example: executing the code (/ 4 9) returns a ratio object 4/9. If instead of dividing such integers, one of the numbers is a `Double`, then the result is also a `Double`. As an example, evaluating `(/ 4.0 9)` returns `0.4444444444444444`.

One final thing of interest: Clojure converts `Integers` that exceed their capacity to `Longs`. Further, when `Longs`, in turn, exceed their capacity, they get converted into `BigIntegers`.

We've covered the basic data types in Clojure, and these are probably familiar to programmers from most backgrounds. We're now going to examine a few that are somewhat unique to the Clojure language. We'll begin with keywords and symbols and then move on to sequences.

2.4.3 Keywords and symbols

Keywords are similar to those in languages like Ruby (where they're called symbols). Some examples of keywords are `:first-name` and `:last-name`. Keywords are symbolic identifiers that always evaluate to themselves. A typical use of keywords is as keys inside hash maps, but they can be used anywhere a unique value is needed.

Keywords have a rather convenient property—they're also functions. They operate on hash maps by looking themselves up in them. We'll say more about this in the next chapter.

Clojure symbols are identifiers that evaluate to something they name. They're used for pretty much everything in Clojure. For instance, consider s-expressions where function parameter names, local names created inside `let` bindings, vars that represent function names or global constants, and so on are all represented symbolically using Clojure symbols. Symbols can have metadata (you'll learn about metadata in the next chapter).

Symbols, like keywords, also have the interesting property of being functions. They accept hash maps and look themselves up in them. You'll learn about these as well in the next chapter. In the chapter on macros, we'll manipulate symbols inside s-expressions in order to manipulate and transform code. In the meantime, we'll look at Clojure sequences, which represent the language's fresh take on Lisps' core data structure: the list.

2.4.4 Sequences

In one sense, Lisp was created to process lists. It's not an overstatement, then, to say that the list is a core data structure in the language (to be more specific, the core data structure is the `cons` cell). Other, more complicated data structures can be created in Lisp by building on the simple list. In general, this isn't a problem. Because most Lisps implement the list in a hardwired way (using the `cons` cell), the usefulness of many Lisp functions is limited to operating on such lists.

Clojure avoids this problem in an elegant way. Instead of providing a concrete implementation of a list data structure, it provides an abstract interface called `ISeq`. Any concrete implementation of `ISeq` is a valid sequence, and all of Clojure's power can be brought to bear on it. This includes library functions, special forms, and macros. Because most of the sequence library in Clojure is lazy, user-defined data structures that implement ISeq can also benefit from this laziness. Examples of sequences are lists, vectors, and hash maps.

The ISeq interface provides three functions: first, rest, and cons. Here's how first and rest work:

```
user=> (first [1 2 3 4 5])
1

user=> (rest [1 2 3 4 5])
(2 3 4 5)
```

They're both pretty straightforward. first returns the first element of the sequence, whereas rest returns the sequences without the first element. cons creates new sequences given an element and an existing sequence. cons, which is short for *construct*, is so named for historical reasons. It works as follows:

```
user=> (cons 1 [2 3 4 5])
(1 2 3 4 5)
```

These three functions, and indeed many others, all work with sequences, aka the ISeq interface. In the remainder of this section, we'll examine the most commonly used data structures that implement this interface. As we discuss each of the following, it will help to keep in mind that all core data structures in Clojure are immutable.

LISTS

Lists are the basic data structure of Clojure. Lists are plain collections of symbols and expressions, surrounded by parentheses. They can be created using the list function:

```
user=> (list 1 2 3 4 5)
(1 2 3 4 5)
```

The conj function can be used to add values to a list:

```
user=> (conj (list 1 2 3 4 5) 6)
[1 2 3 4 5 6]
```

Because lists are immutable, what conj does is return a new list with the additional element. You can check if a data structure is a list by using the list? predicate:

```
user=> (let [a-list (list 1 2 3 4 5)]
          (list? a-list))
true
```

LISTS ARE SPECIAL

As you learned earlier, Clojure code is represented using Clojure data structures. The list is special because each expression of Clojure code is a list. The list may contain other data structures such as vectors, but the list is the primary one.

In practice, this implies that lists are treated differently. Clojure assumes that the first symbol appearing in a list represents the name of a function (or a macro). The remaining expressions in the list are considered arguments to the function. Here's an example:

```
(+ 1 2 3)
```

This list contains the symbol for plus (which evaluates to the addition function), followed by symbols for numbers representing one, two, and three. Once the reader reads and parses this, the list is evaluated by applying the addition function to the numbers 1, 2, and 3. This evaluates to 6, and this result is returned as the value of the expression (+ 1 2 3).

This has another implication. What if you wanted to define three-numbers as a list containing the numbers 1, 2, and 3? Let's try that:

```
user=> (def three-numbers (1 2 3))
; Evaluation aborted.
java.lang.Integer cannot be cast to clojure.lang.IFn
   [Thrown class java.lang.ClassCastException]
```

The reason for this error is that Clojure is trying to treat the list (1 2 3) the same way as it treats all lists. The first element is considered a function, and here the integer 1 isn't a function. What we want here is for Clojure to not treat the list as code. We want to say, "This list is not code, so don't try to apply normal rules of evaluation to it." As you've seen, you can do this by using quotation, and the quote form does exactly this:

```
user=> (def three-numbers (quote (1 2 3)))
#'user/three-numbers
user=> three-numbers
(1 2 3)
```

You also saw the reader macro for quote, which is a shortcut to using quote. Here it is in action again:

```
user=> (def three-numbers '(1 2 3))
#'user/three-numbers
```

The ability to quote lists is important, as you'll see when we generate code using the macro system. Now, having seen the most basic of the various built-in implementations of ISeq, let's examine a similar one, the vector.

VECTORS

Vectors are like lists, except for two things: they're denoted using square brackets, and they're indexed by numbers. Vectors can be created using the vector function or literally using the square bracket notation:

```
user=> (vector 10 20 30 40 50)
[10 20 30 40 50]
user=> (def the-vector [10 20 30 40 50])
#'user/the-vector
```

Being indexed by numbers means that you have random access to the elements inside a vector. The functions that allow you to get these elements are get and nth. If the-vector is a vector of several elements, the following is how you'd use these functions:

```
user=> (get the-vector 2)
30
user=> (nth the-vector 2)
30
```

```
user=> (get the-vector 10)
nil
```

```
user=> (nth the-vector 10)
; Evaluation aborted.
[Thrown class java.lang.IndexOutOfBoundsException]
```

As shown here, the difference between nth and get is that nth throws an exception if the value is not found, whereas get returns nil. There are also several ways to modify a vector (return a new one with the change). The most commonly used one is assoc, which accepts the index at which to associate a new value, along with the value itself:

```
user> (assoc the-vector 5 60)
[10 20 30 40 50 60]
```

Vectors have another interesting property. They're functions that take a single argument. The argument is assumed to be an index, and when the vector is called with a number, the value associated with that index is looked up inside itself. Here's an example:

```
user> (the-vector 3)
40
```

The advantage of this is that vectors can be used where functions are expected. This helps a lot when using functional composition to create higher-level functions. We'll revisit this aspect of vectors in the next chapter. For now, we'll examine another useful implementation of the ISeq interface, the map.

MAPS

Maps are similar to associative arrays or dictionaries in languages like Python, Ruby, and Perl. A map is a sequence of key-value pairs. The keys can be pretty much any kind of object, and a value can be looked up inside a map with its key. Maps are denoted using braces. Here's an example of a map using keywords as keys, which, as it turns out, is a common pattern:

```
user=> (def the-map {:a 1 :b 2 :c 3})
#'user/the-map
```

Maps can also be constructed using the hash-map function.

```
user=> (hash-map :a 1 :b 2 :c 3)
{:a 1, :c 3, :b 2}
```

Here, the-map is a sequence of key-value pairs. The keys are :a, :b, and :c. The values are 1, 2, and 3. Each key-value pair appears in sequence, establishing which value associates with which key. The values can be looked up like this:

```
user=> (the-map :b)
2
```

The reason this is valid Clojure code is because a Clojure map is also a function. It accepts a key as its parameter, which is used to look up the associated value inside itself. As a reminder, Clojure keywords (like `:a` and `:b`) are also functions. They accept a sequence, such as a map, and look themselves up in the sequence, for example:

```
user=> (:b the-map)
2
```

The advantage of both maps and keywords being functions is that it makes function composition more flexible. Both these kinds of objects can be used where functions are needed, resulting in less and clearer code.

Like all Clojure data structures, maps are also immutable. There are several functions that can modify a map, and `assoc` and `dissoc` are the ones commonly used.

```
user=> (def updated-map (assoc the-map :d 4))
#'user/updated-map

user=> updated-map
{:d 4, :a 1, :b 2, :c 3}

user=> (dissoc updated-map :a)
{:b 2, :c 3, :d 4}
```

Before wrapping up this section, let's look at some rather convenient functions that can make working with maps easy. First, let's look at what we want to accomplish. Imagine you had an empty map, and you wanted to store user details in it. With one entry, the map might look like:

```
(def users {:kyle {
                :date-joined "2009-01-01"
                :summary {
                  :average {
                    :monthly 1000
                    :yearly 12000}}}})
```

Note the use of nested maps. If you wanted to update Kyle's monthly average, you'd need to write some code, like this:

```
(defn set-average-in [users-map user type amount]
  (let [user-map (users-map user)
        summary-map (:summary user-map)
        averages-map (:average summary-map)]
    (assoc users-map user
          (assoc user-map :summary
                (assoc summary-map :average
                      (assoc averages-map type amount))))))
```

Tedious as it is to write, the `set-average-in` function could then be used as follows:

```
user=> (set-average-in users :kyle :monthly 2000)
{:kyle {:date-joined "2009-01-01", :summary {:average {:monthly 2000, :yearly
    12000}}}}
```

Somewhat equally tedious is this function to read an average value:

```
(defn average-for [user type]
  (type (:average (:summary (user @users)))))
```

It works but is rather convoluted. This is where those convenience functions mentioned earlier kick in. The first one is called assoc-in, and here it is in action:

```
user=> (assoc-in users [:kyle :summary :average :monthly] 3000)
{:kyle {:date-joined "2009-01-01", :summary {:average {:monthly 3000, :yearly
    12000}}}}
```

This is helpful, because you didn't have to write a new function to set a new value in the rather deep users map. The general form of assoc-in is

```
(assoc-in map [key & more-keys] value)
```

If any nested map doesn't exist along the way, it gets created and correctly associated. The next convenience function reads values out of such nested maps. This function is called get-in:

```
user=> (get-in users [:kyle :summary :average :monthly])
1000
```

(Note that the changes to Kyle's monthly average aren't reflected because Clojure's data structures are immutable. You'll see how to manage state in chapter 6.)

The final function that's relevant to this discussion is called update-in, which can be used to update values in such nested maps. To see it in action, imagine you wanted to increase Kyle's monthly average by 500:

```
user=> (update-in users [:kyle :summary :average :monthly] + 500)
{:kyle {:date-joined "2009-01-01", :summary {:average {:monthly 1500, :yearly
    12000}}}}
```

The general form of update-in is

```
(update-in map [key & more-keys] update-function & args)
```

This works similarly to assoc-in, in that the keys are used to find what to update with a new value. Instead of supplying the new value itself, you supply a function that accepts the old value (and any other arguments that you can supply as well). The function is applied to these arguments, and the result becomes the new value. The + function here does that job—it takes the old monthly average value of 1000 and adds it to the supplied argument of 500.

A lot of Clojure programs use the map as a core data structure. Often, programmers used to objects in the stateful (data) sense of the word use maps in their place. This is a natural choice and works well.

2.5   Summary

This was a long chapter! We started out installing the Clojure runtime and then addressed the basics of writing code in the language. Specifically, we addressed forms that structure code, such as functions, let, looping, and so on. We also looked at execution control forms, such as if, when, cond, and so on. Armed with this knowledge, you can probably write a fair amount of Clojure code to solve fairly complex problems.

We also visited some of the data types and data structures that come built into the language. Understanding these equips you to use and create the right data abstractions in your programs.

In the next chapter, we're going to explore more building blocks of Clojure. We'll begin with a deep dive into functions, in an attempt to understand Clojure's support for functional programming. We'll also explore the idea of scope and show how to organize your programs with namespaces. Finally, we'll explore a concept somewhat unique to Clojure (well, uncommon in imperative languages such as Java and Ruby at least) called destructuring.

The material from the next chapter, combined with this one, should enable you to write almost any program using the core of Clojure. The remainder of this part of the book will focus on the advanced features of the language.

Building blocks of Clojure

This chapter covers

- Clojure functions in more depth
- Scope rules in Clojure
- Clojure namespaces
- Clojure's destructuring feature
- Clojure metadata

When people are good at something already (such as a programming language), and they try to learn something new (such as another programming language), they often fall into what Martin Fowler calls an improvement ravine. For programming, the ravine refers to the drop in productivity experienced when one has to relearn how to do things in the new language. I've been guilty of switching back to a language I'm already good at in order to get the job done. It sometimes takes me several attempts to get over enough of the ravine to get simple things done. The next few chapters aim to do that—we'll review the basics of Clojure in more detail. After reading them, you'll be comfortable enough to solve problems of reasonable complexity. We'll also cover most constructs of the language, most of which will be familiar to programmers who use other common languages.

First, we'll examine functions in some detail. Lisp was born in the context of mathematics, and functions are elemental to it. Clojure uses functions as building blocks, and mastering functions is fundamental to learning Clojure. We'll then look at how namespaces help organize large programs. These are similar to Java packages; they're a simple way to keep code organized by dividing it into logical modules.

The next section will address vars, which represent the notion of globally visible entities in Clojure. Understanding them is critical to using Clojure effectively. You'll also learn how they're special, thanks to their dynamic scoping rules (as opposed to the more familiar lexical scoping rules). This chapter will explore vars and their use in some detail. Next will be a section on destructuring, something that's rather uncommon in most languages. Destructuring is a neat way of accessing interesting data elements from inside a larger data structure.

Finally, we'll conclude this chapter with a section on metadata, which is a unique way to associate orthogonal data with ordinary Clojure objects. Without any further ado, let's review how Clojure creates and uses functions.

3.1   Functions

As discussed in chapter 1, Lisp was born in the context of mathematics and is a functional language. A functional language, among other things, treats functions as first-class elements. This means the following things:

- Functions can be created dynamically (at runtime).
- Functions can be accepted as arguments by other functions.
- Functions can be returned from functions as return values.
- Functions can be stored as elements inside other data structures (for example, lists).

It's worth mentioning again that Clojure functions are objects, and because they follow all the rules mentioned, they can be used in some interesting ways. This section will give you an overview of what functions are and how they work, and you'll see several code examples that illustrate various concepts. We'll begin by defining simple functions, with both a fixed and a variable number of parameters. We'll then show how to use the do construct to allow side effects. After that, we'll examine anonymous functions and a few shortcuts for using them, followed by using recursion as a means of looping. We'll end the section with a discussion on higher-order functions and closures. To get started, let's examine the means that Clojure provides to define your own functions.

3.1.1   Defining functions

Functions are defined using the defn macro. The structure of the defn macro is the following:

```
(defn function-name doc-string? attr-map? [parameter-list]
 conditions-map?
  (expressions))
```

Before discussing the details of this structure, let's take a quick look at an example. This example is quite basic, and you'll see more examples later in this section:

```
(defn total-cost [item-cost number-of-items]
  (* item-cost number-of-items))
```

Here, total-cost is the name of the new function object we defined. It accepts two parameters: item-cost and number-of-items. The body of the function is the s-expression that's the call to the multiply function, which is passed the same two arguments. There's no explicit return keyword in Clojure; instead, the value of the last expression is automatically returned to the caller of the function.

Notice that defn was described as a macro. There's a whole chapter on macros coming up (chapter 7), but it's worth mentioning that the defn form expands to a def. For example, the definition of the total-cost function above is expanded to

```
(def total-cost (fn [item-cost number-of-items]
  (* item-cost number-of-items)))
```

total-cost is what Clojure calls a var. You'll learn about vars later on in this chapter. Note also that the function object is created using the fn special form. Because creating such vars and pointing them to function objects is common, the defn macro was included in the language as a convenience.

If you wanted to, you could add a documentation string to the function, as follows:

```
(defn total-cost
"return line-item total of the item and quantity provided"
[item-cost number-of-items]
  (* item-cost number-of-items))
```

In addition to providing a comment that aids in understanding this function, the documentation string can later be called up using the doc macro. If you called the doc macro on this, you'd get the following output:

```
 (doc total-cost)
-------------------------
user/total-cost
([item-cost number-of-items])
 return line-item total of the item and quantity provided
```

doc is useful when working with unfamiliar functions. Next, you'll learn a little more about function parameters. Specifically, you'll learn how to achieve overloading based on the number of parameters and how to handle a variable number of parameters.

Finally, before moving on, recall the general form of the defn macro from the previous page. It has an optional conditions-map, and you'll now see what it's used for. Consider the following function definition:

```
(defn item-total [price quantity]
  {:pre [(> price 0) (> quantity 0)]
   :post [(> % 0)]}
  (* price quantity))
```

Here, item-total behaves as a normal function that multiplies its two arguments and returns a result. But at runtime, it runs additional checks as specified by the hash with the two keys :pre and :post. The checks it runs before executing the body of the function are the ones specified with the :pre key (hence called preconditions). In this case, there are two checks: one that ensures that price is greater than zero and a second that ensures that quantity is also greater than zero.

Let's try it with valid input:

```
user=> (item-total 20 1)
20
```

Now let's try it with invalid input:

```
user=> (item-total 0 1)
; Evaluation aborted.
Assert failed: (> price 0)
  [Thrown class java.lang.AssertionError]
```

Note that in this case, the function didn't compute the result but instead threw an AssertionError error with an explanation of which condition failed. The Clojure runtime automatically takes care of running the checks and throwing an error if they fail.

Now let's look at the conditions specified by the :post key, called the postconditions. The % in these conditions refers to the return value of the function. The checks are run after the function body is executed, and the behavior in the case of a failure is the same: an AssertionError is thrown along with a message explaining which condition failed.

You've seen how to define pre- and postconditions to functions, so now let's look at a more modular way of approaching this. Consider the following two function definitions:

```
(defn basic-item-total [price quantity]
  (* price quantity))
```

```
(defn with-line-item-conditions [f price quantity]
    {:pre [(> price 0) (> quantity 0)]
     :post [(> % 1)]}
    (apply f price quantity))
```

basic-line-item is defined without any conditions and is clearly focused on only the business logic of calculating the line-item total. with-line-item-conditions is a higher-order function that accepts a function and the same two arguments. Here it is in action with valid arguments:

```
user> (with-line-item-conditions basic-item-total 20 1)
20
```

And here it is with invalid arguments:

```
user> (with-line-item-conditions basic-item-total 0 1)
; Evaluation aborted.
Assert failed: (> (first args) 0)
  [Thrown class java.lang.AssertionError]
```

There's another advantage to this approach apart from keeping basic-item-total clean, and that is with-line-item-conditions can be used with other functions like basic-item-total, allowing these conditions to be reused. Finally, if calling the function as shown previously becomes tedious, you can easily do the following:

```
(def item-total (partial with-line-item-conditions basic-item-total))
```

partial is a higher-order function that returns a new function with some arguments fixed. You'll see it in more detail later in this chapter. The previous usage allows item-total to be used as we did when we defined it in the regular way. Now that you've seen how to add pre- and postconditions to your functions, we're ready to move on. We'll next look at functions that can accept different sets of parameters.

MULTIPLE ARITY

The arity of a function is the number of operands it accepts. Clojure functions can be overloaded on arity. In order to define functions with such overloading, you can define the various forms within the same function definition as follows:

```
(defn function-name
  ([parameter-list-1]
    ;; body
  )
  ([paramter-list-2]
    ;; body
  )
;;more cases
)
```

Let's look at an example:

```
(defn total-cost
  ([item-cost number-of-items]
    (* item-cost number-of-items))
  ([item-cost]
    (total-cost item-cost 1)))
```

Here, we've defined two arities of the total-cost function. The first is of arity 2, and it's the same as the one we defined earlier. The other is of arity 1, and it accepts only the first parameter, item-cost. Note that you can call any other version of the function from any of the other arities. For instance, in the previous definition, we call the dual-arity version of total-cost from the body of the single-arity one.

VARIADIC FUNCTIONS

A variadic function is a function of variable arity. Different languages support this in different ways; for example, C++ has the ellipsis, and Java has varargs. In Clojure, the same is achieved with the & symbol:

```
(defn total-all-numbers [ & numbers]
  (apply + numbers))
```

Here, total-all-numbers is a function that can be called with any number of arguments. All the arguments are packaged into a single list called numbers, which is available to the body of the function. You can use this form even when you do have a few named parameters. The general form of declaring a variadic function is as follows:

```
(defn name-of-variadic-function [param-1 param-2 & rest-args]
  (body-of-function))
```

Here, `param-1` and `param-2` behave as regular named parameters, and all remaining arguments will be collected into a list called `rest-args`.

RECURSIVE FUNCTIONS

Recursive functions are those that either directly or indirectly call themselves. Clojure functions can certainly call themselves using their names, but this form of recursion consumes the stack. If enough recursive calls are made, eventually the stack will overflow. This is how things work in most programming languages. There is a feature in Clojure that circumvents this issue. Let's first write a recursive function that will blow the stack:

```
(defn count-down [n]
  (if-not (zero? n)
    (do
      (if (= 0 (rem n 100))
        (println "count-down:" n))
      (count-down (dec n)))))
```

If you try calling `count-down` with a large number, for instance 100000, you'll get a `StackOverflowError` thrown at you. You'll now see how to ensure that this doesn't happen.

In the last chapter, you saw the `loop/recur` construct that allowed you to iterate through sequences of data. The same `recur` form can be used to write recursive functions. When used in the tail position of a function body, `recur` binds its arguments to the same names as those specified in its parameter list. Let's rewrite `count-down` using recur:

```
(defn count-downr [n]
  (if-not (zero? n)
    (do
      (if (= 0 (rem n 100))
          (println "count-down:" n))
      (recur (dec n)))))
```

This now works for any argument, without blowing the stack. The change is minimal because at the end of the function body, `recur` rebinds the function parameter n to (dec n), which then proceeds down the function body. When n finally becomes zero, the recursion ends. As you can see, writing self-recursive functions is straightforward. Writing mutually recursive functions is a bit more involved, and we'll look at that next.

MUTUALLY RECURSIVE FUNCTIONS

Mutually recursive functions are those that either directly or indirectly call each other. Let's begin this section by examining an example of such a case. Listing 3.1 shows a contrived example of two functions, `cat` and `hat`, that call each other. When given a large enough argument, they'll throw the same `StackOverflowError` you saw earlier. Note that the declare macro calls def on each of its arguments. This is useful in cases where a function wants to call another function that isn't defined yet, as is the case with a pair of mutually recursive functions in the following listing.

Listing 3.1   Mutually recursive functions that can blow the stack

```
(declare hat)

(defn cat [n]
  (if-not (zero? n)
    (do
      (if (= 0 (rem n 100))
          (println "cat:" n))
      (hat (dec n)))))

(defn hat [n]
  (if-not (zero? n)
    (do
      (if (= 0 (rem n 100))
          (println "hat:" n))
      (cat (dec n)))))
```

Let's now fix this problem. We can't use recur because recur is only useful for self-recursion. Instead, let's modify the code to use a special Clojure function called trampoline. In order to do so, we'll make a slight change to the definition of cat and hat. The new functions are shown in the following listing as catt and hatt.

Listing 3.2   Mutually recursive functions that can be called with trampoline

```
(declare hatt)

(defn catt [n]
  (if-not (zero? n)
    (do
      (if (= 0 (rem n 100))
          (println "catt:" n))
      #(hatt (dec n)))))

(defn hatt [n]
  (if-not (zero? n)
    (do
      (if (= 0 (rem n 100))
          (println "hatt:" n))
      #(catt (dec n)))))
```

The difference is so minor that you could almost miss it. Consider the definition of catt, where instead of making the recursive call to hatt, you now return an anonymous function that when called makes the call to hatt. The same change is made in the definition of hatt.

Because these functions no longer perform their recursion directly, you have to use a special higher-order function to use them. That's the job of trampoline, and here's an example of using it:

```
(trampoline catt 100000)
```

This doesn't blow the stack and works as expected.

You've now seen how recursive functions can be written in Clojure. Although using recur and trampoline is the correct and safe way to write such functions, if you're sure that your code isn't in danger of consuming the stack, it's OK to write them without using these. Now that you've seen the basics of defining functions, let's look at a couple of ways to call them.

3.1.2 Calling functions

Because the function object is so fundamental to Clojure, you'll be calling a lot of functions in your programs. The most common way of doing this looks similar to the following:

```
(+ 1 2 3 4 5)
```

Here, the symbol + represents a function that adds its arguments. As a side note, Clojure doesn't have the traditional operators present in other languages. Instead, everything is a first-class function object, defined as any other function. Coming back to the previous example, the + function is variadic, and it adds up all the parameters passed to it and returns 15.

There's another way to evaluate a function. Let's say someone handed us a sequence called list-of-expenses, each an amount such as $39.95. In a language such as Java, you'd have to perform some kind of iteration over the list of expense amounts, combined with collecting the result of adding them. In Clojure, you can treat the list of numbers as arguments to a function like +. The evaluation, in this case, is done using a higher-order function called apply:

```
(apply + list-of-expenses)
```

The apply function is extremely handy, because it's quite common to end up with a sequence of things that need to be used as arguments to a function. This is true because a lot of Clojure programs use the core sequence data structures to do their job.

As you saw, apply is a higher-order function that accepts another function as its first parameter. Higher-order functions are those that accept one or more functions as parameters, or return a function, or do both. You'll now learn a bit more about this powerful concept by looking at a few examples of such functions provided by Clojure.

3.1.3 Higher-order functions

As we discussed in the previous chapter, functions in Clojure are first-class entities. Among other things, this means that functions can be treated similar to data: they can be passed around as arguments and can be returned from functions. Functions that do these things are called higher-order functions.

Functional code makes heavy use of higher-order functions. The map function that you saw in the previous chapter is one of the most commonly used higher-order functions. Other common ones are reduce, filter, some, and every. You saw simple examples of map, reduce, and filter in chapter 2. Higher-order functions aren't just convenient ways of doing things such as processing lists of data but are also the core of a programming technique known as function composition. In this section, we'll examine a few interesting higher-order functions that are a part of Clojure's core library.

EVERY?, SOME

every? is a function that accepts a predicate function and a sequence. It then calls the predicate on each element of the provided sequence and returns true if they all return true; otherwise, it returns false. Here's an example:

```
(def bools [true true true false false])
(every? true? bools)
;; this returns false
```

some has the same interface as every; that is, it accepts a predicate and a sequence. It then calls the predicate on each element in the sequence and returns the first logically true value it gets. If none of the calls return a logically true value, some returns nil. Here's an example, which is a quick and dirty way to check if a particular value exists in a sequence:

```
(some (fn [p] (= "rob" p)) ["kyle" "siva" "rob" "celeste"])
;; returns true
```

CONSTANTLY

constantly accepts a value v and returns a variadic function that always returns the same value v no matter what the arguments.

COMPLEMENT

complement is a simple function that accepts a function and returns a new one that takes the same number of arguments, does the same thing as the original function does, but returns the logically opposite value.

PARTIAL

partial is a higher-order function that accepts a function f and a few arguments to f but fewer than the number f normally takes. partial then returns a new function that accepts the remaining arguments to f. When this new function is called with the remaining arguments, it calls the original f with all the arguments together. Consider the following function that accepts two parameters, threshold and number, and checks to see if number is greater than threshold:

```
(defn above-threshold? [threshold number]
  (> number threshold))
```

To use it to filter a list, you might do this:

```
(filter (fn [x] (above-threshold? 5 x)) [ 1 2 3 4 5 6 7 8 9])
;; returns (6 7 8 9)
```

With partial, you could generate a new function and use that instead:

```
(filter (partial above-threshold? 5) [ 1 2 3 4 5 6 7 8 9])
;; returns (6 7 8 9)
```

MEMOIZE

Memoization is a technique that prevents functions from computing results for arguments that have already been processed. Instead, return values are looked up from a cache. Clojure provides a convenient `memoize` function that does this. Consider the following artificially slow function that performs a computation:

```
(defn slow-calc [n m]
  (Thread/sleep 1000)
  (* n m))
```

Calling it via a call to `time` tells you how long it's taking to run:

```
(time (slow-calc 5 7))
```

This prints the following to the console:

```
(time (slow-calc 5 7))
"Elapsed time: 1000.097 msecs"
35
```

Now, let's make this fast, by using the built-in `memoize` function:

```
(def fast-calc (memoize slow-calc))
```

In order for `memoize` to do its thing, let's call `fast-calc` once with a set of arguments (say 5 and 7). You'll notice that this run appears as slow as before; this time the result has been cached. Now, let's call it once more via a call to `time`:

```
(time (fast-calc 5 7))
```

Here's what Clojure prints to the console:

```
"Elapsed time: 0.035 msecs"
35
```

This is pretty powerful! Without any work at all, we were able to substantially speed up our function. These are some examples of what higher-order functions can do, and these are only a few of those included with Clojure's standard library. Next, you'll learn more about constructing complex functions by building on smaller ones.

WRITING HIGHER-ORDER FUNCTIONS

You can create new functions that use existing functions by combining them in various ways to compute the desired result. For example, consider the situation where you need to sort a given list of user accounts, where each account is represented by a hash map, as shown in the following listing.

Listing 3.3 Function composition using higher-order functions

```
(def users [
  {:username "kyle"
   :balance 175.00
   :member-since "2009-04-16"}

  {:username "zak"
   :balance 12.95
   :member-since "2009-02-01"}
```

```
   {:username "rob"
    :balance 98.50
    :member-since "2009-03-30"}
])

(defn username [user]
  (user :username))

(defn balance [user]
  (user :balance))

(defn sorter-using [ordering-fn]
  (fn [users]
    (sort-by ordering-fn users)))

(def poorest-first (sorter-using balance))

(def alphabetically (sorter-using username))
```

Here, users is a vector of hash maps. Specifically, it contains three users representing Kyle, Zak, and Rob. You define two convenience functions called username and balance, which accept a hash map representing a user and return the appropriate value. With these basics out of the way, let's get to the meat of what we're trying to demonstrate here: the idea of sorting a list of users on the two data elements, username and balance.

You define sorter-using as a higher-order function, one that accepts another function called ordering-fn, which will be used as a parameter to sort-by. sort-by itself is a higher-order function provided by Clojure that can sort a sequence based on a user-provided function. Note here that sorter-using returns a function object, defined by the fn special form that you saw earlier. Finally, you define poorest-first and alphabetically as the two desired functions, which sort the incoming list of users by balance and by username.

The two functions username and balance are used in other places, so defining them the way we did is OK. If the only reason they were created was to use them in the definition of poorest-first and alphabetically, then they can be considered clutter. You'll see a couple of ways to avoid the clutter created by single-use functions, starting with anonymous functions in the next section.

3.1.4   *Anonymous functions*

As you saw in the previous section, there may be times when you have to create functions for single use. A common example is when another higher-order function needs to be passed a function that might be specific to how it works (for example, our sorter-using function defined earlier). Such single-use functions don't even need names, because no one else will be calling them. Functions without names are, well, anonymous functions.

You've seen anonymous functions before, even if we didn't call them out. Consider this code snippet from earlier in the chapter:

```
(def total-cost (fn [item-cost number-of-items]
  (* item-cost number-of-items)))
```

As we discussed earlier, this code assigns the `total-cost` var a value, which is the function object created by the `fn` special form. To be more specific, the function object by itself doesn't have a name; instead, you use the var with the name `total-cost` to refer to the function. The function object itself is anonymous. To sum up, anonymous functions can be created using the `fn` form. Let's consider a situation where you need a list of dates when your members joined (perhaps for a report). You can use the `map` function for this:

```
(map (fn [user] (user :member-since)) users)
```

Here, you pass the anonymous function that looks up the `member-since` data element from inside the `users` hash map into the `map` function to collect the dates. This is a fairly trivial use case, but there are cases where this will be useful. Before we move on, let's look at a reader macro that helps with creating anonymous functions.

A SHORTCUT FOR ANONYMOUS FUNCTIONS
We talked about reader macros in chapter 2. One of the reader macros provided by Clojure allows anonymous functions to be defined quickly and easily. The reader macro character that does this is #.

Let's rewrite the code used to collect a list of member-joining dates using this reader macro:

```
(map #(% :member-since) users)
```

That's much shorter! The `#(% :member-since)` is equivalent to the anonymous function used in the previous version. Let's examine this form in more detail.

The `#()`, with the body of the anonymous function appearing within the parentheses, creates an anonymous function. The `%` symbol represents a single argument. If the function needs to have more than one argument, then `%1`, `%2`, and so on can be used. The body can contain pretty much any code, except for nested anonymous functions defined using another `#()` reader macro.

We'll now show another way to write such functions—a way that will result in even shorter code.

3.1.5 *Keywords and symbols*

You learned about keywords and symbols in chapter 2. They're some of the most heavily used entities in Clojure code, and they have one more property of interest. They're also functions, and their use as functions is quite common in idiomatic Clojure.

Keyword functions take either one or two parameters. The first parameter is a hash map, and the keyword looks itself up in the given hash map. For example, consider one of our user hash maps from earlier:

```
(def person {:username "zak"
             :balance 12.95
             :member-since "2009-02-01"})
```

To find out what username this corresponds to, you'd do the following:

```
(person :username)
```

This would return "zak". But now that you know that keywords behave as functions, you could write the same thing as

```
(:username person)
```

This would also return the same "zak". Why would you want to do such a strange-looking thing? To understand this, consider the code we wrote earlier to collect a list of all dates when members joined our service:

```
(map #(% :member-since) users)
```

Although this is short and easy to read, you could now make this even clearer by using the keyword as a function:

```
(map :member-since users)
```

This is much nicer! Indeed, this is the idiomatic way of working with hash maps and situations such as this one. We said earlier that keyword functions could accept a second optional parameter. This parameter is what gets returned if there is no value in the hash map associated with the keyword. As an example, consider the following two calls:

```
(:login person)
(:login person :not-found)
```

The first call returns nil because person doesn't have a value associated with :login. But if nil was a legitimate value for some key in the hash map, you wouldn't be able to tell if it returned that or it wasn't present. To avoid such ambiguity, you'd use the second form shown here, which will return :not-found. This return value tells you clearly that there was nothing associated with the key :login.

Now let's talk about symbols. In Clojure, *symbols* are identifiers that represent something else. Examples are users and total-cost, which as you've seen represent the list of users and a function. A symbol is the *name* of something. Every time a particular symbol appears in code, it's always the same object. For instance, whenever the symbol total appears, it will always refer to the same *symbol* object. The value it refers to could be different. The Clojure runtime automatically takes care of this, and all programs can rely on this behavior. This is useful when programs manipulate symbolic data.

Normally, when the Clojure runtime sees a symbol like users, it automatically evaluates it and uses the value that the symbol represents. But you may wish to use symbols as is. You may desire to use symbols themselves as values, for instance, as keys in a hash map. To do this, you'd quote the symbols. Everything else works exactly the same as in the case of keywords, including its behavior as a function. Here's an example:

```
(def expense {'name "Snow Leopard"
              'cost 29.95})

(expense 'name) ;; returns "Snow Leopard"
('name expense) ;; also returns "Snow Leopard"
('vendor expense) ;; returns nil
('vendor expense :absent) ;;returns :absent
```

You can see here that symbols behave similar to keywords in this context. The optional parameter that works as the default return value as shown here is a useful technique, which would otherwise require a separate function. Furthermore, it turns out that hash maps and vectors themselves have another interesting property, which is that they're also functions. Hash maps are functions of their keys, so they return the value associated with the argument passed to them. Consider the example from earlier:

```
(person :username)
```

person is a hash map, and this form works because it's also a function. It returns "zak". Incidentally, hash maps also accept an optional second parameter, which is the default value returned when a value associated with the key is not found, for instance:

```
(person :username :not-found)
```

Vectors also behave the same way; they're functions of their indices. Consider the following example:

```
(def names ["kyle" "zak" "rob"])
(names 1)
```

The call to names returns "zak", and this works because the vector names is a function. Note here that vector functions don't accept a second argument, and if an index that doesn't exist is specified, an exception is thrown. The fact that vectors and hash maps are functions proves to be useful when function composition is being used to design code. Instead of writing wrapper functions, these data structures can themselves be passed around as functions. This results in cleaner, shorter code.

In this section, we looked at functions in some detail. As we mentioned earlier, functions are a fundamental aspect of Clojure, and you'll be using them heavily. It's worth spending some time and experimenting with the various ideas explored in this section, because any nontrivial Clojure program will use most of these concepts. A large part of gaining proficiency with a language like Clojure is understanding and gaining proficiency with functional programming. Functional programming languages are great tools for designing things in a bottom-up way, because small functions can easily be combined into more complex ones. Each little function can be developed and tested incrementally, and this also greatly aids rapid prototyping. Having a lot of small, general functions that then combine to form solutions to the specific problems of the domain is also an important way to achieve flexibility.

Having seen how functions work, you're ready to tackle another important element in the design of Clojure programs: its scoping rules. In the next section, we'll explore scope. Scoping rules determine what is visible where, and understanding this is critical to writing and debugging Clojure programs.

3.2 Scope

Now that you've seen the basics of defining functions, we'll take a bit of a detour and show how scope works in Clojure. *Scope*, as it's generally known, is the enclosing context where names resolve to associated values. Clojure, broadly, has two kinds of scope: static (or lexical) scope and dynamic scope. Lexical scope is the kind that programming languages such as Java and Ruby offer. A *lexically scoped variable* is visible only inside the textual block that it's defined in (justifying the term *lexical*) and can be determined at compile time (justifying the term *static*).

Most programming languages only offer lexical scoping, and this is the most familiar kind of scope. The Lisp family has always also offered what are called special variables that follow a different set of rules for scope called dynamic scope. We'll examine both in this section. We'll first explore vars and how they can operate as special variables with dynamic scope. Then, we'll examine lexical scope and how to create new lexically scoped bindings.

3.2.1   *Vars and binding*

Vars in Clojure are, in some ways, similar to globals in other languages. Vars are defined at the top level, using the def special form. Here's an example:

```
(def MAX-CONNECTIONS 10)
```

After this call, the MAX-CONNECTIONS var is available to other parts of the program. The value of a var is determined by what's called its binding. In this example, MAX-CONNECTION is bound to the number 10, and such an initial binding is called a *root binding*. A var can be defined without any initial binding at all, in the following form:

```
(def RABBITMQ-CONNECTION)
```

Here, RABBITMQ-CONNECTION is said to be unbound. If another part of the code tries to use its value, an exception will be thrown saying that the var is unbound. To set a value for an unbound var, or to change the value bound to a var, Clojure provides the binding form:

```
(binding [MAX-CONNECTIONS 20
          RABBITMQ-CONNECTION (new-connection)]
    (
      ;; do something here
    ))
```

The general structure of the binding form is that it begins with the symbol binding, followed by a vector of even number of expressions. The first of every pair in the vector is a var, and it gets bound to the value of the expression specified by the second element of the pair. Binding forms can be nested, which allows new bindings to be created within each other.

As you saw earlier in this chapter, the defn macro expands to a def form, implying that functions defined using defn are stored in vars. Functions can be redefined using a binding form as well. This is useful for things like implementing aspect-oriented programming or stubbing out behavior for unit tests. You'll see examples of this in part 2 of this book.

SPECIAL VARIABLES

There's one thing to note about vars: they're not lexically scoped but are dynamically scoped. To understand what this means, let's again consider the following var:

```
(def *db-host* "localhost")
```

If you now call a function like expense-report, which internally uses *db-host* to connect to the database, you'd see numbers retrieved from the local database. For now, let's use test this with a function that prints the binding to the console:

```
(defn expense-report [start-date end-date]
  (println *db-host*)) ;; can do real work
```

Now, once you've tested things to your satisfaction, you can have the same code connect to our production database by setting up an appropriate binding:

```
(binding [*db-host* "production"]
    (expense-report "2010-01-01" "2010-01-07"))
```

This will run the same code as defined in the expense-report function but will connect to the production database. You can prove that this happens by running the previous code; you'd see "production" printed to the console.

Note here that you managed to change what the expense-report function does, without changing the parameters passed to it (the function connects to a database specified by the binding of the *db-host* var.) This is called *action at a distance*, and people regard this as something that must be done with caution. The reason is that it can be similar to programming with global variables that can change out from underneath you. Used with caution, it can be a convenient way to alter the behavior of a function.

Such vars that need to be bound appropriately before use are called *special* variables. A naming convention is used to make this intent clearer: these var names begin and end with an asterisk.

DYNAMIC SCOPE

You've seen how vars in general (and special variables in specific) can be bound to different values. We'll now explore our earlier statement that vars aren't governed by lexical scoping rules. We'll implement a simple form of aspect-oriented programming, specifically a way to add a log statement to functions when they're called. You'll see that in Clojure this is a simple thing to do, thanks to dynamic scope.

Scope determines which names are visible at certain points in the code and which names shadow which other ones. Lexical scope rules are simple to understand; you can tell the visibility of all lexically scoped variables by looking at the program text (hence the word *lexical*). Ruby and Java are lexically scoped.

Dynamic scope doesn't depend on the lexical structure of code; instead, the value of a var depends on the execution path taken by the program. If a function rebinds a var using a binding form, then the value of the var is changed for all code that executes from that point on, including other functions called. This works in a nested manner, too. If a function were to then use another binding form later on in the call stack, then from that point on, all code would see this second value of the var. When the second binding form completes (execution exits), the previous binding takes over for all code that executes from there onward. Look at the contrived example in the following listing.

Listing 3.4   Listing 3.4 Dynamic scope in action

```
(def *eval-me* 10)

(defn print-the-var [label]
  (println label *eval-me*))

(print-the-var "A:")

(binding [*eval-me* 20] ;; the first binding
        (print-the-var "B:")
        (binding [*eval-me* 30] ;; the second binding
          (print-the-var "C:"))
        (print-the-var "D:"))

(print-the-var "E:")
```

Running this code will print the following:

```
A: 10
B: 20
C: 30
D: 20
E: 10
```

Let's walk through the code. First, you create a var called *eval-me* with a root binding of 10. The print-the-var function causes the A: 10 to be printed. The first binding form changes the binding to 20, causes the following B: 20 to be printed. Then the second binding kicks in, causing the C: 30. Now, as the second binding form exits, the previous binding of 20 gets restored, causing the D: 20 to be printed. When the first binding exits after that, the root binding is restored, causing the E: 10 to be printed.

We'll contrast this behavior with the let form in the next section. In the meantime, let's implement a kind of aspect-oriented logging functionality for function calls. Consider the following code.

Listing 3.5   A higher-order function for aspect-oriented logging

```
(defn twice [x]
  (println "original function")
  (* 2 x))

(defn call-twice [y]
  (twice y))

(defn with-log [function-to-call log-statement]
  (fn [& args]
```

```
    (println log-statement)
    (apply function-to-call args)))

(call-twice 10)

(binding [twice (with-log twice "Calling the twice function")]
    (call-twice 20))

(call-twice 30)
```

If you run this, the output will be

```
original function
20

Calling the twice function
original function
40

original function
60
```

`with-log` is a higher-order function that accepts another function and a log statement. It returns a new function, which when called, prints the log statement to the console and then calls the original function with any arguments passed in. Note the action at a distance behavior modification of the `twice` function. It doesn't even know that calls to it are now being logged to the console, and, indeed, it doesn't need to. Any code that uses `twice` also can stay oblivious to this behavior modification, and as `call-twice` shows, everything works. Note that when the `binding` form exits, the original definition of `twice` is restored. In this way, only certain sections of code (to be more specific, certain call chains) can be modified using the `binding` form.

We will now examine one more property of bindings.

THREAD-LOCAL STATE

As we mentioned in chapter 1, Clojure has language-level semantics for safe concurrency. It supports writing lock-free multithreaded programs. Clojure provides several ways to manage state between concurrently running parts of your programs, and vars is one of them. We'll say a lot more about concurrency and Clojure's support for lock-free concurrency in chapter 6. Meanwhile, we'll look at the dynamic scope property of vars with respect to thread-local storage.

A var's root binding is visible to all threads, unless a binding form overrides it in a particular thread. If a thread does override the root binding via a call to the `binding` macro, that binding isn't visible to any other thread. Again, a thread can create nested bindings, and these bindings exist until the thread exits execution. You'll see more interaction between `binding` and threads in the chapter on concurrency.

LAZINESS AND SPECIAL VARIABLES

We mentioned Clojure's lazy sequences in chapter 1 and talked about how functions like `map` are lazy. This laziness can be a source of frustration when interplay with dynamic vars isn't clearly understood. Consider the following code:

```
(def *factor* 10)

(defn multiply [x]
  (* x *factor*))
```

This simple function accepts a parameter and multiplies it by the value of `*factor*`, which is determined by its current binding. Let's collect a few multiplied numbers using the following:

```
(map multiply [1 2 3 4 5])
```

This returns a list containing five elements: `(10 20 30 40 50)`. Now, let's use a binding call to set `*factor*` to 20, and repeat the `map` call:

```
(binding [*factor* 20]
  (map multiply [1 2 3 4 5]))
```

Strangely, this also returns `(10 20 30 40 50)`, despite the fact that you clearly set the binding of `*factor*` to 20. What explains this?

The answer is that a call to `map` returns a lazy sequence and this sequence isn't realized until it's needed. Whenever that happens (in this case. as the REPL tries to print it), the execution no longer occurs inside the binding form, and so `*factor*` reverts to its root binding of 10. This is why you get the same answer as in the previous case. To solve this, you need to force the realization of the lazy sequence from within the binding form:

```
(binding [*factor* 20]
  (doall (map multiply [1 2 3 4 5])))
```

This returns the expected `(20 40 60 80 100)`. This shows the need to be cautious when mixing special variables with lazy forms. `doall` is a Clojure function that forces realization of lazy sequences, and it's invaluable in such situations.

In this section, we looked at dynamic scope and the associated `binding`. Next, we'll take another look at the `let` form we saw earlier. Since they look so similar, we'll also explore the difference between the `let` and `binding` forms.

3.2.2   *The let form revisited*

We briefly explored the `let` form in chapter 2, where we used it to create local variables. Let's quickly look at another example of using it:

```
(let [x 10
      y 20]
  (println "x, y:" x "," y))
```

Here, x and y are locally bound values. Locals such as these are local because the lexical block of code they're created in limits their visibility and extent (the time during which they exist). When execution leaves the local block, they're no longer visible and indeed get garbage collected.

Clojure allows functions to be defined locally, inside a lexically scoped `let` form. Here's an example:

```
(defn upcased-names [names]
  (let [up-case (fn [name]
                  (.toUpperCase name))]
    (map up-case names)))
```

Here, upcased-names is a function that accepts a list of names and returns a list of the same names, all in uppercase characters. up-case is a locally defined function that accepts a single string and returns an up-cased version of it. The .toUpperCase function (with a prefixed dot) is Clojure's way of calling the toUpperCase member function on a Java object (in this case a string). You'll learn about Java interop in chapter 5.

Now, let's examine the difference between the structurally similar let and binding forms. To do this, let's first reexamine the behavior of binding via the use of *factor*, as follows:

```
(def *factor* 10)

(binding [*factor* 20]
  (println *factor*)
  (doall (map multiply [1 2 3 4 5])))
```

This prints 20 and then returns (20 40 60 80 100), as expected. Now, let's try the same thing with a let form:

```
(let [*factor* 20]
  (println *factor*)
  (doall (map multiply [1 2 3 4 5])))
```

This prints 20 as expected but returns (10 20 30 40 50). This is because although the let changes the binding of *factor* to 20 inside the let itself, it has no effect on the dynamic scope of the *factor* var. Only the binding form can affect the dynamic scope of vars.

Now that you know how the let form works and what it can be used for, let's look at a useful feature of Clojure that's possible thanks to two things: lexical scope and the let form.

3.2.3 Lexical closures

Let's begin our exploration of what a lexical closure is by understanding what a free variable is. A variable is said to be free inside a given form if there's no binding occurrence of that variable in the lexical scope of that form. Consider the following example:

```
(defn create-scaler [scale]
  (fn [x]
    (* x scale)))
```

In this example, within the anonymous function being returned, scale doesn't appear in any kind of binding occurrence—specifically, it's neither a function parameter nor created in a let form. Within the anonymous function, therefore, scale is a free variable. Only lexically scoped variables can be free, and the value of the form in which they appear depends on their value. Forms that enclose over free variables (such as the anonymous function shown previously) are called closures. Closures are an extremely powerful feature of languages such as Clojure—in fact, even the name Clojure is a play on the word.

How do you use a closure? Consider the following code:

```
(def percent-scaler (create-scaler 100))
```

Here, we're binding the `percent-scaler` var to the function object that gets returned by the `create-scaler` call. As you saw earlier, the parameter `scale` gets closed over and now lives on inside the `percent-scaler` closure. You can see this when you make a call to the `percent-scaler` function:

```
(percent-scaler 0.59)
;; returns 59.0
```

This trivial example shows how closures are easy to create and use. A closure is an important construct in Clojure (it's no coincidence that the name of the language sounds like the word!). It can be used for information hiding (encapsulation) because nothing from outside the closure can touch the closed-over variables. Because Clojure data structures are immutable (reducing the need to make things private), macros, closures, and multimethods allow for powerful paradigms in which to create programs. It makes traditional object-oriented ideas (a la Java or C++) feel rather confining. You'll learn about multimethods in chapter 4 and more about macros in chapter 7. We'll also look at closures a lot more in chapter 13, which takes a deeper look at functional programming concepts.

Now that you understand several basic structural aspects of writing Clojure code, we'll address an organizational construct of Clojure: the namespace. Understanding how to use namespaces will aid you in writing larger programs that need to be broken into pieces for the sake of modularity and manageability.

3.3   Namespaces

When a program becomes larger than a few functions, computer languages allow the programmer to break it up into parts. An example of this facility is the package system in Java. Clojure provides the concept of namespaces for the same purpose. Programs can be broken up into parts, each being a logical collection of code—functions, vars, and the like.

Another reason why namespaces are useful is to avoid name collisions in different parts of programs. Imagine that you were writing a program that dealt with students, tests, and scores. If you were to then use an external unit-testing library that also used the word *test*, Clojure might complain about redefinition! Such problems can be handled by writing code in its own namespace.

3.3.1   ns

The `*ns*` var is bound to the currently active namespace. The ns macro sets the current namespace to whatever is specified. Here's the general form of the ns macro:

```
(ns name & references)
```

The `name`, as mentioned previously, is the name of the namespace being made current. If it doesn't already exist, it gets created. The `references` that follows the name are optional and can be one or more of the following: use, `require`, `import`, `load`, or `gen-class`. You'll see some of these in action in this section and in chapter 5, which covers Java interop. First, let's look at an example of defining a namespace:

```
(ns org.currylogic.damages.calculators)

(defn highest-expense-during [start-date end-date]
 ;; (logic to find the answer)
)
```

`highest-expense-during` is now a function that lives in the namespace with the name of `org.currylogic.damages.calculators`. In order to use it, code outside this namespace would need to make a call (directly or indirectly) to `use`, `require`, or `import` (if the library is compiled into a JAR). We'll explore these now through an example.

> ### Public versus private functions
> Before moving on to the next section, let's take a quick look at private functions versus public functions. In Clojure, all functions belong to a namespace. The `defn` macro creates public functions, and these can be called from any namespace. In order to create private functions, Clojure provides the `defn-` macro, which works exactly the same, but such functions can only be called from within the namespace they're defined in.

USE, REQUIRE

Let's imagine that we we're writing an HTTP service that responds to queries about a user's expenses. Let's further imagine that we're going to deal with both XML and JSON. In order to handle XML, we can use the Clojure-provided XML functions that live in the `clojure.xml` namespace.

As far as handling JSON is concerned, ideally we wouldn't have to write code to handle the format. It turns out that Dan Larkin has written an excellent library for this purpose; it's called `clojure-json` and lives on github.com. Clojure enjoys incredible support as far as libraries are concerned. Often, either a pure Clojure library exists for the purpose under question or a suitable Java library can be wrapped with Clojure.

Once you've downloaded the libraries, put the JAR files somewhere convenient (usually inside the lib folder), and ensure that they're on the JVM's classpath. The following listing shows what the code looks like now that you've picked the two libraries you need.

Listing 3.6 Using external libraries by calling `use`

```
(ns org.currylogic.damages.http.expenses)

(use 'org.danlarkin.json)
(use 'clojure.xml)
```

```
(defn import-transactions-xml-from-bank [url]
  (let [xml-document (parse url)]
    ;; more code here

(defn totals-by-day [start-date end-date]
  (let [expenses-by-day (load-totals start-date end-date)]
    (encode-to-str expenses-by-day)))
```

Here, parse and encode-to-str are functions that come from the clojure.xml and clojure-json libraries. The reason they're available is that we called use on their namespaces. use takes all public functions from the namespace and includes them in the current namespace. The result is as though those functions were written in the current namespace. Although this is easy, and sometimes desirable, it often makes the code a little less understandable in terms of seeing where such functions are defined. require solves this problem, as shown in here.

Listing 3.7   Using external libraries by calling `require`

```
(ns org.currylogic.damages.http.expenses)

(require '(org.danlarkin [json :as json-lib]))
(require '(clojure [xml :as xml-core]))

(defn import-transactions-xml-from-bank [url]
  (let [xml-document (xml-core/parse url)]
    ;; more code here

(defn totals-by-day [start-date end-date]
  (let [expenses-by-day (load-totals start-date end-date)]
    (json-lib/encode-to-str expenses-by-day)))
```

require makes functions available to the current namespace, as use does, but doesn't include them the same way. They must be referred to using the full namespace name or the aliased namespace using the as clause, as shown in listing 3.7.

RELOAD AND RELOAD-ALL

As described in chapter 1, typical programming workflow in Clojure involves building up functions in an incremental fashion. As functions are written or edited, the namespaces that they belong to need to be reloaded in the REPL so they can be tested. You can do this by using the following:

```
(use 'org.currylogic.damages.http.expenses :reload)
```

```
(require '(org.currylogic.damages.http [expenses :as exp]) :reload)
```

:reload can be replaced with :reload-all to reload all libraries that are used either directly or indirectly by the specified library.

Before wrapping up this section on namespaces, we'll explore some options that Clojure provides to work with them programmatically.

3.3.2 *Working with namespaces*

Apart from the convenience offered by namespaces in helping keep code modular (and guarding from name collisions), Clojure namespaces can be accessed programmatically. In this section, we'll review a few useful functions to do this.

CREATE-NS, IN-NS

`create-ns` is a function that accepts a symbol and creates a namespace named by it if it doesn't already exist. `in-ns` is a function that accepts a single symbol as argument and switches the current namespace to the one named by it. If it doesn't exist, it's created.

ALL-NS, FIND-NS

The no-argument function `all-ns` returns a list of all namespaces currently loaded. The `find-ns` function accepts a single symbol as argument and checks to see if it names a namespace. If so, it returns `true`, else `nil`.

NS-INTERNS, NS-PUBLICS

`ns-interns` is a function that accepts a single argument, a symbol that names a namespace, and returns a map containing symbols to var mappings from the specified namespace. `ns-publics` is similar to `ns-interns` but instead of returning a map that contains information about all vars in the namespace, it returns only the public ones.

NS-RESOLVE, RESOLVE

`ns-resolve` is a function that accepts two arguments: a symbol naming a namespace and another symbol. If the second argument can be resolved to either a var or a Java class in the specified namespace, the var or class is returned. If it can't be resolved, the function returns `nil`. `resolve` is a convenience function that accepts a single symbol as its argument and tries to resolve it (such as `ns-resolve`) in the current namespace.

NS-UNMAP, REMOVE-NS

`ns-unmap` accepts a symbol naming a namespace and another symbol. The mapping for the specified symbol is removed from the specified namespace. `remove-ns` accepts a symbol naming a namespace and removes it entirely. This doesn't work for the `clojure.core` namespace.

These are some of the functions provided by Clojure to programmatically work with namespaces. They're useful in controlling the environment in which certain code executes. An example of this will appear in the last chapter, on domain-specific languages.

So far, you've seen a lot of the basics of Clojure and should now be in a position to read and write programs of reasonable complexity. In the next section, you'll see a feature that isn't found in languages such as Java and Ruby, namely, destructuring.

3.4 *Destructuring*

Several programming languages provide a feature called pattern matching, which is a form of function overloading based on structural patterns of arguments (as opposed to their number or types). Clojure has a somewhat less-general form of pattern matching called *destructuring*. In Clojure, destructuring lets programmers bind names to only those parts of sequences that they care about. To see how this works, look at the following code, which doesn't use destructuring:

```
(defn describe-salary [person]
  (let [first (:first-name person)
        last (:last-name person)
        annual (:salary person)]
    (println first last "earns" annual)))
```

Here, the `let` form doesn't do much useful work—it sets up local names for parts of the incoming `person` sequence. By using Clojure's destructuring capabilities, such code clutter can be eliminated:

```
(defn describe-salary-2 [{first :first-name
                         last :last-name
                         annual :salary}]
  (println first last "earns" annual))
```

Here, the incoming sequence (in this case a hash map) is destructured, and useful parts of it are bound to names within the function's parameter-binding form. In fact, extracting values of certain keys from inside hash maps is so common that Clojure provides an even more convenient way of doing this. You'll see that and more ways to destructure hash maps in section 3.4.2, but before that let's examine destructuring vectors.

3.4.1 *Vector bindings*

Vector destructuring supports any data structure that implements the `nth` function, including vectors, lists, seqs, arrays, and strings. This form of destructuring consists of a vector of names, each of which is assigned to the respective elements of the expression, looked up via the `nth` function. An example will make this clear:

```
(defn print-amounts [[amount-1 amount-2]]
  (println "amounts are:" amount-1 "and" amount-2))

(print-amounts [10.95 31.45])

;;this prints the following -
amounts are: 10.95 and 31.45
```

This implementation of `print-amounts` is short and clear: you can read the parameter list and see that the single argument will be broken into two parts named `amount-1` and `amount-2`. The alternative is to use a `let` form inside the function body to set up `amount-1` and `amount-2` by binding them to the first and last values of the incoming vector.

There are several options when it comes to using vector bindings. Let's imagine that the function `print-amounts` takes a vector that could contain two or more amounts (instead of only two in our contrived example). Here's how you could deal with that situation:

USING & AND :AS

Consider the following example of destructuring:

```
(defn print-amounts-multiple [[amount-1 amount-2 & remaining]]
  (println "Amounts are:" amount-1 "," amount-2 "and" remaining))
```

If you make the following call

```
(print-amounts-multiple [10.95 31.45 22.36 2.95])
```

Clojure would print the following:

```
Amounts are: 10.95 , 31.45 and (22.36 2.95)
```

As shown here, the name following the & symbol gets bound to a sequence containing all the remaining elements from the sequence being destructured.

Another useful option is the :as keyword. Here's another rather contrived example:

```
(defn print-all-amounts [[amount-1 amount-2 & remaining :as all]]
  (println "Amounts are:" amount-1 "," amount-2 "and" remaining)
  (println "Also, all the amounts are:" all))
```

When we call this function as follows

```
(print-all-amounts [10.95 31.45 22.36 2.95])
```

it results in the following being printed to the console:

```
Amounts are: 10.95 , 31.45 and (22.36 2.95)
Also, all the amounts are: [10.95 31.45 22.36 2.95]
```

Destructuring vectors makes it easy to deal with the data inside them. What's more, Clojure allows nesting of vectors in destructuring bindings.

NESTED VECTORS

Suppose you had a vector of vectors. Each inner vector was a pair of data—the first being a category of expense and the second the amount. If you wanted to print the category of the first expense amount, you could do the following:

```
(defn print-first-category [[[category amount] & _ ]]
  (println "First category  was:" category)
  (println "First amount was:" amount))
```

Running this with an example

```
(def expenses [[:books 49.95] [:coffee 4.95] [:caltrain 2.25]])
(print-first-category expenses)
```

results in Clojure printing the following:

```
First category  was: :books
First amount was: 49.95
```

You've seen how vector destructuring is done, and it's quite powerful. Note that in the argument list of print-first-category, we used & _ to ignore the remaining elements of the vector that we didn't care about. One thing to remember is that destructuring can take place in any binding form including function parameter lists and let forms. Another thing to remember is that vector destructuring works for any data type that supports the nth and nthnext functions. On a practical level, for instance, if you were to implement the ISeq interface and create your own sequence data type, you'd be able to natively use not only all of Clojure's core functions but also such destructuring.

Before closing out this section on destructuring, let's look at another useful form of destructuring binds—the one that uses hash maps.

3.4.2   *Map bindings*

You saw how convenient it is to destructure vectors into relevant pieces and bind only those instead of the whole vector. Clojure supports similar destructuring of maps. To be specific, Clojure supports destructuring of any associative data structure, which includes maps, strings, vectors, and arrays. Maps, as you know, can have any key, whereas strings, vectors, and arrays have integer keys. The destructuring binding form looks similar to ones you saw earlier; it's a map of key-expression pairs, where each key name is bound to the value of the respective initialization expression.

Let's look at an the example from earlier:

```
(defn describe-salary-2 [{first :first-name
                          last :last-name
                          annual :salary}]
    (println first last "earns" annual))
```

As we noted earlier, `first`, `last`, and `annual` get bound to the respective values from the hash map passed to `describe-salary-2`. Let's now suppose that you also want to bind a bonus percentage, which may or may not exist. Clojure provides a convenient option in map destructuring bindings to handle such optional values, using the `:or` keyword:

```
(defn describe-salary-3 [{first :first-name
                          last :last-name
                          annual :salary
                          bonus :bonus-percentage
                          :or {bonus 5}}]
    (println first last "earns" annual "with a" bonus "percent bonus"))
```

When called with arguments that do contain all keys that are being destructured, it works similar to the previous case:

```
(def a-user {:first-name "pascal"
             :last-name "dylan"
             :salary 85000
             :bonus-percentage 20})

(describe-salary-3 a-user)
```

This prints the following to the console:

```
pascal dylan earns 85000 with a 20 percent bonus
```

Here's how it works if you call the function with an argument that doesn't contain a bonus:

```
(def another-user {:first-name "basic"
                   :last-name "groovy"
                   :salary 70000})

(describe-salary-3 another-user)
```

This binds bonus to the default value specified via the :or option. The output is

```
basic groovy earns 70000 with a 5 percent bonus
```

Finally, similar to the case of vectors, map bindings can use the :as option to bind the complete hash map to a name. Here's an example:

```
(defn describe-person [{first :first-name
                        last :last-name
                        bonus :bonus-percentage
                        :or {bonus 5}
                        :as p}]
  (println "Info about" first last "is:" p)
  (println "Bonus is:" bonus "percent"))
```

An example of using this function is

```
(def third-user {:first-name "lambda"
                 :last-name "curry"
                 :salary 95000})
(describe-person third-user)
```

This causes the following to be echoed on the console:

```
Info about lambda curry is: {:first-name lambda,
                             :last-name curry,
                             :salary 95000}
Bonus is: 5 percent
```

This is all convenient and results in short, readable code. Clojure provides a couple of options that make it even more easy to destructure maps: the :keys, :strs, and :syms keywords. Let's look the how to use :keys by writing a small function to greet our users:

```
(defn greet-user [{:keys [first-name last-name]}]
  (println "Welcome," first-name last-name))
```

When you run this, first-name and last-name get bound to values of :first-name and :last-name from inside the argument map. Let's try it:

```
(def roger {:first-name "roger" :last-name "mann" :salary 65000})
(greet-user roger)
```

The output might look like this:

```
Welcome, roger mann
```

If your keys were strings or symbols (instead of keywords as in these examples), you'd use :strs or :syms.

We covered various ways that Clojure supports destructuring large, complex data structures into their components. This is a useful feature because it results in code that's shorter and clearer. It improves the self-documentation nature of well-written code, because the destructuring binding tells the reader exactly what parts of the incoming data structure are going to be used in the code that follows.

Our final stop in this chapter will be to explore another neat feature of Clojure—that of metadata.

3.5   *Metadata*

Metadata means data about data. Clojure supports tagging data (for example, objects like maps and lists) with other data, which can be completely unrelated to the tagged data. For instance, you might want to tag some data that was read over an insecure network.

For example, let's use the tags :safe and :io to determine if something is considered a security threat and if it came from an external I/O source. Here's how you might use metadata to represent such information:

```
(def untrusted (with-meta {:command "clean-table" :subject "users"}
                          {:safe false :io true}))
```

Objects with metadata can be used like any other objects. The additional metadata doesn't affect their values. In fact, if you were to check what untrusted was at the REPL, the metadata won't even appear:

```
user=> untrusted
{:command "clean-table", :subject "users"}
```

If you do want to examine the metadata associated with the object, you can use the meta function:

```
user=> (meta untrusted)
{:safe false, :io true}
```

As mentioned earlier, the metadata isn't part of the logical value of the data, so it also doesn't affect equality. Further, when new objects are created from those that have metadata, the metadata carries over, for example:

```
user=> (def still-suspect (assoc untrusted :complete? false))
#'user/still-suspect

user=> (meta still-suspect)
{:safe false, :io true}
```

Functions and macros can also be defined with metadata. Here's an example:

```
(defn
  testing-meta "testing metadata for functions"
  {:safe true :console true}
  []
  (println "Hello from meta!"))
```

Let's try using the meta function to check that the metadata was set correctly:

```
user=> (meta testing-meta)
nil
```

This returns nil because the metadata is associated with the var testing-meta not the function object itself. To access the metadata, you'd have to pass the testing-meta var to the meta function. You can do this as follows:

```
user=> (meta (var testing-meta))
{:ns #<Namespace user>,
 :name testing-meta,
```

```
:file "NO_SOURCE_FILE",
:line 1, :arglists ([]),
:console true,
:safe true,
:doc "testing metadata for functions"}
```

Metadata is useful in many situations where you want to tag things for purposes orthogonal to the data they represent. Annotations are one example where you might perform certain tasks if objects are annotated a certain way, such as if their metadata contains a certain key and value. Clojure internally uses metadata quite a lot; for example, the :doc key is used to hold the documentation string for functions and macros, the :macro key is set to true for functions that are macros, the :file key is used to keep track of what source file something was defined in, and so on.

3.6 *Summary*

This was another long chapter! We explored a few important aspects of writing code in Clojure. We looked at functions, which form the basis of the language, and we saw several ways to create and compose functions. We also examined scope—both lexical and dynamic—and how it works in Clojure. We also showed that once programs start getting large, namespaces can be used to break up and organize them. Finally, we looked at the destructuring capabilities of Clojure—a feature that comes in handy when writing functions or let forms.

Between the previous chapter and this one, we covered most of the basic features of the language. You can write fairly non-trivial programs with what you've learned so far. The next few chapters focus on a few features that are unique to Clojure—things like Java interoperability, concurrency support, multimethods, the macro system, and more.

In the next chapter, you'll learn about multimethods. You'll see how inheritance-based polymorphism is an extremely limited way of achieving polymorphic behavior and how multimethods are an open-ended system to create your own version of polymorphism that could be specific to your problem domain. By combining ideas from the next chapter with those we explored in this one, such as higher-order functions, lexical closures, and destructuring, you can create some rather powerful abstractions.

Polymorphism
with multimethods

Many years ago, when I was learning the Java programming language, I read a book by Bruce Eckel called *Thinking in Java*. Although I thought it was a great book and learned a lot from it, over the years I've realized that the title of the book is a specific instance of a common curse. It's a curse that afflicts a majority of programmers—if programmers know only a specific language, they soon begin to think only in terms of what's possible (expressible) in that language.

In our industry, this is manifested in several ways. The most common is that, on average, a programmer fluent in several languages is a better programmer than a programmer who knows only one language. This correlation is because each language has slightly (sometimes very) different concepts and models that programs are expressed in (for instance, objects in Java/C++, prototypes in JavaScript, functions in Haskell, and so on). The corollary to this observation is that a programmer familiar with many different languages is often an even better programmer than the programmer who's familiar with several similar ones.

There's a point to this introduction, and it's that popular OO languages such as Java and C++ mold the general notion of what is and what isn't object-oriented. Here is what Alan Kay said about this: "Actually, I invented the term 'object-oriented', and I can tell you I did not have C++ in mind."

As mentioned in chapter 1, the truth is that the idea of objects is far more nuanced than the common notions of it, and by the end of this book, you'll hopefully have a rather different opinion of objects than the one you might have today. We'll start off this chapter by exploring a pillar of OO—polymorphism—and see how Clojure deals with it.

4.1 Polymorphism

The word *polymorphism* derives from ancient Greek, where *poly* means many and *morph* means form. In programming languages, polymorphism is the idea that values of different data types can be treated in the same way. Often, this is manifested via class inheritance, where classes in a hierarchy can have methods of the same name. When such a method is called on an object, the right code is executed at runtime depending on which class the object is an instance of. There are various ways of achieving polymorphic behavior, and inheritance is only one such way. The diagram in figure 4.1, taken from a paper published

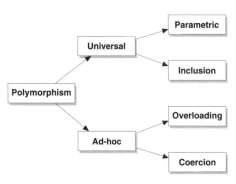

Figure 4.1 There are several types of polymorphism. Subtype polymorphism (a form of inclusion) is the most common (Java/C++) kind of polymorphism but is only one of several.

by Luca Cardelli in 1985 (http://lucacardelli.name/Papers/OnUnderstanding.pdf), shows a high-level classification of polymorphism.

We won't get into the details of all these types of polymorphism (the previously mentioned paper is highly recommended). Instead, we'll concentrate on subtype polymorphism (which is a form of inclusion polymorphism), because it's the most commonly implemented form of polymorphism. Examples of languages that offer this type include Java, C++, and Ruby. The following sections offer a primer that paves the way to understanding how Clojure approaches polymorphism. Specifically, we'll explore basic subtype polymorphism, followed by duck typing. Then we'll look at method dispatch, starting with the commonly available single dispatch, followed by double and multiple dispatches. Then, you'll be ready to deal with Clojure.

4.1.1 Subtype polymorphism

Subtype polymorphism, as illustrated in figure 4.2, is a form of inclusion polymorphism that establishes the basis of polymorphic behavior through an inheritance relationship. Languages such as Java express such a relationship using the `extends` keyword.

This is the famous *dynamic polymorphism* that's common in literature about Java and C++. In a situation where there's an inheritance hierarchy, and a particular method has been overridden across parts of it, which method is executed depends on the type of the receiver (the object on which a method is called). It's dynamic because this determination of the type of the receiver happens at runtime.

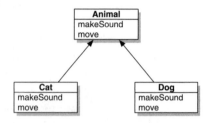

Figure 4.2　An example of the commonly found subtype polymorphism. Which `makeSound` gets called depends on the type of receiver and is determined at runtime.

To be as clear as possible, let's imagine a function `recordSound` that accepted an argument named `anAnimal` of the `Animal` type. When the `makeSound` method is called on the `anAnimal` object, the correct method is called, thanks to subtype polymorphism. Although this form of polymorphism is present in several programming languages, Clojure doesn't support it. (To be specific, it doesn't support it out of the box. We'll create our own little subtype-polymorphic DSL later.)

As we said earlier, this isn't the only way languages implement polymorphism. Languages such as Ruby have another form of polymorphism called duck typing.

4.1.2　Duck typing

Duck typing describes a form of dynamic polymorphism similar to the one we talked about previously but without inheritance. James Whitcomb Riley (who has nothing to do with computer science) coined the term when he noted, "When I see a bird that walks like a duck and swims like a duck and quacks like a duck, I call that bird a duck" (http://en.wikipedia.org/wiki/Duck_test).

In a weakly typed language, the `recordSound` function from the previous example could work on any type of object as long as it implemented a `makeSound` method. There need be no special relationship between objects that can be accepted as arguments here; all they have to do is respond appropriately to the `makeSound` method call. Languages such as Ruby and Python support duck typing.

The disadvantage is that duck typing alone is insufficient to implement more than one method of the same name that accepts different types of arguments. To do that, subtype polymorphism is needed once again. Clojure isn't duck typed either, because Clojure doesn't have the traditional concept of objects.

Now that you've seen two commonly found variants of polymorphism, let's examine the underlying mechanism that allows polymorphism to work—the concept of method dispatch.

4.2　Method dispatch

The key to all this dynamic behavior—which method is executed when a polymorphic method is called—is the mechanism of dynamic method dispatch. It's a fancy way of saying that when a method is called, the name of the method is mapped to a concrete implementation at runtime.

4.2.1 Single and double dispatch

Languages such as Java support only single dispatch. What this means is that at runtime, the type of receiver is the only thing that determines which method is executed. To demonstrate this, we'll use another commonly cited but well-suited example of a program that needs to process an abstract syntax tree (AST). Let's imagine our AST is implemented in a Java-like OO language and is modeled via the classes shown in figure 4.3.

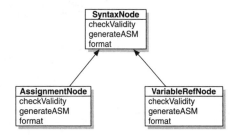

Figure 4.3 A simplistic hierarchy representing an AST. Each node is a subclass of a generic `SyntaxNode` and has functions for various tasks that a compiler or IDE might perform.

When an IDE needs to format the source code being edited, it calls `format` on the AST representation of the code text. Internally, the AST delegates the `format` call to each component. This walks the tree and ultimately calls `format` on each node in the AST.

This is straightforward enough. Even though the AST is made up of different kinds of concrete nodes, the operation `format` is defined in the generic base class and is called using a reference to that base class. Dynamically, the receiver type is determined, and the appropriate method is executed. This is called single-dispatch because only the type of receiver is used to determine which code to run. If any of these methods were to accept arguments, the types of those wouldn't determine the method that needs to execute.

Single dispatch can lead to unexpected situations. We'll explore one such issue with the following example. Consider a Java interface for a `Person`, in the domain of pet lovers:

```
public interface Person {
    public void pet(Dog d);
    public void pet(Cat c);
}
```

Let's now define a couple of implementations of this interface. First, we'll define `Man`, which might look as follows:

```
public class Man implements Person {
  public void pet(Dog d) {
    System.out.println("Man here, petting dog:" + d.makeSound());
  }

  public void pet(Cat c) {
    System.out.println("Man here, petting cat:" + c.makeSound());
  }
}
```

Let's also add another implementation of the same interface, in the form of the Woman class:

```
public class Woman implements Person{
  public void pet(Dog d) {
    System.out.println("Woman here, petting dog:" + d.makeSound());
  }

  public void pet(Cat c) {
      System.out.println("Woman here, petting cat:" + c.makeSound());
  }
}
```

The purpose of the code so far is to construct a class hierarchy that we can then use to deal with a different one: that of the Animals. We'll start with the interface:

```
public interface Animal {
    public String makeSound();
}
```

We'll create the two implementations we referred to in our Person interface, the Dog and the Cat:

```
public class Dog implements Animal{
    public String makeSound() {
        return "Bow, wow";
    }
}

public class Cat implements Animal {
    public String makeSound() {
        return "Meow";
    }
}
```

Finally, let's imagine we want to use all these classes together. We'll create a Park class where we might have instances of our Person interface hanging out with instances of our Animal interface. It might look like this:

```
public class Park {
  public static void main(String[] args) {
    Person p = new Man();
    Animal a = new Dog();
    p.pet(a);
  }
}
```

Unfortunately, this Java code won't even compile. The compiler will say that there's no such method pet that accepts an instance of the Animal class. What we'd like (and what we intended) is for Java to accept this and then at runtime discern that p is of type Man and a is of type Dog. We'd then like for it to call the right method inside the Man class.

But it can't. Java can only look at the type of the receiver (the object p). In this case, it's declared as Person and is determined to be Man at runtime. In order to find out what method to call, Java would need to know the *runtime* type of a (which in this case is `Dog`). But it doesn't do that. Because a is declared to be of type `Animal`, it looks for a method inside `Man` with the signature `pet(Animal)` and doesn't find it. This results in the compiler error.

This is the whole single-dispatch problem, and it occurs only when you have more than one hierarchy (as we do: `Animal` and `Person`). The visitor pattern is an attempt to work around it, and it does so by using a callback. We'll examine this in the next section.

4.2.2 *The visitor pattern (and simulating double dispatch)*

Our `Park` class doesn't work because only the type of the receiver object is used to determine which method to call. The type of the `Animal` object is ignored in a single-dispatch scenario. In a language that resolved methods through double dispatch, the types of the receiver *and* the first argument would be used to find the method to execute. This would then work as desired.

We can simulate double dispatch in Java and other languages that suffer from single dispatch. That's exactly what the visitor pattern does. We'll examine that here, and later you'll see why it's not needed in Clojure.

Consider the program we mentioned earlier that needed to process an AST. The implementation from there implemented things like `checkValidity` and `generate-ASM` inside each concrete implementation of `SyntaxNode`. The problem with this approach is that adding new operations like this is quite invasive, because every type of node needs to be touched. The visitor pattern allows such operations to be separated from the data object hierarchy (which, in this case, is the `SyntaxNode` hierarchy). Let's take a quick look at the modification needed, as shown in figure 4.4, followed by the new visitor classes. Figure 4.5 shows the new visitor classes.

The infrastructure method `accept(NodeVisitor)` in each `SyntaxNode` is required because of the need to simulate a double dispatch. Inside it, the visitor itself is called back using an appropriate visit method. Here's some more Java code showing an example involving `AssignmentNode`:

```
public void accept(NodeVisitor visitor) {
  visitor.visitAssignment(this);
}
```

This is a lot of indirection for something that ought to be simple. Unfortunately, the limitation of single dispatch requires this forced simulation of double dispatch. Again,

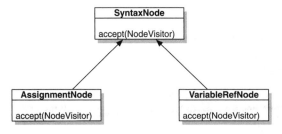

Figure 4.4 A modification is needed to simulate double dispatch. The `accept` **method is a somewhat unclear but required method in each node, which will call back the visitor.**

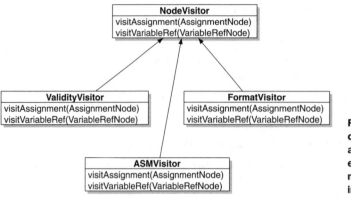

Figure 4.5   Each visitor class does one operation and knows how to process each kind of node. Adding new kinds of operation involves adding new visitors.

if the language natively supported double dispatch, all this boilerplate code would be unnecessary. Further, the NodeVisitor hierarchy needs to know about all the classes in the SyntaxNode hierarchy, which makes it a more coupled design.

Still, now that you know about double dispatch, the obvious question is, what about triple dispatch? What about dispatching on any number of argument types?

4.2.3   *Multiple dispatch*

In essence, multiple dispatch takes the idea of double dispatch to its logical end. A language that supports multiple dispatch can look up methods based on the type of the receiver and all the arguments passed to it.

A language that supports this feature doesn't need the convoluted visitor pattern. Simple and straightforward calls with multiple arguments of different types work fine. Figure 4.6 shows how this arrangement might look.

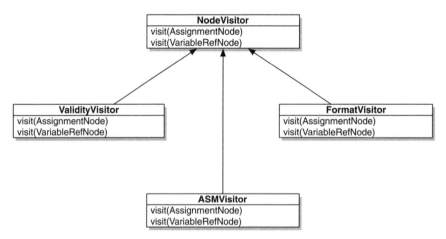

Figure 4.6   With multiple dispatch, visitors can have a straightforward, polymorphic visit method (off the type of SyntaxNodes**), and** SyntaxNode **doesn't need the accept method infrastructure.**

Languages such as Dylan, Nice, R, and Common Lisp support multiple dispatch. Clojure also supports multiple dispatch through its multimethods feature.

4.3 Multimethods

Now that you've seen how method polymorphism works underneath, we're finally ready to look at Clojure's multimethod feature. Clojure multimethods support not only multiple dispatch but much more. Indeed, once you look past multiple dispatch, a commonly asked question is whether a language can dispatch on things other than the types of values. With Clojure's multimethods, methods can be made to dispatch based on any arbitrary rule.

A multimethod is defined using `defmulti`. A multimethod by itself isn't useful; it needs candidate implementations from which to choose when it's called. The `defmethod` macro is used to define implementations. Let's take a look.

4.3.1 Without multimethods

Consider the situation where our expense-tracking service has become popular. We've started an affiliate program where we pay referrers if they get users to sign up for our service. Different affiliates have different fees. Let's begin with the case where we have two main ones: mint.com and the universal google.com.

We'd like to create a function that calculates the fee we pay to the affiliate. For the sake of illustration, let's decide we'll pay our affiliates a percentage of the annual salary the user makes. We'll pay Google 0.01%, we'll pay Mint 0.03%, and everyone else gets 0.02%. Let's write this without multimethods first:

```
(defn fee-amount [percentage user]
  (float (* 0.01 percentage (:salary user))))

(defn affiliate-fee-cond [user]
  (cond
    (= :google.com (:referrer user)) (fee-amount 0.01 user)
    (= :mint.com (:referrer user)) (fee-amount 0.03 user)
    :default (fee-amount 0.02 user)))
```

The trouble with this way of writing this function is that it's painful to add new rules about affiliates and percentages. The `cond` form will soon get messy. We'll now rewrite it using Clojure's multimethods.

4.3.2 Using multimethods

Before we implement the same functionality using multimethods, let's take a moment to understand how they work. As mentioned earlier, multimethods are declared using the `defmulti` macro. Here's a simplified general form of this macro:

```
(defmulti name dispatch-fn & options)
```

The `dispatch-fn` function is a regular Clojure function that accepts the same arguments that are passed in when the multimethod is called. The return value of dispatch-fn is what is called a *dispatching value*. Before moving on, let's look at the previously mentioned defmethod macro:

```
(defmethod multifn dispatch-value & fn-tail)
```

This creates a concrete implementation for a previously defined multimethod. The multifn identifier should match the name in the previous call to defmulti. The dispatch-value will be compared with the return value of the dispatch-fn from earlier in order to determine which method will execute. This will be clearer through an example, so let's rewrite the affiliate-fee function using multimethods:

```
(defmulti affiliate-fee :referrer)

(defmethod affiliate-fee :mint.com [user]
  (fee-amount 0.03 user))

(defmethod affiliate-fee :google.com [user]
  (fee-amount 0.01 user))

(defmethod affiliate-fee :default [user]
  (fee-amount 0.02 user))
```

That looks a lot cleaner than the cond form, because it separates each case into its own method (which looks somewhat similar to a plain function). Let's set up some test data, so you can try it out:

```
(def user-1 {:login "rob" :referrer :mint.com :salary 100000})
(def user-2 {:login "kyle" :referrer :google.com :salary 90000})
(def user-3 {:login "celeste" :referrer :yahoo.com :salary 70000})
```

And now try a few calls to affiliate-fee:

```
(affiliate-fee user-1)
30.0
(affiliate-fee user-2)
9.0
    (affiliate-fee user-3)
14.0
```

This works as expected. When a call is made to affiliate-fee, the multimethod first calls the dispatch-fn. In this case, we used :referrer as the dispatch-fn. The arguments to the dispatch-fn are the same as the arguments to the multimethod, which in this case is the user hash map. Calling :referrer on the user object returns something like :google.com and is considered the dispatch-value. The various methods are then checked over, and when a match is found, it's executed.

If a match isn't found, then the default case is picked. The default value for this catchall case is :default, but you can specify anything you want when calling defmulti, as so:

```
(defmulti affiliate-fee :referrer :default :else)
```

After you change the default value with such a call, the default case method would need to use the same value:

```
(defmethod affiliate-fee :else [user]
  (fee-amount 0.02 user))
```

It's that simple! Now, to add new cases, you add new methods, which is far cleaner than ending up with a long-winded cond form. Now let's try to stretch this example a bit by expanding the capabilities of our system.

4.3.3 Multiple dispatch

Imagine that our service is even more successful than before and that the affiliate program is working great. So great, in fact, that we'd like to pay more profitable users a higher fee. This would be a win-win situation for the affiliate network and our service, so let's get started by quantifying a user's level of profitability. Consider the following dummy implementation of this functionality:

```
(defn profit-rating [user]
  (let [ratings [::bronze ::silver ::gold ::platinum]]
    (nth ratings (rand-int (count ratings)))))
```

This is quite the dummy implementation, as you can see; it doesn't even use the user parameter. It serves our purpose nicely, because it demonstrates that this function could be doing anything (number crunching, database access, web-service calls, whatever you like). In this case, it returns one of the four possible ratings out of ::bronze, ::silver, ::gold, or ::platinum. The extra colon resolves each of these keywords to the namespace it's used in. As you'll see shortly, creating ad hoc hierarchies in Clojure requires the use of namespace-qualified keywords if they're used as dispatch values.

Now let's consider the business rules shown in table 4.1.

Table 4.1 Affiliate fee business rules

Affiliate	Profit rating	Fee (% of salary)
mint.com	Bronze	0.03
mint.com	Silver	0.04
mint.com	Gold/platinum	0.05
google.com	Gold/platinum	0.03

From the rules it's clear that there are two values based on which fee percentage is calculated: the referrer and the profit rating. In a sense, the combination of these two values is the affiliate fee type. Because we'd like to dispatch on this virtual type, comprising two values, let's create a function that computes the pair:

```
(defn fee-category [user]
  [(:referrer user) (profit-rating user)])
```

This returns a vector containing two values, for instance, [:mint.com ::bronze], [:google.com ::gold], and [:mint.com ::platinum]. We can use these as dispatch values in our methods, as follows:

```
(defmulti profit-based-affiliate-fee fee-category)
(defmethod profit-based-affiliate-fee [:mint.com ::bronze] [user]
  (fee-amount 0.03 user))
(defmethod profit-based-affiliate-fee [:mint.com ::silver] [user]
  (fee-amount 0.04 user))
(defmethod profit-based-affiliate-fee [:mint.com ::gold] [user]
  (fee-amount 0.05 user))
(defmethod profit-based-affiliate-fee [:mint.com ::platinum] [user]
  (fee-amount 0.05 user))
(defmethod profit-based-affiliate-fee [:google.com ::gold] [user]
  (fee-amount 0.03 user))
(defmethod profit-based-affiliate-fee [:google.com ::platinum] [user]
  (fee-amount 0.03 user))
(defmethod profit-based-affiliate-fee :default [user]
  (fee-amount 0.02 user))
```

This reads a lot like our table with business rules, and adding new rules is still quite easy and doesn't involve modifying existing code.

On a separate note, this is a form of double dispatch because we're dispatching on two values. The `affiliate-id` and `profit-level`, even though they aren't types in the class-based sense of the word, behave as types in this domain. This Clojure code performs a double dispatch based on types in our domain. There's nothing to stop you from dispatching on any number of such types if you wanted to; the mechanism is straightforward.

> **Simulating single dispatch with multimethods**
>
> Incidentally, it's trivial to simulate single dispatch in Clojure—all that's needed is a dispatch function that ignores all but the first argument. If the first argument is a data type (or a class), you can even simulate Java-style single-dispatch.

Although we've shown polymorphic behavior in these examples, we've not mentioned inheritance at all. This shows that inheritance isn't a necessary condition for polymorphism. But inheritance can be quite convenient, as you'll see in the next section.

4.3.4 *Ad hoc hierarchies*

Now that we have the profit-rating infrastructure in place, we might want to expose the ratings to our members in a form similar to airlines' membership status. We could treat bronze as an entry-level status, and members could graduate to silver and higher levels. We could also treat gold and platinum as premier statuses, affording such members a higher class of service. This classification might look like that shown in figure 4.7.

We can codify this hierarchy using Clojure's `derive` function, as follows:

```
(derive ::bronze ::basic)
(derive ::silver ::basic)
(derive ::gold ::premier)
(derive ::platinum ::premier)
```

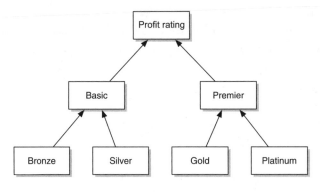

Figure 4.7　Our domain demands a hierarchy of membership statuses. We can use this external-facing classification to simplify our code by defining an ad hoc hierarchy reflecting this structure.

This is why we namespace-qualified the keywords; we can now use them in hierarchies as shown here. Having done so, we can programmatically ensure it works as expected using the isa? function:

```
(isa? ::platinum ::premier)
true

(isa? ::bronze ::premier)
false
```

Because we now have a hierarchy, we can redefine the multimethod to calculate the affiliate fee as follows:

```
(defmulti affiliate-fee-for-hierarchy fee-category)
(defmethod affiliate-fee-for-hierarchy [:mint.com ::bronze] [user]
  (fee-amount 0.03 user))
(defmethod affiliate-fee-for-hierarchy [:mint.com ::silver] [user]
  (fee-amount 0.04 user))
(defmethod affiliate-fee-for-hierarchy [:mint.com ::premier] [user]
  (fee-amount 0.05 user))
(defmethod affiliate-fee-for-hierarchy [:google.com ::premier] [user]
  (fee-amount 0.03 user))
(defmethod affiliate-fee-for-hierarchy :default [user]
  (fee-amount 0.02 user))
```

This is even more succinct; it also captures the intent that acquiring a premier member from an affiliate partner is more expensive.

JAVA CLASS HIERARCHY

Although we've shown that it's easy enough to create ad hoc hierarchies, Clojure goes one step further to make things simpler by providing support for Java classes out of the box. When Java classes are used as dispatch values, inheritance relationships are automatically respected, relieving the need for the hierarchy to be created again via calls to derive.

This ensures that both javax.swing.JComboBox and javax.swing.JFileChooser automatically treat javax.swing.JComponent as a parent. A method that uses the JComponent as a dispatch value will match if the dispatching function returns either a JFileChooser or a JComboBox. The programmer doesn't have to do anything special for this to work.

THE VISITOR PATTERN REVISITED

Now that you know how multimethods solve the dispatch problem, let's rewrite the AST program using multimethods. Imagine we represent a couple of syntax nodes as so:

```
(def aNode {:type :assignment :expr "assignment"})
(def vNode {:type :variable-ref :expr "variableref"})
```

We'll use the appropriately named :type value of the hash map to behave as the type on which we'll dispatch our multimethod. Here's the implementation of checkValidity:

```
(defmulti checkValidity :type)
(defmethod checkValidity :assignment [node]
  (println "checking :assignment, expression is" (:expr node)))
(defmethod checkValidity :variable-ref [node]
  (println "checking :variable-ref, expression is" (:expr node)))
```

Similarly, here's the multimethod for generateASM:

```
(defmulti generateASM :type)
(defmethod generateASM :assignment [node]
  (println "gen ASM for :assignment, expr is" (:expr node)))
(defmethod generateASM :variable-ref [node]
  (println "gen ASM for :variable-ref, expr is" (:expr node)))
```

This is much simpler than creating the whole double-dispatch mechanism in a language like Java or C++ that doesn't support it. In order to add new types of operations on the AST, you create a new multimethod.

We've covered creation and usage of multimethods. Before moving on, let's look at the situation where more than one dispatching value matches, which confuses the multimethod.

RESOLVING CONFLICTS

Sometimes, a hierarchy may involve what looks like multiple inheritance. Consider the situation where a programmer can be both an employee and a geek, as shown in figure 4.8.

To reflect this, you'd call derive with the following:

```
(derive ::programmer ::employee)
(derive ::programmer ::geek)
```

Such multiple-inheritance relationships are perfectly valid in several domains, and Clojure doesn't stop the programmer from creating or using them. But when methods are created with dispatch values of ::employee and ::geek, and the dispatch function returns ::programmer, the multimethod doesn't know which one to pick because they're both valid.

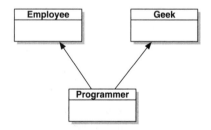

Figure 4.8 A hierarchy could lead to multiple inheritance. Clojure doesn't do anything to prevent this, but it provides an elegant way to break a tie if multiple dispatch values match.

This multiple-inheritance problem is by no means unique to Clojure. Languages like Java avoid it by disallowing classes from being derived from more than one parent class. In Clojure, you can break the tie by specifying your order of preference using the `prefer-method` function. Here's how you'd specify that being a geek trumps being employed:

```
(prefer-method multimethod-name ::geek ::employee)
```

Read this as a preference of `::geek` over `::employee`.

We've covered the mechanics of multimethods and shown how they're a superior way of achieving polymorphism to what languages limited to single dispatch can ever provide. Having said that, multimethods aren't used much, mostly because the functional programming style makes this kind of polymorphism less needed. When there's a need, they can be an elegant solution. In the next section, we'll examine an example of where multimethods are used to great effect.

4.3.5 *Redis-clojure*

Redis is a key-value database. It is fast and persistent. Redis-clojure is a Clojure client for the Redis server written by Ragnar Dahlen. The library is open source and is hosted on github.com. It uses a multimethod to parse responses sent by the server as the client communicates with it.

When the server sends a response, it prefaces the data being asked for with a single character. These control characters are shown in table 4.2. Ragnar has created a multimethod called `parse-reply`, which processes the responses from the server.

```
(defmulti parse-reply reply-type :default :unknown)
```

From what we showed earlier, the default dispatch value has been set to `:unknown`.

Table 4.2 Control characters sent by the Redis server

Character	Meaning
–	An error
+	Single-line reply
$	Bulk data
*	Multi-bulk data
:	Integer number

There are six implementations (methods) of this multimethod—one for each of the five control characters and one for the default case. The following listing shows relevant parts of the code (only the multimethod portion is listed). The choice of a multimethod here keeps the code in the next listing clean, easy to read, and easy to modify.

Listing 4.1   Implementing the Redis protocol using multimethods

```clojure
(defmulti parse-reply reply-type :default :unknown)

(defmethod parse-reply :unknown
  [#^BufferedReader reader]
  (throw (Exception. (str "Unknown reply type:"))))

(defmethod parse-reply \-
  [#^BufferedReader reader]
  (let [error (read-line-crlf reader)]
    (throw (Exception. (str "Server error: " error)))))

(defmethod parse-reply \+
  [#^BufferedReader reader]
  (read-line-crlf reader))

(defmethod parse-reply \$
  [#^BufferedReader reader]
  (let [line (read-line-crlf reader)
        length (parse-int line)]
    (if (< length 0)
      nil
      (let [#^chars cbuf (char-array length)]
        (do
          (do-read reader cbuf 0 length)
          (read-crlf reader) ;; CRLF
          (String. cbuf))))))

(defmethod parse-reply \*
  [#^BufferedReader reader]
  (let [line (read-line-crlf reader)
        count (parse-int line)]
    (if (< count 0)
      nil
      (loop [i count
             replies []]
        (if (zero? i)
          replies
          (recur (dec i) (conj replies (read-reply reader))))))))

(defmethod parse-reply \:
  [#^BufferedReader reader]
  (let [line (trim (read-line-crlf reader))
        int (parse-int line)]
    int))
```

You've seen the basics of multimethods. We're now ready to move on; the next chapter shows how easy Clojure makes interoperability with its host language, Java.

4.4   Summary

As you've seen, what's generally referred to as polymorphism in the context of languages such as Java and C++ is a rather specific variety called subtype polymorphism. Further, the implementation in such languages is limited to single dispatch, which is again a specific case of the far more general possibility of multiple dispatch.

These languages subscribe to a view of OOP that demands methods (and data) *belong* to the enclosing class. It's probable that this is the reason these languages support only single dispatch—they dispatch only on the receiver because it's the class that *owns* the potentially polymorphic method.

In Clojure, a multimethod doesn't belong to anything. The concrete methods instead belong to the multimethod, and they can be dispatched based off any number of types. In fact, the `dispatch` function is an ordinary function written by the programmer, and it can do anything the programmer wants. It's by no means limited to only the type of the arguments, opening up possibilities that can't even be dreamed of in other languages. After all, if you think only in a singular dispatched language, you can't imagine a world of multimethods.

This chapter covered an interesting feature of Clojure, and using it in the right situation will make your programs richer. The next chapter will focus on another great innovation of Clojure: seamless interoperability with Java code.

Clojure and Java interop

This chapter covers

- Introduction to Clojure's Java Interop functionality
- Calling Java from Clojure
- Compiling Clojure down to byte code
- Calling Clojure from Java

Java is the new COBOL. This pronouncement has been made year after year for a few years now, but hasn't quite come to pass. Java was originally designed in the early nineties, was officially released in the mid-nineties, and went on to become one of the most significant technologies of its time. Today, the Java stack is probably one of the most popular in the industry. It isn't going away anytime soon.

With the sheer amount of Java code in production (and more being written every day), no modern programming language can hope to succeed without being able to interoperate with it. Rich Hickey chose well when he picked the JVM to host the Clojure language. Not only does Clojure benefit from the state-of-the-art technology (raw performance, HotSpot, just-in-time compilation, adaptive optimization, garbage collection, and more), but also it makes the goal of seamless Java interoperability easier to achieve. The result is that Java interop with Clojure is both elegant and easy to use. We'll explore this facility in this chapter.

We'll start out by demonstrating how to use Java classes from our Clojure code. Clojure provides a lot of convenient macros that make the resulting code simple and clean. After that, we'll see how our Clojure code can be converted into Java byte code via the compilation facility provided by Clojure. Before wrapping up this chapter, we'll take a brief look at how Clojure code can be called from Java programs.

This chapter talks about several macros that are provided by the Clojure language. We haven't addressed macros so far, so for now, you can think of these as features of the language itself. Once you learn how to write your own macros in chapter 7, you'll be able to appreciate the elegance of the macros from this chapter even more. In any case, by the end of this chapter, you'll have mastered another extremely powerful feature of Clojure—that of being able to use the extensive set of Java libraries out there from within your Clojure programs.

5.1   Calling Java from Clojure

The availability of a good set of standard libraries can make or break a programming language. This is why Clojure has such a great advantage; being hosted on the JVM means that programs have instant access to literally thousands of libraries and frameworks. It's a bit like having the privilege of living most of your programming life in the advanced environment of Clojure but being able to cherry-pick any Java library to use when you need to. So let's begin our exploration of Clojure's Java interop features by learning how to use external Java classes in your programs.

5.1.1   Importing Java classes into Clojure

Writing large programs in any language quickly reaches a point where code needs to be organized into logical units. This is a simple way of managing complexity, because it breaks things down into more understandable chunks of code. In Clojure, the basic unit of code organization is namespaces, and we explored them in chapter 3. We also showed how to `require` and `use` namespaces. In Java, the analogous unit of code organization is called the package. The `import` statement is used to import complete packages or specific classes from inside packages into Java programs that need them. In keeping with that, Clojure also provides the `import` function. Here's the general form:

```
(import & import-symbols-or-lists)
```

As you can tell, `import` takes a variable number of arguments. Each argument is a list, where the first part of the list is a Java package name, followed by the names of those classes from inside that package that you want to import. Here's an example:

```
(import
  '(org.apache.hadoop.hbase.client HTable Scan Scanner)
  '(org.apache.hadoop.hbase.filter RegExpRowFilter StopRowFilter))
```

This code snippet uses the Hadoop HBase client library, and the first line imports the HTable, Scan, and Scanner classes from the org.apache.hadoop.hbase.client package. This makes them available to the rest of the code in the namespace. The recommended way to import Java classes into a namespace is to use the :import option in the namespace declaration:

```
(ns com.clojureinaction.book
  (:import (java.util Set)))
```

Once classes have been imported, they can be used easily in the rest of the code. You can do almost anything you can do in Java from within Clojure. We'll explore all the common things you might need to do in the following sections, beginning with how to create new instances of Java classes and how to access methods and fields of Java objects.

5.1.2 *Creating instances and accessing methods and fields*

In this section, we'll quickly demonstrate the basics of Java interop, specifically ways in which to create new objects from Java classes and to access methods and fields on these objects. We'll also show some conveniences that Clojure provides to make things easier when working with Java. For instance, once you're familiar with the macros that Clojure provides for creating and using Java classes and objects, you might decide it's easier to use Java classes from Clojure than from Java itself! Let's start with instantiating classes.

CREATING INSTANCES

Let's create a new instance of a Java class. Consider the following code:

```
(import '(java.text SimpleDateFormat))
(def sdf (new SimpleDateFormat "yyyy-MM-dd"))
```

After the call to def, the sdf var has a root binding that's a new instance of the class SimpleDateFormat. The new special form works similarly to the new keyword in Java: it accepts a class name and arguments that can be a applied to a matching constructor.

Clojure also has an alternative to using the new form via its support of a special notation for symbols containing a dot (.). If the first symbol in a list ends with a dot, that symbol is assumed to be a class name, and the call is assumed to be to a constructor of that class. The remaining symbols are assumed to be arguments to the matching constructor. This form gets converted into the equivalent new form.

Here's the previous example again, rewritten to use this macro syntax:

```
(def sdf (SimpleDateFormat. "yyyy-MM-dd"))
```

Note the dot at the end of "SimpleDateFormat.". Now that you know how to create new Java objects, let's examine accessing their members.

MEMBER ACCESS

In Java, member access refers to accessing methods and fields of objects. Doing this from within Clojure is easy because Clojure provides another convenient dot macro to do this. Consider the following code:

```
(defn date-from-date-string [date-string]
  (let [sdf (SimpleDateFormat. "yyyy-MM-dd")]
    (.parse sdf date-string)))
```

You first create a `SimpleDateFormat` object as you did earlier. To call the parse method on that object, you use the dot form by prefixing a dot to the symbol `parse`. The first operand in that form is the object on which the instance member is being called. The remaining operands are arguments to that instance method.

Calling static methods on classes is slightly different but just as easy:

```
(Long/parseLong "12321")
```

Here, `parseLong` is a static method on the class `Long`, which accepts a string containing a long number. This example returns `12321` as an instance of `java.lang.Long`. Calling a static method in general has the following form:

```
(Classname/staticMethod args*)
```

The first element of this list is a class name and static method combination like `Long/parseLong`, whereas the remaining elements in the list are arguments to that method.

Accessing static fields is similar to calling static methods. Here's an example:

```
(import '(java.util Calendar))
```

```
Calendar/JANUARY
Calendar/FEBRUARY
```

These two examples access the static fields `JANUARY` and `FEBRUARY` from the `Calendar` class.

THE DOT SPECIAL FORM

In Clojure, all underlying Java access is done via the dot operator. The macro forms we just discussed get converted into forms using this dot operator. The Clojure documentation says that the dot operator can be read as "in the scope of." That means that the member access is happening in the scope of the value of the first symbol.

Let's examine how it works. Consider the following pair of general forms:

```
(. Classname-symbol method-symbol args*)
(. Classname-symbol (method-symbol args*))
```

These forms allows static methods to be called on classes specified as the first argument. Here's an example of using them:

```
(. System getenv "PATH")
(. System (getenv "PATH"))
```

Both these forms return the system path as a string. The second form uses parentheses to enclose the name of the method being called. This is convenient when such a call is being made inside other macros (it's easy to generate lists of things). Typically in code, if you do use the dot operator directly, the first form is preferred. Having said that, idiomatic code uses the form described in the previous section, "Member access."

Now let's look at another example that's similar but operates on instances of Java classes (objects) as opposed to classes. Here are the general forms:

```
(. instance-expr method-symbol args*)
(. instance-expr (method-symbol args*))
```

The following example illustrates both these forms:

```
(import '(java.util Random))
(def rnd (Random. ))

(. rnd nextInt 10)
(. rnd (nextInt 10))
```

Again, they both return a number, randomly picked between 0 and 10. The second form, with the extra parentheses, is useful when this kind of call is made inside other macros. This is convenient because it's easy to generate lists of things in Clojure. Also as pointed out in the previous section, when using the dot operator in this way, the first option is preferred. The forms described in the previous section are the idiomatic way to access members of Java objects.

Finally, let's consider the following two general forms:

```
(. Classname-symbol member-symbol)
(. instance-expr member-symbol)
```

These access public fields from either a class or an instance of a class. Here's an example of accessing a static field from the `Calendar` class that you saw earlier, rewritten using the dot operator:

```
(. Calendar DECEMBER)
```

Now that you've seen how the dot operator works, it's worth repeating that it's idiomatic to use the regular forms as described in the previous section. The dot operator is usually reserved for use within macros. We'll now look at another couple of convenience macros, the dot dot macro (two dots) and `doto`.

.. (DOT DOT)

Java code tends to be verbose. It isn't only the syntax; the mutable state, its idea of object orientation, and the lack of higher-order functions all contribute to its verbosity. One common pattern is a series of methods that need to be called on the same object. Another is a sequence of methods that need to be chained together, each operating on the result of the previous. The `doto` macro helps with the former, and the .. (dot dot) macro helps with the latter.

Consider the following code snippet:

```
(import '(java.util Calendar TimeZone))
(. (. (Calendar/getInstance) (getTimeZone)) (getDisplayName))
```

Depending on where in the world you are, this might return something like "Pacific Standard Time". But writing that code is a bit unwieldy—where the dots and the brackets go can get confusing. Imagine if you had another method call to make! You can simplify this by using the form without the extra parentheses as described earlier, to make it a little cleaner:

```
(. (. (Calendar/getInstance) getTimeZone) getDisplayName)
```

This is better but not by much. This is where the dot dot form comes in. It's a convenient macro that chains together method calls. The previous code can be rewritten using this macro as follows:

```
(.. (Calendar/getInstance) (getTimeZone) (getDisplayName))
```

This can be simplified (without the extra parentheses, because we're passing no arguments to either getTimeZone or getDisplayName methods) to the following:

```
(.. (Calendar/getInstance) getTimeZone getDisplayName)
```

If we were using method signatures that accepted arguments, we'd do so as follows:

```
(..
  (Calendar/getInstance)
  (getTimeZone)
  (getDisplayName true TimeZone/SHORT))
```

This might return something like "PDT", again depending on where you are. Note that the code reads better, too, because the sequence of method calls is clearer. Having examined this convenience macro, let's look at another way to write clearer code in such situations.

DOTO

As mentioned earlier, the doto macro helps write code where multiple methods are called on the same Java object. Consider this contrived function that starts with the current time and works out the most recent midnight:

```
(import '(java.util Calendar))
(defn the-past-midnight-1 []
  (let [calendar-obj (Calendar/getInstance)]
    (.set calendar-obj Calendar/AM_PM Calendar/AM)
    (.set calendar-obj Calendar/HOUR 0)
    (.set calendar-obj Calendar/MINUTE 0)
    (.set calendar-obj Calendar/SECOND 0)
    (.set calendar-obj Calendar/MILLISECOND 0)
    (.getTime calendar-obj)))
```

As you can see, there's tedious repetition of the symbol calendar-obj in this code. The doto macro eliminates this sort of duplication. Here's an example:

```
(defn the-past-midnight-2 []
  (let [calendar-obj (Calendar/getInstance)]
    (doto calendar-obj
      (.set Calendar/AM_PM Calendar/AM)
      (.set Calendar/HOUR 0)
```

```
      (.set Calendar/MINUTE 0)
      (.set Calendar/SECOND 0)
      (.set Calendar/MILLISECOND 0))
  (.getTime calendar-obj)))
```

In general, it accepts a symbol followed by a body of forms. The symbol is spliced into the form without the doto. This kind of macro used to eliminate duplication is quite common in Clojure code.

Before wrapping up this section, let's look at a couple of macros that make life easier when dealing with Java code. We'll first talk about memfn, which is a convenient way to convert Java instance methods into Clojure functions. We'll then cover bean, a super-convenient way to convert a Java bean object into a Clojure map.

5.1.3   *memfn*

Let's say you wanted to collect the byte arrays that compose a few strings. Here's how you might do it:

```
(map (fn [x] (.getBytes x)) ["amit" "rob" "kyle"])
```

This can be simplified using the reader macro for anonymous functions:

```
(map #(.getBytes %) ["amit" "rob" "kyle"])
```

Creating this anonymous function is necessary because a member function like get-Bytes can't be used as a regular higher-order Clojure function. But there is a convenient macro called memfn that makes it easy to convert such a member function into a Clojure function. This is necessary because Java methods aren't first class, so they can't be used without this conversion in places that need functions. Our previous use of the higher-order function map is a typical example of such usage. Here's an example of using memfn:

```
(memfn getBytes)
```

Using it in the context of map, for instance, looks like this:

```
(map (memfn getBytes) ["amit" "rob" "kyle"])
```

memfn also works with member functions that accept more than one argument. Consider the following call to the subSequence member function on a String object:

```
(.subSequence "Clojure" 2 5)
```

This returns "oju". The equivalent form is

```
((memfn subSequence start end) "Clojure" 2 5)
```

This also returns "oju". The Clojure function returned by the call to (memfn sub-Sequence start end) can be used as a regular function in all the usual constructs. Now we'll look at bean, another macro that's quite useful when working with Java code.

5.1.4 *bean*

bean is another convenient macro that's useful when dealing with Java code, especially Java beans, which are classes that conform to a simple standard involving exposing their data via getter and setter methods. Instead of having to deal with calling the getters via the macros described previously (which can get tedious rather quickly if you're dealing with large objects), you could use the Clojure-provided bean macro to convert the object into a hash map. Consider the following examples:

```
(bean (Calendar/getInstance))
```

This returns a Clojure map that contains all its bean properties. Being a Clojure data structure, it's immutable. It looks like the following:

```
{:timeInMillis 1257466522295,
 :minimalDaysInFirstWeek 1,
 :lenient true,
 :firstDayOfWeek 1,
 :class java.util.GregorianCalendar

;; other properties
}
```

This map is a lot easier to work with when compared to calling getters on the original object. Next we'll look at Clojure's mechanism for dealing with arrays.

> **Number of parentheses**
>
> People often talk about the sheer number of parentheses that Clojure uses. Despite the advantages this syntax offers, first-time Clojure programmers can find the code a bit hard to read.
>
> This is why it's somewhat amusing to note that when compared to Java code, Clojure code often has fewer parentheses, all used and placed in a consistent and regular manner. It's true that the placement of the parentheses is different, but it's a point worth noticing.

5.1.5 *Arrays*

A Java array is a container object that holds values of the same type. It's a random-access data structure that uses integers as its keys. Although not used as often as other container classes from the standard Java library, it's common in Java programs. Clojure has native support for dealing with Java arrays. Consider the following snippet:

```
(def tokens (.split "clojure.in.action" "\\."))
```

tokens is a Java array of String objects.

Let's now look at a few of the functions that Clojure provides that help in working with Java arrays:

- (alength tokens)—alength returns the size of the array, which in this case returns 3.
- (aget tokens 2)—aget returns the element of the array at the index specified, which in this case returns the string "action".
- (aset tokens 2 "actionable")—This mutates the tokens array so that the last token is now actionable.

It's worth remembering at this point that unlike any of Clojure's core data structures, Java arrays are mutable. This is true for all Java objects. You'll see in chapter 6 how mutability can cause problems in multithreaded programs, and you'll also learn about Clojure's approach to dealing with concurrency.

Clojure also provides several other functions that allow sequences to be converted into Java arrays (to-array, to-array-2d, and into-array) and one that allows arbitrary new Java arrays to be created (make-array). There are also array-specific versions of the previously seen map and reduce functions, called amap and areduce.

All these functions make working with Java arrays easy. Having said that, because arrays need special handling and are a bit unwieldy compared to regular sequences, you should limit their use to situations where they're absolutely needed.

We've covered quite a few aspects of Clojure's support for interoperating with the world of Java code. We're nearly finished; the last thing we'll discuss is how to implement Java interfaces and extend Java classes from within Clojure code. By the end of the next section, you'll have a mostly complete Java interop toolkit under your belt.

5.1.6 *Implementing interfaces and extending classes*

When working with Java libraries and framework, it's often necessary to define new classes that implement certain interfaces or extend certain classes. It would be a shame if any of that required writing Java code. Luckily, Clojure has a macro called proxy that allows you to do this from within Clojure code.

Consider, for instance, the Grizzly project. It's a server application framework that takes advantage of Java's NIO API and allows programmers to write highly scalable server applications for various services. An abstract class that's provided by the framework is the GrizzlyAdapter class, which can be used for simple services. The only abstract method on the class is

```
abstract void service(GrizzlyRequest req, GrizzlyResponse res)
```

The request and response objects are what you'd expect. Here's a contrived example of creating an instance of a class that extends GrizzlyAdapter and implements the service method:

```
(import '(com.sun.grizzly.tcp.http11 GrizzlyAdapter))
(proxy [GrizzlyAdapter] []
    (service [req res]
      "Service was called!"))
```

Please note that you'll need the Grizzly JARs on the classpath for this to work. The general form of the proxy macro is

```
(proxy [class-and-interfaces] [args] fs+)
```

This shows that the proxy form accepts a vector of Java classes and interfaces, followed by a vector of arguments (possibly empty) that will be passed to the superclass constructor, followed by any methods being defined. In the previous example, the Grizzly-Adapter interface is specified, and only the single method service is implemented.

This section was quite dense and filled with a lot of detail! You're now in a position to use any kind of Java library in your Clojure programs. This is a great feature of the Clojure language and is quite critical to writing real-world programs. We'll do that later, when we use HBase to store data and communicate between Clojure programs over a message bus.

Now that you understand Clojure's support for Java interoperability, we're ready to move on. You'll now see how to generate static Java classes from Clojure code.

5.2 Compiling Clojure code to Java byte code

As you saw in chapter 1, Clojure doesn't have an interpreter. Code is evaluated one s-expression at a time. During that process, if something needs to be compiled, the Clojure runtime does so. Ultimately, because Clojure is hosted on the JVM, everything is converted to Java byte code before execution, and the programmer doesn't have to worry about when and how this happens.

Clojure provides a mechanism to do this compilation ahead of time (AOT). AOT compilation has its advantages. Packaging the code lets you deliver it as a class file (without the source code being included) for use by other Java applications, and it speeds up the program's startup time. In this section, we'll examine how to AOT compile Clojure code.

5.2.1 Example–a tale of two calculators

In this example, we'll examine some code that implements a couple of financial calculators that you might use to manage investments in stocks and bonds. We'll lay out our code in a directory structure for easy organization of code—one that's somewhat idiomatic in the Clojure world. Figure 5.1 shows this organization.

Note that calculators.clj is located in the src/com/curry/utils folder and is the file that contains the namespace of our current interest. Here are the contents:

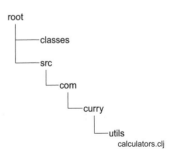

Figure 5.1 Typical organization of a Clojure project. The src directory contains the source code, organized in a similar way to Java packages.

```
(ns com.curry.utils.calculators
  (:gen-class))

(defn present-value [data]
  (println "calculating present value..."))
```

This code can be compiled from a REPL that has both classes and src directories on the classpath. The compile function is used to do this, and it accepts the namespace to be compiled:

```
(compile 'com.curry.utils.calculators)
```

If successful, this function returns the name of the namespace that was compiled. Let's now examine what the output of this compilation process is, what class files are generated, and where they're located.

GENERATED CLASSES

As noted, the compile function compiles the specified namespace. In this case, it generates class files for the com.curry.utils.calculators namespace. Three class files that get generated here are calculators_init.class, calculators.class, and calculators$present_value__xx.class, and they're located in the classes/com/curry/utils directory.

A class file is created for each Clojure function. In this case, the present-value function causes the calculators$present_value__xx.class to be created, the name of which will vary each time the namespace is recompiled (because it's a generated name). A class file is also generated for each gen-class, and in this case this corresponds to the calculators.class file.

Finally, the class files that have the __init in their names contain a loader class, and one such file is generated for every Clojure source file. Typically, this loader class doesn't need to be referenced directly, because use, require, and load calls figure out which file to use when they're called.

:gen-class has a lot of options that allow control over various aspects of the generated code. These are explored in section 5.2.2. Now that we've covered the basics of compilation, let's try to compile a namespace that's spread across files.

ADDITIONAL FILES

Let's add a couple more calculators to our calculators namespace. You'll create two more files in order to do this, one for each new calculator function. The resulting file structure is shown in figure 5.2.

The contents of dcf.clj are

```
(in-ns 'com.curry.utils.calculators)
(defn discounted-cash-flow [data]
  (println "calculating discounted cash flow..."))
```

And the contents of fcf.clj are

```
(in-ns 'com.curry.utils.calculators)
(defn free-cash-flow [data]
  (println "calculating free cash flow..."))
```

Note that they both use in-ns to ensure that these files all belong to the same namespace. calculators.clj is modified as follows:

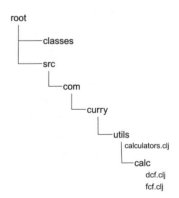

Figure 5.2 Adding two new files, dcf.clj and fcf.clj, in a subdirectory of utils that have code for the same com.curry.utils .calculators namespace.

```
(ns com.curry.utils.calculators
  (:gen-class))

(load "calc/fcf")
(load "calc/dcf")

(defn present-value [data]
  (println "calculating present value..."))
```

Note the use of load using relative paths, because the fcf.clj and dcf.clj files are inside the calc subdirectory of utils. Calling compile, as you did before, results in new class files being generated in the classes directory. Two files, namely dcf__init.class and fcf__init.class, are generated in the classes/com/curry/utils/calc folder. New files are also created for the new functions, namely discounted-cash-flow and free-cash-flow in the classes/com/curry/utils directory.

COMPILE-PATH

In case you're curious as to why the generated code is being output to the classes directory, it's because it's the default value of the global var *compile-path*. It's easy to change this by calling set! to alter the value of the var or to call compile inside a binding form with *compile-path* bound to something appropriate. The thing to remember is that the directory must exist, and it should be on the classpath.

5.2.2 *Creating Java classes and interfaces using gen-class and gen-interface*

Clojure also has a standalone utility for generating Java classes and interfaces in the gen-class and gen-interface macros. When code containing these calls is compiled, it generates byte code for the specified classes or interfaces and writes them into class files as you saw earlier. In this section, you'll see an example of how gen-class works. Consider the following listing, which is a contrived example of an abstract Java class that we'll use to illustrate gen-class.

> **Listing 5.1 An abstract Java class that will be used to illustrate gen-class**

```
package com.gentest;

public abstract class AbstractJavaClass {

    public AbstractJavaClass(String a, String b) {
        System.out.println("Constructor: a, b");
    }

    public AbstractJavaClass(String a) {
        System.out.println("Constructor: a");
    }

    public abstract String getCurrentStatus();

    public String getSecret() {
        return "The Secret";
    }
}
```

Once `AbstractJavaClass` is compiled, it needs to be on Clojure's classpath. After ensuring that the Clojure runtime can see the class, you can use `gen-class` as shown in this next listing.

Listing 5.2   `gen-class` generates a Java class to reference `AbstractJavaClass`

```
(ns com.gentest.gen-clojure
  (:import (com.gentest AbstractJavaClass))
  (:gen-class
    :name com.gentest.ConcreteClojureClass
    :extends com.gentest.AbstractJavaClass
    :constructors {[String] [String]
                   [String String] [String String]}
    :implements [Runnable]
    :init initialize
    :state localState
    :methods [[stateValue [] String]]
    ))

(defn -initialize
    ([s1]
      (println "Init value:" s1)
        [[s1 "default"] (ref s1)])
    ([s1 s2]
      (println "Init values:"  s1 "," s2)
      [[s1 s2] (ref s2)]))

(defn -getCurrentStatus [this]
  "getCurrentStatus from - com.gentest.ConcreteClojureClass")

(defn -stateValue [this]
  @(.localState this))

(defn -run [this]
  (println "In run!")
  (println "I'm a" (class this))
  (dosync (ref-set (.localState this) "GO")))

(defn -main []
  (let [g (new com.gentest.ConcreteClojureClass "READY")]
    (println (.getCurrentStatus g))
    (println (.getSecret g))
    (println (.stateValue g)))
  (let [g (new com.gentest.ConcreteClojureClass "READY" "SET")]
    (println (.stateValue g))
    (.start (Thread. g))
    (Thread/sleep 1000)
    (println (.stateValue  g))))
```

Now, let's go over the code in listing 5.2 to understand what's going on. The call to `ns` should be familiar by now. It uses `:import` to pull in `AbstractJavaClass` from listing 5.1. This was why it needs to be on the classpath. The next option, `:gen-class`, is our primary interest. It can take several options, some of which are used in this example and some aren't. Table 5.1 describes the options used in listing 5.2.

Table 5.1 `gen-class` **options used in listing 5.2**

Option	Description
`:name`	The name of the class that will be generated when this namespace is compiled.
`:extends`	The fully qualified name of the superclass.
`:constructors`	Explicit specification of constructors via a map where each key is a vector of types that specifies a constructor signature. Values are similar vectors that identify the signature of a superclass constructor.
`:implements`	A vector of classes that the class implements.
`:init`	The name of a function that will be called with the arguments to the constructor. Must return a vector of two elements, the first being a vector.
`:methods`	Specifies the signatures of additional methods of the generated class. Implemented interface or extended superclass public methods are generated by default.

Functions such as `-initialize`, `-getCurrentStatus`, and `-run` implement or override interface or superclass methods. The reason they're prefixed with a dash (-) is so that they can be identified via convention. The prefix can be changed using the `:prefix` option (see table 5.2). Now that you understand what each option in the example does, you're ready to run it.

RUNNING IT

The classpath needs to have clojure.jar on it as well as the locations of com.gentest .AbstractJavaClass and com.gentest.ConcreteClojureClass. The following command assumes the CLASSPATH environment variable has been set up appropriately. The command to test our generated class is

```
java com.gentest.ConcreteClojureClass
```

This outputs the following to the console:

```
Init value: READY
Constructor: a
getCurrentStatus from - com.gentest.ConcreteClojureClass
The Secret
READY
Init values: READY , SET
Constructor: a, b
SET
In run!
I'm a com.gentest.ConcreteClojureClass
GO
```

As the code shows, you've used both constructor signatures to create instances of our generated class. You've also called a superclass method `getSecret` and the overridden method `getCurrentStatus`. Finally, you've also run the second instance as a thread and checked the mutating state `localState`, which changed from `"SET"` to `"GO"`.

Table 5.2 shows the other options available to `gen-class`.

Table 5.2 More `gen-class` options

Option	Description
`:post-init`	Name of the function that's called with the newly created instance as the first argument and that's called each time an instance is created, after all constructors have run.
`:main`	Defaults to `true`—specifies whether a main method should be generated.
`:factory`	Specifies the name of the factory function(s) that will have the same signature as the constructors. A public final instance of the class will also be created. An `:init` function will also be needed in order to supply the initial state.
`:exposes`	Used to expose protected fields inherited from the superclass. The value is a map where the keys are the name of the protected field and the values are maps specifying the names of the getters and setters. The format is `:exposes {protected-field-name {:get name :set name}, ...}`
`:exposes-methods`	Exposes overridden methods from the superclass via the specified name. The format of this is `:exposes-methods {super-method-name exposed-name, ...}`
`:prefix`	Defaults to the dash (`-`). When methods like `getCurrentStatus` are called, they will be looked up by prefixing this value (for example, `getCurrentStatus`).
`:impl-ns`	Defaults to the current namespace but can be specified here if the methods being implemented or overridden are in a different namespace.
`:load-impl-ns`	Defaults to `true`; causes static initializer of generated class to reference the load code of the implementing namespace. Can be turned to `false` if the code needs to be loaded in a more controlled manner.

This is quite an exhaustive set of options, and it lets the programmer influence nearly every aspect of the generated code. `gen-interface` works in a similar fashion to `gen-class` but has fewer options because it's limited to defining an interface.

Now that you've seen how to compile and generate Java code from our Clojure source, we're ready to move on. Next, you're going to see how to go the other way: to call our Clojure functions from Java programs. This will allow you to write appropriate parts of our application in Clojure using all the facilities provided by the language and then use it from other Java code.

5.3   *Calling Clojure from Java*

One of the great things about most languages hosted on the JVM is that they can be embedded into other Java programs. This is useful when you need the ability to script the larger system. Let's review how to call Clojure functions from Java code.

Consider the following Clojure function, defined in the `clj.script.examples` namespace:

```
(ns clj.script.examples)

(defn print-report [user-name]
  (println "Report for:" user-name)
  10)
```

If this Clojure code is in a file named clojure_script.clj, you can now call the print-report function from a Java method, as shown in the following code:

```
public class Driver {
    public static void main(String[] args) throws Exception {
        RT.loadResourceScript("clojure_script.clj");
        Var report = RT.var("clj.script.examples", "print-report");
        Integer result = (Integer) report.invoke("Siva");
        System.out.println("Result: " + result);
    }
}
```

Here, RT is the class that represents the Clojure runtime. You initialize it by calling the static method loadResourceScript on the RT class. It accepts the name of the Clojure script file and loads the code defined within. The RT class also has a var static method, which accepts a namespace name along with a var name (both as strings). It looks up a var as specified and returns a Var object, which can then be invoked using the invoke method. The invoke method can accept an arbitrary number of arguments.

As you can see, the basics of calling Clojure from Java are quite straightforward. This is by design; Clojure was created to embrace the JVM, and does so in a seamless, user-friendly manner.

5.4 Summary

This chapter explored Clojure's excellent support for interoperability with Java. This is an important feature, because it gives programmers instant access to thousands of libraries and frameworks. As you'll see in later parts of the book, this is a huge advantage when it comes to building real-world systems in Clojure. You can write your application-specific code in Clojure and use well-tested, production-quality Java libraries for infrastructure-related requirements, for example, accessing HBase (an open-source implementation of Google's BigTable) and using RabbitMQ (an extremely fast messaging system).

This availability of a large number of well-tested, production-ready libraries and frameworks makes a huge difference to a new language such as Clojure. Apart from making all this functionality available to use from Clojure, the Java interop also makes it possible to write code that coexists with and leverages existing investments in Java systems. This allows Clojure to be brought into environments and organizations in an incremental fashion. Lastly, the elegance of the interop makes it easy to use Java code from within Clojure. All these factors contribute to making Clojure's embrace of the Java platform a huge plus when considering the adoption of the language.

State and the concurrent world

This chapter covers

- The problems with mutable state
- Clojure's approach to state
- Refs, agents, atoms, and vars
- Futures and promises

> *State—you're doing it wrong.*
>
> Rich Hickey

The above quote is from a presentation by Rich Hickey in which he mentions Clojure's approach to concurrency and state. He means that most languages use an approach to modeling state that doesn't work. To be precise, it used to work when computers were less powerful and ran programs in a single-threaded fashion. In today's world of increasingly multicore and multi-CPU computers, the model has broken down.

This is evidenced by the difficulty of writing bug-free multithreaded code in typical object-oriented languages like Java and C++. Still, programmers continue to make the attempt. You can see why this is so: the demands on today's software require that it take advantage of all available CPU cores. As software needs grow in complexity, parallelism is becoming an implicit requirement. This chapter is about concurrent programs and the problems they face in dealing with state. We'll first examine what these problems are and then look at the traditional solutions to these problems. We'll then look at Clojure's approach to dealing with these issues and show that when trying to solve difficult problems, it's sometimes worth starting with a fresh slate.

6.1 The problem with state

State is the current set of values associated with things in a program. For example, a payroll program might deal with employee objects. Each employee object represents the state of the employee, and every program usually has a lot of such state. There's no problem with state, per se, or even with mutating state. The real world is full of perceived changes: people change, plans change, the weather changes, and the balance in bank accounts changes. The problem occurs when concurrent (multithreaded) programs share this sort of state among different threads and then attempt to make updates to it. When the illusion of single-threaded execution breaks down, the code encounters all manner of inconsistent data. In this section, we'll look at a solution to this problem. But before we do, let's recap the issues faced by concurrent programs operating on shared data.

6.1.1 Common problems with shared state

Most problems with multithreaded programs happen because changes to shared data aren't correctly protected. The book *Java Concurrency in Practice*, by Brian Goetz, does an incredible job of throwing light on these issues. The book uses Java to illustrate examples, so it isn't directly useful, but it's still highly recommended. For purposes of this chapter, we'll summarize the issues as follows.

LOST OR BURIED UPDATES

Lost updates occur when two threads update the same data one after the other. The update made by the first thread is lost because it's overwritten by the second one. A classic example is two threads incrementing a counter whose current value is 10. Because execution of threads is interleaved, both threads can do a read on the counter and think the value is 10, and then both increment it to 11. The problem is that the final value should have been 12, and the update done by one of the threads was lost.

DIRTY AND UNREPEATABLE READS

A *dirty read* happens when a thread reads data that another thread is in the process of updating. When the updating thread is done, the data that was read by the other thread is inconsistent (dirty). Similarly, an *unrepeatable read* happens when a thread reads a particular set of data, but because other threads are updating it, the thread can never do another read that results in it seeing the same data again.

PHANTOM READS

A *phantom read* happens when a thread reads data that's been deleted (or more data is added). The reading thread is said to have performed a phantom read because it has summarily read data that no longer exist.

6.1.2 *The traditional solution*

The most obvious solution to these problems is to impose a level of control on those parts of the code that mutate shared data. This is done using *locks*, which are constructs that control the execution of sections of code, ensuring that only a single thread runs a lock-protected section of code at a time. When using locks, a thread can execute a destructive method (one that mutates data) that's protected with a lock only if it's able to first obtain the lock. If a thread tries to execute such code while some other thread holds the lock, it blocks until the lock becomes available again. The blocking thread is allowed to resume execution only after it obtains the lock at a later time.

This approach might seem reasonable, but it gets complicated the moment more than one piece of mutable data needs a coordinated change. When this happens, each thread that needs to make those changes must obtain multiple locks, leading to more contention and resulting in concurrency problems. It's difficult to ensure correctness of multithreaded programs that have to deal with multiple mutating data structures. Further, finding and fixing bugs in such programs is difficult thanks to the inherent nondeterministic nature of multithreaded programs.

Still, programs of significant complexity have been written using locks. It takes a lot more time and money to ensure things work as expected and a larger maintenance budget to ensure things continue to work properly while changes are being made to the program. It makes you wonder if there isn't a better approach to solving this problem.

This chapter is about such an approach. Before we get into the meat of the solution, we'll examine a couple of things. First, we'll look at the general disadvantages of using locks in multithreaded programs. Then, we'll take a quick overview of the new issues that arise from the presence of locking.

DISADVANTAGES OF LOCKING

The most obvious disadvantage of locking is that code is less multithreaded than it was before the introduction of locks. When one thread obtains and holds a lock, no other thread can execute that code, causing other threads to wait. This can be wasteful, and it reduces throughput of multithreaded applications.

Further, locks are an excessive solution. Consider the case where a thread only wants to read some piece of mutable data. To ensure that no other thread makes changes while it's doing its work, the reader thread must lock all concerned mutable data. This causes not only writers to block but other readers too. This is unnecessarily wasteful.

Lastly, another disadvantage of locking is that, well, the programmer must remember to lock! If someone introduces a bug that involves a forgotten lock, it can be difficult to track down and fix. There are no automatic mechanisms to flag this situation and no compile-time or runtime warnings associated with such situations, other than the fact that the program behaves in an unexpected manner! The knowledge of what to lock and in what order to lock things (so that the locks can be released in the reverse order) can't be expressed within program code—typically, it's recorded in technical documentation. Everyone in the software industry knows how well documentation works.

Unfortunately, these aren't the only disadvantages with using locks; it causes new problems too. We'll examine some of them now.

THE NEW PROBLEMS WITH LOCKING

When a single thread needs to change more than one piece of mutable data, it needs to obtain locks for all of them. This is the only way for a lock-based solution to offer coordinated changes to multiple items. The fact that threads need to obtain locks to do their work causes contention for these locks. This contention results in a few issues that are typically categorized as shown in table 6.1.

Table 6.1   Issues that arise from the use of locks

Issue	Description
Deadlock	This is the case where two or more threads wait for the other to release locks that they need. This cyclic dependency results in all concerned threads being unable to proceed.
Starvation	This happens when a thread is not allocated enough resources to do its job, causing it to starve and never complete.
Livelock	This is a special case of starvation, and it happens when two threads continue executing (changing their states) but make no progress toward their final goal. A typical example used to visualize this is of two people meeting in a hallway and each trying to pass the other. If they both wait for the other to move, it results in a deadlock. If they both keep moving for the other, they end up still blocking each other from passing. This situation results in a livelock, because they're both doing work and changing states but are still unable to proceed.
Race condition	This is a general situation where the interleaving of execution of threads causes an undesired computational result. Such bugs are difficult to debug because race conditions happen in relatively rare scenarios.

With all these disadvantages and issues that accompany the use of locks, you must wonder if there isn't a better solution to the problem of concurrency and state. We'll explore this in the next section, beginning with a fresh look at modeling state itself.

6.2   *Identities and values*

Now that we've explored the landscape of some of the common problems of concurrent programs and shared state, including the popular solution to them, we're ready to examine an alternative point of view. Let's begin by reexamining a construct offered by most popular programming languages to deal with state—that of objects. Object-oriented languages like Java, C++, Ruby, and Python offer the notion of *classes* that contain state and related operations. The idea is to provide the means to encapsulate things in order to separate responsibility among various abstractions, allowing for cleaner design. This is a noble goal and is probably even achieved once in a while. But most languages have a flaw in this philosophy that causes problems when these same programs need to run as multithreaded applications. And most programs eventually do need multithreading, either because requirements change or to take advantage of multicore CPUs.

The flaw is that these languages conflate the idea of what Rich Hickey calls identity with that of state. Consider a person's favorite set of movies. As a child, this person's set might contain films made by Disney and Pixar. As a grown-up, the person's set might contain other movies such as ones directed by Tim Burton or Robert Zemeckis. The entity represented by "favorite movies" changes over time. Or does it?

In reality, there are two different sets of movies; at one point (earlier) `favorite-movies` referred to the set containing children's movies. At another point (later), it referred to a different set that contained other movies. What changes over time, therefore, is not the set itself but which set the entity "favorite movies" refers to. Further, at any given point, a set of movies itself doesn't change. The time line demands different sets containing different movies over time, even if some movies appear in more than one set.

To summarize, it's important to realize that we're talking about two distinct concepts. The first is that of an identity—someone's favorite movies. It's the subject of all the action in the associated program. The second is the sequence of values that this identity assumes over the course of the program. These two ideas give us an interesting definition of state—the value of an identity at a particular point time.

This idea of state is different from what traditional implementations of object-oriented languages provide out of the box. For example, in a language like Java or Ruby, the minute a class is defined with stateful fields and destructive methods (those that change a part of the object), concurrency issues begin to creep into the world and can lead to many of the problems discussed earlier. This approach to state might have worked a few years ago when everything was single threaded; it doesn't work anymore.

Now that you understand some of the terms involved, let's further examine the idea of using a series of immutable values to model the state of an identity.

6.2.1   *Immutable values*

An immutable object is one that can't change once it has been created. In order to simulate change, you'd have to create a whole new object and replace the old one. In the light of our discussion so far, this means that when the identity of "favorite movies" is being modeled, it should be defined as a reference to an immutable object (a set, in this case). Over time, the reference would point to different (also immutable) sets. This ought to apply to objects of any kind, not only sets. Several programming languages already offer this mechanism in some of their data types, for instance, numbers and strings. As an example, consider the following assignment:

```
x = 101
```

Most languages treat the number 101 as an immutable value. Languages provide no constructs to do the following, for instance:

```
x.setUnitsDigit(3)
x.setTensDigit(2)
```

No one expects this to work, and no one expects this to be a way to transform 101 into 123. Instead, you might do the following:

```
x = 101 + 22
```

At this point, x points to the value 123, which is a completely new value and is also immutable. Some languages extend this behavior to other data types. For instance, Java strings are also immutable. In programs, the identity represented by x refers to different (immutable) numbers over time. This is similar to the concept of favorite-movies referring to different immutable sets over time.

6.2.2 *Objects and time*

As you've seen, objects (such as x or favorite-movies) don't have to physically change in order for programs to handle the fact that something has happened to them. As discussed previously, they can be modeled as references that point to different objects over time. This is the flaw that most OO languages suffer from: they conflate identities (x or favorite-movies) and their values. Most such languages make no distinction between an identity such as favorite-movies and the memory location where the data relating to that identity is stored. A variable kyle, for example, might directly point to the memory location containing the data for an instance of the Person class.

In typical OO languages, when a destructive method (or procedure) executes, it directly alters the contents of the memory where the instance is stored. Note that this doesn't happen when the same language deals with primitives, such as numbers or strings. The reason no one seems to notice this difference in behavior is that most languages have conditioned programmers to think that composite objects are different from primitives such as strings and numbers. But this is not how things should be, and there's another way.

Instead of letting programs have direct access to memory locations via pointers such as favorite-movies and allowing them to change the content of that memory location, programs should have only a special reference to immutable objects. The only thing they should be allowed to change is this special reference itself, by making it point to a completely different, suitably constructed object that's also immutable. This concept is illustrated in figure 6.1.

This should be the default behavior of all data types, not only select ones like numbers or strings. Custom classes defined by a programmer should also work this way.

Now that we've talked about this new approach to objects and mutation over time, let's see why this might be useful and what might be special about such references to immutable objects.

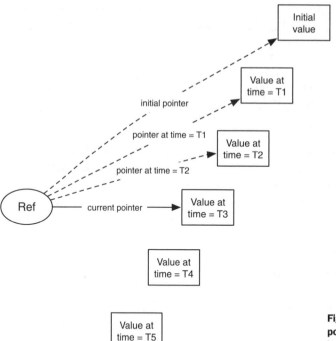

Figure 6.1 **A reference that points to completely different immutable values over time**

6.2.3 *Immutability and concurrency*

It's worth remembering that the troubles with concurrency happen only when multiple threads attempt to update the same shared data. In the first part of this chapter, we reviewed the common problems that arise when shared data is mutated incorrectly in a multithreaded scenario. The problems with mutation can be classified into two general types: losing updates (or updating inconsistent data) and reading inconsistent data.

If all data is immutable, then we eliminate the second issue. If a thread reads something, it's guaranteed to never change while it's being used. The concerned thread can go about its business, doing whatever it needs to with the data—calculating things, displaying information, or using it as input to other things. In the context of our example concerning favorite movies, a thread might read someone's favorite set of movies at a given point and use it in a report about popular movies. Meanwhile, a second thread might update a person's favorites. In this scenario, because the sets are immutable, the second thread would create a new set of movies, leaving the first thread with valid and consistent (and merely stale) data.

We've glossed over some of the technicalities involved in ensuring that this works, and we'll explore Clojure's approach in much greater depth in the following sections. In particular, threads should be able to perform repeated reads correctly, even if another thread updated some or all of the data. Assuming things do work this way, the read problem in a multithreaded situation can be considered solved. It leaves only the issue of when two or more threads try to update the same data at the same time.

Solving this second problem requires some form of supervision by the language runtime and is where the special nature of references comes into play. Because no identity has direct access to the contents of various memory locations (that in turn contain the data objects), the language runtime has a chance of doing something to help supervise writes. Specifically, because identities are modeled using special references, as mentioned previously, the language can provide constructs that allow supervised changes to these indirect references. These constructs can have concurrency semantics, thereby making it possible for multiple threads to update shared data correctly. The semantics can ensure more than safe writes; they can signal errors when writes fail or enforce certain other constraints when a write is to be made.

This isn't possible in most other popular languages today, because they allow direct access to (and mutation of) memory locations. A language that satisfies two requirements can hope to solve the concurrency problem: the first is that identities not point directly to memory locations but do so indirectly via managed references, and the second is that data objects themselves be immutable. This separation of identity and state is the key. You'll see Clojure's flavor of this approach over the next few sections.

6.3 *The Clojure way*

As you saw in the previous section, there's an alternative when it comes to modeling identities and their state. Instead of letting an identity be a simple reference (direct access to a memory location and its contents), it can be a managed reference that points to an immutable value. Over the course of the program, this reference can be made to point to other immutable values as required by the program logic. If state is modeled this way, then the programming language facilities that allow a managed reference to point to different things can support concurrency semantics—it can check for modified data, can enforce validity, can enforce that other programming constructs be used (such as transactions), and so forth. This is exactly the Clojure way.

Clojure provides managed references to state, as described previously. It provides four different kinds of managed references, each suitable in different situations. It also provides language-level constructs that help in changing what these references point to. Further, to coordinate changes to more than one reference, Clojure exposes an interesting take on a software transactional memory (STM) system. We'll examine each of these in detail now.

Before we do so, it's useful to talk about one more thing. In order for any language to work this way (managed references, immutable objects), an important requirement must be met—that of performance. Working with this model of state and mutation needs to be as fast as the old way of in-place mutation. Traditional solutions to this issue have been unsatisfactory, but Clojure solves it in an elegant way.

6.3.1 *Requirements for immutability*

Let's again consider our example concerning movies and multiple threads. Imagine that the first thread is dealing with Rob's set of favorite movies when he was a child. If a second thread were to update his favorites to a new set, the data seen by the first thread should still be valid. One way to achieve this is to make a copy of the object being updated so that readers still have valid (if old) data while the writer updates it to the new object.

The problem with this approach is that naively copying something over in this manner is extremely inefficient. Often, the speed of such a copy operation grows linearly with the size of the objects being copied. If every write involved such an expensive operation, it would be impossible to use in a production environment. Therefore, given that an approach that involves blind copying of data is not viable, the alternative must involve sharing the data structures in question. Specifically, the new and updated objects must in some way point to the old values, while making additional changes required to perform updates.

To make the performance requirements clearer, such an implementation must have approximately the same performance characteristics as the old mutable implementation. For example, a hash table must behave in a constant time (or near enough) manner. This performance guarantee must be satisfied, in addition to satisfying the previous constraint that the older version still be usable. This would allow other threads that had read the data prior to the update to continue with their job. In summary, the requirements are that the immutable structures do the following:

- Leave the old version of itself in a usable state when it mutates
- Satisfy the same performance characteristics as the mutable versions of themselves

You'll now see how Clojure satisfies these requirements.

PERSISTENT DATA STRUCTURES

The common usage of the word *persistence* in computer science refers to persisting data into a nonvolatile storage system, such as a database. But there's another way that term is used, one that's quite common in the functional programming space. A persistent data structure is one that preserves the previous version of itself when it's modified. Older versions of such data structures persist after updates. Such data structures are inherently immutable, because update operations yield new values every time.

All of the core data structures offered by Clojure are persistent. These include maps, vectors, lists, and sets. These persistent data structures also perform extremely well because instead of using copying, they share structure when an update needs to be done. Specifically, they maintain nearly all the performance guarantees that are made by such data structures, and their performance is on par with or extremely close to that of similar data structures that are provided by the Java language.

With this implementation, Clojure has the means to provide the managed reference model for mutating state. We'll examine this in the next section.

6.3.2 Managed references

Given Clojure's efficient implementation of persistent data structures, the approach of modeling state through managed references becomes viable. Clojure has four distinct offerings in this area, each useful in certain scenarios. Table 6.2 gives an overview of the options available.

Table 6.2 Clojure provides four different types of managed references.

Managed reference type	Useful for
ref	Shared changes, synchronous, coordinated changes
agent	Shared changes, asynchronous, independent changes
atom	Shared changes, synchronous, independent changes
var	Isolated changes

Clojure provides a managed reference for the different situations that arise when writing programs that use multiple threads. This ranges from the case that needs to isolate any change to within the thread making it to the case when threads need to coordinate changes that involve multiple shared data structures. In the next few sections, we'll examine each one in turn.

In the first section of this chapter, we examined the problems faced by multithreaded programs when shared data is involved. These problems are typically handled using locks, and we also examined the problems associated with locks.

Managed references and language-level support for concurrency semantics offer an alternative to locks. In the next section, we'll examine the first of Clojure's managed references—the ref—and show how the language provides lock-free concurrency support.

6.4 Refs

Clojure provides a special construct in ref (short for *reference*) to create a managed reference that allows for *synchronous* and *coordinated* changes to mutable data. A ref holds a value that can be changed in a synchronous and coordinated manner. As an example, let's consider our expense-tracking domain. You'll create a ref to hold all the users of our imaginary system. The following is an example of this, and we've initialized the ref with an empty map:

```
(def all-users (ref {}))
```

At this point, all-users is a ref, which points to our initial value of an empty map. You can check this by dereferencing it using the deref function:

```
(deref all-users)
{}
```

Clojure also provides a convenient reader macro to dereference such a managed reference: the @ character. The following works the same way as calling `deref`:

```
@all-users
{}
```

Now that you know how to create and read back a ref, you're ready to see how you can go about changing what it points to.

6.4.1 *Mutating refs*

Now, you'll write a function that adds a new user to our existing set. Clojure's refs can be changed using the `ref-set`, `alter`, or `commute` functions. `ref-set` is the most basic of these; it accepts a ref and a new value and replaces the old value with the new. Try the following to see it in action:

```
(ref-set all-users {})
;; No transaction running
;; [Thrown class java.lang.IllegalStateException]
```

Because refs are meant for situations where multiple threads need to coordinate their changes, the Clojure runtime demands that mutating a ref be done inside an STM transaction. STM stands for software transactional memory, and an STM transaction is analogous to a database transaction but for changes to in-memory objects. You'll learn more about Clojure's STM system in the following section; for now, you'll start an STM transaction using a built-in macro called `dosync`. You can check that this works by trying your previous call to `ref-set` but this time inside the scope of a `dosync`:

```
(dosync
  (ref-set all-users {}))
{}
```

That worked as expected, and you can use `ref-set` like this to reset your list of users. `dosync` is required for any function that mutates a ref, including the other two we mentioned earlier, `alter` and `commute`.

ALTER

Typically, a ref is mutated by using its current value, applying a function to it, and storing the new value back into it. This read-process-write operation is a common scenario, and Clojure provides the `alter` function that can do this as an atomic operation. The general form of this function is

```
(alter ref function & args)
```

The first and second arguments to `alter` are the ref that's to be mutated and the function that will be applied to get the new value of the ref. When the function is called, the first argument will be the current value of the ref, and the remaining arguments will be the ones specified in the call to `alter` (`args`).

Before examining the `commute` function, let's get back to our intention of writing a function to add a new user to our list of existing users. First, here's a function to create a new user:

```
(defn new-user [id login monthly-budget]
  {:id id
   :login login
   :monthly-budget monthly-budget
   :total-expenses 0})
```

This uses a Clojure map to represent a user—a common pattern used where traditional objects are needed. We've deliberately kept the representation simple; in real life your users would probably be a lot more, well, real. Next, here's the add-user function:

```
(defn add-new-user [login budget-amount]
  (dosync
    (let [current-number (count @all-users)
          user (new-user (inc current-number) login budget-amount)]
      (alter all-users assoc login user))))
```

Note the use of dosync. As mentioned previously, it starts an STM transaction, which allows us to use alter. In the previous code snippet, alter is passed the all-users ref, which is the one being mutated. The function you pass it is assoc, which takes a map, a key, and a value as parameters. It returns a new map with that value associated with the supplied key. In our case, our newly created user gets associated with the login name. Note that the first argument to assoc is the current value of the ref all-users (the map that contains the existing set of users).

Further note that we chose to include the entire let form inside the transaction started by dosync. The alternative would have been to call only alter inside the dosync. Clojure wouldn't have complained because dereferencing a ref (@all-users) doesn't need to happen inside a transaction. The reason you do it this way, is to ensure that you see a consistent set of users. You want to avoid the buried update problem where two threads read the count, and one thread commits a new user (increasing the real count), causing the other thread to commit a new user with a duplicate id.

One final note: in the previous example, it doesn't matter in what order you add users. If two threads were both trying to add a user to our system, you wouldn't care in what order they're added. Such an operation is said to be *commutative*, and Clojure has optimized support for commutes.

COMMUTE

When two threads try to mutate a ref using either ref-set or alter, and one of them succeeds (causing the other to fail), the second transaction starts over with the latest value of the ref in question. This ensures that a transaction doesn't commit with inconsistent values. The cost of this mechanism is that a transaction may be tried multiple times.

For those situations where it doesn't matter what the most recent value of a ref is (only that it's consistent and recent), Clojure provides the commute function. The name derives from the commutative property of functions, and you might remember this from math class. A function is commutative if it doesn't matter in which order the arguments are applied. For example, addition is commutative, whereas subtraction is not:

```
a + b = b + a
a - b != b - a
```

The `commute` function is useful where the order of the function application isn't important. For instance, imagine that a number was being incremented inside a transaction. If two threads were to go at it in parallel, at the end of the two transactions, it wouldn't matter which thread had committed first. The result would be that the number was incremented twice.

When the `alter` function is applied, it checks to see if the value of the ref has changed because of another committed transaction. This causes the current transaction to fail and for it to be retried. The `commute` function doesn't behave this way; instead, execution proceeds forward and all calls to `commute` are handled at the end of the transaction. The general form of `commute` is similar to `alter`:

```
(commute ref function & args)
```

As explained earlier, the function passed to `commute` should be commutative. Similar to `alter`, the `commute` function also performs the read-apply-write operation on one atomic swoop.

You've now seen the three ways in which a ref can be mutated. In showing these, we've mentioned STM transactions quite a bit. In the next section, you'll learn a little more about Clojure's implementation of the STM system.

6.4.2 *Software transactional memory*

A common solution to the problems of shared data and multithreading is the (careful) use of locks. But this approach suffers from several problems, and we examined common ones in section 6.1.2. These issues make using locks messy and error prone while also making code based on locks infamously difficult to debug.

Software transactional memory (STM) is a concurrency control mechanism that works in a fashion similar to database transactions. Instead of controlling access to data stored on disks, inside tables and rows, STMs control access to shared memory. Using an STM system offers many advantages to multithreaded programs, the most obvious being that it's a lock-free solution. You can think of it as getting all the benefits of using locks but without any of the problems. You also gain increased concurrency because this is an optimistic approach compared with the inherently pessimistic approach of locking.

In this section, you'll get a high-level overview of what STM is and how it works.

STM TRANSACTIONS

Lock-based solutions prevent more than one thread from executing a protected part of the code. Only the thread that acquired the right set of locks is allowed to execute code that has been demarcated for use with those locks. All other threads that want to execute that same code, block until the first thread completes and relinquishes those locks.

An STM system takes a nearly opposite approach. First, code that needs to mutate data is put inside a transaction. In the case of Clojure, this means using the `dosync` macro. Once this is done, the language runtime takes an optimistic approach in letting threads execute the transaction. Any number of threads are allowed to begin the transaction. Changes made to refs within the transaction are isolated, and only the threads that made the changes can see the changed values.

The first thread that completely executes the block of code that's the transaction is allowed to commit the changed values. Once a thread commits, when any other thread attempts to commit, that transaction is aborted and the changes are rolled back.

The commit performed when a transaction is successful is atomic in nature. This means that even if a transaction makes changes to multiple refs, as far as the outside world is concerned, they all appear to happen at the same instant (when the transaction commits). STM systems can also choose to retry failed transactions, and many do so until the transaction succeeds. Clojure also supports this automatic retrying of failed transactions, up to an internal limit.

Now that you know how transactions work at a high level, let's recap an important set of properties that the STM system exhibits.

ATOMIC, CONSISTENT, ISOLATED

The Clojure STM system has ACI properties (atomicity, consistency, isolation). It doesn't support durability because it isn't a persistent system and is based on volatile, in-memory data. To be specific, if a transaction mutates several refs, the changes become visible to the outside world at one instant. Either all the changes happen, or, if the transaction fails, the changes are rolled back and no change happens. This is how the system supports *atomicity*.

When refs are mutated inside a transaction, the changed data are called *in-transaction values*. This is because they're visible only to the thread that made the changes *inside* the transaction. In this manner, transactions *isolate* the changes within themselves (until they commit).

Clojure's refs (and also agents and atoms) accept validator functions when created. These functions are used to check the consistency of the data when changes are made to them. If the validator function fails, the transaction is rolled back. In this manner, the STM system supports *consistency*.

Before moving onto the other types of managed references in Clojure, we'll make one final point about the STM.

MVCC

Clojure's STM system implements multiversion concurrency control (MVCC). This is the type of concurrency supported by several database systems such as Oracle and PostgreSQL. In an MVCC system, each contender (threads in the case of Clojure) is given a snapshot of the mutable world when it starts its transaction.

Any changes made to the snapshot are invisible to other contenders until the changes are committed at the end of a successful transaction. But thanks to the snapshot model, readers never block writers (or other readers), increasing the inherent concurrency that the system can support. In fact, writers never block readers either, thanks to the same isolation. Contrast this with the old locking model where both readers and writers block while one thread does its job.

Having seen the way the ref managed reference works in Clojure and also how the associated mechanism of the software transactional memory works, you can write multithreaded programs that need to coordinate changes to shared data. In the next section, we'll examine a method to mutate data in an uncoordinated way.

6.5   *Agents*

Clojure provides a special construct called an `agent` that allows for *asynchronous* and *independent* changes to shared mutable data. The `agent` function allows the creation of agents, which hold values that can be changed using special functions. Clojure provides two functions, `send` and `send-off`, that result in mutating the value of an agent. Both accept the agent that needs to be updated, along with a function that will be used to compute the new value. The application of the function happens at a later time, on a separate thread. By corollary, an agent is also useful to run a task (function) on a different thread, with the return value of the function becoming the new value of the agent. The functions sent to agents are called actions.

Creating an agent is similar to creating a ref:

```
(def total-cpu-time (agent 0))
```

Dereferencing an agent to get at its current value is similar to using a ref:

```
(deref total-cpu-time)
0
```

Clojure also supports the `@` reader macro to dereference agents, so the following is equivalent to calling `deref`:

```
@total-cpu-time
0
```

Having created an agent, let's see how you can mutate it.

6.5.1   *Mutating agents*

As described in the preceding paragraphs, agents are useful when changes to them can be made in an asynchronous fashion. The changes are made by sending an action (a regular Clojure function) to the agent, which runs on a separate thread at a later time. There are two flavors of this, and we'll examine them both.

SEND
The general form of the `send` function is as follows:

```
(send the-agent the-function & more-args)
```

As an example, consider adding a few hundred milliseconds to the `total-cpu-time` agent you created earlier:

```
(send total-cpu-time + 700)
```

The addition operator in Clojure is implemented as a function, no different from regular functions. The action function sent to an agent should accept one or more parameters. When it runs, the first parameter it's supplied is the current value of the agent, and the remaining parameters are the ones passed via send.

In this example, the + function is sent to the total-cpu-time agent, and it uses the current value of the agent (which is 0) as the first argument and 700 as the second argument. At some point in the future, although it isn't noticeable in our example because it will happen almost immediately, the addition function will execute and the new value of total-cpu-time will be set as the value of the agent. You can check the current value of the agent by dereferencing it:

```
(deref total-cpu-time)
700
```

If the action took a long time, it might be a while before dereferencing the agent shows the new value. Dereferencing the agent before the agent runs will continue to return the old value. The call to send itself is nonblocking, and it returns immediately.

Actions sent to agents using send are executed on a fixed thread pool maintained by Clojure. If you send lots of actions to agents (more than the number of free threads in this pool), they get queued and will run in the order in which they were sent. Only one action runs on a particular agent at a time. This thread pool doesn't grow in size, no matter how many actions are queued up. This is why you should use send for actions that are CPU intensive and don't block, because blocking actions will use up the thread pool. But for blocking actions, Clojure does provide another function, and we'll look at that now.

SEND-OFF

The general form of the send-off function is exactly the same as for send:

```
(send-off the-agent the-function & more-args)
```

The semantics of what happens when send-off is called are the same as that of send, the only difference being that send-off can handle potential blocking actions. This is because it uses a different thread pool from the one used by send, and this thread pool can grow in size to accommodate more actions sent using send-off. Again, only one action runs on a particular agent at a time.

We'll now look at a few convenient constructs provided by Clojure that are useful when programming using agents.

6.5.2 *Working with agents*

This section will examine a few functions that come in rather handy when working with agents. A common scenario when using agents to do work asynchronously is that several actions are sent (using either send or send-off), and then one waits until they all complete. Clojure provides two functions that help in this situation. We'll also look at ways to test agents for errors.

Another common use case is that a notification is desired when an action sent to an agent completes successfully. This is where watchers come in. Finally, you'll see how the value of an agent can be kept consistent by validating it with some business rules each time an attempt is made to change it.

AWAIT AND AWAIT-FOR

await is a function that's useful when execution must stop and wait for actions that were previously dispatched to certain agents to be completed. The general form is

```
(await & the-agents)
```

As an example, let's say you had agents named agent-one, agent-two, and agent-three. Let's also say you sent several actions to these three agents, either from your own thread or from another agent. At some point, you could cause the current thread to block until all actions sent to your three agents completed, by doing the following:

```
(await agent-one agent-two agent-three)
```

await blocks indefinitely, so if any of the actions didn't return successfully, the current thread wouldn't be able to proceed. In order to avoid this, Clojure also provides the await-for function. The general form looks similar to that of await, but it accepts a maximum timeout in milliseconds:

```
(await-for timeout-in-millis & the-agents)
```

Using await-for is safer in the sense that the max wait time can be controlled. If the timeout does occur, await-for returns nil. An example of using it is shown here:

```
(await-for 1000 agent-one agent-two agent-three)
```

This will abort the blocking state of the thread if the timer expires before the actions have completed. It's common to check if the actions succeeded or not by testing the agents for any errors after using await-for.

AGENT ERRORS

When an action doesn't complete successfully (it throws an exception), the agent knows about it. If you try to dereference an agent that's in such an error state, Clojure will throw another exception. Take a look:

```
(def bad-agent (agent 10))
```

This sets up an agent with an initial value of 10. You'll now send it an action that will cause an exception to be thrown, leaving the agent in an error state.

```
(send bad-agent / 0)
```

This is caused by the classic divide-by-zero error. If you now try to dereference bad-agent

```
(deref bad-agent)
Agent has errors
  [Thrown class java.lang.Exception]Agent has errors
```

you can discern the error is by using the `agent-errors` function:

```
(agent-errors bad-agent)
(#<ArithmeticException java.lang.ArithmeticException: Divide by zero>)
```

`agent-errors` returns a list of exceptions thrown during the execution of the actions that were sent to the agent. The objects in this list are instances of the particular exception class corresponding to the error that happened, and they can be queried using Java methods, for example:

```
(use 'clojure.contrib.str-utils)
(let [e (first (agent-errors bad-agent))
      st (.getStackTrace e)]
  (println (.getMessage e))
    (println (str-join "\n" st)))
```

If an agent has errors, you can't send it any more actions. If you do, Clojure throws the same exception, informing you that the agent has errors. In order to make the agent usable again, Clojure provides the `clear-agent-errors` function:

```
(clear-agent-errors bad-agent)
```

The agent is now ready to accept more actions.

VALIDATIONS

The complete general form of the `agent` function that creates new agents is

```
(agent initial-state & options)
```

The options allowed are

```
:meta metadata-map
:validator validator-fn
```

If the `:meta` option is used, then the map supplied with it will become the metadata of the agent. If the `:validator` option is used, it should be accompanied by either `nil` or a function that accepts one argument. The `validator-fn` is passed the intended new state of the agent, and it can apply any business rules in order to allow or disallow the change to occur. If the validator function returns `false` or throws an exception, then the state of the agent is not mutated.

You've now seen how agents can be used in Clojure. Before moving on to the next kind of managed reference, you'll see how agents can also be used to cause side effects from inside STM transactions.

6.5.3 *Side effects in STM transactions*

We said earlier that Clojure's STM system automatically retries failed transactions. After the first transaction commits, all other transactions that had started concurrently will abort when they, in turn, try to commit. Aborted transactions are then started over. This implies that code inside a `dosync` block can potentially execute multiple times before succeeding, and for this reason, such code should be without side effects.

As an example, if there was a call to `println` inside a transaction, and the transaction was tried several times, the `println` will be executed multiple times. This behavior would probably not be desirable.

There are times when a transaction does need to generate a side effect. It could be logging or anything else such as writing to a database or sending a message on a queue. Agents can be used to facilitate such intended side effects. Consider the following pseudo code:

```
(dosync
   (send agent-one log-message args-one)
   (send-off agent-two send-message-on-queue args-two)
   (alter a-ref ref-function)
     (some-pure-function args-three))
```

Clojure's STM transactions hold all actions that need to be sent to agents until they succeed. In the pseudo code shown here, `log-message` and `send-message-on-queue` are actions that will be sent only when the transaction succeeds. This ensures that even if the transaction is tried multiple times, the side effect causing actions gets sent only once. This is the recommended way to produce side effects from within a transaction.

This section walked through the various aspects of using agents. To recap, agents allow asynchronous and independent changes to mutable data. The next kind of managed reference is called an atom, and it's the subject of the next section.

6.6   *Atoms*

Clojure provides a special construct in atom that allows for *synchronous* and *independent* changes to mutable data. The difference between an atom and an agent is that updates to agents happen asynchronously at some point in the future, whereas atoms are updated synchronously (immediately). Atoms differ from refs in that changes to atoms are independent from each other and can't be coordinated so that they either all happen or none do.

Creating an atom looks similar to creating either refs or agents:

```
(def total-rows (atom 0))
```

`total-rows` is an atom that starts out being initialized to zero. You could use it to hold the number of database rows inserted by a Clojure program as it restores data from a backup, for example. Reading the current value of the atom uses the same dereferencing mechanism used by refs and agents

```
(deref total-rows)
0
```

or by using the @ reader macro:

```
@total-rows
0
```

Now that you've seen how to create atoms and read their values, let's address mutating them.

6.6.1 *Mutating atoms*

Clojure provides several ways to update the value of an atom. There's an important difference between atoms and refs, in that changes to one atom are independent of changes to other atoms. Therefore, there's no need to use transactions when attempting to update atoms.

RESET!

The general form of the reset! function follows:

```
(reset! atom new-value)
```

The reset! function doesn't use the existing value of the atom and sets the provided value as the new value of the atom. This might remind you of the ref-set function, which also does the same job but for refs.

SWAP!

The swap! function has the following general form:

```
(swap! the-atom the-function & more-args)
```

You could pass swap! the addition function whenever you finish inserting a batch of rows:

```
(swap! total-rows + 100)
```

Here, in a synchronous manner, the + function is applied to the current value of total-rows (which is zero) and 100. The new value of total-rows becomes 100. If you were to use a mutation function that didn't complete before another thread changed the value of the atom, swap! would then retry the operation until it did succeed. For this reason, mutation functions should be free of side effects.

Clojure also provides a lower-level function called compare-and-set! that can be used to mutate the value of an atom. swap! internally uses compare-and-set!

COMPARE-AND-SET!

Here's the general form of the compare-and-set! function:

```
(compare-and-set! the-atom old-value new-value)
```

This function atomically sets the value of the atom to the new value, if the current value of the atom is equal to the supplied old value. If the operation succeeds, it returns true; else it returns false. A typical workflow of using this function is to dereference the atom in the beginning, do something with the value of the atom, and then use compare-and-set! to change the value to a new one. If another thread had changed the value in the meantime (after it had been dereferenced), then the mutation would fail.

The swap! function does that internally: it dereferences the value of the atom, applies the provided mutation function, and attempts to update the value of the atom using compare-and-set! by using the value that was previously dereferenced. If compare-and-set! returns false (the mutation failed because the atom was updated elsewhere), the swap! function will reapply the mutation function until it succeeds.

Atoms can be used whenever there's need for some state but not for coordination with any other state. Using refs, agents, and atoms, all situations that demand mutation of shared data can be handled. Our last stop will be to study vars, because they're useful when state needs to be mutated but not shared.

6.7   *Vars*

We looked at vars in chapter 3, specifically in section 3.2.1. In this section, we'll take a quick look at how vars can be used to manage state in an isolated (thread-local) manner.

Vars can be thought of as pointers to mutable storage locations, which can be updated on a per-thread basis. When a var is created, it can be given an initial value, which is referred to its root binding:

```
(def *hbase-master* "localhost")
```

In this example, *hbase-master* is a var that has a root binding of "localhost". The starting and ending asterisks are conventions that denote that this var needs to be rebound before use. This can be enforced by not specifying any root binding, causing the Clojure system to throw an exception when an attempt is made to use the var before binding. Here's an example:

```
(def *hbase-master* "localhost")
(println "Hbase-master is:" *hbase-master*)
```

This prints "Hbase-master is: localhost" to the console. Now let's attempt to use a var without a root binding:

```
(def *rabbitmq-host*)
(println "RabbitMQ host is:" *rabbitmq-host*)
Var user/*rabbitmq-host* is unbound.
  [Thrown class java.lang.IllegalStateException]
```

Whether a var has a root binding or not, when the binding form is used to update the var, that mutation is visible only to that thread. If there was no root binding, other threads would see no root binding; if there was a root binding, other threads would see that value. Let's look at an example. You'll create a function that will fetch the number of rows in a users table from different databases: test, development, and staging. Imagine that you define the database host using a var like so:

```
(def *mysql-host*)
```

This var has no root binding, so it will need to be bound before use. You'll do that in a function that's meant to do a database query, but for the purposes of this example it will return some dummy data such as the length of the hostname. In the real world, you'd run the query against the database using something like a JDBC library:

```
(defn db-query [db]
  (binding [*mysql-host* db]
    (count *mysql-host*)))
```

Next, you'll create a list of the hosts you want to run your fake function against:

```
(def mysql-hosts ["test-mysql" "dev-mysql" "staging-mysql"])
```

Finally, you could run your query function against all the hosts

```
(pmap db-query mysql-hosts)
```

which returns `(10 9 13)`.

pmap works like `map`, but each time the supplied function is called on an element of the list, it's done so on an available thread from an internally maintained thread pool. The call to binding sets up `*mysql-host*` to point to a different host, and the query function proceeds appropriately. Each execution of the `db-query` function sees a different value of `*myql-host*`, as expected.

Now you've seen how vars work, and we've covered the four different options that Clojure offers when it comes to concurrency, state, and performing updates. The various options, namely, refs, agents, atoms, and vars, are each useful in different scenarios. You'll eventually run into a situation where one of these will be a good fit, and you'll be grateful for Clojure's language-level support for lock-free concurrency.

6.8   *State and its unified access model*

This section is a quick recap of the constructs Clojure offers for managing state. We covered each of them over the past few sections, and it's now possible to make an observation. All of the constructs for managing state enjoy a unified access model that allows the used functions to manage them similarly. This is true whether the managed reference is a ref, an agent, or an atom. Let's take another quick look at these functions.

CREATING
Here are the functions that can create each type of managed reference:

```
(def a-ref (ref 0))
(def an-agent (agent 0))
(def an-atom (atom 0))
```

Notice how each accepts an initial value during creation.

READING
All three kinds of references can be dereferenced the same way:

```
(deref a-ref) or @a-ref
(deref an-agent) or @an-agent
(deref an-atom) or @an-atom
```

This uniformity makes Clojure's references easier to use, because they work in such a similar manner. Let's also recap how their values can be changed.

MUTATION
Changing a managed reference in Clojure always follows the same model: a function is applied to the current value, and the return value is set as the new value of the reference. Table 6.3 shows the functions that allow such mutation.

TRANSACTIONS
Finally, there's the question of which references need transactions and which don't. Because refs support coordinated changes, mutating them needs the protection of

Table 6.3 Ways to mutate refs, agents, and atoms

Refs	Agents	Atoms

`(ref-set ref new-value)`
 	
`(alter ref function & args)`
 	
`(commute ref function & args)`
	`(send agent function & args)`
	
	`(send-off agent function & args)`
		`(reset! atom new-value)`
		
		`(swap! atom function & args)`
		
		`(compare-and-set! atom old-value new-value)`

STM transactions: all such code needs to be inside the dosync macro. Agents and atoms don't need STM transactions. Functions used to calculate new values of refs or atoms must be free of side effects, because they could be retried several times.

While we're on the topic of mutation, it's worthwhile to note that Clojure provides a hook, which can be used to run arbitrary code when a reference changes state. This mechanism works for refs, agents, atoms, and vars.

6.9   *Watching for mutation*

Sometimes it's useful to add an event listener that gets notified when the value of a stateful construct changes. Clojure provides the add-watch function for this purpose. It allows you to register a regular Clojure function as a "watcher" against any kind of reference. When the value of the reference changes, the watcher function is run.

The watcher must be a function of four arguments: a key to identify the watcher, the reference it's being registered against, the old value of the reference, and finally, the new value of the reference. Here it is in action:

```
(def adi (atom 0))

(defn on-change [the-key the-ref old-value new-value]
  (println "Hey, seeing change from" old-value "to" new-value))

(add-watch adi :adi-watcher on-change)
```

Now that it's all set up, you can test it. Let's check the current value of adi and then update it:

```
user> @adi
0

user> (swap! adi inc)
Hey, seeing change from 0 to 1
1
```

As mentioned before, this can be used for all of Clojure's special managed references. It's also possible to remove a watch if it's no longer required. Clojure provides the remove-watch function to do this. Using it is simple:

```
(remove-watch adi :adi-watcher)
```

So far, we've covered several options provided by Clojure to manage the mutation of state. In the next section, we'll examine another couple of constructs that aid the development of concurrent programs.

6.10 Futures and promises

A *future* is an object that represents code that will eventually execute on a different thread. A *promise* is an object that represents a value that will become available at some point in the future. We'll explore the usage of futures first.

6.10.1 Futures

A future is a simple way to run code on a different thread, and it's useful for long-running computations or blocking calls that can benefit from multithreading. To understand how to use it, let's examine this contrived function that takes over five seconds to run:

```
(defn long-calculation [num1 num2]
  (Thread/sleep 5000)
  (* num1 num2))
```

Now that we have this slow-running function, let's imagine you needed to run multiple such computations. The code might look like the following:

```
(defn long-run []
  (let [x (long-calculation 11 13)
        y (long-calculation 13 17)
        z (long-calculation 17 19)]
    (* x y z)))
```

If you run this in the REPL and use `time` to see how long this takes, you might see something like this:

```
user=> (time (long-run))
"Elapsed time: 14998.165 msecs"
10207769
```

Now, you can see the `long-run` will benefit from being multithreaded. That's where futures come in. The general form of a future is

```
(future & body)
```

It returns an object that will invoke `body` on a separate thread. The returned object can be queried for the return value of the body. In case the computation hasn't completed yet, the threading asking for the value will block. The result of the computation is cached, so subsequent queries for the value are immediate. Let's write a faster version of the `long-run` function:

```
(defn fast-run []
  (let [x (future (long-calculation 11 13))
        y (future (long-calculation 13 17))
        z (future (long-calculation 17 19))]
    (* @x @y @z)))
```

Let's test this using the `time` function as well:

```
user> (time (fast-run))
"Elapsed time: 5000.078 msecs"
10207769
```

As you can see, futures are a painless way to get things to run on a different thread. Here are a few future-related functions Clojure provides:

- `future?`—Checks to see if the object is a future, returns `true` if it is.
- `future-done?`—Returns `true` if the computation represented by this future object is completed.
- `future-cancel`—Attempts to cancel this future. If it has already started executing, it doesn't do anything.
- `future-cancelled?`—Returns `true` if the future has been canceled.

You've seen the basics of using futures in this section. The next section will talk about promises.

6.10.2 Promises

A promise is an object that represents a commitment that a value will be delivered to it. You create one using the no-argument `promise` function:

```
(def p (promise))
```

In order to ask for the promised value, you can dereference it:

```
(def value (deref p))
```

Or, as usual, you can use the reader macro version of dereferencing:

```
@p
```

The way the value delivery system works is via the use of the `deliver` function. The general form of this function is

```
(deliver promise value)
```

Typically, this function is called from a different thread, so it's a great way to communicate between threads. The `deref` function (or the reader macro version of it) will block the calling thread if no value has been delivered to it yet. The thread automatically unblocks when the value becomes available. The concept of promises finds a lot of use in things such as data-flow programming.

Together, futures and promises are ways to write concurrent programs that need to pass data between threads in a simple way. They are a nice, complementary addition to all the other concurrency options you saw earlier in this chapter.

6.11 Summary

We've covered some heavy material in this chapter! We began with a look at the new reality of an increasing number of cores inside CPUs and the need for increasingly multithreaded software. We then looked at the problems that are encountered when programs have more than one thread of execution, specifically when these threads need to make changes to shared data. We looked at the traditional way of solving these problems—using locks—and then briefly looked at the new problems that they introduce.

Finally, we looked at Clojure's approach to these issues. It has a different approach to state, one that involves immutability. Changes to state are modeled by carefully changing managed references so that they point to different immutable values over time. And because the Clojure runtime itself manages these references, it's able to offer the programmer a great deal of automated support in their use.

First, data that needs to change must use one of the four options that Clojure offers. This makes it explicit to anyone reading the code in the future. Next, it offers a software transactional memory (STM) system that helps in making coordinated changes to more than one piece of data. This is a huge win, because it's a lock-free solution to a hairy problem!

Clojure also offers agents and atoms, which allow independent changes to mutable data. These are different in that they're asynchronous and synchronous, respectively, and each is useful in different situations. Finally, Clojure offers vars that can be used where changes to data need to be isolated within threads. The great thing is that despite offering options that are quite different from each other, they have a uniform way of creating and accessing the data inside them.

Clojure's approach to state and mutation is an important step forward in terms of the current status quo of dealing with state and multithreaded programming. As we discussed in section 6.2, most popular object-oriented languages confuse identities and state, whereas Clojure keeps them distinct. This allows Clojure to provide language-level semantics that make concurrent software easier to write (and read and maintain!) and more resilient to bugs that afflict lock-based solutions.

7

Evolving Clojure through macros

This chapter covers

- Introduction to macros
- Macro examples from within Clojure
- Writing your own macros

Macros are the most distinguishing feature of Clojure when compared to languages such as Java and Ruby. Macros make possible things that can only be dreamed of in other languages. The macro system is why Lisp is known as the programmable programming language, and you'll see how you can grow your own language on top of Clojure. Macros are a useful ingredient in bottom-up programming, the approach where an application is written by first modeling low-level entities in a domain and then combining them to create complex ones. Understanding and using macros well is the key to becoming a master Clojure programmer.

If you talk to seasoned Lisp or Clojure programmers, you'll find that opinion about the use of macros varies a great deal. Some say that macros are too powerful and that they should be used with great caution. I've always thought that any feature of a programming language can be misused when it isn't fully understood. Further, the advantages of using macros far outweigh the perceived disadvantages. After all, the whole point of Clojure being homoiconic is to make the macro system possible.

This chapter discusses macros are and how to use them. We'll begin by writing an example macro, which will help you explore Clojure's macro-writing facilities. Then, we'll dig into the Clojure source code to examine a few well-written macros. It's inspiring to learn that parts of Clojure itself are written as macros and that you can use this facility in your own programs. Finally, you'll write a few macros of your own. We'll begin with explaining what a macro is and why a language might need a macro system.

7.1 Macro basics

In order to explain what a macro is, we'll take a step back and examine language runtimes again. Recall from chapter 1 that the Clojure runtime processes source code differently when compared to most other languages. Specifically, there's a read phase followed by an evaluation phase. In the first phase, the Clojure reader converts a stream of characters (the source code) into Clojure data structures. These data structures are then evaluated to execute the program. The trick that makes macros possible is that Clojure offers a hook between the two phases, allowing the programmer to process the data structures representing the code before they're evaluated. Figure 7.1, which you also saw in chapter 1, illustrates these phases.

Code is converted into data structures and these data structures are then evaluated. Macros are functions that the programmer can write that act upon these data structures before they're evaluated. Macros allow code to be modified programmatically before evaluation, making it possible to create whole new kinds of abstractions. Macros operate at the syntactic level by operating on the code itself. Consequently, you can use them to add features to the Clojure language itself. You'll see examples of this in this chapter.

7.1.1 Textual substitution

As an example, imagine that you had a `ref` called `a-ref`:

```
(def a-ref (ref 0))
```

Now, imagine that you wanted to change the value of `a-ref` to 1. You might do something like this:

```
(dosync
  (ref-set a-ref 1))
```

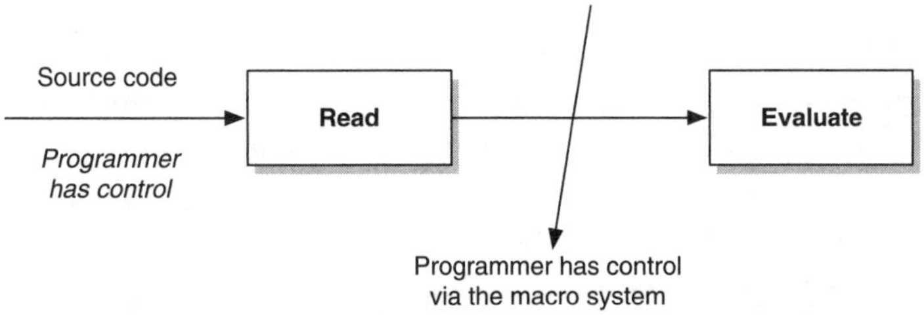

Figure 7.1 Phases of the Clojure runtime. This separation is what makes the macro system possible.

Remember that code is data, which means that this code snippet is just a list containing symbols and other lists—the first one being dosync, followed by a nested list where the symbols are ref-set, a-ref, and 1.

Even if your program used only the single ref shown here, the need to wrap every call to ref-set in a dosync would quickly become tedious. In the real world, you could use an atom, but using a ref is acceptable for the purposes of this example. You could write something called sync-set that wouldn't need a dosync when called and then would do what ref-set does.

You could implement this using a macro called sync-set that manipulates the code as data to insert the required dosync in the appropriate place. The following call would be transformed into the previous one:

```
(sync-set a-ref 1)
```

Let's write the macro. Recall that new lists can be created using the list function and that things can be quoted using the ' macro character.

```
(defmacro sync-set [r v]
  (list 'dosync
    (list 'ref-set r v)))
```

A macro definition looks like a function definition. Internally, macros are functions, tagged as macros via metadata. The difference between functions and macros is that functions execute to return a value, whereas macros execute to return s-expressions that in turn are evaluated to return a value.

An important point to note is that macros operate well before evaluation time and have no notion of what values might be passed in as arguments later on. For instance, you couldn't dereference a-ref and output different kinds of s-expressions depending on the value, because during macro expansion time there's no ref, just the symbols r and v. Macros operate on symbols directly, and this is why they're useful for symbolic manipulation of code.

All this might seem a bit much to achieve the functionality provided by sync-set, because it would be trivial to write it as a function instead. In fact, in the real world, you would indeed write it as a function. Now you know what macros do: they transform or generate arbitrary s-expressions. We'll now look at something macros can do that functions can't.

7.1.2 *The unless example*

Since the book *The C Programming Language* came out, almost all programming language books have used the "Hello, world!" program as an introductory example. There's a similar tradition when it comes to explaining macros, and it involves adding the unless control structure to the language. unless is kind of the opposite of the if form. Here's the general if form, as a reminder:

```
(if test then else)
```

If the test expression returns true, the then expression is evaluated. The optional else expression will be evaluated if the test returns false. Here's an example:

```
(defn exhibits-oddity? [x]
  (if (odd? x)
    (println "Very odd!")))
```

The Ruby programming language provides an unless form, which is also a conditional that can be used in similar functions. Clojure doesn't provide unless, but if it were there, it might work as follows:

```
(defn exhibits-oddity? [x]
  (unless (even? x)
    (println "Very odd, indeed!")))
```

Obviously, trying this won't work in Clojure because it will complain that it's unable to resolve the symbol unless. Our first attempt at fixing this error will involve writing a function.

THE UNLESS FUNCTION

Let's define a function that implements unless:

```
(defn unless [test then]
  (if (not test)
    then))
```

After defining unless as shown here, the definition of exhibits-oddity? will work without a problem. It will even work correctly, as is evident if you test it at the REPL by calling it with an odd number like 11:

```
user=> (exhibits-oddity? 11)
Very odd, indeed!
nil
```

Trouble arises when it's tested with an even number, such as 10:

```
user=> (exhibits-oddity? 10)
Very odd, indeed!
nil
```

It appears that exhibits-oddity? declares all numbers as odd. The reason for this is that unless is a function, and all functions execute according to the following rules:

1 Evaluate all arguments passed to the function call form.
2 Evaluate the function using the values of the arguments.

Step 1 causes the arguments to be evaluated. In the case of our unless function, that's the test and then expressions. This happens *before* execution of the if form even begins. Because all functions follow these rules, there's no way that you can use a function to implement your desired functionality for unless. No matter what you try, the arguments would be evaluated first.

You could cheat a little by insisting that your callers not pass in raw expressions such as (println "Odd! ") but instead pass them in wrapped in functions. Consider the following new definition of our unless function:

```
(defn unless [test then-thunk]
  (if (not test)
    (then-thunk)))
```

Here, then-thunk is a function that is evaluated only if the test condition isn't true. You can rewrite exhibits-oddity? as follows:

```
(defn exhibits-oddity? [x]
  (unless (even? x)
    #(println "Rather odd!")))
```

Recall that the #() reader macro characters create an anonymous function. This function now works as expected:

```
user=> (exhibits-oddity? 11)
Rather odd!
nil
user=> (exhibits-oddity? 10)
nil
```

This solution still isn't quite satisfactory. It forces callers to wrap the then expression inside a function. Using the #() reader macro involves just one extra character, but the language gives no warning if the caller forgets to use it. What you want is something that works similar to if, which is a special form built into Clojure. Now, let's write a macro to solve this problem.

THE UNLESS MACRO

You know that the if form can be used to write the unless form, as long as you can avoid the evaluation of the then argument, unless it's needed. You tried the approach of delaying evaluation using the function wrapper in the previous section, but you can do a lot better with a macro. Consider the following definition:

```
(defmacro unless [test then]
  (list 'if (list 'not test)
    then))
```

This generates an s-expression of the form (if (not test) then) when the macro is expanded. Let's rewrite exhibits-oddity? using this macro:

```
(defn exhibits-oddity? [x]
  (unless (even? x)
    (println "Very odd, indeed!")))
```

This works as expected. The unless form is replaced by the new expression generated by the macro expansion. You can check this at the REPL using the macroexpand function:

```
user=>(macroexpand
        '(unless (even? x) (println "Very odd, indeed!")))
(if (not (even? x)) (println "Very odd, indeed!"))
```

Once this expanded form of unless replaces the unless form itself, it's in turn evaluated to produce the right result. This final definition of unless works as expected, and the callers don't need to know that there's anything special about it. In fact, as far as callers are concerned, unless could have been supplied by the Clojure language itself.

---

macroexpand and macroexpand-1

macroexpand-1 is a useful function when writing macros, because it can be used to check if the transformation of s-expressions is working correctly. macroexpand-1 expands an s-expression by evaluating the macro named by the first symbol in the form. If the first symbol doesn't name a macro, the form is returned as is.

macroexpand is a function that repeatedly calls macroexpand-1 until the first symbol of the expanded form is no longer a macro. It can be used to test cases where macros expand to forms that in turn call macros.

If it isn't obvious already, you just added a feature to the Clojure language. That's neat! What's more, such macros are quite common. For instance, Clojure provides when, when-not, cond, if-not, and so on that are all constructs that allow conditional execution of code and are all implemented as macros. This is cool; after all, if macros are good enough to create parts of Clojure itself, then they're good enough for your programs.

The example in this section showed you the basics of creating a control-flow macro. But the way you generated s-expressions in the previous unless macro can become unwieldy quickly. Clojure provides a more convenient way to write macros that doesn't involve constructing lists using the list function. This approach involves generating code via templates.

7.1.3 Macro templates

Let's consider our unless macro again. Here it is, for convenience:

```
(defmacro unless [test then]
  (list 'if (list 'not test)
    then))
```

This is a tiny macro, and the s-expression it generates is quite simple. If you wanted to generate or transform a large, nested s-expression, the repeated calls to list would become quite tedious. It would also be hard to see the structure of the s-expression being generated because the repeated occurrence of the symbol list would be in the way of reading the structure easily. Clojure provides a way out through its back-quote reader macro, which we'll explore now.

TEMPLATING

Anyone who has programmed a web application in the last few years knows what a templating system is. It allows HTML generation from a sort of blueprint. Some parts are fixed and some are to be filled in when the template is expanded. Examples are JSP (Java Server Pages) and RHTML (Rails HTML) pages.

If generating HTML code can be made easier using templates, you can imagine the same thing would be true for generating Clojure code. This is why the macro system supports templates through the backquote (`) reader macro. Let's see it in action by rewriting the unless macro from before:

```
(defmacro unless [test then]
  `(if (not ~test)
     ~then))
```

> ### Redefining macros
> By the way, when you redefine a macro, you have to reevaluate any functions that use it. If you don't, such functions will appear to use the old definition of the macro. This happens because macro expansion happens only once, and in the case of such function definitions, the expansions were from the older definition. Remember to reevaluate your functions when you change a macro used by any of them.

Our new macro definition certainly looks much clearer! The exact form is immediately obvious, minus a few characters: the backquote and the unquote (~). The backquote starts the template. The template will be expanded into an s-expression and will be returned as the return value of the macro. Clojure calls the backquote the *syntax quote character.*

Symbols that appear inside the template are used as is when the template is expanded. In the JSP analogy, these might be fixed text that doesn't change each time the page is rendered. Things that do need to change, say, parameters passed to the macro, are unquoted using the ~ character. Unquoting is the opposite of quoting. Because the whole template is inside a backquote (a quote), the ~ is used to undo that quotation so that values can be passed through.

Imagine if we hadn't unquoted the then parameter in our macro definition:

```
(defmacro unless [test then]
  `(if (not ~test)
     then))
```

This would cause the symbol then to appear in the s-expression returned by this macro. That could cause Clojure to throw an error when the macro is used in a definition, complaining that it was unable to resolve the then symbol. You can see why this would happen by examining the output of the macro:

```
user=>(macroexpand
        '(unless (even? x) (println "Very odd, indeed!")))
(if (clojure.core/not (even? x)) user/then)
```

Based on this expansion, you can infer that if this macro were used, Clojure would complain that user/then is an unknown var. This is why you need to unquote anything that must be replaced with its value in the template. Next, we'll look at another form of unquoting.

SPLICING

You'll now try to use our `unless` macro to do more than one thing if the `test` condition is satisfied. Consider the following new definition of `exhibits-oddity?`:

```
(defn exhibits-oddity? [x]
  (unless (even? x)
    (println "Odd!")
    (println "Very odd!")))
```

This won't work, because `unless` accepts only two parameters, and you're attempting to pass it more arguments. You can overcome this using the `do` form that you learned about in chapter 2:

```
(defn exhibits-oddity? [x]
  (unless (even? x)
    (do
      (println "Odd!")
      (println "Very odd!"))))
```

This works but is a bother; you have to use the `do` form everywhere you want more than one thing in the `then` part of your `unless` form. To make things more convenient for the callers of your macro, you can include the `do` form in the expansion:

```
(defmacro unless [test & exprs]
  `(if (not ~test)
     (do ~exprs)))
```

Now the `unless` macro accepts multiple expressions that will be executed if the test condition fails, and they'll be enclosed inside a `do` form. Let's try it with our latest `exhibits-oddity?` function:

```
user=> (exhibits-oddity? 11)
Odd!
Very odd!
; Evaluation aborted.
No message.
   [Thrown class java.lang.NullPointerException]
```

Hmm, that's strange. It does print text from both calls but then aborts with an exception. The previously seen function `macroexpand-1` can help you debug this situation:

```
user=>(macroexpand-1 '(unless (even? x)
                        (println "Odd!")
                        (println "Very odd!")))

(if (clojure.core/not (even? x))
  (do ((println "Odd!") (println "Very odd!"))))
```

There's an extra pair of parentheses around the expressions you passed into the `unless` macro as `then`. The return value of `println` is `nil`, which causes the `then` clause to reduce to `(nil nil)`. The extra parentheses cause this expression to be interpreted as a function call, throwing the `NullPointerException` that you saw earlier.

The solution is to eliminate the extra pair of parentheses. But because then is passed in as the remaining arguments to unless, it's a list. This is where the unquote splice reader macro (~@) comes in. Instead of taking a list and unquoting it as is using the unquote (~), the unquote splicing macro splices the contents of the list into the container list. Let's rewrite the unless macro using it:

```
(defmacro unless [test & exprs]
  `(if (not ~test)
     (do ~@exprs)))
```

With this definition of unless, our exhibits-oddity? function works just fine. This use of do that wraps the returned expressions from a macro is quite common, and it's a convenience all the callers of your macros will appreciate.

One final aspect of writing macros that we'll consider before moving on is that of variable capture.

GENERATING NAMES

In most Lisps, writing macros can get tricky. Well, they can get tricky in Clojure too, but the language makes things easier than other Lisps. Consider the following (incorrect) example:

```
(defmacro def-logged-fn [fn-name args & body]
  `(defn ~fn-name ~args
     (let [now (System/currentTimeMillis)]
       (println "[" now "] Call to" (str (var ~fn-name)))
       ~@body)))
```

The idea behind this macro is to create a function that logs the fact that it was called. Although Clojure allows the macro to be defined, using it throws an exception:

```
user=> (def-logged-fn printname [name]
         (println "hi" name))
; Evaluation aborted.
Can't let qualified name: user/now
  [Thrown class java.lang.Exception]
```

The problem is that the macro attempts to use a namespace-qualified name in the let binding, which is illegal. You can confirm this using macroexpand-1:

```
user> (macroexpand-1 '(def-logged-fn printname [name]
         (println "hi" name)))
(clojure.core/defn printname [name]
  (clojure.core/let [user/now (java.lang.System/currentTimeMillis)]
    (clojure.core/println "[" user/now ":] Call to"
      (clojure.core/str (var printname)))
    (println "hi" name)))
```

The let form can't use qualified names like user/now, and that's what Clojure is complaining about. If Clojure didn't expand now into a namespace qualified user/now (where user is the current namespace), then now might shadow another value with the same name. This situation is illustrated here, where daily-report is a function that might run a report for a given day:

```
(def-logged-fn daily-report [the-day]
 ;; code to generate a report here
)
```

Now, let's see what happens if we use the function in the following way:

```
(let [now "2009-10-22"]
  (daily-report now))
```

This doesn't work as expected, because the value of now that the `daily-report` function sees isn't `"2009-10-22"` but a number like `1259828075387`. This is because the value set up in the previous `let` form is captured by the one in the `let` form generated by the macro. This behavior is known as *variable capture*, and it can happen in most Lisps.

To avoid this, Clojure expands the names into their fully qualified names, causing the exception you saw earlier. So how do you use the `let` form to introduce new names? This is where the reader macro # comes in. It generates unique names that won't conflict with others that might be used in the code that's passed into the macro. This facility is called `auto-gensym`, because it automatically generates a symbol that's unique enough to be used as a name for things. Here's our `def-logged-fn` that uses this facility:

```
(defmacro def-logged-fn [fn-name args & body]
  `(defn ~fn-name ~args
     (let [now# (System/currentTimeMillis)]
       (println "[" now# "] Call to" (str (var ~fn-name)))
       ~@body)))
```

It's that simple. The `auto-gensym` uses the specified prefix when generating a name. For example, now# might expand to now__14187__auto__. Clojure will replace all occurrences of each use of `auto-gensym` with the same generated symbol.

This new definition of `def-logged-fn` will create a function that logs calls to it correctly. Redefine the previously defined `printname` function, and try calling it now:

```
user=> (printname "celeste")
[ 1259955655338 ] Call to #'user/printname
hi celeste
nil
```

Variable capture is a fact of life in all Lisps, and you need to avoid it when it's undesired. Clojure makes this easier than most Lisps through this `auto-gensym` facility. In chapter 15, you'll see why you might want the effect of variable capture when we explore anaphoric macros.

We've covered a lot of macro basics so far. Before moving on, let's take a moment to summarize the reasons to use macros.

7.1.4 Recap—why macros?

As you saw in the previous section, macros can be more powerful than functions because they can do things functions can't: delay (or even choose not to do) the execution of code, change the normal flow of execution, add syntactic forms, add brand-new abstractions to the language, or just make things convenient for callers. This chapter has examples of some of these uses. Macros can also move parts of computation from runtime to compile time, and you'll see examples of this in chapter 15.

In this section, we'll discuss the possibilities offered by a programming language that features a macro system.

CODE GENERATION

Generating or transforming code is a rather common way of dealing with certain aspects of writing programs. Most programmers use code generation, even if they aren't always cognizant of doing so. The most obvious example is the use of a compiler: it takes source code and generates some form of executable code, either machine language or byte code for a virtual machine. Parts of compilers are themselves often generated from descriptions of the language grammar. XSLT transforms are often used to convert one kind of structured XML document to other types of documents.

There are many other examples. API documentation is often created via an automated process that extracts annotated comments from the source code. Database access layers often generate all the SQL they need from high-level descriptions of tables or the model classes themselves. User interface toolkits often have associated programs that can generate code to create GUI layouts. Web service frameworks can generate standards-compliant interfaces from descriptions. Web application frameworks usually include template-based systems that generate HTML code.

Sometimes programs are written to explicitly generate source code files in order to handle some kind of pattern in the main application under development. For instance, in a multitier Java system, you might generate code for JavaBean classes from some other set of domain classes. Such programs often manipulate strings of text to do their job.

This kind of metaprogramming is primitive, and languages such as Ruby improve on it by providing language-level facilities to define classes and methods at runtime. Clojure provides almost an ultimate form of metaprogramming by allowing the programmer to generate or manipulate code as data.

SYNTAX AND DSLs

We've already looked at how you can use macros to add syntactic forms to Clojure. When combined with bottom-up design and domain-specific abstractions, macros can transform the solution space into one or more domain-specific languages (DSLs) with which to code the application. We'll examine examples of such a design approach in later chapters of this book.

PLAIN CONVENIENCE

Macros can make life easy for the callers of your functions. Things like the implicit do form that you saw in the previous section are common additions to macros. In the next section, you'll see some examples of macros. This will give you an idea of how people use them and how you might use them in your own programs.

7.2 Macros from within Clojure

In this section, we'll look at some macros. Many come from the source code of the Clojure language itself; some are from elsewhere. These examples should give you a flavor of macro style and ideas about how to use macros in your own code.

Let's begin our journey with examples from the Clojure language itself. As mentioned in the previous section, much of Clojure is implemented in Clojure itself, and a lot of that code is macros. This allows the core language to remain small; Clojure has only about a dozen special forms. This approach allows most other features of the language to be developed in Clojure itself. We'll examine a few macros now.

7.2.1 comment

The comment macro is a great one to start with, because it's so simple. Here's the complete implementation:

```
(defmacro comment [& body])
```

The comment macro does nothing—literally. This is an example of ignoring code altogether, as opposed to changing the flow of execution or delaying it. The comment macro returns nil. The comment macro allows you to comment out parts of your program or to add comments to your code.

7.2.2 declare

Here's a macro that does a little bit more. The declare macro accepts one or more symbols, in order to let Clojure know that there may be references to them in the code that follows. The macro goes through each argument and creates a var with that name. Typically, these vars are redefined at a later point in the program.

```
(defmacro declare [& names]
  `(do
     ~@(map #(list 'def %) names)))
```

Let's see how it works by using the macroexpand function:

```
user=> (macroexpand '(declare add multiply subtract divide))
(do
  (def add)
  (def multiply)
  (def subtract)
  (def divide))
```

The formatting, isn't part of the macro expansion. This is just a simple way to get rid of duplication from having to define multiple vars. You couldn't accomplish this with a function, by the way, because def is a special form that accepts only a symbol. Inside of macros, all special forms become available because we're operating at the s-expression (or symbolic) level. This is an important advantage of macros.

7.2.3   *defonce*

We'll now look at a macro that evaluates conditional expressions. defonce is a macro that accepts the name of a var and an initialization expression. But if the var has already been initialized once (has a root binding), it won't be reinitialized. The implementation of this macro is straightforward, so we don't even need to use macro expansion to see what's going on:

```
(defmacro defonce [name expr]
  `(let [v# (def ~name)]
     (when-not (.hasRoot v#)
       (def ~name ~expr))))
```

7.2.4   *and*

Let's now look at a slightly more complex example. In most languages, and (and other logical operators) are implemented as special forms. In other words, they're built into the core of the language. In Clojure, and is just another macro:

```
(defmacro and
  ([] true)
  ([x] x)
  ([x & next]
   `(let [and# ~x]
      (if and# (and ~@next) and#))))
```

This is an elegant piece of code! When and is called with no arguments, it returns true. When called with a single argument, the return value is the argument itself (remember that anything other than nil or false is treated as true). When there are multiple arguments, the macro evaluates the first argument. It then tests it with the if form. If the value is logically true, the macro calls itself with the remaining arguments. The process then repeats. If the evaluation of any argument returns a logical false, the if form returns that value as is.

Let's use macroexpand to see what happens:

```
user=>(macroexpand '(and (even? x) (> x 50) (< x 500)))
(let* [and__4357__auto__ (even? x)]
  (if and__4357__auto__
    (clojure.core/and (> x 50) (< x 500))
    and__4357__auto__))
```

You may see something slightly different because the auto-gensym will create different names for the local symbols. Also, remember that macroexpand doesn't expand macros contained in subexpressions. In reality, the macro will be completely expanded, and the final expanded s-expression will replace the original call to and.

7.2.5   *time*

This is a rather handy macro, useful for quick checks on how slow or fast your code is running. It accepts an expression, executes it, prints the time it took to execute, and then returns the result of the evaluation. Here's an example:

```
user=> (time (* 1331 13531))
"Elapsed time: 0.04 msecs"
18009761
```

Using the `time` macro isn't as sophisticated as using a profiler, for instance, but can be quite useful for quick benchmarks of your code. Here's how it's implemented:

```
(defmacro time [expr]
  `(let [start# (. System (nanoTime))
         ret# ~expr]
    (prn
      (str "Elapsed time: "
           (/ (double (- (. System (nanoTime)) start#)) 1000000.0)
           " msecs"))
    ret#))
```

As you can see, the macro starts a timer before evaluating the expression passed in. The value of the expression is captured and returned after the timer is stopped and the duration printed to the console.

These are just a few macros that can be found in Clojure's source code. As mentioned earlier, it's advantageous for a language to have a small core and have all other features built on top of it using regular code. Clojure does this in an elegant fashion, and reading through the source code is a great way to learn the tricks of the trade. You'll now write some macros of our own.

7.3   *Writing your own macros*

So far, you've learned the basic theory of Clojure's macro system. You also saw some macros that form part of the Clojure language. You'll now write a few of your own to see how you might use macros in your own programs. The first is a simple macro called `infix`—to help you get started. Then you'll write one called `randomly`, which will appear to add a new control structure to Clojure. The next is `defwebmethod`, which could be the beginning of a DSL for writing web applications. The final is `assert-true`, which could be the beginning of a unit-testing framework for Clojure.

7.3.1   *infix*

In chapter 1, we talked about an `infix` macro, which would allow you to call mathematical operators using infix notation. Here's how you might implement it:

```
(defmacro infix [expr]
  (let [[left op right] expr]
    (list op left right)))
```

It's a trivial implementation: it just rearranges the function symbol and the arguments back into prefix notation. It's also a fairly naïve implementation because it supports only two terms and doesn't do any kind of error checking. Still, it's a fun little macro.

7.3.2   *randomly*

This is an example of a control-flow macro. There are often situations where you want
to randomly pick a path of execution. Such a requirement might arise, for instance, if
you wanted to introduce some randomness into your code.

randomly accepts any number of s-expressions and picks one at random. Here's
the implementation:

```
(defmacro randomly [& exprs]
  (let [len (count exprs)
        index (rand-int len)
        conditions (map #(list '= index %) (range len))]
    `(cond ~@(interleave conditions exprs))))
```

rand-int is a function that returns a random integer between zero and its argument.
Here you pass the length of the incoming exprs to the rand-int function. You then
use nth to pick out an expression to evaluate. Let's test it:

```
user=>(randomly
         (println "amit") (println "deepthi") (println "adi"))
adi
nil
```

Let's try it one more time:

```
user=>(randomly
         (println "amit") (println "deepthi") (println "adi"))
deepthi
nil
```

And once more:

```
user=>(randomly
         (println "amit") (println "deepthi") (println "adi"))
adi
nil
```

The macro works as expected, evaluating only one of the three expressions. Obviously,
given the randomization, your output will look different. Here's what the macro transforms the passed in s-expressions into:

```
user=>(macroexpand-1 '(randomly
                        (println "amit")
                        (println "deepthi")
                        (println "adi")))
(clojure.core/cond
  (= 0 0) (println "amit")
  (= 0 1) (println "deepthi")
  (= 0 2) (println "adi"))
```

Again, given the randomization, your expansion may look different. Indeed, if you
expand it several times, you'll see that the condition clauses in the cond form change.
Incidentally, there's an easier way to achieve the same effect. Consider the following
implementation:

```
(defmacro randomly-2 [& exprs]
  (nth exprs (rand-int (count exprs))))
```

Try it at the REPL to confirm that it works. There's one unintended consequence of this macro, and I'll leave figuring it out as an exercise for the reader. Hint: what happens when it's called from within the body of a function definition?

7.3.3 *defwebmethod*

You'll now write a macro that has nothing to do with changing the flow of execution of your code but is a convenience macro that makes life easier for those who use it. It will also appear to add a feature that's specific to building web applications to Clojure.

In essence, the web is made dynamic through programs that generate different HTML documents based on certain input parameters. You can use Clojure functions for this purpose, where each function might correspond to something the user requests. For instance, you could write a function that accepts a username and a date and returns a report of that day's expenses. The parameters of the request might be bundled in a hash map and given to each function as a request object. Each function could then query the request object for the parameters it needs, process the request as required, and then return appropriate HTML. Here's what such a function might look like:

```
(defn login-user [request]
  (let [username (:username request)
        password (:password request)]
    (if (check-credentials username password)
      (str "Welcome back, " username ", " password " is correct!")
      (str "Login failed!"))))
```

Here, check-credentials might be a function that would look up authentication information from a database. For your purposes, let's define it as follows:

```
(defn check-credentials [username password]
  true)
```

Also, login-user would return real HTML as opposed to the strings you're returning. It should give a general idea about the structure of such functions, though. Let's try it:

```
(def request {:username "amit" :password "123456"})

user=> (login-user request)
"Welcome back, amit, 123456 is correct!"
```

The trouble with this is that every function like login-user must manually query values out of the request map. The example here needs two parameters—username and password—but you can certainly imagine functions that need many more. It would be quite tedious to have to pull them out from the request map each time. Consider the following macro:

```
(defmacro defwebmethod [name args & exprs]
  `(defn ~name [{:keys ~args}]
     ~@exprs))
```

Let's now use this macro to define a new version of `login-user` as follows:

```
(defwebmethod login-user [username password]
  (if (check-credentials username password)
    (str "Welcome, " username ", " password " is still correct!")
    (str "Login failed!")))
```

You can try this version of the function on the REPL:

```
user=> (login-user request)
"Welcome, amit, 123456 is still correct!"
```

For programmers who don't know the internals of `defwebmethod`, it appears that it's literally a new language abstraction, designed specifically for web applications. Any names specified in the parameters list are automatically pulled out of the request map and set up with the right value (the function defined still takes the same argument). You can specify the names of the function parameters in any order, which is a nice convenience.

You can imagine other domain-specific additions to Clojure written this way.

7.3.4   *assert-true*

For our last example, let's write a macro that you can use to assert that an s-expression evaluates to `true`. Let's see how you might use it:

```
user=> (assert-true (= (* 2 4) (/ 16 2)))
true
```

```
user=> (assert-true (< (* 2 4) (/ 18 2)))
true
```

You might use `assert-true` in a set of unit tests. You might be tempted to have multiple such assertions in a single unit test, all verifying related functionality. The trouble with having several assertions in one unit test is that when something fails, it isn't immediately obvious what failed. Line numbers are useful, as are custom error messages that some unit-testing frameworks allow. In our little macro, we'd like to see the code that failed. It might work as follows:

```
user=> (assert-true (>= (* 2 4) (/ 18 2)))
(* 2 4) is not >= 9
  [Thrown class java.lang.RuntimeException]
```

Using literal code like this is a natural fit for macros. Here's the macro:

```
(defmacro assert-true [test-expr]
  (let [[operator lhs rhs] test-expr]
    `(let [lhsv# ~lhs rhsv# ~rhs ret# ~test-expr]
       (if-not ret#
         (throw (RuntimeException.
                  (str '~lhs " is not " '~operator " " rhsv#)))
         true))))
```

It's quite a straightforward implementation. A binding form is used to tease apart `test-expr` into its constituent `operator`, `lhs`, and `rhs` parts. The generated code then uses these to do their thing, best understood by looking at a sample macro expansion:

```
user=> (macroexpand-1 '(assert-true (>= (* 2 4) (/ 18 2))))
(clojure.core/let [lhsv__11965__auto__ (* 2 4)
                   rhsv__11966__auto__ (/ 18 2)
                   ret__11967__auto__ (>= (* 2 4) (/ 18 2))]
    (clojure.core/if-not ret__11967__auto__
      (throw (java.lang.RuntimeException.
        (clojure.core/str (quote (* 2 4))
            " is not " (quote >=) " " rhsv__11966__auto__)))
    true))
```

As mentioned earlier, this macro is extremely straightforward. You can improve it by adding some semantic error checking to handle some situations where invalid expressions are passed. Consider the following definition:

```
(defmacro assert-true [test-expr]
  (if-not (= 3 (count test-expr))
    (throw (RuntimeException.
        "Argument must be of the form
            (operator test-expr expected-expr)")))
  (if-not (some #{(first test-expr)} '(< > <= >= = not=))
    (throw (RuntimeException.
      "operator must be one of < > <= >= = not=")))
  (let [[operator lhs rhs] test-expr]
    `(let [lhsv# ~lhs rhsv# ~rhs ret# ~test-expr]
      (if-not ret#
        (throw (RuntimeException.
          (str '~lhs " is not " '~operator " " rhsv#)))
        true)))))
```

This works for the two situations where someone passes a malformed expression into the macro:

```
user=> (assert-true (>= (* 2 4) (/ 18 2) (+ 2 5)))
; Evaluation aborted.
Argument must be of the form (operator test-expr expected-expr)
  [Thrown class java.lang.RuntimeException]
```

It also checks for the case where someone tries to use an operator that isn't supported:

```
user=> (assert-true (<> (* 2 4) (/ 16 2)))
; Evaluation aborted.
operator must be one of < > <= >= = not=
  [Thrown class java.lang.RuntimeException]
```

This example shows how macros can make it easy to perform domain-specific semantic checking of not just values but of the code itself. In other languages, this might have required some serious parsing. Clojure's code-as-data approach pays off in this scenario.

7.4 Summary

We said in the beginning of this chapter that macros distinguish Clojure (and other Lisps) from most other programming languages. Macros allow the programmer to add new language features to Clojure. Indeed, you can build whole new layers of functionality on top of Clojure, which makes it appear that an entire new language has been created. An example of this is Clojure's concurrency system: it isn't part of the language per se; it's implemented as a set of Java classes and associated Clojure functions and macros.

Macros truly blur the distinction between the language designer and the application programmer, allowing you to add to the language as you see fit. For instance, should you feel that Clojure lacks a construct that would allow you to express something, you don't have to wait for the next version of the language or wish you were using a different language. You can add that feature yourself.

We've covered most of the basics of Clojure the language, and we're ready to start exploring some real-world applications.

Part 2

Getting real

The first part of this book focuses on basics. You're now ready to use your new knowledge to build things. In this part of the book, we'll focus on a number of things that you'll likely encounter as you work on your real-world projects. Specifically, we'll focus on unit testing, database access, creating web services, working with messaging systems, and more.

After this, we'll concentrate on data-processing applications of Clojure by exploring the Map/Reduce paradigm. This will help strengthen your grasp of functional programming. We'll even build our own little parallel, distributed programming framework to process streams of data. We'll also address the notion of object-oriented programming in order to really understand what it means. In order to prove that Clojure transcends traditional OO, we'll build our own OO framework. Finally, we'll look at advanced uses for macros and domain-specific languages (DSLs).

At the end of these chapters, you'll be ready to build large-scale systems using Clojure. Perhaps more important, you'll be proficient enough in Clojure to use it in all your work. Indeed, you may be spoiled for any other programming language.

Test-driven
development and more

This chapter covers
- Introduction to unit-testing Clojure
- Writing test-driven Clojure code
- Mocking and stubbing code in Clojure
- Improving test organization

Test-driven development (TDD) has become something of the norm on most software development projects. It's easy to understand why, because TDD has several advantages. It allows the programmer to look at code being developed from the point of view of a consumer, which results in a more useful design when compared with a library that might be designed in relative isolation. Further, because code developed using TDD must be testable (by definition), the resulting design is often better in terms of low coupling as well. Finally, the suite of tests that results from the process is a good way to ensure that functionality doesn't regress in the face of enhancements and bug fixes.

Clojure has excellent support for unit testing. Further, because Clojure is a Lisp, it's also extremely well suited for rapid application development. The REPL supports this by offering a means to develop code in an incremental manner. In this chapter, as you learn about TDD, you'll use the REPL for quick experiments and

169

such (you visited the REPL in chapter 2, and in this chapter, you'll see a lot more of it). As you'll discover, this combination of TDD and the REPL makes for a productive development environment. The specific unit-testing framework you'll explore is called test-is, and it comes as a standard part of the Clojure distribution. Finally, you'll look into mocking and stubbing needs that you might run into, and you'll write code to handle such situations.

8.1 Getting started with TDD

In this section, you'll develop some code in a test-first manner. The first example is a set of functions that help with strings that represent dates. Specifically, you'll write functions to increment and decrement such date strings. Such operations are often needed in many applications, so this functionality may prove useful as a utility.

Although this example is simple, it illustrates the technique of writing unit tests and then getting them to pass, while also using the REPL to make the process quicker. The example in the next section will be a little more involved and will deal with a situation that demands mocking and stubbing of functions. Let's get started.

8.1.1 Example: dates and string

In test-driven development, you begin by writing a test. Obviously, because no code exists to support the test, it will fail. Making that failing test pass becomes the immediate goal, and this process repeats. So the first thing you'll need is a test. The test you'll write is for a function that can accept a string containing a date in a particular format, and you'll check to see if you can access its internals.

THE FIRST ASSERTION

In this initial version of the test, you'll check that the day portion is correct. Consider the following code (remember to put it in a file called date_operations_spec.clj in a folder named chapter08 within your source directory):

```
(ns chapter08.date-operations-spec
  (:use chapter08.date-operations)
  (:use clojure.test))

(deftest test-simple-data-parsing
  (let [d (date "2009-1-22")]
    (is (= (day-from d) 22))))
```

You're using the test-is unit-testing framework for Clojure, which began life as an external library and later was included as part of the distribution. The first evidence that you're looking at a unit test is the use of the deftest macro. Here's the general form of this macro:

```
(deftest [name & body])
```

It looks somewhat like a function definition, without any parameters. The body here represents the code that will run when the unit test is executed. The test-is library provides a couple of assertion macros, the first being is, which was used in the previous example. You'll see the use of the other in the following paragraphs.

Meanwhile, let's return to our test. If you try to evaluate the test code at the REPL, Clojure will complain that it can't find the chapter08.date-operations namespace. The error might look something like the following:

```
Could not locate chapter08/date_operations__init.class or
  chapter08/date_operations.clj on classpath:
  [Thrown class java.io.FileNotFoundException]
```

To move past this error, create a new namespace in an appropriately located file. This namespace has no code in it, so your test code still won't evaluate, but the error will be different. It will complain that it's unable to find the definition of a function named date:

```
Unable to resolve symbol: date in this context
  [Thrown class java.lang.Exception]
```

Getting past this error is easy; define a date function in your new date-operations namespace. To begin with, it doesn't even have to return anything. The same goes for the day-from function:

```
(ns chapter08.date-operations)

(defn date [date-string])

(defn day-from [d])
```

This will cause your tests to evaluate successfully, leaving them ready to be run. You can also do this from the REPL, like so:

```
user> (use 'clojure.test)
nil
user> (run-tests 'chapter08.date-operations-spec)

Testing chapter08.date-operations-spec

FAIL in (test-simple-data-parsing) (NO_SOURCE_FILE:1)
expected: (= (day-from d) 22)
  actual: (not (= nil 22))

Ran 1 tests containing 1 assertions.
1 failures, 0 errors.
{:type :summary, :test 1, :pass 0, :fail 1, :error 0}
```

Now you're set. You have a failing test that you can work on, and once you have it passing, you'll have the basics of what you want. To get this test to pass, you'll write some real code in the chapter08.date-operations namespace. One way to implement this functionality is to use classes from the JDK standard library (there are other options as well, such as the excellent Joda Time library available as open source). You'll stick with the standard library, specifically with the GregorianCalendar and the SimpleDate-Format classes. You can use these to convert strings into dates. You can experiment with them on the REPL:

```
user> (import '(java.text SimpleDateFormat))
java.text.SimpleDateFormat
```

```
user> (def f (SimpleDateFormat. "yyyy-MM-dd"))
#'user/f
```

```
user> (.parse f "2010-08-15")
#<Date Sun Aug 15 00:00:00 PDT 2010>
```

So you know `SimpleDateFormat` will work, and now you can check out the `Gregorian-Calendar`:

```
user> (import '(java.util GregorianCalendar))
java.util.GregorianCalendar
```

```
user> (def gc (GregorianCalendar. ))
#'user/gc
```

Now that you have an instance of a `GregorianCalendar` in hand, you can set the time by parsing a date string and then calling `setTime`:

```
user> (def d (.parse f "2010-08-15"))
#'user/d
```

```
user> (.setTime gc d)
nil
```

Because `setTime` returns `nil`, you're going to have to explicitly pass back the calendar object. Having performed this experiment, you can write the code, which ends up looking like this:

```
(ns chapter08.date-operations
  (:import (java.text SimpleDateFormat)
           (java.util Calendar GregorianCalendar)))

(defn date [date-string]
  (let [f (SimpleDateFormat. "yyyy-MM-dd")
        d (.parse f date-string)]
    (doto (GregorianCalendar.)
      (.setTime d))))
```

Also, you have to figure out the implementation of `day-from`. A look at the API documentation for `GregorianCalendar` will reveal that the `get` method is what you're need. You can try it at the REPL:

```
user> (import '(java.util Calendar))
java.util.Calendar
```

```
user> (.get gc Calendar/DAY_OF_MONTH)
15
```

Again, you're all set. The `day-from` function can be

```
(defn day-from [d]
  (.get d Calendar/DAY_OF_MONTH))
```

The tests should pass now. Remember that in order for the REPL to see the new definitions of the code in the `date-operations` namespace, you may need to reload it (using the `:reload` option). Here's the output:

```
user> (run-tests 'chapter08.date-operations-spec)

Testing chapter08.date-operations-spec

Ran 1 tests containing 1 assertions.
0 failures, 0 errors.
{:type :summary, :test 1, :pass 1, :fail 0, :error 0}
```

Now that you can create date objects (represented by instances of GregorianCalendar) and can access the day from these objects, you can implement accessors for month and year. Again, you'll begin with tests.

MONTH-FROM, YEAR-FROM

The tests for getting the month and year are similar to what you wrote before. You can include these assertions in the previous test:

```
(deftest test-simple-data-parsing
  (let [d (date "2009-01-22")]
    (is (= (month-from d) 1))
    (is (= (day-from d) 22))
    (is (= (year-from d) 2009)))))
```

This won't evaluate until you at least define the month-from and year-from functions. You'll skip over the empty functions and write the implementation as

```
(defn month-from [d]
  (inc (.get d Calendar/MONTH)))

(defn year-from [d]
  (.get d Calendar/YEAR))
```

With this code in place, the tests should pass:

```
user> (run-tests 'chapter08.date-operations-spec)

Testing chapter08.date-operations-spec

Ran 1 tests containing 3 assertions.
0 failures, 0 errors.
{:type :summary, :test 1, :pass 3, :fail 0, :error 0}
```

Again, you're ready to add more features to your little library. Let's add an as-string function that can convert your date objects into the string format.

AS-STRING

The test for this function is quite straightforward, because it's the same format you began with:

```
(deftest test-as-string
  (let [d (date "2009-01-22")]
    (is (= (as-string d) "2009-01-22"))))
```

Because you have functions to get the day, month, and year from a given date object, it's trivial to write a function that constructs a string containing words separated by dashes. Here's the implementation, which will compile and run after you include clojure .contrib.str-utils in the namespace via a use clause:

```
(defn as-string [date]
  (let [y (year-from date)
        m (month-from date)
        d (day-from date)]
    (str-join "-" [y m d])))
```

You can confirm that this works by running it at the REPL:

```
user> (def d (date "2010-12-25"))
#'user/d
```

```
user> (as-string d)
"2010-12-25"
```

So that works, which means your test should pass. Running the tests now gives the following output:

```
user> (run-tests 'chapter08.date-operations-spec)

Testing chapter08.date-operations-spec

FAIL in (test-as-string) (NO_SOURCE_FILE:1)
expected: (= (as-string d) "2009-01-22")
  actual: (not (= "2009-1-22" "2009-01-22"))

Ran 2 tests containing 4 assertions.
1 failures, 0 errors.
{:type :summary, :test 2, :pass 3, :fail 1, :error 0}
```

The test failed! The problem is that instead of returning "2009-01-22", your as-string function returns "2009-1-22", because the various parts of the date are returned as numbers without leading zeroes even when they consist of only a single digit. You'll either have to change your test (which is fine, depending on the problem at hand) or pad such numbers in order to get your test to pass. You'll do the latter:

```
(defn pad [n]
  (if (< n 10) (str "0" n) (str n)))
```

```
(defn as-string [date]
  (let [y (year-from date)
        m (pad (month-from date))
        d (pad (day-from date))]
    (str-join "-" [y m d])))
```

Running the tests now should show a better response:

```
user> (run-tests 'chapter08.date-operations-spec)

Testing chapter08.date-operations-spec

Ran 2 tests containing 4 assertions.
0 failures, 0 errors.
{:type :summary, :test 2, :pass 4, :fail 0, :error 0}
```

So, you now have the ability to create date objects from strings, get at parts of the dates, and also convert the date objects into strings. You can either continue to add features or take a breather to refactor your code a little.

INCREMENTING, DECREMENTING

Because you're just getting started and don't want to lose momentum, we'll postpone refactoring until after adding one more feature. You'll add functionality to advance and turn back dates. You'll start with addition, and as usual, you'll write a test:

```
(deftest test-incrementing
  (let [d (date "2009-10-31")
        n-day (increment-day d)]
    (is (= (as-string n-day) "2009-11-01"))))
```

This test will fail, citing the inability to find the definition of increment-day. You can implement this function using the add method on the GregorianCalendar class, which you can check on the REPL:

```
user> (def d (date "2009-10-31"))
#'user/d

user> (.add d Calendar/DAY_OF_MONTH 1)
nil

user> (as-string d)
"2009-11-01"
```

So that works quite nicely, and you can convert this into a function, as follows:

```
(defn increment-day [d]
  (doto d
    (.add  Calendar/DAY_OF_MONTH 1)))
```

Now, you can add a couple more assertions to ensure you can add not only days but also months and years. The modified test looks like this:

```
(deftest test-incrementing-date
  (let [d (date "2009-10-31")
        n-day (increment-day d)
        n-month (increment-month d)
        n-year (increment-year d)]
    (is (= (as-string n-day) "2009-11-01"))
    (is (= (as-string n-month) "2009-11-30"))
    (is (= (as-string n-year) "2010-10-31"))))
```

The code to satisfy this test is simple, now that you already have increment-day:

```
(defn increment-month [d]
  (doto d
    (.add  Calendar/MONTH 1)))

(defn increment-year [d]
  (doto d
    (.add  Calendar/YEAR 1)))
```

Running this results in the following output:

```
user> (run-tests 'chapter08.date-operations-spec)

Testing chapter08.date-operations-spec
```

```
FAIL in (test-incrementing-date) (NO_SOURCE_FILE:1)
expected: (= (as-string n-day) "2009-11-01")
  actual: (not (= "2010-12-01" "2009-11-01"))

FAIL in (test-incrementing-date) (NO_SOURCE_FILE:1)
expected: (= (as-string n-month) "2009-11-30")
  actual: (not (= "2010-12-01" "2009-11-30"))

FAIL in (test-incrementing-date) (NO_SOURCE_FILE:1)
expected: (= (as-string n-year) "2010-10-31")
  actual: (not (= "2010-12-01" "2010-10-31"))

Ran 4 tests containing 8 assertions.
3 failures, 0 errors.
{:type :summary, :test 4, :pass 5, :fail 3, :error 0}
```

The tests failed! Even the one that was passing earlier (incrementing the date by a day) is now failing. Looking closely, all three failures are because the incremented date seems to be "2010-12-01". It appears that "2009-10-31" was incremented first by a day, then by a month, and then by a year! You've been bitten by the most-Java-objects-are-not-immutable problem. Because d is a mutable object, and you're calling increment-day, increment-month, and increment-year on it, you're accumulating the mutations, resulting in a final date of "2010-12-01". As a side note, this also illustrates how easy it is to get used to Clojure's immutability and then to expect everything to behave like Clojure's core data structures. Within a few days of using Clojure, you'll begin to wonder why you ever thought mutable objects were a good idea!

In order to address this problem, you'll return a new date from each mutator function. The clone method in Java does this, and you can use it in your new definitions:

```
(defn increment-day [d]
  (doto (.clone d)
    (.add  Calendar/DAY_OF_MONTH 1)))

(defn increment-month [d]
  (doto (.clone d)
    (.add  Calendar/MONTH 1)))

(defn increment-year [d]
  (doto (.clone d)
    (.add  Calendar/YEAR 1)))
```

With this change, the tests all pass, allowing us to tackle decrementing. Again, start with the test:

```
(deftest test-decrementing-date
  (let [d (date "2009-11-01")
        n-day (decrement-day d)
        n-month (decrement-month d)
        n-year (decrement-year d)]
    (is (= (as-string n-day) "2009-10-31"))
    (is (= (as-string n-month) "2009-10-01"))
    (is (= (as-string n-year) "2008-11-01"))))
```

To get this test to pass, you can go with the same structure of functions that did the incrementing. The code might look like the following:

```
(defn decrement-day [d]
  (doto (.clone d)
    (.add Calendar/DAY_OF_MONTH -1)))

(defn decrement-month [d]
  (doto (.clone d)
    (.add Calendar/MONTH -1)))

(defn decrement-year [d]
  (doto (.clone d)
    (.add Calendar/YEAR -1)))
```

This passes the tests. You now have code that works and a library that can accept date strings and return dates as strings. It can also increment and decrement dates by days, months, and years. But the code isn't quite optimal, and we're now going to improve it.

REFACTOR MERCILESSLY

Extreme programming (XP) is an agile methodology that espouses several specific guidelines. One of them is to "refactor mercilessly." It means that you should continuously strive to make code (and design) simpler by removing clutter and needless complexity. An important part of achieving such simplicity is to remove duplication. You'll do that with the code you've written so far.

Before you start, it's pertinent to make an observation. There's one major requirement to any sort of refactoring; in order for it to be safe, there needs to be a set of tests that can verify that nothing broke because of the refactoring. This is another benefit of writing tests (and TDD in general). Our tests from the previous section will serve this purpose.

Let's begin our refactoring by addressing the duplication in the increment/decrement functions. Here's a rewrite of those functions:

```
(defn date-operator [operation field]
  (fn [d]
    (doto (.clone d)
      (.add field (operation 1)))))

(def increment-day (date-operator + Calendar/DAY_OF_MONTH))

(def increment-month (date-operator + Calendar/MONTH))

(def increment-year (date-operator + Calendar/YEAR))

(def decrement-day (date-operator - Calendar/DAY_OF_MONTH))

(def decrement-month (date-operator - Calendar/MONTH))

(def decrement-year (date-operator - Calendar/YEAR))
```

After replacing all six of the old functions with this code, the tests still pass. You've removed the duplication from the previous implementation and also made the code more declarative: the job of each of the six functions is clearer with this style. The benefit may seem small in this example, but for more complex code, it can be a major boost in readability, understandability, and maintainability. This refactored version can be reduced more via some clever use of convention, but it may be overkill for this particular task. As it stands, you've reduced the number of lines from 18 to 10, showing that the old implementation was a good 80% larger than this new one.

You could imagine a similar refactoring being applied to the month-from, day-from, and year-from functions, but the decision to do that and the implementation are left as an exercise for you.

This section showed the usage of the built-in Clojure unit-testing library called test-is. As you saw through the course of building our example, using the REPL is a critical element to writing Clojure code. You can use the REPL to quickly check how things work and then write code once you understand the APIs. It's great for such short experiments and allows for incrementally building up code for larger, more complex functions. When a unit-testing library is used alongside a REPL, the combination can result in an ultra-fast development cycle while keeping quality high. In our next section, you'll see how you can write a simple mocking and stubbing framework to make your unit testing even more effective.

8.2   *Mocking and stubbing things*

Unit testing is testing at a unit level, which in the case of Clojure is the function. Functions are often composed of other functions, and there are times when testing such upper-level functions that it's useful to mock out calls to certain underlying functions. *Mocking* functions is a useful technique (often used during unit testing) where a particular function is replaced with one that doesn't do anything. This allows you to focus only on those parts of the code where the unit test is being targeted.

At other times, it's useful to *stub* the calling of a function, so instead of doing what it's implemented to do, the stubbed function returns canned data.

You'll see examples of both of these in this section. You'll also write a simple library to handle mocking and stubbing functions in this manner. Clojure, being the dynamic functional language that it is, makes this extremely easy to do.

8.2.1   *Example: expense finders*

In this example, you'll write a few functions to load expense objects from a data store and to filter them based on some criteria (such as greater than a particular amount). Because you're dealing with money, you'll also throw in a requirement that your functions must log to an audit log. This example is a bit contrived, but it will serve our purposes quite well.

Also, the focus of this section isn't the TDD that you saw in the previous section. This section will focus on the need to stub calls to certain functions. The following is the code you're trying to test.

> **Listing 8.1   Example code that fetches and filters expenses from a data store**

```
(ns chapter08.expense-finders
  (:use clojure.contrib.str-utils))

(defstruct expense :amount :date)
```

```
(defn log-call [id & args]
  (println "Audit - called" id "with:" (str-join ", " args))
  ;;do logging to some audit data-store
)

(defn fetch-all-expenses [username start-date end-date]
  (log-call "fetch-all" username start-date end-date)
  ;find in data-store, return list of expense structs
)

(defn expenses-greater-than [expenses threshold]
  (log-call "expenses-greater-than" threshold)
  (filter #(> (:amount %) threshold) expenses))

(defn fetch-expenses-greater-than [username start-date end-date threshold]
  (let [all (fetch-all-expenses username start-date end-date)]
    (expenses-greater-than all threshold)))
```

Here, the expense struct map is used to represent expense objects. The `log-call` function presumably logs calls to some kind of an audit database. The two `fetch` functions both depend on loading expenses from some sort of data store. In order to write a test for, say, the `fetch-expenses-greater-than` function, you'll need to populate the data store to ensure it's loaded from the test via the `fetch-all-expenses` call. In case any test alters the data, you must clean it up so subsequent runs of the tests also work.

This is a lot of trouble. Moreover, it couples your tests to the data store and the data in it. Presumably, you've tested the persistence of data to and from the data store elsewhere in your code, so having to deal with hitting the data store in this test is a distraction and plain unnecessary. It would be nice if you could stub the call and return canned data. You'll implement this stubbing functionality next. Further, you'll look at dealing with another distraction, the `log-call` function in the following section.

8.2.2 Stubbing

In your test for `fetch-expenses-greater-than`, it would be nice if you could do the following:

```
(let [filtered (fetch-expenses-greater-than "" "" "" 15.0)]
  (is (= (count filtered) 2))
  (is (= (:amount (first filtered)) 20.0))
  (is (= (:amount (last filtered)) 30.0)))
```

You're passing blank strings to `fetch-expenses-greater-than` because you don't care what the values are (you could have passed anything). Inside the body of `fetch-expenses-greater-than`, they're used only as arguments to `fetch-all-expenses`, and you want to stub the call to this latter function (the one parameter that you do pass correctly is the last one, with a value of `15.0`). What you'd also like is for the stubbed call to return canned data, which you might define as follows:

```
(def all-expenses [(struct-map expense :amount 10.0 :date "2010-02-28")
                   (struct-map expense :amount 20.0 :date "2010-02-25")
                   (struct-map expense :amount 30.0 :date "2010-02-21")])
```

So, the question is how do you express the requirement for these two things: the call to fetch-all-expenses is faked out (stubbed) and that it returns all-expenses? In order to make the process of stubbing functions feel as natural as possible, you'll create a new construct for your tests and give it the original name stubbing. After you have it all implemented, you'll be able to say something like this:

```
(deftest test-fetch-expenses-greater-than
  (stubbing [fetch-all-expenses all-expenses]
    (let [filtered (fetch-expenses-greater-than "" "" "" 15.0)]
      (is (= (count filtered) 2))
      (is (= (:amount (first filtered)) 20.0))
      (is (= (:amount (last filtered)) 30.0)))))
```

The general form of the stubbing macro is as follows:

```
(stubbing [function-name1 stubbed-return-value1
           function-name2 stubbed-return-value2...]
    code-body)
```

This reads a little like the let and binding forms, and whenever you add such constructs to your code, it makes sense to make them look and feel like one of the built-in features of Clojure to keep things easy for others to understand. Now let's see how you might implement it.

IMPLEMENTING STUBBING

Clojure makes implementing this quite easy. Because it's a functional language, you can easily create a dummy function on the fly, one that accepts an arbitrary number of parameters and returns whatever you specify. Next, because function definitions are held in vars, you can then use the binding form to set them to your newly constructed stub functions. This makes it almost trivial, and here's the implementation:

```
(ns chapter08.stubbing)

(defmacro stubbing [stub-forms & body]
  (let [stub-pairs (partition 2 stub-forms)
        returns (map last stub-pairs)
        stub-fns (map #(list 'constantly %) returns)
        real-fns (map first stub-pairs)]
    `(binding [~@(interleave real-fns stub-fns)]
       ~@body)))
```

Considering that many languages have large, complex libraries for stubbing functions and methods, this code is almost disappointingly short. Admittedly, it doesn't do everything a fuller-featured stubbing framework might, but it gets the job done. Before you look at a sample expansion of this macro, let's look at an example:

```
(defn calc-x [x1 x2]
  (* x1 x2))

(defn calc-y [y1 y2]
  (/ y2 y1))

(defn some-client []
  (println (calc-x 2 3) (calc-y 3 4)))
```

Let's see how `some-client` behaves under normal conditions:

```
user> (some-client)
6 4/3
nil
```

And here's how it behaves using our new stubbing macro:

```
user> (stubbing [calc-x 1
                 calc-y 2]
        (some-client))
1 2
```

So now that we've confirmed this works as expected, let's look at how it does so:

```
user> (macroexpand-1' (stubbing [calc-x 1 calc-y 2]
        (some-client)))
  (clojure.core/binding [calc-x (constantly 1)
                         calc-y (constantly 2)]
    (some-client))
```

The `constantly` function does the job well, but in order to make things easier for you later on, you'll introduce a function called `stub-fn`. It's a simple higher-order function that accepts a value and returns a function that returns that value no matter what arguments it's called with. Hence, it is equivalent to `constantly`. The rewritten code is shown here:

```
(defn stub-fn [return-value]
  (fn [& args]
    return-value))

(defmacro stubbing [stub-forms & body]
  (let [stub-pairs (partition 2 stub-forms)
        returns (map last stub-pairs)
        stub-fns (map #(list 'stub-fn %) returns)
        real-fns (map first stub-pairs)]
    `(binding [~@(interleave real-fns stub-fns)]
       ~@body)))
```

This extra layer of indirection will allow you to introduce another desirable feature into this little framework (if you can even call it that!)—mocking, the focus of the next section.

8.2.3 Mocking

Let's begin by going back to what you were doing when you started the `stubbing` journey. You wrote a test for `fetch-expenses-greater-than`, a function that calls `expenses-greater-than`. This function does two things: it logs to the audit log, and then it filters out the expenses based on the threshold parameter. You should be unit testing this lower-level function as well, so let's look at the following test:

```
(ns chapter08.expense-finders-spec
  (:use chapter08.expense-finders
        clojure.test))
```

```
(deftest test-filter-greater-than
  (let [fetched [(struct-map expense :amount 10.0 :date "2010-02-28")
                 (struct-map expense :amount 20.0 :date "2010-02-25")
                 (struct-map expense :amount 30.0 :date "2010-02-21")]
        filtered (expenses-greater-than fetched 15.0)]
    (is (= (count filtered) 2))
    (is (= (:amount (first filtered)) 20.0))
    (is (= (:amount (last filtered)) 30.0)))))
```

Running the test gives the following output:

user> (run-tests 'chapter08.expense-finders-spec)

Testing chapter08.expense-finders-spec
Audit - called expenses-greater-than with: 15.0

Ran 1 tests containing 3 assertions.
0 failures, 0 errors.
{:type :summary, :test 1, :pass 3, :fail 0, :error 0}

It works, and the test passes. The trouble is that the audit function also runs as part of the test (as can be seen from the text Audit - called expenses-greater-than with: 15.0 that was printed by the log-call function. In the present case, all it does is print some text, but in the real world, it could do something useful—perhaps write to a database or send a message on a queue.

Ultimately, it causes our tests to be dependent on an external system such as a database server or a message bus. It makes the tests less isolated, and it detracts from the unit test itself, which is trying to check whether the filtering works correctly.

One solution is to not test at this level at all but to write an even lower-level function that tests only the filtering. But you'd like to test at least at the level that clients of the code will work at, so you need a different solution. One approach is to add code to the log-call function so that it doesn't do anything when running in test mode. But that adds unnecessary code to functions that will run in production, and it also clutters the code. In more complex cases, it will add noise that will detract from easily understanding what the function does.

Luckily, you can easily fix this problem in Clojure by writing a simple mocking framework.

8.2.4 *Mocks versus stubs*

A mock is similar to a stub because the original function doesn't get called when a function is mocked out. A stub returns a canned value that was set up when the stub was set up. A mock records the fact that it was called, with a specific set of arguments. Later on, the developer can programmatically verify if the mocked function was called, how many times it was called, and with what arguments.

Now that you have a separate function called stub-fn, you can modify this to add mocking capabilities. You'll begin by creating an atom called mock-calls that will hold information about the various mocked functions that were called:

```
(def mock-calls (atom {}))
```

Now, you'll modify stub-fn to use this atom:

```
(defn stub-fn [the-function return-value]
  (swap! mock-calls assoc the-function [])
  (fn [& args]
    (swap! mock-calls update-in [the-function] conj args)
    return-value))
```

When stub-fn is called, an empty vector is stored in the atom against the function being stubbed. Later, when the stub is called, it records the call in the atom (as shown in chapter 6), along with the arguments it was called with. It then returns the return-value it was created with, thereby working as before in that respect. Now that you've changed the way stub-fn works, you have to also slightly refactor the stubbing macro in order for it to stay compatible:

```
(defmacro stubbing [stub-forms & body]
  (let [stub-pairs (partition 2 stub-forms)
        real-fns (map first stub-pairs)
        returns (map last stub-pairs)
        stub-fns (map #(list 'stub-fn %1 %2) real-fns returns)]
    `(binding [~@(interleave real-fns stub-fns)]
      ~@body)))
```

OK, now you've laid the basic foundation on which to implement the mocking features. Because a mock is similar to a stub, you can use stub-fn to create a new one. You don't care about a return value, so you'll use nil:

```
(defn mock-fn [the-function]
  (stub-fn the-function nil))
```

Now for some syntactic sugar. You'll create a new macro called mocking, which will behave similar to stubbing, except that it will accept any number of functions that need to be mocked:

```
(defmacro mocking [fn-names & body]
  (let [mocks (map #(list 'mock-fn (keyword %)) fn-names)]
    `(binding [~@(interleave fn-names mocks)]
      ~@body)))
```

Now that you have the basics ready, you can rewrite your test:

```
(deftest test-filter-greater-than
  (mocking [log-call]
    (let [filtered (expenses-greater-than all-expenses 15.0)]
      (is (= (count filtered) 2))
      (is (= (:amount (first filtered)) 20.0))
      (is (= (:amount (last filtered)) 30.0)))))
```

When you run this test, it won't execute the log-call function, and the test is now independent of the whole audit-logging component. As noted earlier, the difference between mocking and stubbing, so far, is that you don't need to provide a return value when using mocking.

Although you don't want the log-call function to run as is, it may be important to verify that the code under test calls a function by that name. Perhaps such calls are part of some security protocol in the overall application. It's quite easy for you to verify this, because you're recording all calls to your mocked functions in the mock-calls atom.

VERIFYING MOCKED CALLS

The first construct that you'll provide to verify mocked function usage will confirm the number of times they were called. Here it is:

```
(defmacro verify-call-times-for [fn-name number]
  `(is (= ~number (count (@mock-calls ~(keyword fn-name)))))))
```

This makes it easy to see if a mocked function was called a specific number of times. Another way to verify the mocked calls would be to ensure they were called with specific arguments. Because you're recording that information as well, it's quite easy to provide verification functions to do this:

```
(defmacro verify-first-call-args-for [fn-name & args]
  `(is (= '~args (first (@mock-calls ~(keyword fn-name)))))))
```

Let's look at these two verification mechanisms in action:

```
(deftest test-filter-greater-than
  (mocking [log-call]
    (let [filtered (expenses-greater-than all-expenses 15.0)]
      (is (= (count filtered) 2))
      (is (= (:amount (first filtered)) 20.0))
      (is (= (:amount (last filtered)) 30.0)))
    (verify-call-times-for log-call 1)
    (verify-first-call-args-for log-call "expenses-greater-than" 15.0)
    (verify-nth-call-args-for 1 log-call "expenses-greater-than" 15.0)))
```

What you now have going is a way to mock any function so that it doesn't get called with its regular implementation. Instead, a dummy function is called that returns nil and lets the developer also verify that the calls were made and with particular arguments. This makes testing code with various types of dependencies on external resource much easier. The syntax is also not so onerous, making the tests easy to write and read.

Finally, because a mocked function may be called multiple times by the code under test, here's a macro to verify any of those calls:

```
(defmacro verify-nth-call-args-for [n fn-name & args]
  `(is (= '~args (nth (@mock-calls ~(keyword fn-name)) (dec ~n)))))
```

You can now also refactor verify-first-call-args-for in terms of verify-nth-call-args-for as follows:

```
(defmacro verify-first-call-args-for [fn-name & args]
  `(verify-nth-call-args-for 1 ~fn-name ~@args))
```

So that's the bulk of it! Listing 8.2 shows the complete mocking and stubbing implementation. It allows functions to be dynamically mocked out or stubbed, depending on the requirement. It also provides a simple syntactic layer in the form of the mocking and stubbing macros, as shown previously.

Listing 8.2 Simple stubbing and mocking functionality for Clojure tests

```clojure
(ns chapter08.mock-stub
  (:use clojure.test))

(def mock-calls (atom {}))

(defn stub-fn [the-function return-value]
  (swap! mock-calls assoc the-function [])
  (fn [& args]
    (swap! mock-calls update-in [the-function] conj args)
    return-value))

(defn mock-fn [the-function]
  (stub-fn the-function nil))

(defmacro verify-call-times-for [fn-name number]
  `(is (= ~number (count (@mock-calls ~(keyword fn-name))))))

(defmacro verify-first-call-args-for [fn-name & args]
  `(verify-nth-call-args-for 1 ~fn-name ~@args))

(defmacro verify-nth-call-args-for [n fn-name & args]
  `(is (= '~args (nth (@mock-calls ~(keyword fn-name)) (dec ~n)))))

(defmacro mocking [fn-names & body]
  (let [mocks (map #(list 'mock-fn (keyword %)) fn-names)]
    `(binding [~@(interleave fn-names mocks)]
      ~@body)))

(defmacro stubbing [stub-forms & body]
  (let [stub-pairs (partition 2 stub-forms)
        real-fns (map first stub-pairs)
        returns (map last stub-pairs)
        stub-fns (map #(list 'stub-fn %1 %2) real-fns returns)]
    `(binding [~@(interleave real-fns stub-fns)]
      ~@body)))
```

That's not a lot of code: under 30 lines. But it's sufficient for our purposes and indeed as a basis to add more complex functionality. We'll now look at a couple more things before closing this section.

CLEARING RECORDED CALLS

After a test run such as the previous one, our `mock-calls` atom contains all the recorded calls to mocked functions. The verification macros you create work against this to ensure that your mocks were called the way you expected. When all is said and done though, the data that remains is useless. Let's add a function to clear out the recorded calls:

```clojure
(defn clear-calls []
  (reset! mock-calls {}))
```

On a separate note, in case you wondered why running the same test multiple times doesn't cause an accumulation in the `mock-calls` atom, it's because the call to `stub-fn` resets the entry for that function. Further, this global state will cause problems if you happen to run tests in parallel, because the recording will no longer correspond to a single piece of code under test. The atom will, instead, contain a mishmash of all calls to various mocks from all the tests. This isn't what's intended, so you can fix this by making the state local.

REMOVING GLOBAL STATE

By removing the global mock-calls atom, you'll be able to improve the ability of tests that use mocking to run in parallel. The first thing you'll do is to get rid of the global binding for mock-calls:

```
(def mock-calls)
```

Next, in order for things to continue to work as they did, you have to reestablish the binding at some point. You'll create a new construct called defmocktest, which will be used instead of deftest. Its only job is to create a binding for mock calls before delegating back to good old deftest:

```
(defmacro defmocktest [test-name & body]
  `(deftest ~test-name
     (binding [mock-calls (atom {})]
       (do ~@body))))
```

After this, your previously defined tests would need to be redefined using defmocktest:

```
(defmocktest test-fetch-expenses-greater-than
  (stubbing [fetch-all-expenses all-expenses]
    (let [filtered (fetch-expenses-greater-than "" "" "" 15.0)]
      (is (= (count filtered) 2))
      (is (= (:amount (first filtered)) 20.0))
      (is (= (:amount (last filtered)) 30.0)))))
```

And here's the other one:

```
(defmocktest test-filter-greater-than
  (mocking [log-call]
    (let [filtered (expenses-greater-than all-expenses 15.0)]
      (is (= (count filtered) 2))
      (is (= (:amount (first filtered)) 20.0))
      (is (= (:amount (last filtered)) 30.0)))
    (verify-call-times-for log-call 1)
    (verify-first-call-args-for log-call "expenses-greater-than" 15.0)))
```

The trade-off is that you have to necessarily include the calls to your verify macros inside the scope of the call to defmocktest. This is because the mock calls are recorded inside the atom bound by the binding created by the defmocktest macro, and outside such scope there's nothing bound to mock-calls.

You've completed what you set out to do: you started by exploring the test-is framework and then added functionality to allow simple stubbing and mocking of functions. Our final stop will be to look at another couple of features of test-is.

8.3 Organizing tests

A couple of other constructs that are part of the test-is unit-testing framework are worth knowing about. They help with organizing asserts inside the body of a test function. Although it's usually better to keep the number of asserts in each test to the lowest possible number, sometimes it's logical to add asserts to existing tests rather than adding new tests.

When a test does have several assertions, it often becomes more difficult to understand and maintain. When an assertion fails, it isn't always clear what the specific failure is and what specific functionality is breaking. The testing macro comes in handy by documenting groups of asserts.

Finally, the are macro does two things: it removes duplication when several assertions using is are used with minor variations, and it groups such assertions together.

8.3.1 Testing

Let's revisit our test-filter-greater-than test from the previous section. There are two distinct sets of things you're checking for here: the fact that that filtering itself works and that the call to log-call happens correctly. You'll use the testing macro to group these according to those goals:

```
(defmocktest test-filter-greater-than
  (mocking [log-call]
    (let [filtered (expenses-greater-than all-expenses 15.0)]
      (testing "the filtering itself works as expected"
        (is (= (count filtered) 2))
        (is (= (:amount (first filtered)) 20.0))
        (is (= (:amount (last filtered)) 30.0))))
    (testing "Auditing via log-call works correctly"
      (verify-call-times-for log-call 2)
      (verify-first-call-args-for log-call "expenses-greater-than" 15.0)))))
```

We've deliberately changed the number of times log-call is expected to be called to 2, so you can see how things look when this test fails:

```
user> (test-filter-greater-than)
FAIL in (test-filter-greater-than) (NO_SOURCE_FILE:1)
Auditing via log-call works correctly
expected: (clojure.core/= 2 (clojure.core/count ((clojure.core/deref
    chapter08.mock-stub2/mock-calls) :log-call)))
  actual: (not (clojure.core/= 2 1))
```

As you can see, now when anything within a group of assertions fails, the testing string is printed along with the failure. It gives immediate feedback about what the problem is and also makes reading and understanding the test much easier.

Now let's look at the are macro.

8.3.2   *are*

We'll now look at an additional construct to group assertions with, one that also helps remove unnecessary duplication. Imagine that you had to create a function to upper case a given string:

```
(deftest test-to-upcase
  (is (= "RATHORE" (to-upper "rathore")))
  (is (= "1" (to-upper 1)))
  (is (= "AMIT" (to-upper "AMIT")))))
```

Here's a function that will satisfy this test:

```
(defn to-upper [s]
  (.toUpperCase (str s)))
```

You can remove the duplication in this test by using the are macro:

```
(deftest test-to-upcase
  (are [l u] (= u (to-upper l))
     "RATHORE" "RATHORE"
     "1" "1"
     "amit" "AMIT"))
```

Using the are macro combines several forms into a single assertion. When any of them fail, the failure is reported as a single assertion failure. This is one reason why it should be used for related assertions, not as a means to remove duplication.

8.4   *Summary*

In this chapter, we looked at test-driven development in Clojure. As you saw, TDD in a language such as Clojure, can work as well as it does in other dynamic languages. In fact, when combined with the REPL, it gets an additional boost of productivity. You can write a failing unit test and try out various implementation ideas at the REPL. When it's clear what approach to take, it's easy to write the code to pass the test. Similarly, it's easy to test implementations quickly at the REPL and then to copy the code over to the test files to add additional assertions and tests.

You then wrote a simple framework to stub functions, and then you added functionality to mock functions and verify the calls made to them. Clojure made it extremely easy—and the complete code for this clocked in at fewer than thirty lines of code. Although it probably didn't satisfy every requirement from a stubbing and mocking library, it served our purposes well and it can be used as the basis for something more complex. It certainly showed how easily, seemingly complex things can be implemented in Clojure.

Overall, this chapter demonstrated that the natural productivity boost that comes from using a modern and functional Lisp is significantly amplified by using the REPL and test-driven development.

Data storage with Clojure

This chapter covers

- Using Clojure with MySQL for simple needs
- Using Clojure with HBase for big data
- Using Clojure with Redis for key-value storage

This chapter begins an exciting journey. We're going to use all the concepts you've learned so far and apply them to applications that might be useful in the real world. We'll start by discussing a simple requirement common to most nontrivial applications, that of storing data.

First, we'll look at relational database systems because many applications need a standard relational database. MySQL fits the bill for most people, and we'll examine an open source project that provides functionality to allow Clojure programs to talk to MySQL.

After discussing MySQL, we'll look at communicating with HBase, which is an open source implementation of Google's BigTable. These are column-oriented databases that can handle extremely large datasets, often measured in petabytes. The term *big data* has been used recently to describe such systems, and HBase is one answer to such large-scale data storage requirements.

Finally, we'll wrap up the chapter by examining Redis, a new key-value store designed for extremely fast lookups. We'll write code to create a convenient

Clojure abstraction that makes dealing with Redis easy and transparent. It will allow you to map Clojure data structures into and out of Redis.

9.1   MySQL & clj-record

In this section, we're going to work with a MySQL database using the `clj-record` library. We'll first look at a quick example of the library in action, followed by a look under the hood at its inner workings.

9.1.1   ActiveRecord, users, and charges

Martin Fowler documented the active record design pattern in his book *Patterns of Enterprise Application Architecture.* In this pattern, a class or a module corresponds directly to a single database table. Methods or functions are created that allow the usual CRUD (create, read, update, and delete), along with other convenience methods to look things up using different columns of the table, and accessor methods to read column values. Although this is a simple pattern, it turns out to be applicable in a large percentage of cases; domain objects are mapped to tables in a straightforward manner. As an example, this is the pattern used in the eponymous `ActiveRecord` library that forms an integral part of the Ruby on Rails web application framework. Now that you understand this pattern at a high level, let's look at an example.

SETTING UP THE TABLES

Let's imagine you're dealing with users and charges. Let's further imagine that you have a MySQL table called `users` for this purpose and that it has the structure shown in table 9.1.

Table 9.1   The structure of the `users` table

Column name	Data type	Description
`id`	int	The identity column for each row
`login`	varchar	The username of the user
`first_name`	varchar	The first name of the user
`last_name`	varchar	The last name of the user
`password`	varchar	The user's password
`email_address`	varchar	The user's email address

This is a simple table, and our use of the active record pattern will support code to create records for new users, find records pertaining to existing users via their id or other attributes, update such records, and also delete them. As mentioned earlier, we're going to use the open-source library `clj-record` in order to implement this.

Let's also create another table for the all the charges. We'll call it `charges` and give it the structure shown in table 9.2.

Table 9.2   The structure of the `charges` table

Column name	Data type	Description
id	int	The identity column for each row
user_id	int	The user to whom this charge belongs
amount_dollars	int	The dollar part of the charge amount
amount_cents	int	The cents part of the charge amount
category	varchar	The category of this charge
vendor_name	varchar	The vendor of this item or service
date	datetime	The date this charge was billed

Having established these two tables, you can now use `clj-record` to access them.

GETTING STARTED WITH CLJ-RECORD

The `clj-record` project was created by John Hume and is located at http://github.com/duelinmarkers/clj-record. Once you've downloaded it and put it on the Clojure classpath, you can use it in your programs via calls to `require`. You'll now write code to implement your user and `charge` entities.

9.1.2   *The user model*

The `clj-record` library is based on Clojure namespaces. In order to define a model class (such as `user`, in this case), you define a namespace that ends with that name. Further, by including the `clj-record.boot` namespace, you pull in all the required code to use the library. Consider the following example:

```
(ns org.rathore.amit.damages.model.user
  (:require clj-record.boot))
```

Requiring `clj-record.boot` pulls in several different namespaces, including `core`, `associations`, and `validation`. In order to get things going, you only need to call the `init-model` function from the `clj-record.core` namespace. But it depends on the existence of a var named `db`, which must contain the database configuration information. Here's an example of what such a configuration might look like:

```
(def db
  {:classname "com.mysql.jdbc.Driver"
   :subprotocol "mysql"
   :user "root"
   :password "password"
   :subname "//localhost/damages_dev"})
```

`clj-record` supports a few databases: Apache Derby, MySQL, and PostgreSQL among them. In this example, we've specified MySQL. In typical applications, the configuration information might be specified in a dedicated configuration file, and a function would read it from there.

Now that you have your database configuration ready, you can call init-model. This can be simple as the following:

```
(clj-record.core/init-model)
```

Note that, by default, the clj-record library makes an assumption about the table that the model is going to use. In this case, because the model name is user, the table will be assumed to be users. You can override this using the :table-name option, as shown here:

```
(clj-record.core/init-model
 :table-name "members")
```

You're now ready to start accessing the database, and it's quite simple. In the following section, you'll see how to create, read, update, and delete rows of the users table. After that, you'll see how to handle associations, validations, and so on.

CREATING RECORDS

Let's import the user namespace. As you've seen several times over the past few chapters, this is as simple as the following:

```
(require '(org.rathore.amit.damages.model [user :as user]))
```

Remember that all the functions that were defined when you called init-model are in the user namespace. Here's how you can create a user:

```
user=> (user/create {:login "rob"
                      :first_name "Robert"
                      :last_name "Berger"
                      :password "secret"
                      :email_address "rob@runa.com"})
{:email_address "rob@runa.com", :password "secret", :last_name "Berger",
    :first_name "Robert", :login "rob", :id 1}
```

Note that the id field gets populated automatically, and you don't have to figure out what it should be. Let's create another one:

```
user=> (user/create {:login "rob2"
                      :first_name "Robert"
                      :last_name "Stevenson"
                      :password "friday"
                      :email_address "rob@crusoe.com"})
{:email_address "rob@crusoe.com", :password "friday", :last_name
    "Stevenson", :first_name "Robert", :login "rob2", :id 2}
```

Now that you have a couple of records in your table, let's look at reading them back out.

READING RECORDS

You've seen how to create new users; now let's use a few more functions provided by the clj-record library to read them out. If the id of the record you're looking for is known, then you can use the get-record function:

```
user=> (user/get-record 1)
{:email_address "rob@runa.com", :password "secret", :last_name "Berger",
    :first_name "Robert", :login "rob", :id 1}
```

If you don't know the exact row-id and would like to search for records based on some other attributes, you can do that using the `find-records` function:

```
user=> (user/find-records {:first_name "robert"})
({:email_address "rob@runa.com", :password "secret", :last_name "Berger",
    :first_name "Robert", :login "rob", :id 1}
 {:email_address "rob@crusoe.com", :password "friday", :last_name "Steven-
    son", :first_name "Robert", :login "rob2", :id 2})
```

`find-records` accepts a map of attributes and will find records whose columns match all those attributes specified in the map.

The `clj-record` library supports other finder functions such as `find-record` and `find-by-sql`. You can find more information on these on the `clj-record` project page.

UPDATING RECORDS

Updating a record is just as simple. You use the `update` function for this purpose, which accepts a map of attributes that need updating. The map must include the `id` attribute so that the correct record can be found. Here's an example:

```
user=> (user/update {:login "stevenson" :id 2})
{:id 2, :login "stevenson"}
```

You can confirm that it worked by reading the complete record again:

```
user=> (user/get-record 2)
{:email_address "rob@crusoe.com", :password "friday", :last_name
    "Stevenson", :first_name "Robert", :login "stevenson", :id 2}
```

Finally, let's look at deleting rows.

DELETING RECORDS

The final piece of CRUD is deletion, and you'll now see how to delete some of the records you just created. The `clj-record` library provides the function `destroy-record` for this purpose, which accepts a map that must contain an `:id` key. Here's an example:

```
user=> (user/destroy-record {:id 2})
(1)
```

You can confirm it was deleted by trying to read it back:

```
user=> (user/find-records {:id 2})
()
```

Our next stop in exploring `clj-record` is to explore associations. In order to do so, you'll set up the second model in your system: `charges`.

9.1.3 Associations

Database systems like MySQL are relational; they support relationships between tables. In this section, you'll examine the `clj-record` support for two kinds of such relationships: `belongs-to` and `has-many`.

First, let's set up a namespace to handle the charges tables that you defined earlier. As you did for the user model, you'll define a namespace that ends in `charge`:

```
(ns org.rathore.amit.damages.model.charge
  (:require clj-record.boot)
```

You're ready to call `init-model` now, but you'll use the associations support provided by `clj-record` in order to specify that each `charge` belongs to your `user` model.

```
(clj-record.core/init-model
 (:associations
  (belongs-to user)))
```

Testing this at the REPL will involve calling `require`:

```
(require '(org.rathore.amit.damages.model [charge :as charge]))
```

Let's now create a charge for your user "rob":

```
user=> (charge/create {:user_id 1, :amount_dollars 11 :amount_cents 50
        :category "books" :vendor_name "amazon" :date "2010-01-15"})
{:date #<Timestamp 2010-01-15 00:00:00.0>, :vendor_name "amazon", :category
    "books", :amount_cents 50, :amount_dollars 11, :user_id 1, :id 1}
```

And one more, just to be sure:

```
user=> (charge/create {:user_id 1, :amount_dollars 27 :amount_cents 91
        :category "meals" :vendor_name "stacks" :date "2010-01-15"})
{:date #<Timestamp 2010-01-15 00:00:00.0>, :vendor_name "stacks", :category
    "meals", :amount_cents 91, :amount_dollars 27, :user_id 1, :id 2}
```

Similarly, you can update the definition of your user model to say that your users have many charges:

```
(ns org.rathore.amit.damages.model.user
  (:require clj-record.boot))

 (clj-record.core/init-model
 (:associations
  (has-many charges)))
```

Let's now see the associations in action. You'll first use `get-record` to load your user object and then load the charges associated with it:

```
user=> (let [rob (user/get-record 1)]
        (user/find-charges rob))
({:date #<Timestamp 2010-01-15 00:00:00.0>, :vendor_name "amazon", :category
    "books", :amount_cents 50, :amount_dollars 11, :user_id 1, :id 1}
{:date #<Timestamp 2010-01-15 00:00:00.0>, :vendor_name "stacks", :category
    "meals", :amount_cents 91, :amount_dollars 27, :user_id 1, :id 2})
```

This makes it convenient to work with graphs of related data. `clj-record` also provides similar support for deleting associations. Our next stop will be a quick tour of some convenient aspects of this library.

9.1.4 *Validations and callbacks*

The `clj-record` library supports features beyond what you've seen so far. This section will look at a couple of features: validations and callbacks. *Validations* are a mechanism to ensure that the integrity of data in each record is maintained. Callbacks are a way to run arbitrary code whenever certain things happen to a record, such as saving to the database, loading from the database, and so on.

VALIDATIONS

Let's add a check to our charge model, so that you can guard against expenses with amounts less than zero. Here's the change to the call to `init-model`:

```
(clj-record.core/init-model
 (:associations
  (belongs-to user))
 (:validation
  (:amount_dollars "Must be positive!" #(>= % 0))
  (:amount_cents "Must be positive!" #(>= % 0))))
```

You can now use the `validate` function to check if there are any errors:

```
user=> (let [errors (charge/validate {:amount_dollars 0
                                       :amount_cents -10
                                       :date "2010-01-10"
                                       :vendor_name "amazon"})]
         (println errors))
{:amount_cents [Must be positive!]}
```

This way, you can easily ensure business rules are being satisfied before persisting things into the database.

CALLBACKS

A *callback* is a function that gets called when a particular event occurs. The `clj-record` library supports three kinds of callbacks: `before-save`, `before-update`, and `after-load`. The specified function is handed the record that's being processed and must return a possibly modified version of the record. Here's an example of our charge model's `init-model` function:

```
(clj-record.core/init-model
 (:callbacks
  (:before-save (fn [record]
                  (if-not (:category record)
                    (assoc record :category "uncategorized")
                    record)))))
```

And here it is in action:

```
user=> (charge/create {:amount_cents 0 :amount_dollars 10 :vendor_name
       "amazon" :date "2010-01-01"})
{:date #<Timestamp 2010-01-01 00:00:00.0>, :vendor_name "amazon", :category
    "uncategorized", :amount_cents 0, :amount_dollars 10, :user_id nil,
    :id 6}
```

Okay! You've been through a whirlwind introduction to the `clj-record` library, and by now, you're able to add database persistence support to your applications. Our last stop in this part of the chapter is a peek under the covers of this nifty library, to see how it's implemented.

9.1.5 *A look under the hood*

This section has two related purposes: to get a high-level understanding of how clj-record is implemented and to learn tricks you can then use in your own programs. With that, I'd like to bring your attention to a few points about the implementation.

CLJ-RECORD.BOOT

As you've seen in the past several examples, the way to get started with the clj-record library is to require the clj-record.boot namespace. Internally, the library is made up of several different namespaces that contain code related to things like associations, validations, callbacks, and serialization. Instead of having the client programmer require all these namespaces, clj-record.boot does something convenient: it requires all these other namespaces. Here's the relevant line (minus the doc string):

```
(ns clj-record.boot
  (:require
    (clj-record core callbacks associations validation serialization)))
```

This is a convenient way to allow users of a library to quickly get started with as little clutter as possible.

CLJ-RECORD.CORE

The most interesting (and certainly most directly useful) thing about the core namespace is the init-model macro. As you saw in previous sections, it can accept several options, and it generates a large amount of code. It generates all the methods that you've seen in the previous sections: get-record, find-records, destroy-records, create, update, and so on. The following listing shows what it looks like.

> **Listing 9.1 The init-model macro from clj-record.core**

```
(defmacro init-model [& init-options]
  (let [model-name (last (str-utils/re-split #"\."           ❶ Extract model name
                           (name (ns-name *ns*))))]             from namespace
        [top-level-options option-groups] (split-out-init-options
                                             init-options)
        tbl-name (or (top-level-options :table-name)
                     (pluralize model-name))
        optional-defs (defs-from-option-groups model-name
                        option-groups)]
    `(do                                                      ◁
      (init-model-metadata ~model-name)                         ┐
      (set-db-spec ~model-name ~'db)                            │ Generate code for
      (set-table-name ~model-name ~tbl-name)                    │ multiple function
      (def ~'table-name (table-name ~model-name))             ❷ │ definitions
      (defn ~'model-metadata [& args#]
        (apply model-metadata-for ~model-name args#))
      (defn ~'table-name [] (table-name ~model-name))
      (defn ~'get-record [id#]
        (get-record ~model-name id#))
      (defn ~'find-records [attributes#]
        (find-records ~model-name attributes#))
      (defn ~'find-record [attributes#]
```

```
      (find-record ~model-name attributes#))
  (defn ~'find-by-sql [select-query-and-values#]
    (find-by-sql ~model-name select-query-and-values#))
  (defn ~'create [attributes#]
    (create ~model-name attributes#))
  (defn ~'insert [attributes#]
    (insert ~model-name attributes#))
  (defn ~'update [attributes#]
    (update ~model-name attributes#))
  (defn ~'destroy-record [record#]
    (destroy-record ~model-name record#))
  (defn ~'validate [record#]
    (clj-record.validation/validate ~model-name record#))
  ~@optional-defs)))
```

The code in listing 9.1 won't work as is on the REPL, because it depends on a lot of other things defined in `clj-record`. Let's look at a couple of points of note. The model name is parsed out from the current namespace ❶. This is how it builds the model around the namespace in which you call `init-model`.

The second is that the `init-model` macro expands to several calls to the `defn` macro, all wrapped inside a do ❷ block. The expansion occurs in the namespace that the model is being defined around, and that's how all those functions are made available. It makes it easy to put all related functions in the same namespace (such as `user` or `charge`), because database access functions are readily available.

CODE ORGANIZATION

As mentioned earlier, the `clj` library has separate namespaces for things like associations, validations, callbacks, serialization, and so on. This organization makes the code easy to navigate, understand, and maintain.

That wraps up our tour of `clj-record`. It's a straightforward library and works well enough in systems that need access to databases that aren't looking to implement complex schemas. It also has a `find-by-sql` function, which allows straight SQL access to the database. For larger projects, many people are now looking beyond relational databases, and our next stop is going to be the first NoSQL data store we're going to look at in this chapter.

9.2 HBase

HBase, which is the open source version of Google's BigTable, is a rather interesting data-storage technology. As opposed to a traditional relational database (RDBMS), Google describes BigTable as a "sparse, distributed, persistent multi-dimensional sorted map." Let's further examine what that means and how it's different from working with relational databases.

9.2.1 Meet HBase

In this section, we'll quickly explore HBase. If you're familiar with relational databases, you'll notice that things in HBase are significantly different from that world. We'll start by addressing scalability and then talk about schema design. It takes a little time to get your head wrapped around the column-oriented approach, so we'll explore a simple example.

SCALABILITY

Most people come to HBase for its scalability. Anyone who has had to scale, say, MySQL knows it's a lot of work. Up to a point, adding machines to a master-slave setup can satisfy scalability requirements. For serious scaling requirements, data must be sharded across multiple servers. *Sharding* is a technique in which a large dataset is broken into sections, each stored on a different server. This allows the system to scale the data storage beyond what a single database server can handle comfortably. This sharding has to be done at the application level, using some strategy, and it affects code that writes to or reads from the database. Any code that relied on joins will need to be rewritten to reflect the sharding strategy. This approach to scaling adds a lot of complexity to the application. HBase makes this unnecessary.

HBase can scale to support petabytes of data, and it does so by scaling across thousands of commodity servers. With HBase, application code that accesses the data doesn't have to change as the data store is scaled up. HBase runs on top of the Hadoop Distributed File System (HDFS), and all data gets replicated across several nodes in a transparent manner. Not only does this allow the system to grow to use thousands of nodes, but it also adds a tremendous amount of reliability in the case where nodes fail (as they will).

COLUMN ORIENTED

HBase differs from traditional relational databases in the way that tables are defined and also in the manner in which rows are created and used. In the normal RDBMS world, a table is defined with a fixed set of columns, and these can't be changed in any particularly dynamic manner. Further, each row of such a table always has the same set of columns as defined in the table. One of the columns is defined to contain the primary key and is unique across all rows of the table. The primary key can be used to identify a single row.

In HBase, data is still stored in rows, and each row has a row-id. Inside each HBase table, rows can have any number of columns. This is possible because HBase is a column-oriented data store, implying that underneath it, data for each column is stored contiguously. This sparse but efficient storage allows wide variation in the columns of each row.

This makes designing schemas for column-oriented data stores different for folks coming from a traditional RDBMS background. In the next section, you'll see an example of what this looks like. For now, it's enough to know that each HBase column contains two parts: a statically defined (during table creation) column family name and a dynamically defined qualifier. Putting the two pieces together, a complete column name looks like the following:

```
<column-family>:<qualifier>
```

As mentioned, the column families of an HBase table are the only things that are defined at table creation time. They can also be changed (or new ones created)

using administrative tools provided with HBase. This is analogous to using alter statements to modify the structure of tables in the SQL world. The qualifier portion of
the column name can be created at program runtime, without having to declare it
earlier. HBase supports millions of qualifiers in each column family and hundreds of
column families.

There's one more element that we need to talk about before we're ready to look at
an example—versions.

VERSIONS

So far, you've seen that each HBase row has a row-id and a variable set of columns via
the combination of column families and qualifiers. Another dimension is added to
this by the fact that each cell of an HBase row can contain multiple versions of data.
The version keys are timestamps, and a new version of data is created every time a cell
is written to. The default number of versions is three, but this can be set to any number when the table is created.

To get something out of the a table, you have to follow this trail:

```
row-id > column-family > column-qualifier > version
```

This is what is meant by a multidimensional data store. Now that you understand the
anatomy of an HBase table, you're ready to look at an example.

SCHEMA DESIGN

Designing for column-oriented data stores feels rather odd when you're used to relational database systems. Here's a traditional example, used both in Google's BigTable
paper and in the HBase documentation. Imagine working on an Internet search
engine. This domain would require you to store web pages in a table, which might be
designed as shown in table 9.3.

Table 9.3   Example of an HBase table storing web pages

Row key	contents	anchor				mime
		cnnsi.com	my.look.ca	bbc.com	bbc.co.uk	
"com.cnn.www"	<html>...	"CNN"	"CNN.com"			"text/html"
"com.bbc.www"	<html>...			"BBC US"	"BBC UK"	"text/html"
		... and more rows ...				

Note that `contents`, `anchor`, and `mime` are column families. The `anchor` column family
has been used along with several qualifiers: `cnnsi.com`, `my.look.ca`, `bbc.com`, and so
on, and these are different for different rows. As mentioned earlier, because data is
stored sparsely, these seemingly null values in each row pose no efficiency overhead.

We're now ready to write some Clojure code to access HBase.

9.2.2   *Using Clojure to access HBase*

HBase is written in Java, so the Java client library that it ships with is perfect for your Clojure programs. For the remainder of this section on HBase, you'll need to have HBase 0.20.2 installed and running on your system. You'll also need to have the HBase JAR file on your Clojure classpath. We'll first learn about accessing an HBase table directly, and then we'll propose an abstraction that will make life easier for most Clojure programs.

Configuring hbase-site.xml

One piece of XML-driven configuration needs to be configured before your Clojure programs can access the HBase system. A file called hbase-site.xml lives in the conf directory inside the HBase root folder. This file will need to be copied into a location on the JVM's classpath and will need to contain some information regarding your particular installation of HBase. Listing 9.2 shows the content of the file for a standalone installation, as an example.

Listing 9.2   Contents of a sample hbase-site.xml for a standalone HBase system

```
<configuration>
  <property>
    <name>hbase.master</name>
    <value>localhost:60000</value>
  </property>
  <property>
    <name>hbase.rootdir</name>
    <value>hdfs://localhost:50001/hbase</value>
  </property>
  <property>
    <name>hbase.zookeeper.quorum</name>
    <value>localhost</value>
  </property>
  <property>
    <name>hbase.cluster.distributed</name>
    <value>false</value>
  </property>
</configuration>
```

DIRECT ACCESS

Imagine you had a table called clojure_test that had a column family named meta. This can be done by creating it at the HBase shell using the following command:

```
create "clojure_test", "meta"
```

In order to do any of the following, you'll need to import the necessary libraries. The following code imports all that's required:

```
(ns chapter12
  (:import (java.util Set)
           (org.apache.hadoop.hbase HBaseConfiguration)
```

```
        (org.apache.hadoop.hbase.client Put Get HTable)
        (org.apache.hadoop.hbase.util Bytes)))
```

The first function is a utility function to allow you to get a handle to your HBase table:

```
(defn hbase-table [table-name]
  (HTable. (HBaseConfiguration.) table-name))
```

Let's begin by writing something to the table and then follow it up with reading it back out. Consider the following couple of functions:

```
(defn add-to-put [p object column-family]
  (let [name-of (fn [x]
                    (if (keyword? x) (name x) (str x)))]
    (doseq [[k v] object]
      (.add p (Bytes/toBytes column-family)
             (Bytes/toBytes (name-of k))
             (Bytes/toBytes (str v))))))

(defn put-in-table [object table-name column-family row-id]
  (let [table (hbase-table table-name)
        p (Put. (Bytes/toBytes row-id))]
    (add-to-put p object column-family)
    (.put table p)))
```

You can test it at the REPL like so:

```
chapter12=> (put-in-table {:a "x" :b "y"}
                          "clojure_test"
                          "meta"
                          "repl")
nil
```

This writes a single row into the clojure_test table, which has a single column family of meta, and the values x and y are stored with column qualifiers a and b, respectively. You can verify this by running the following command at the HBase shell:

```
scan "clojure_test"
```

Issuing this command will cause HBase to print a bunch of text at the shell, as shown in figure 9.1.

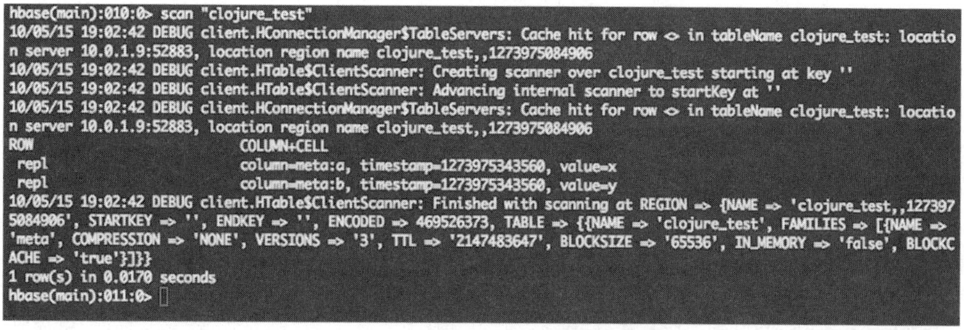

Figure 9.1 Output from the scan "clojure_test" command issued at the HBase shell

The part of the text shown in the image that you're interested in is the following:

```
ROW                     COLUMN+CELL
repl                    column=meta:a, timestamp= 1273975343560, value=x
repl                    column=meta:b, timestamp= 1273975343560, value=y
```

This shows that a row with the row-id of repl has two columns populated: meta:a and meta:b.

Let's now write a function to read your data back out of the table. Here's the function that does it:

```
(defn print-from-table [table-name row-id column-family]
  (let [table (hbase-table table-name)
        g (Get. (Bytes/toBytes row-id))
        r (.get table g)
        nm (.getFamilyMap r (Bytes/toBytes column-family))]
    (doseq [[k v] nm]
      (println (String. k) ":" (String. v)))))
```

You can confirm that this works by attempting to print the row you just inserted into the table from the REPL:

```
chapter12=> (print-from-table "clojure_test" "repl" "meta")
a : x
b : y
nil
```

Similar code can be written to scan across tables, something that's quite a common operation because HBase doesn't support any SQL-like querying mechanism. The API to do this is built on the Scan class. Writing code to perform scans is left as an exercise to you.

Let's now talk a little about the Get/Put classes that you used to do your reads and writes. This interface is simple (and may remind some folks of RESTful APIs from the world of web services), but it can get tedious to use if you have to drop down to using such Java classes every time you want to talk to HBase. This calls for building a higher-level abstraction that's friendlier to Clojure. We'll examine this in this next section.

A DATA MAPPER

A data mapper is a layer of code that moves data between objects and a data store, while keeping each independent of the other. In the case of Clojure, maps are the most commonly used form of (traditional) objects. In this section, you'll specify what you'd like your data mapper to do and what limitations it will have.

Most Clojure programs use simple hash maps to represent things like employees, customers, and buildings, depending on the domain. Contrast this with other languages such as Java or Ruby where you might use classes and objects. The advantage of using Clojure data structures is that you gain simplicity and get to use Clojure's entire sequence library.

Imagine that you were working on a program that dealt with paintings and that a typical description of a painting might look like this:

```
(def painting
    {:trees ["cedar", "maple", "oak"],
```

```
:houses 4,
:cars [{:make "honda", :model "fit", :license "ah12001"},
       {:make  "toyota", :model  "yaris",
                                  :license  "xb34544"}],
:road {:name "101N" :speed 65}})
```

You'd like to store these types of maps in HBase, in a table named `paintings`. Note that the map isn't deep and that there are some restrictions in the data mapper you're about to define. The values in such maps can be simple primitives like 4 or lists containing other primitives (for example, `["cedar", "maple", "oak"]`). The values can also be other hash maps such as the value for `:road` in this example, but such maps can't themselves be deep. Finally, the value can be a list of simple hash maps, such as the value for the `:cars` key.

Although this may sound arbitrarily restrictive, it turns out that many applications do fine within these constraints. Besides, you can certainly modify the mapper for more complex, nested maps.

In the previous section, you saw how simple maps can be persisted to an HBase table. Your job now is to transform this nested map into a simple one that's easy to insert into a single HBase row. For instance, you could transform the previous map into one that looks like this:

```
{ "road:name"  "101N",
  "road:speed"  65,
  "houses:"  4,
  "trees:cedar"  "cedar",
  "trees:maple"  "maple",
  "trees:oak"  "oak",
  "cars_model:ah12001"  "fit",
  "cars_model:xb34544"  "yaris",
  "cars_make:ah12001"  "honda",
  "cars_make:xb34544"  "toyota"}
```

This flattened map is simple to store into an HBase table that has the following column families: road, houses, trees, and cars. The key to any such transformation is that it be reversible, so that when you want to read back your data from the HBase row, you can convert it back into the familiar Clojure data structure that you started out with. Let's examine the transformed map.

The idea is simple. The keys of your transformed hash map will contain parts of your data. For instance, our original map has a key `:road` that has a value of `{:name "101N" :speed 65}`. In the transformed map, the equivalent keys are `"road:name"` and `"road:speed"`, and their values are `"101N"` and 65, respectively. Similar transforms are made for the `:houses` and `:trees` keys.

Transforming values that are primitives, lists of primitives, or a simple map is straightforward. Handling values that are lists of maps is a little trickier. This situation is analogous to a has-many relationship: our painting has many cars in it, and each car has a few data elements. In order to flatten this structure, you need to pick a primary key inside each car. Here, we've picked `:license` for this role. The flattening then takes place in a similar fashion as before, but the value for the primary key is tacked onto all the other keys for each car. For example, consider this car:

```
{:make "honda"
 :model "fit"
 :license "ah12001"}
```

The value of the primary key is `"ah12001"`, and this is tacked onto each key when the flattening occurs:

```
{"cars_make:ah12001"  "honda"
 "cars_model:ah12001"  "fit"}
```

The primary key and its value are implicitly represented in this map; there's no separate need to add them on their own. When you reverse the transform, you'll use the knowledge that the primary key was `:license` and add the keys back as needed. In this manner, you can flatten out a value that's a series of maps. Our next stop will be to look at some code that will allow you to flatten maps this way, and after that we'll talk about reading back things from HBase.

DATAMAPPER—WRITING TO HBASE

As you saw in the previous section, you want to convert your Clojure maps (up to a certain depth, as described earlier) into flattened maps, which are easy to store in a single HBase row. There are two ways to store a flattened map in an HBase table row, and the one you choose depends on your table design.

The first method defines your HBase table using multiple column families. In our painting example from earlier, this might mean you define column families named `houses`, `roads`, `cars`, and `trees`. This might be useful in situations where you might need to read only a subset of your object (say, `cars`), and this can be done without reading all the columns. Remember that data under a column family is stored contiguously, so reading one is more efficient that reading multiple. This table design, means that if another attribute is added to your object, you'd have to use the HBase admin tools to alter the schema to add a new column family.

The other option is to use only one column family, named something general like `meta`. This will allow you to be flexible in what attributes your objects have, but it means that your flattening process will have to ensure that the transformed map has keys that can be stored within a single column family. Our data mapper will handle both these options.

Let's first see what using the functions might look like. In order to do so, let's recap what we said about handling map values that are themselves lists of maps (the has-many-maps analogy). We said we'd pick a primary key and use the value of the primary key to mark up the keys in the transformed map. See the earlier painting example to refresh your memory. Sometimes, there may be no clear, single primary key. In that case, you'll pick one, write a function to return a value unique to each map, and use that to mark up the keys instead. To generalize, this transform process can be represented by a function. In the case where there's a clear primary key, this function would return the value of that key. In our paintings example from before, this function would be the following:

```
(fn [painting-map]
  (:license painting-map))
```

This can be abbreviated to #(:license %) or even :license.

In addition to the function, the flattening process needs to know which key is the one that has multiple maps as its value and what the primary key itself is. The config-for function is used for this:

```
(config-for :cars :license :license)
```

This says that the :cars key has a value that's a list of maps, and inside the inner maps :license is the primary key. Further, the value to be used to mark up the keys for the flattened map should be obtained by applying the function provided (which, as described earlier, in this case is the value of :license itself). Although this looks redundant in the call to config-for, in other cases the function could be arbitrarily complex.

Multiple such keys can be configured using the config-for function and then bundled together using the config-keys function. In the case of our painting example, the single :cars key can have a sequence of hash maps as its key. We refer to this process of transforming a generic map into a flattened one as *encoding*. The reverse process would be defined as *decoding*. This complementary set of information can be bundled together inside a simple map with the keys :encode and :decode. Here's the encoding part of this configuration:

```
(def keys-config
  {:encode (config-keys
            (config-for :cars :license :license))})
```

To recap, the general form of this is

```
{:encode (config-keys
                (config-for …)
                (config-for …)
                …)
 :decode (config-keys
                (config-for …)
                (config-for …)
                …)
}
```

keys-config, as defined here, contains only the encode part, which is sufficient to go one way—in the direction of flattening. The code for all of this flattening is shown in the following listing.

Listing 9.3 Transforming Clojure maps into ones suitable for insertion into HBase rows

```
(ns chapter12.datamapper
  (:import (org.apache.hadoop.hbase HBaseConfiguration)
           (org.apache.hadoop.hbase.client Put Get HTable)
           (org.apache.hadoop.hbase.util Bytes)))
```

```
(def *single-column-family?*)
(def *primary-keys-config*)                          Special variable
(def *hbase-single-column-family*)                   for configuration

(defstruct key-config :qualifier :functor)

(defn config-for [key-name qualifier functor]
  {key-name (struct key-config qualifier functor)})

(defn config-keys [& encoders]
  (apply merge encoders))

(defn column-name-delimiter []
  (if *single-column-family?* "__" ":"))

(defn single-column-prefix []
  (str *hbase-single-column-family* ":"))

(defn encoding-keys []
  (*primary-keys-config* :encode))

(defn qualifier-for [key-name]
  (((encoding-keys) (keyword key-name)) :qualifier))      Calling a function
                                                          returned by a
(defn encoding-functor-for [key-name]                     function
  (((encoding-keys) (keyword key-name)) :functor))

(defn symbol-name [prefix]
  (if (keyword? prefix)
    (name prefix)
    (str prefix)))

(defn new-key [part1 separator part2]
  (str (symbol-name part1) separator (symbol-name part2)))

(defn prepend-to-keys [prefix separator hash-map]
  (reduce (fn [ret key]
            (assoc ret
              (new-key prefix separator key)              Pass reduce an
              (hash-map key)))                            anonymous
          {} (keys hash-map)))                            function

(defn process-map [initial-prefix final-prefix single-map]
  (let [all-keys (to-array (keys single-map))]
    (areduce all-keys idx ret {}
      (assoc ret
        (str initial-prefix "_" (symbol-name (aget all-keys idx))
        (column-name-delimiter) final-prefix)
        (single-map (aget all-keys idx))))))

(defn process-maps [key maps]
  (let [qualifier (qualifier-for key)
        encoding-functor (encoding-functor-for key)]
    (apply merge (map
                   (fn [single-map]
                     (process-map (symbol-name key)
                       (encoding-functor single-map)       Merge maps
                       (dissoc single-map qualifier)))     returned
                   maps))))                                 by map
```

```
(defn process-strings [key strings]
  (reduce (fn [ret the-string]
            (assoc ret
                   (new-key key (column-name-delimiter) the-string)
                   the-string))
          {} strings))
(defn process-multiple [key values]
  (if (map? (first values))
    (process-maps key values)
    (process-strings key values)))
(defn process-key-value [key value]
  (cond
    (map? value) (prepend-to-keys key (column-name-delimiter)
                                  value)
    (vector? value) (process-multiple key value)
    :else {(new-key key (column-name-delimiter) "") value}))
(defn prepend-keys-for-single-column-family [flattened]
  (if-not *single-column-family?*
    flattened
    (let [prefix (single-column-prefix)
          key-prepender (fn [[key value]]
                          {(str prefix key) value})]
      (apply merge (map key-prepender flattened)))))
(defn flatten [bloated-object]
  (let [f (apply merge (map
                         (fn [[k v]]
                           (process-key-value k v))
                         bloated-object))]
    (prepend-keys-for-single-column-family f)))
```

◁ **Dispatch based on bound value**

Let's now use this configuration to flatten our previously defined painting object into a map suitable to be inserted into an HBase table with multiple column families:

```
chapter12.datamapper=> (binding [*single-column-family?* false
          *primary-keys-config* keys-config]
  (flatten painting))
{"road:name" "101N",
 "houses:" 4,
 "road:speed" 65,
 "trees:cedar" "cedar",
 "trees:maple" "maple",
 "trees:oak" "oak",
 "cars_model:ah12001" "fit",
 "cars_model:xb34544" "yaris",
 "cars_make:ah12001" "honda",
 "cars_make:xb34544" "toyota"}
```

If you wanted to flatten this into a map suitable for an HBase table with a single column family called meta, you could do that too:

```
chapter12.datamapper=> (binding [*single-column-family?* true
                       *hbase-single-column-family* "meta"
                       *primary-keys-config* keys-config]
                  (flatten painting))
```

```
{"meta:road__name" "101N",
"meta:houses__" 4,
"meta:cars_model__ah12001" "fit",
"meta:cars_model__xb34544" "yaris",
"meta:cars_make__ah12001" "honda",
"meta:cars_make__xb34544" "toyota",
"meta:road__speed" 65,
"meta:trees__cedar" "cedar",
"meta:trees__maple" "maple",
"meta:trees__oak" "oak"}
```

Both these maps can easily be persisted into HBase, using the function insert-into-hbase, as shown in the following listing.

Listing 9.4   Inserting a Clojure map into an HBase row

```
(defn hbase-table [table-name]
  (HTable. (HBaseConfiguration.) table-name))

(defn add-to-insert-batch [put flattened-list]      Use doseq for
  (doseq [[column value] flattened-list]            side effect
    (let [[family qualifier] (.split column ":")]    method add
      (.add put (Bytes/toBytes family)
                (Bytes/toBytes (or qualifier ""))
                (Bytes/toBytes value)))))

(defn insert-into-hbase [object-to-save hbase-table-name row-id]
  (let [table (hbase-table hbase-table-name)
        put (Put. (Bytes/toBytes row-id))
        flattened (flatten object-to-save)]
    (add-to-insert-batch put flattened)
    (.put table put)))
```

Here it is in action:

```
chapter12.datamapper=>
    (binding [*single-column-family?* true
              *hbase-single-column-family* "meta"
              *primary-keys-config* keys-config]
      (insert-into-hbase painting "clojure_test" "flatten-test"))
nil
```

Our next stop will be to explore reading this back out.

DATAMAPPER—READING FROM HBASE

In order to get your Clojure map back from the HBase table, you need to do two things. The first is to read from the HBase table and convert the resulting Result object into the flattened map you put into the row in the first place. Then you'd need to convert the flattened map into your original map, like the one defined earlier as painting.

The first part of the solution is in the next listing. It shows code that reads the data from the HBase row.

Listing 9.5 Reading the flattened map back out from HBase

```
(defn hbase-object-as-hash [hbase-result]
  (let [extractor (fn [kv]
                    {(String. (.getColumn kv))
                     (String. (.getValue kv))})
        key-values-objects (.list hbase-result)]
    (apply merge (map extractor key-values-objects))))

(defn read-row [hbase-table-name row-id]
  (let [table (hbase-table hbase-table-name)
        hbase-get-row-id (Get. (Bytes/toBytes row-id))]
    (.get table hbase-get-row-id)))

(defn get-flattened-map [hbase-table-name row-id]
  (hbase-object-as-hash (read-row hbase-table-name row-id)))
```

And here it is in action:

```
chapter12.datamapper=>
  (get-flattened-map "clojure_test" "flatten-test")
{"meta:road__name" "101N",
 "meta:houses__" "4",
 "meta:cars_model__ah12001" "fit",
 "meta:cars_model__xb34544" "yaris",
 "meta:cars_make__ah12001" "honda",
 "meta:cars_make__xb34544" "toyota",
 "meta:road__speed" "65",
 "meta:trees__cedar" "cedar",
 "meta:trees__maple" "maple",
 "meta:trees__oak" "oak"}
```

Note how all values come out as strings (because HBase stores everything as an uninterpreted byte array). You could write code to convert the values into other types (such as numbers).

As far as the second part of this problem goes, converting a flattened map back into the original hydrated one, we won't solve that here. The code is available along with the rest of the code for this book from http://manning.com/ClojureinAction.

What follows, is an example of this hydration process, starting with an updated keys-config object that now includes the :decode key:

```
(def keys-config
  {:encode (config-keys
             (config-for :cars :license :license))
   :decode (config-keys
             (config-for :cars :license #(first (.split % "@"))))})
```

And now let's see the hydration in action. Again, note that the values are still strings, and some wrapper code might convert them into more appropriate types (one approach might be to use the Clojure reader, via a call to read-string).

```
chapter12.datamapper=>
  (binding [*single-column-family?* true
```

```
               *hbase-single-column-family* "meta"
               *primary-keys-config* keys-config]
  (read-as-hydrated "clojure_test" "flatten-test"))
{:cars [{:make "toyota", :model "yaris", :license "xb34544"}
        {:make "honda", :model "fit", :license "ah12001"}],
 :trees ["maple" "oak" "cedar"],
 :road {:name "101N", :speed "65"},
 :houses "4"}
```

This was a long section! You saw the basics of HBase table design and then used Clojure to do some basic read and write operations. You didn't look in any detail at the scan operations, but you did write the beginnings of a simple data mapper that can persist (and read back) Clojure maps into HBase rows. Our final stop in this chapter is going to be Redis.

9.3   Redis

The previous section talked about HBase, a sort of heavy artillery for big data. Often, applications need some form of data storage that's lighter in weight and extremely fast. Redis is one such choice, a sort of light saber of key-value stores. It's described as an advanced, extremely performant key-value store, similar to memcached but persistent. Further, values can be strings, lists, sets, maps, and sorted sets. These features make it extremely suitable as a sort of "data structure server." In fact, in this chapter, you'll create your own abstraction on top of it, which will allow you to more easily move data into and out of Redis. To get started, you'll download and install Redis and then using an open source Clojure library to read and write values into it.

9.3.1   Installing Redis

Redis is open source software made available under the BSD license. It's hosted at http://redis.io. Installing it is quite easy on most UNIX/Linux or Mac OS systems. You download the compressed distribution, and unzip it into a directory of your choice. The software uses the standard compilation tool chain, and running make compiles and gets it ready for use. Following that, executing the redis-server script file starts the server. And that's it! Once you've done this you'll be ready to start writing to and reading from Redis.

9.3.2   Accessing Redis from Clojure programs

Several libraries have been written to access Redis from a variety of languages. From our point of view, there are a couple of choices: you can either use something written in Java or look for options written in Clojure. Luckily, there are two Java libraries, JDBC-redis and JRedis, and one Clojure library, redis-clojure. We're going to use redis-clojure, which is written in idiomatic Clojure that makes it easy and fun to use.

GETTING STARTED

In chapter 4, we mentioned the `redis-clojure` library as an example of using multi-methods. It's hosted at http://github.com/ragnard/redis-clojure and can be easily compiled using lein. To do so, check out the source, change to the directory, and run

```
lein jar
```

You'll need leiningen (found at https://github.com/technomancy/leiningen) for this to work. The previous command builds the `redis-clojure` JAR file, which can then be put on the JVM classpath to ensure that Clojure can see it. Or you can just put the src directory of the Redis-clojure project on your classpath. To get started using it, you need to refer to the `redis` namespace, as follows:

```
(ns chapter12.redis
  (:require redis))
```

In order to talk to the Redis server, you need to establish a connection to it. `redis-clojure` provides the convenient `with-server` macro that does this. It accepts a map containing the Redis server configuration, followed by code, which will execute in the context of a connection to Redis. Here's an example:

```
chapter12.redis=>
  (redis/with-server {:host "127.0.0.1" :port 6379 :db 0}
        (redis/ping))
"PONG"
```

As you might have guessed, the `redis` namespace has all the functions that allow communication with the Redis server, and the `ping` function just checks to see if the Redis server is up (which replies with the string `"PONG"`).

STRINGS

As mentioned earlier, Redis supports several data types, namely strings, lists, sets, maps, and sorted sets. There are also different functions that deal with setting and getting these data types as the values for various keys. Let's start by looking at setting and getting strings. I've omitted the REPL prompt for the following examples:

```
(redis/with-server {:host "127.0.0.1" :port 6379 :db 0}
  (redis/set "name" "deepthi"))
"OK"

(redis/with-server    {:host "127.0.0.1" :port 6379 :db 0}
  (redis/get "name" ))
"deepthi"
```

LISTS

Here's an example of using the list data type. Let's start by setting a couple of values in a list:

```
(redis/with-server    {:host "127.0.0.1" :port 6379 :db 0}
  (redis/rpush "names" "adi"))
"OK"
  (redis/with-server    {:host "127.0.0.1" :port 6379 :db 0}
    (redis/rpush "names" "punit"))
"OK"
```

And now, let's read them back:

```
(redis/with-server   {:host "127.0.0.1" :port 6379 :db 0}
  (redis/lindex "names" 0))
"adi"
 (redis/with-server   {:host "127.0.0.1" :port 6379 :db 0}
   (redis/lindex "names" 1))
"punit"
```

SETS

Let's also look at dealing with sets, which are similar to lists but can't have duplicates:

```
(redis/with-server   {:host "127.0.0.1" :port 6379 :db 0}
  (redis/sadd "names-set" "amit"))
true

(redis/with-server   {:host "127.0.0.1" :port 6379 :db 0}
  (redis/sadd "names-set" "adi"))
true

(redis/with-server   {:host "127.0.0.1" :port 6379 :db 0}
  (redis/sadd "names-set" "adi"))
false

(redis/with-server   {:host "127.0.0.1" :port 6379 :db 0}
  (redis/smembers "names-set"))
#{"adi" "amit"}
```

Similarly, there are functions to handle sorted sets. A full reference to all the commands it supports is here: http://redis.io/commands.

OTHER

Redis also supports a lot of other things, such as atomically incrementing the integer value of a key. This can be used to automatically assign IDs to Redis objects, similar to the autoincrement feature found in relational databases.

There are ways to atomically pop a value from a list-type collection, to get a random member of a set, to perform set operations (such as intersections and unions), or to sort a list or set. Again, more information is at the command reference mentioned previously.

Working with individual key values is easy but can be a little tedious in programs that make extensive use of Redis. Let's now look at building a little abstraction on top of Redis so you can work more naturally with Clojure maps.

9.3.3   *A Redis data mapper*

The inspiration for this mapper comes from the fact that most ORM (object-relational mapping) libraries make life easier for the developer. They hide the details of the database and SQL from code that's trying to get a job done and hence also make the code clearer and shorter. It also often feels more natural to work in the native data structures of the language while letting the library handle converting them to a format suitable for storage in the underlying database engine.

We'd like to do something similar when working with Redis (even though it's already quite easy, especially with the redis-clojure library). We'd like to work with Clojure maps, for instance, and not have to worry about how to break them down into key-value pairs that can be stored in Redis. Or we'd like to read them out as key pairs and construct the original map by reversing the breakdown process. In this manner, this is analogous to the HBase data mapper you saw earlier.

For the sake of variety, we'll take a different approach to implementing this mapper. The approach involves the use of a concept called let-over-lambda, and the reason for this name will become obvious shortly. Let's get started.

DEF-REDIS-TYPE

We'd like to define a higher-level abstraction that represents something that's "Redis aware." The following REPL conversation shows what you'll implement:

```
user> (use 'chapter12-redis-datamapper)
nil

user> (def-redis-type consumer
        (string-type :id :merchant-id :start-time :timezone)
        (list-type :cart-items)
        (primary-key :id :merchant-id))
#'user/consumer
```

This defines the idea of a Redis-aware consumer type. (To work with this, you'll need to get code from listings 9.6 and 9.7.) You could then query it like so:

```
user> (consumer :name)
consumer

user> (consumer :format)
:clj-str
user> (consumer :key-separator)
"___"

user> (consumer :primary-key)
(:id :merchant-id)
```

The :format here refers to the format in which the values will be stored in Redis. We'd like to support the Clojure built-in clj-str format (which will allow you to use the Clojure reader to deserialize things) and also JSON, so that if other, non-Clojure programs want to read the values, they can do so by using a JSON parser. The format defaults to clj-str but can be overridden using the :format option. This is also true for the key separator, which will be used to construct keys that will store pieces of the Redis-aware objects. Here's how the overriding works:

```
user> (def-redis-type consumer
        (string-type :id :merchant-id :start-time :timezone)
        (list-type :cart-items)
        (primary-key :id :merchant-id)
        (format :json)
        (key-separator "##"))
#'user/consumer
```

And to confirm

```
user> (consumer :format)
:json
user> (consumer :key-separator)
"##"
```

For now, we'll support only a limited set of data types—specifically, strings and lists. Extending the types to include others will be easy, once you understand how the rest work, and we'll leave such extensions as an exercise to you.

INSTANTIATING AND USING REDIS OBJECTS

Now let's see how you'd use these abstractions. First, we'll show how to set simple string-type data:

```
user> (def c (consumer :new))
#'user/c

user> (c :set! :id "adi")
"adi"

user> (c :set! :merchant-id "14")
"14"

user> (c :set! :start-time (System/currentTimeMillis))
1264582286124
```

Here's how to add list types:

```
user> (c :add! :cart-items {:sku "XYZ" :cost 10.95})
{:sku "XYZ", :cost 10.95}

user> (c :add! :cart-items {:sku "ABC" :cost 22.40})
{:sku "ABC", :cost 22.4}
```

Finally, here's how to get data out of these objects:

```
user> (c :get :merchant-id)
"14"

user> (c :get :cart-items)
({:sku "ABC", :cost 22.4} {:sku "XYZ", :cost 10.95})
```

Our last stop before we dive into the implementation is to show how to save these to Redis and how to get them back out.

PERSISTENCE

Here's how to save an object into Redis:

```
user> (redis/with-server    {:host "127.0.0.1" :port 6379 :db 0}
        (c :save!))
true
```

Let's look at how you'd go about loading one from Redis at a later time. You'll need the primary key(s) and use the :find command:

```
user> (redis/with-server {:host "127.0.0.1" :port 6379 :db 0}
          (def d (consumer :find "adi" "14")))
#'user/d
```

And to confirm that it indeed has the right data, do this:

```
user> (d :get :id)
"adi"
user> (d :get :merchant-id)
"14"
user> (d :get :cart-items)
({:cost 22.4, :sku "ABC"} {:cost 10.95, :sku "XYZ"})
```

So that's the broad usage. You're now ready to see how this is implemented.

IMPLEMENTATION

The code is divided into two namespaces. Listing 9.6 shows a namespace called chapter12-redis-datamapper, which contains most of the code for all the examples you've seen so far. Listing 9.7 contains a namespace called chapter12-redis-persistence, which contains the code that implements the persistence of Clojure maps into Redis and also deserializing it back out.

Listing 9.6 Namespace containing functions exposed to users of this library

```
(ns chapter12-redis-datamapper
  (:require redis)
  (:use clojure.contrib.str-utils)
  (:use chapter12-redis-persistence))

(defn primary-key-value [redis-obj]
  (let [pk-keys ((redis-obj :type) :primary-key)
        separator ((redis-obj :type) :key-separator)
       values (map #(redis-obj :get %) pk-keys)]
    (str-join separator values)))

(defn new-redis-object [redis-type]
  (let [state (ref {})]                          ◁─┐ Return a
    (fn thiz [accessor & args]                       │ closure
      (condp = accessor
        :type redis-type
        :set! (let [[k v] args]
                (redis-type :valid-key? k)
                (dosync
                 (alter state assoc k v))
                v)
        :set-all! (let [[kv-map] args]
                    (doseq [kv kv-map]
                      (let [[k v] kv]
                        (thiz :set! k v))))
        :copy-from-redis-object (let [from (first args)
                                      attribs (rest args)]
                                  (doseq [attrib attribs]
                                    (thiz :set! attrib (from :get attrib))))
        :add! (let [[k v] args
                    add-to-inner-list (fn [current-state ke valu]
                                        (update-in current-state [ke] conj valu))]
                (dosync
                 (alter state add-to-inner-list k v))
                v)
```

```
          :get (let [[k] args]
                 (redis-type :valid-key? k)
                 (state k))
          :primary-key-value (primary-key-value thiz)
          :save! (persist thiz)
          :get-state @state
          :replace-state (let [[new-state] args]
                           (dosync
                             (ref-set state new-state)))))))))

(defn key-type-for [key-name string-types list-types]
  (if (some #(= % key-name) string-types)
    :string-type
    (if (some #(= % key-name) list-types)
      :list-type)))

(defn keys-for [keys separator values]
  (let [pk-value (str-join separator values)]
    (map #(str pk-value separator %) keys)))

(defn check-key-validity [key redis-type string-attribs list-attribs]
  (if-not (some #(= % key) string-attribs)
    (if-not (some #(= % key) list-attribs)
      (throw (RuntimeException.
        (str "Attempt to use unknown key " key
              " in redis-object of type " (redis-type :name))))))
    true)

(defn new-redis-type [name separator format primary-keys
                                    string-attribs list-attribs]
  (fn redis-type [accessor & args]
    (condp = accessor
      :name name
      :format format
      :key-separator separator
      :primary-key primary-keys
      :key-type (let [[k] args]
                  (key-type-for k string-attribs list-attribs))
      :valid-key? (let [[key] args]
                    (check-key-validity key redis-type
                                        string-attribs list-attribs))
      :string-keys (let [[values] args]
                     (keys-for string-attribs separator values))
      :list-keys (let [[values] args]
                   (keys-for list-attribs separator values))
      :new (new-redis-object redis-type)
      :new-with-state (let [[new-state] args
                            nh (new-redis-object redis-type)]
                        (nh :replace-state new-state)
                        nh)
      :find (find-by-primary-key redis-type args)
      :exists? (let [key-value (str-join separator args)
                     key-value (str key-value separator
                                    (first primary-keys))]
                 (redis/exists key-value))
      :attrib-exists? (let [attrib-key (first args)
                            pk-value (str-join separator (rest args))]
```

Set a form of runtime type safety

Name the anonymous function

Simulate message passing

Define another function as the "type"

Refer to the anonymous function

```
                                   (redis/exists (str pk-value
                                                      separator attrib-key))))))

(defn specs-for [redis-datatype specs]
  (let [type-spec? #(= redis-datatype (first %))
        extractor (comp next first)]
    (extractor (filter type-spec? specs))))

(defmacro def-redis-type [name & specs]
  (let [string-types (specs-for 'string-type specs)
        list-types (specs-for 'list-type specs)
        pk-keys (specs-for 'primary-key specs)
        format (or (first (specs-for 'format specs)) :clj-str)
        separator (or (first (specs-for 'key-separator specs)) "___")]
    `(def ~name
       (new-redis-type '~name ~separator ~format
                       '~pk-keys '~string-types '~list-types))))
```

Listing 9.7 Namespace containing functions to persist and read back maps from Redis

```
(ns chapter12-redis-persistence
  (:require redis)
  (:require (org.danlarkin [json :as json])))
```
                                                    Serialization defined
                                                    as a multimethod
```
(defmulti serialize (fn [format key-type value]
                      [format key-type]))

(defmethod serialize [:json :string-type]
                     [format key-type value]
  (json/encode-to-str value))

(defmethod serialize [:json :list-type]
                     [format key-type value]
  (map json/encode-to-str value))

(defmethod serialize [:clj-str :string-type]
                     [format key-type value]
  (pr-str value))

(defmethod serialize [:clj-str :list-type]
                     [format key-type value]
  (map pr-str value))
```
                                                    Deserialization also
                                                    a multimethod
```
(defmulti deserialize (fn [format key-type serialized]
                        [format key-type]))

(defmethod deserialize [:json :string-type]
                       [format key-type serialized]
  (json/decode-from-str serialized))

(defmethod deserialize [:json :list-type]
                       [format key-type serialized]
  (map json/decode-from-str serialized))

(defmethod deserialize [:clj-str :string-type]
                       [format key-type serialized]
  (read-string serialized))

(defmethod deserialize [:clj-str :list-type]
                       [format key-type serialized]
```

```
        (map read-string serialized))

(def inserters {                          Redis insert functions
  :string-type redis/set                  stored in a map
  :list-type redis/rpush
})

(def fetchers {                                     Redis fetchers also
  :string-type (fn [key]                            stored in a map
                 {key {:value (redis/get key)
                       :key-type :string-type}})
  :list-type (fn [key]
               {key {:value (redis/lrange key 0 (redis/llen key))
                     :key-type :list-type}})})

(defn insert-into-redis [persistable]
  (let [inserter (fn [[k v]]
                   (cond
                   (= (v :key-type) :string-type)
                    ((inserters :string-type) k (v :value))
                   (= (v :key-type) :list-type)
                    (doall (map #((inserters :list-type) k %)
                                               (v :value)))))]
      (doall (map inserter persistable)))))
                                                  doall forces
(defn persistable-for [redis-object]              side effects
  (let [redis-type (redis-object :type)
        separator (redis-type :key-separator)
        format (redis-type :format)
        pk-value (redis-object :primary-key-value)
        kv-persister (fn [[k v]]
                   (let [key-type (redis-type :key-type k)]
                 {(str pk-value separator k)
                    {:value (serialize format key-type v)
                     :key-type key-type}}))]
      (apply merge (map kv-persister (redis-object :get-state)))))

(defn persist [redis-object]
  (insert-into-redis (persistable-for redis-object))
  true)

(defn deserialize-state [serialized redis-type]
  (let [format (redis-type :format)
        separator (redis-type :key-separator)
        key-from (fn [k] (read-string (last (.split k separator))))
        deserializer (fn [[k {:keys [key-type value]}]]
                       (if-not value
                   {}
                   {(key-from k) (deserialize format
                                                key-type value)}))]
      (apply merge (map deserializer serialized))))

(defn find-by-primary-key [redis-type pk-values]
  (let [string-keys (redis-type :string-keys pk-values)
        list-keys (redis-type :list-keys pk-values)
        string-maps (apply merge (map #((fetchers :string-type) %)
                             string-keys))
```

```
        list-maps (apply merge (map #((fetchers :list-type) %)
                                                        list-keys))
      serialized (merge string-maps list-maps)
      deserialized (deserialize-state serialized redis-type)]
   (if (every? empty? (vals deserialized))
     nil
     (redis-type :new-with-state deserialized))))
```

UNDER THE HOOD

There are a couple of things to talk about regarding the implementation. The first is the use of closures to represent Redis types and Redis objects. The second is the persistence side of things. The macro `def-redis-type` accepts the specification as expressed by the developer and converts it into a function. This function is created by calling `new-redis-type`, and the return value is held in a var (which is given the name specified in the macro call). Let's look into this in a little more detail.

The `new-redis-type` function returns an anonymous function. Clojure functions are lexical closures, and this fact is used by the returned function to hang onto the parameters that were passed to `new-redis-type` (things like the name of the Redis type, options, and so on). The anonymous function itself is variadic: the first parameter is a command name, followed by any number of other arguments. It uses a `condp` form to execute specific code depending on what the command word is. For example, if the command is `:name`, it returns the name of the Redis type. Or if the command is `:new`, it calls `new-redis-object`, which gets returned to the caller, for use as a Redis-aware object.

`new-redis-object` is another function that returns a similar anonymous function. This technique of returning a function that accepts commands with arguments makes things look like traditional objects (albeit with a different syntax). You'll see this approach again later when we implement our own flavor of traditional OO on top of Clojure.

The second namespace is the one that handles persistence, and most of the code here is rather straightforward. Of interest are the serialize and deserialize multimethods, which make it easy to add support for more Redis data types (strings, lists, sets, sorted sets, and the like) and for more formats in which to store values (`clj-str`, json, and so on.) The other thing to note is the inserters and fetchers maps that contain as values functions that will be called when needed. This lookup table makes it easy to write generic code to handle inserting things into Redis and fetching things from it. It's a simple sort of polymorphism.

So there it is, a fairly workable solution to map Clojure maps into and out of Redis.

9.4   *Summary*

This chapter showed three ways in which data can be stored in your Clojure applications. Despite the fact that your data needs are growing and you need faster and faster access to your data, a traditional relational database like MySQL is sometimes just the right database for the job. We also looked at a solution that handles large volumes of data: the Apache HBase project, which is an implementation of Google's own Big-Table. Finally, we looked at a new key-value data store named Redis, which is quickly gaining popularity among the developer community thanks to its support for higher-level data structures (such as lists and sets) and its extremely good performance and ease of use.

Hopefully, one of these will be suitable for your applications. The Clojure code we looked at to access these data stores is simple, compact, and easy to maintain and extend. That's the promise of Clojure—making it easy to write code that does much more than the lines of code might signify.

Clojure and the web

HTTP is the lingua franca of the internet. If your project involves creating a dynamic website, you'll need to use a suitable web application framework to get your job done. Even if you aren't creating a website for end users to visit, writing an HTTP interface to your application can provide an easy-to-use API for other applications. In this chapter, we'll explore doing that. First, we'll write some framework code, and then we'll use some open source libraries to enhance what we wrote. Specifically, after writing our own little framework, we'll explore the Ring and Compojure projects. We'll also look at clj-html, another open source library that allows HTML generation via Clojure code.

We'll write own little web framework to demonstrate how easy and straightforward Clojure is. This exercise will also serve as a segue to how you might use open source alternatives for web services in a production environment. Along the way, you'll see some more idiomatic Clojure, which should help in other programs you might be writing. Let's get started with our own take on an HTTP service in Clojure.

10.1 An HTTP interface from scratch

In this section, we'll write some code to make your Clojure functions available as HTTP services. The goal is to show how simply this can be accomplished in Clojure; there's nothing complicated about it. Our solution won't be full featured, but will work quite well. If your goal is to get something simple up and running quickly, this will do the trick.

Instead of providing features that will allow someone to write a full-featured web application, we'll write enough to enable a developer to create a simple web service. The difference is that our program won't provide a UI to an end user but instead can be used as an HTTP API end point by other programs. Let's start by picking an off-the-shelf HTTP server to embed your code in.

10.1.1 The HTTP engine

The first thing you'll need is a way to understand HTTP and to accept requests and respond in kind. You needn't write any code to do this, because this is a solved problem. You can use one of several open source projects that have HTTP servers built in, hitching a ride on top. In this section, we'll pick the Grizzly project, which came out of the Glassfish project at Sun Microsystems (now Oracle). The reason for this choice is that it's based on the Java NIO (new IO) framework, which makes it possible to write Java servers that can scale up to support thousands of users.

The first thing we'll do is create a way to attach Clojure functions to the `Grizzly-Adapter` interface, which will allow you to handle HTTP requests. We'll then write some code to register our functions on web addresses, to allow you to create HTTP services that you can then advertise. Lastly, we'll make it easier for your functions to work with the request parameters.

GRIZZLY

The Grizzly NIO and Web Framework project was created to create Java server-based applications that could scale to thousands of concurrent users. It does this via the use of the NIO libraries that are now part of the Java software development kit (SDK). In order to write truly scalable applications, you can use the asynchronous adapters provided by Grizzly, but for the purposes of this example, we'll use the simpler synchronous option.

The specific Java components of interest to you are an interface called `Grizzly-Adapter` and a class called `GrizzlyWebServer`. You'll use Clojure's `proxy` macro to wrap your functions in an implementation of the `GrizzlyAdapter` interface. You'll then use an instance of `GrizzlyWebServer` to listen for requests and service them. The code is shown in the following listing. We'll discuss a few salient points about the code in the following paragraphs.

Listing 10.1 A simple way to expose Clojure functions as web services

```clojure
(ns chapter13-webbing
  (:import (com.sun.grizzly.http.embed GrizzlyWebServer)
           (com.sun.grizzly.tcp.http11 GrizzlyAdapter)))

(defn route-for [request handlers]
  (let [registered (keys handlers)
        uri-string (.getRequestURI request)]
    (first (filter #(.startsWith uri-string %) registered))))

(defn handler-for [request handlers]
  (handlers (route-for request handlers)))

(defn singularize-values [a-map]
  (let [kv (fn [[k v]] {k (aget v 0)})]
    (reduce merge {} (map kv a-map))))

(defn params-map-from [request]
  (singularize-values (into {} (.getParameterMap request))))

(defn without-query-string? [request]
  (empty? (params-map-from request)))

(defn parsed-params-from-uri [request handlers]
  (let [uri-string (.getRequestURI request)
        requested-route (route-for request handlers)
        params-string (.substring uri-string (count requested-route))]
    (rest (.split params-string "/"))))

(defn params-for [request handlers]
  (if (without-query-string? request)
    (parsed-params-from-uri request handlers)
    (params-map-from request)))
```
◁— **Convert HTTP params into Clojure map**

```clojure
(defn response-from [handler params without-query-string]
  (try
   (if without-query-string
     (apply handler params)
     (handler params))
   (catch Exception e
     (println "Error! Unable to process, reason -")
     (.printStackTrace e))))
```
◁— **Ensure exception doesn't kill the server**

```clojure
(defn service-http-request [handler-functions request response]
  (let [requested-route (route-for request handler-functions)
        handler (handler-for request handler-functions)]
    (if handler
      (let [params (params-for request handler-functions)
            without-query-string (without-query-string? request)
            response-text (response-from handler params
                                         without-query-string)]
        (.println (.getWriter response) response-text))
      (println "Unable to respond to" (.getRequestURI request)))))
```
◁— **Call handler only if found**

```clojure
(defn grizzly-adapter-for [handler-functions-as-route-map]
  (proxy [GrizzlyAdapter] []
```
◁— **Implement Java interface using proxy**

```
    (service [req res]
      (service-http-request handler-functions-as-route-map req res))))
```

```
(defn boot-web-server [handler-functions-map port]          Use stable Grizzly
  (let [gws (GrizzlyWebServer. port)]                   ⊲   web server library
    (.addGrizzlyAdapter gws (grizzly-adapter-for
                                    handler-functions-map))
    (println "Started http-gateway on port" port)
    (.start gws)))
```

Let's now see how you might use your newly written system. First, you'll define a couple of functions that you'll want to expose as HTTP services. After ensuring that the library is included in your program through an appropriate call to :use or :require, the following code sets up the server:

```
(defn greet [name]
  (str "hello, " name))

(defn judge-credentials [{u "username" p "password"}]
  (str u "/" p " is a good combo!"))

(def routes {
  "/test/greet" greet
  "/judge/creds" judge-credentials
})

(boot-web-server routes 10000)
```

Testing that your system works as advertised is easy using a tool like curl (or by typing the URLs in a web browser):

```
~ > curl "http://localhost:10000/test/greet/amit"
hello, amit
```

```
~ > curl "http://localhost:10000/judge/creds?username=amit&password=override"
amit/override is a good combo!
```

This isn't too shabby, because you managed to implement this functionality in less than 60 lines of code. You can handle URLs with explicit query strings or parse out parameters from the URL itself, in a RESTful fashion. Your routing logic is also straightforward: if the requested URL begins with a registered path in your routes map, the associated function is selected as the handler.

We can now look into adding a couple of more small features to your little web service framework—specifically, handling JSONP calls and reading/writing cookies.

ADDING JSONP SUPPORT

With the advent of AJAX and rich internet applications, many websites need to get data from backend HTTP servers and process/display them in the browser. Often, JSON is used as the lightweight format to send data to and from the browser. Because of security restrictions, web pages can't talk to any backend server other than the one they originated from. The JSONP pattern is popular because it allows you to get around this restriction.

As usual, it uses JSON for communication, but the request is made with an extra parameter (conventionally called jsonp). The backend server wraps the return JSON with extra padding (hence the *p* in jsonp) that translates to a JavaScript function call inside the browser. If a request is made as follows:

http://localhost:10000/some/json/request?arg1=a&arg2=b&jsonp=xxx

If the traditional response is {w: 12, z: 20}, it's wrapped in the padding mentioned earlier to become xxx({w: 12, z: 20}).

Let's add this feature to our web service framework. We'll look for a parameter called jsonp, and if it's found, we'll wrap our return to conform to the JSONP format shown previously. We'll edit our program from listing 10.1 and make the modifications shown in the following listing.

Listing 10.2 Extending our basic web service framework to support JSONP callbacks

```
(ns chapter13-webbing-jsonp
  (:import (com.sun.grizzly.http.embed GrizzlyWebServer)
           (com.sun.grizzly.tcp.http11 GrizzlyAdapter))
  (:require (org.danlarkin [json :as json])))

(defn route-for [request handlers]
  (let [registered (keys handlers)
        uri-string (.getRequestURI request)]
    (first (filter #(.startsWith uri-string %) registered))))

(defn handler-for [request handlers]
  (handlers (route-for request handlers)))

(defn singularize-values [a-map]
  (let [kv (fn [[k v]] {k (aget v 0)})]
    (reduce merge {} (map kv a-map))))

(defn params-map-from [request]
  (singularize-values (into {} (.getParameterMap request))))

(defn only-jsonp-param? [params-map]            ◁── Check for jsonp
  (and (= 1 (count params-map))                     parameter in request
       (= "jsonp" (first (keys params-map)))))

(defn without-query-string? [request]
  (let [params-map (params-map-from request)]
    (or (empty? params-map)
        (only-jsonp-param? params-map))))

(defn parsed-params-from-uri [request handlers]
  (let [uri-string (.getRequestURI request)
        requested-route (route-for request handlers)
        params-string (.substring uri-string (count requested-route))]
    (rest (.split params-string "/"))))

(defn params-for [request handlers]
  (if (without-query-string? request)
    (parsed-params-from-uri request handlers)
    (params-map-from request)))
```

```
(defn jsonp-callback [request]
  ((params-map-from request) "jsonp"))
```

Get name of JavaScript
jsonp callback function

```
(defn prepare-response [response-text request]
  (if (jsonp-callback request)
    (str (jsonp-callback request)
         "(" (json/encode-to-str response-text) ")")
    response-text))
```

Create output
as JavaScript
function call

```
(defn response-from [handler params without-query-string]
  (try
   (if without-query-string
     (apply handler params)
     (handler params))
   (catch Exception e
     (println "Error! Unable to process, reason -")
     (println (.printStackTrace e)))))
```

```
(defn service-http-request [handler-functions request response]
  (let [requested-route (route-for request handler-functions)
        handler (handler-for request handler-functions)]
    (if handler
      (let [params (params-for request handler-functions)
            without-query-string (without-query-string? request)
            response-text (response-from handler params
                                         without-query-string)]
        (println "Responding to" requested-route "with params:" params)
        (.println (.getWriter response)
                  (prepare-response response-text request)))
      (println "Unable to respond to" (.getRequestURI request)))))
```

```
(defn grizzly-adapter-for [handler-functions-as-route-map]
  (proxy [GrizzlyAdapter] []
    (service [req res]
      (service-http-request handler-functions-as-route-map req res))))
```

```
(defn boot-web-server [handler-functions-map port]
  (let [gws (GrizzlyWebServer. port)]
    (.addGrizzlyAdapter gws (grizzly-adapter-for handler-functions-map))
    (println "Started http-gateway on port" port)
    (.start gws)))
```

To test this, change your registered functions to ones that might return reasonable
JSON output. Here's the new routes map:

```
(defn js-judge-credentials [{u "username" p "password"}]
  {:judgement (str u "/" p " is a good combo!")})

(defn js-greet [name]
  {:greeting (str "hello, " name)})

(def routes {
  "/test/js_greet" js-greet
  "/judge/js_creds" js-judge-credentials
})

(boot-web-server routes 10000)
```

Let's test these two new services with curl at the shell:

```
~/labs/projectx(master) > curl
    "http://localhost:10000/test/js_greet/amit?&jsonp=asd"
asd({"greeting":"hello, amit"})
```

Let's also test the other one:

```
~/labs/projectx(master) > curl
    "http://localhost:10000/judge/js_creds?username=amit
                                &password=override&jsonp=asd"
asd({"judgement":"amit/override is a good combo!"})
```

So there you are; with about a dozen lines of code, you've added support for JSONP requests. Clients of our services don't have to do anything special; if they include a parameter named `jsonp`, it will work as desired. Further, from a developer standpoint, no extra code needs to be written, only a regular Clojure data structure can be returned (such as a map), which will be converted to JSON format using the JSON library we included (`clojure-json` by Dan Larkin, available from GitHub.com).

Our next adventure will be to support reading and writing of cookies.

SUPPORTING COOKIES

In this section, we'll implement a simple solution to read and write cookies. We won't support a comprehensive solution that offers fine-grain control but just enough to make it useful and to demonstrate the approach. The code is in the following listing, but instead of replicating the entire program again, it shows only the additional functions needed and the modified `service-http-request` function.

Listing 10.3 Changes needed to support simple cookie handling

```
(declare *the-request* *the-response*)

(defn cookie-hash []                                    Call .getCookies on special
  (let [cookies (.getCookies *the-request*)             variable *the-request*
        kv (fn [c] {(.getName c) (.getValue c)})]
    (apply merge (map kv cookies))))                    Convert set of cookies
                                                        into Clojure map
(defn add-cookie [name value]
  (let [c (Cookie. name value)]
    (.setPath c "/")
    (.addCookie *the-response* c)))                     Call .addCookie on
                                                        special variable
(defn read-cookie [name]
  (let [cookies (cookie-hash)]
    (if-not (empty? cookies)
      (cookies name))))                                 Bind *the-request*
                                                        and special variables
(defn service-http-request [handler-functions request response]
  (binding [*the-request* request *the-response* response]
    (let [requested-route (route-for request handler-functions)
          handler (handler-for request handler-functions)]
      (if handler
        (let [params (params-for request handler-functions)
              without-query-string (without-query-string? request)
              response-text (response-from handler params
                                           without-query-string)]
```

```
        (println "Responding to" requested-route "with params:" params)
        (.println (.getWriter response)
                  (prepare-response response-text request)))
        (println "Unable to respond to" (.getRequestURI request))))))
```

You can test it by making slight modifications to the functions you've used as HTTP services so far:

```
(defn greet [name]
  (add-cookie "greeting" "hello")
  (str "hello, " name))

(defn judge-credentials [{u "username" p "password"}]
  (println "greeting cookie:" (read-cookie "greeting"))
  (str u "/" p " is a good combo!"))

(def routes {
  "/test/greet" greet
  "/judge/creds" judge-credentials
})

(boot-web-server routes 10000)
```

Here, the greet function sets a cookie, and the judge-credentials function reads it. This is easiest to test from a web browser. Let's go ahead and test with the following two URLs:

http://localhost:10000/test/greet/amit

and

http://localhost:10000/judge/creds?username=amit&password=override

Because you're printing your inner workings to the console, you can see the following output when you test with these URLs:

```
Responding to /test/greet with params: (amit)
```

This is followed by

```
greeting cookie: hello
Responding to /judge/creds with params: {password override, username amit}
```

That's it. As mentioned earlier, it doesn't allow you much control over the way cookies are set, for instance, but works well enough to be useful. One example of its inflexibility is that it always sets a cookie to the / path. It's now easy enough to build on top of this code and extend the functionality. It's also easy to expose more functionality from the underlying HTTP library, for instance, to do set headers.

Notice also the use of binding to set *the-request* and *the-response* to the appropriate request and response objects and that this happens for each request handled. It avoids passing these two around to all your helper functions. There aren't many such functions right now, but as you add functionality, this might prove convenient.

This section showed that converting your Clojure functions into HTTP services is a rather trivial task. The code didn't do everything you might need in a production-ready system, but it gives you the general idea. The next section will explore a few open source options from the Clojure ecosystem.

10.2 Ring

Ring is a project by Mark McGranaghan that aims to abstract away HTTP so that basic web services can be written in Clojure. It isn't, and doesn't aim to be, a full-featured web application framework. Instead, out-of-the-box, it implements only basic HTTP support, and by featuring a concise, modular design, it allows extensibility through the use of what are called middleware plug-ins.

The Ring project is hosted on GitHub, at http://github.com/mmcgrana/ring. There are instructions on the site about downloading and installing it onto your computer. For the remainder of this section, we'll assume that you have it running (you have Ring's src and lib directories on your JVM classpath).

10.2.1 Understanding Ring

Using Ring is easy. Here's a simple example, a function that says hello:

```
(ns chapter13-ring
  (:use ring.adapter.jetty))

(defn hello [req]
  {:body "hello world!"})

(run-jetty hello {:port 8080})
```

This particular example uses the Jetty adapter, but you can use others, and you can write your own. To understand what an adapter is, it will be useful to get a quick high-level overview of the design of the Ring framework.

THE COMPOSITION OF RING

The diagram in figure 10.1 shows how a request travels through the various pieces of Ring. We'll discuss each component next; this figure also shows where the name Ring comes from.

A Ring request is an abstraction over an HTTP request that makes it easy to deal with from Clojure. It's a map with well-defined keys such as `:request-method`, `:query-string`, and `:headers`.

A handler is a Clojure function that processes a Ring request and produces a Ring response. In our simple example earlier, the function `hello` was the handler.

A Ring response is a Clojure map with well-defined keys such as `:status`, `:body`, and `:headers`.

None of these components care about the HTTP protocol itself, because their job is to abstract those details away from the programmer. Someone in the picture ultimately needs to speak HTTP, and that's where adapters fit in. Their job is to implement HTTP, invoke the handler with Ring requests, and take their return values as Ring responses. Adapters can use other HTTP server libraries to do their work, and as you saw in our example, Ring comes bundled with support for Jetty.

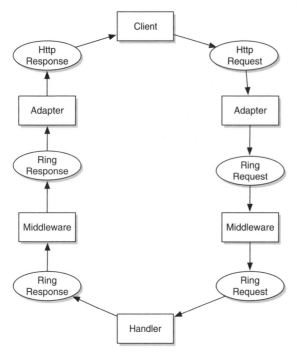

Figure 10.1   How an HTTP request flows through the Ring framework

10.2.2 *Middleware*

So far, we haven't talked about middleware. Ring middleware is a plug-in system that allows the programmer to mix and match modules that augment the functionality of the handlers in some specified way. To understand them, let's look at the following example that doesn't use any middleware. It's a function that echoes a query parameter named echo:

```
(defn echo [req]
  (let [qs (:query-string req)
        params (apply hash-map (.split qs "="))]
    {:body (params "echo")}))

(run-jetty echo {:port 8080})
```

If you go to the localhost URL http://localhost:8080/?echo=hellooooo, you'll see that our echo function behaves as desired. As shown here, we had to manually parse the query string, and you can imagine this would become rather tedious if we had to keep doing it. Even if we abstracted it away as a function, we'd still have to call it in our handlers. It would be nice if we could enhance Ring in some way so that it would hand us the parsed parameters.

Ring middleware modules play exactly this role. They're functions that can be used to enhance the functionality of Ring's handlers. Let's rewrite our previous echo example using the params middleware that comes with Ring:

```
(ns chapter13-ring
  (:use ring.adapter.jetty)
  (:use ring.middleware.params))

(defn new-echo [req]
  (println "new")
  {:body (get-in req [:query-params "echo"])})

(def echo-app (wrap-params new-echo))

(run-jetty echo-app {:port 8080})
```

Notice how you were able to use a new key on the Ring request map called :query-params. This is because echo-app is a function that's returned from wrap-params, a middleware that processes the incoming request, grabs the parameters (either from a query string or from a form body), and makes it all available via new keys in the regular Ring request. By the time our handler is called, the query parameters are all parsed and ready to use.

AVAILABLE MIDDLEWARE

The advantage of this design is that Ring itself can stay lean and focused. It provides a framework that hides the details of the HTTP protocol, so that developers can work with Clojure abstractions such as maps. Other web frameworks can be built on top of Ring that are more full featured; for example, they might provide routing, templating, and the like.

Ring comes with several middleware modules; here are a few of them:

- params—You saw this one in our previous example. It parses the parameters from incoming requests and makes them available in the Ring request map.
- cookies—This works in a similar fashion to params, but makes cookies available in the Ring request map.
- file—This one allows a specified directory to be checked for a static file (and returned if found). If the file doesn't exist, it passes the request onto the handler being wrapped.
- file-info—This adds content-type and content-length headers to a file being served, if those headers aren't already present.
- reload—This allows the source code to be reloaded for each request. This makes it easier to develop because the server doesn't have to be restarted for each change.
- stacktrace—This middleware is also helpful during development because it catches any exceptions thrown during handler processing and displays them in a debugging-friendly manner.

Writing Ring middleware is easy, and you can write specific functions for your application as needed. The general API of a middleware function is

```
(function-name handler options)
```

where handler is the handler being augmented, and options is a map that can contain configuration switches for the middleware.

That's pretty much all there is to Ring. If you need to create your own web service framework, building it on top of Ring is a great option. It does a lot of the basic work for you, and you can use the many available middleware functions to get more features for free. Our next stop will be Compojure, a full-featured web application framework that you can use if you need to create a dynamic website in Clojure.

10.3   Compojure

Compojure is presently the leading web-application framework for writing web apps in idiomatic Clojure. It was inspired by the Ruby web-application framework called Sinatra, but it's growing into a comprehensive solution in its own right. In this section, we'll look at how to use it to create a simple web service.

10.3.1   Using Compojure

Compojure is built on top of Ring, so parts of it will be familiar. The request and response maps, in particular, use the same keys you saw in the previous section. Compojure uses a few middleware components, for instance, `params` and `cookies` that enhance the requests.

Compojure is hosted on GitHub, at http://github.com/weavejester/compojure, and can be downloaded via Git in the usual manner. We're going to deal with version 0.3. Once you have it downloaded, run the following commands to build the application:

```
ant deps
ant
```

The first command downloads the dependencies as a compressed archive and unpacks them into a folder called deps. The second kicks off the Ant build, which leaves a freshly created copy of compojure.jar in the root folder.

For the rest of this section, you'll need all the JAR files in the deps folder on your JVM classpath, along with compojure.jar itself. Let's now start with a simple introductory example of creating a web application using Compojure.

HELLO, WORLD!

Here's what a simple Compojure web application looks like:

```
(ns chapter13-compojure
  (:use compojure))

(defroutes hello
  (GET "/"
    (html [:h1 "Hello, world!"]))
  (ANY "*"
      [404 "Page Not Found!"])))

(run-server {:port 8080}
  "/*" (servlet hello))
```

Try testing this using curl:

```
~ > curl "http://localhost:8080/"
<h1>Hello, world!</h1>
```

```
~ > curl "http://localhost:8080/some/other/route"
```
Page Not Found!

Compojure provides forms such as GET, PUT, POST, and so on to handle HTTP requests made with corresponding HTTP methods. Now that you have the basics working, let's look at some more features of the framework.

HANDLING PARAMETERS

Let's add some interactivity. We'll reimplement the echo service we wrote in the last section by adding the following to the hello routes we've defined so far:

```
(GET "/echo"
  (html [:h2 "You said " (params :message)]))
```

Here it is in action:

```
~ > curl "http://localhost:8080/echo?message=hiya"
```
<h2>You said hiya</h2>

Notice that you were able to access the parameters via a map named params. It's initialized to a map containing parameters from the query string and any form parameters that were passed along with the request. Compojure has other such special names for convenient access to things like cookies and session.

10.3.2 *Under the hood*

There are several interesting things to learn from the Compojure codebase. Let's start by looking at the implementation of defroutes. It's defined in the source file called routes.clj in the http directory. As you can imagine, it's a macro. The definition is quite short; here it is without the doc string:

```
(defmacro defroutes [name doc? & routes]
  (let [[name & routes] (apply-doc name doc? routes)]
    `(def ~name
       (routes ~@routes))))
```

Here, apply-doc is a helper function that applies the doc? doc string to each defined route. It isn't important for our discussion here. The routes function takes the route specifications passed in (an example being the s-expression starting with the symbol GET) and combines them all into a new Ring handler function (Compojure is built on top of Ring). Here's the definition of routes:

```
(defn routes [& handlers]
  (-> (apply routes* handlers)
    with-request-params
    with-cookies))
```

The creation of the handler is delegated to the routes* function (not shown here). Observe that the handler is being wrapped with two Ring middleware plug-ins: with-request-params and with-cookies. The thread-first macro (you saw it in chapter 2) makes the code easy to read; it's clear that the handler is being enhanced to add parameter processing and cookie handling.

MAGIC VARIABLES

Let's now skip over the code a bit and examine the `with-request-bindings` macro. Here it is:

```
(defmacro with-request-bindings [request & body]
  `(let [~'request ~request
         ~'params  (:params  ~'request)
         ~'cookies (:cookies ~'request)
         ~'session (:session ~'request)
         ~'flash   (:flash   ~'request)]
     ~@body))
```

Force variable capture to allow special names in let

This macro wraps the body specified in the call to `defroutes`. To be specific, let's look at our parameter-handling example from earlier:

```
(GET "/echo"
  (html [:h2 "You said " (params :message)]))
```

The second line of code is the body. If you wondered how `params` are made available to the body, because they need to be unique for each request, the `with-request-bindings` macro explains it. It sets up local bindings for five things: `request`, `params`, `cookies`, `session`, and `flash`. Notice how the macro uses the unquote followed by the quote reader macro to force using a name like `params`. Without it, Clojure would expand it into a namespace-qualified name, forcing the usage of the `auto-gensym` reader macro, the hash (#).

This trick of forcing variable capture lets the programmer allow users of a function to use special names in their code. Because they're local bindings and not dynamically bound vars, they won't be available in a function you call from within the handler. You'd have to pass whatever you need to any function you call. This is a limitation, and this behavior will probably change in the future. Incidentally, GET, POST, and so on are also macros, which ultimately expand into code that calls `with-request-bindings`.

THE COMPOJURE RESPONSE

Let's now examine another part of Compojure—the part that takes the return value of the request handler to construct the final Ring response. The function in question is called `create-response`, and it's defined in `response.clj`. Here it is:

```
(defn create-response
  "Create a new response map from an update object, x."
  [request x]
  (update-response request default-response x))
```

Here `default-response` is defined as

```
{:status 200, :headers {}}
```

What's interesting about `create-response` is that it calls `update-response`, which is a multimethod. Here's how it's defined:

```
(defmulti update-response (fn [request reponse update]
                            (class update)))
```

The dispatch function is the class of the update parameter, which is the parameter named x in create-response. This x is the return value of a handler (as defined in defroutes). This allows the individual handler to return several different kinds of objects (such as URL or File), knowing that update-response will handle them correctly. Here are a couple of examples of the methods defined for update-response:

```
(defmethod update-response URL
  [request response url]
  (assoc response :body (.openStream url)))

(defmethod update-response Integer
  [request response status]
  (assoc response :status status))
```

This is convenient, because, for instance, it allows you to return a number such as 404 or 200, and it will be set as the value for the status header in response.

COMPOJURE SESSIONS

Let's now look briefly at the mechanism of Compojure's session handling. The middleware that does this is with-session, and it's defined in the file session.clj. Using it is simple; you wrap your handler with with-session, similar to any other middleware. Here's an example of setting a value inside the session:

```
(GET "/set-session"
    [(session-assoc :some-key (params :name)) "Set!"])
```

As shown in this example, the function to set a value in the session is session-assoc. Although calling this function is quite easy, the syntax for using it inside a handler is a bit awkward. Specifically, notice that we had to wrap the call to session-assoc and the final response string inside a vector. This is because Compojure attempts to avoid state changes until the end by delaying such mutation. It manages this because functions like session-assoc don't do anything immediately but return functions that, when called later, do effect the requested mutation. Here's how session-assoc is implemented:

```
(defn alter-session [func & args]
  (fn [request]
    (set-session
      (apply func (request :session) args))))

(defn session-assoc [& keyvals]
  (apply alter-session assoc keyvals))
```

This approach of delaying computation by returning functions that will be evaluated later can be useful. You can use the technique to collect actions that can all be performed at a later point (or not), in any order desired. Hence, it's a useful technique to control evaluation of code.

In the case of Compojure, the current implementation makes using sessions rather unintuitive, and the implementation will probably change as the framework evolves. Meanwhile, here's an example of how you might get a value out from the session:

```
(GET "/get-session"
    (html [:h3 "some-key is" (session :some-key)]))
```

There's a lot more to learn from the Compojure codebase; you can get many ideas for other applications from reading it. It's in active development, so a lot may have changed by the time you read this.

Our last stop in this chapter will be to explore a couple of ways to generate HTML in Clojure web apps.

10.4 Generating HTML

So far, you've seen several approaches to handling HTTP requests. As you saw, this is easy to do, with minimum ceremony (or even none—we didn't have to create any XML files or other configuration files). We neatly wrote Clojure functions that were mapped to the incoming request, and any parameters either came in via named function arguments or as a convenient Clojure map.

The code you've seen here can be useful in creating HTTP APIs that allow Clojure programs to communicate and interact with other programs (written either in Clojure or any other language). The one thing we haven't discussed so far is how to create UIs that can be used by end users. What you need to make this happen is a way to generate HTML, which can then be used to render your web UI. The previous sections used an interesting set of forms to generate HTML. Here's an example from the section on Compojure:

```
(GET "/echo"
  (html [:h2 "You said " (params :message)]))
```

The `html` function is part of the `clj-html` library, which is the library we'll examine in the following section.

10.4.1 clj-html

`clj-html` is an open source templating library written by Mark McGranaghan, who also wrote the Ring library we looked at in section 10.2. It's hosted on GitHub at http://github.com/mmcgrana/clj-html. In order to use it, you have to do the usual: download it and put it on your classpath.

The central piece of the library is the `html` macro (or the associated `defhtml` macro, which can be used to create named templates). The following section shows a few examples of using it.

USAGE

Using it is quite simple, as you saw in our examples so far. The simplest case accepts a literal and returns it as a string:

```
user=> (html "something")
"something"
user=> (html 1)
"1"
```

If you pass a vector as the argument to `html`, then the first element must be a keyword. This keyword will be the tag name that will be generated by the evaluation. Here's an example:

```
user=> (html [:div])
"<div />"
```

The tag-name keyword supports the CSS-style syntax for specifying its ID and CLASS attributes. Here are a few examples that demonstrate this usage:

```
user=> (html [:div#topseller])
"<div id=\"topseller\" />"

user=> (html [:div.product])
"<div class=\"product\" />"

user=> (html [:div#topseller.product])
"<div id=\"topseller\" class=\"product\" />"
```

The second element of the vector can be a map containing any other attributes that should be part of the expansion, for instance:

```
user=> (html [:div#topseller.product {:runa_type "product"}])
"<div runa_type=\"product\" id=\"topseller\" class=\"product\" />"
```

This map containing extra attributes is optional and can be omitted. The second argument can be the content of the tag expansion, as shown here:

```
user=> (html [:div#topseller.product "Baby T-Shirt"])
"<div id=\"topseller\" class=\"product\">Baby T-Shirt</div>"
```

You can specify both, as shown in the following:

```
user=> (html [:div#topseller.product
               {:runa_type "product"}
               "Baby T-Shirt"])
"<div runa_type=\"product\"
      id=\"topseller\"
      class=\"product\">Baby T-Shirt</div>"
```

Nesting the vectors, as in this example, can generate nested tags:

```
user=> (html [:span [:div "Baby T-Shirts!"]])
"<span><div>Baby T-Shirts!</div></span>"
```

Also, the tag content can evaluate to a single string, such as those you've seen so far, or a sequence of strings. Here's an example:

```
user=> (html [:ul {:type "romans"}
           (for [char '("iii" "iv" "v")]
             [:li char])])
"<ul type=\"romans\"><li>iii</li><li>iv</li><li>v</li></ul>"
```

HTMLI

Finally, one point about html must be noted: it expects the optional map containing the extra tag attributes to be a literal map. This is because html uses this optional map in its macro expansion. If you need to pass in an expression that evaluates to a map instead, you need to use htmli. An example follows:

```
(defn optional-tags [description price]
      {:desc description :price price})
```

```
user=> (htmli [:div.product (optional-tags "Top seller!" 19.95)
         "Baby T-Shirt"])
"<div class=\"product\" desc=\"Top seller!\"
         price=\"19.95\">Baby T-Shirt</div>"
```

Let's now look at a couple of implementation points about clj-html.

10.4.2 *Under the hood*

Because Clojure's macro system uses Clojure as its implementation language, and Clojure code is represented in Clojure's own data structures, Clojure macros can themselves be large Clojure programs. The implementation of the html macro is a much larger than any you've seen so far in this book.

Overall, the design of clj-html is divided into two portions. The first part is the html macro that we've used extensively in this section. The other is htmli, which is the interpreter underneath that handles dynamic content.

The html macro does as much as it can during expansion. For example, let's look at the following call, which we'll examine via the macroexpand-1 function:

```
(macroexpand-1 '(html [:div#topseller.product
                        {:runa_type "product"} "Baby T-Shirt"]))
(clojure.core/let [html-builder (java.lang.StringBuilder.)]
  (.append html-builder "<div runa_type=\"product\"
     id=\"topseller\" class=\"product\">Baby T-Shirt</div>")
  (.toString html-builder))
```

Here, most of the work is done during expansion. When the function is called, the StringBuilder appends the fully constructed string and then returns it using the call to toString.

This kind of computation done during macro expansion time can result in efficient functions that don't have to do as much during runtime. Let's look at another example, this time with nested vectors:

```
(macroexpand-1 '(html [:span [:div "Baby T-Shirts!"]]))
(clojure.core/let [html-builder (java.lang.StringBuilder.)]
  (.append html-builder "<span><div>Baby T-Shirts!</div></span>")
  (.toString html-builder))
```

As you can see in the expansion, the html macro does almost all the work in the expansion in this case as well. Macros ought to do as much as possible during expansion time, and this is determined by the forms that are passed to them. It's important to remember that macros operate on the symbolic expressions themselves and not the values of the expressions (the values are available only at runtime).

Here's a case where it's far more difficult to programmatically determine that all information is available at macro expansion time. To handle this case, the macro expands to a let binding (if-let, to be specific), so that part of the computation happens at runtime:

```
macroexpand-1 '(html [:ul {:type "romans"}
                 (for [char '("iii" "iv" "v")]
                   [:li char])]))
```

```
(clojure.core/let [html-builder (java.lang.StringBuilder.)]
  (.append html-builder "<ul type=\"romans\">")
  (clojure.core/if-let [content__2207__auto__ (for [char
                          (quote ("iii" "iv" "v"))] [:li char])]
    (.append html-builder (clj-html.core/flatten-content
                                  content__2207__auto__)))
  (.append html-builder "</ul>") (.toString html-builder))
```

Obviously, if you try this in your own REPL, you'll see a different name than
content__2207__auto__ because it's generated internally using gensym. Notice how
the list comprehension using for is inserted into an if-let block, and it occurs during runtime.

Finally, it's worth pointing out that flatten-content, a helper function, ultimately
calls htmli, which we used directly in the previous section. As mentioned earlier, html
operates on symbolic forms. This is why instead of passing a literal map containing
extra attributes, if you pass an expression that returns the map instead, the html
macro can't handle it. It's why htmli is exposed to clients as an available API.

10.5 Summary

This chapter was about interfacing with the outside world over HTTP. In the first section, we wrote some simple code that allowed you to expose your Clojure functions as
web services with little fuss. We didn't handle things like authentication, or any form
of security, and so on, but we did get the basics up and running quickly. We leveraged
an existing Java library (from the Grizzly project) that allowed us to use an existing
HTTP server. We also used a simple Clojure map to hold routes and Clojure functions
that are mapped to those routes. This implementation is easy in a functional language
like Clojure.

We then looked at Ring, an open source Clojure framework that makes writing
other HTTP frameworks easy. It does so by abstracting away most of the common
things that most HTTP application frameworks need to deal with: requests and responses.
It also provides a pluggable API for adding functionality to the HTTP request handlers,
such as for handling parameters, cookies, and the like. We then also looked at another
open source web application development framework called Compojure, which happens to be built on top of Ring.

Our final stop in this chapter was a look at clj-html, an HTML generation library
for Clojure. It has an innovative design using macros to enable efficient generation
of HTML.

Writing web services in Clojure can be easy and painless. The fact that Clojure is
functional helps in designing and testing web applications (as it does in applications
of all kinds). We can test handler functions completely in isolation using simple Clojure
maps as inputs and outputs and then expect things to work when plugged into, say,
Ring or Compojure. As you saw, Java interop also helps considerably, because it enables
us to use battle-tested Java web servers to run our web applications. Clojure makes this
easy as well.

Scaling through messaging

11

This chapter covers

- A quick overview of messaging
- Using RabbitMQ with Clojure
- A framework for distributed parallel programming

Messaging has a place in system architecture for many reasons. The most obvious is to communicate between different applications or various subsystems of a single application. Using a messaging system in this manner allows for loose coupling and flexibility: message structure can be changed as needed, or messages can be transformed in the middle as required. There are many design patterns for integrating applications using messaging in this manner.

Another use of messaging is to introduce asynchronous processing into applications. Instead of handling complete requests in a synchronous manner, a message can be dropped onto a queue of some kind, which would eventually be picked up and processed later. This makes the application respond quicker to the end user, while allowing for higher request throughput.

Messaging systems can also be used as a basis for more general-purpose distributed computing. Various computing elements can communicate with each other

over a messaging system in order to coordinate parts of the work they need to participate in. This can lead to elegantly scalable architecture that can grow by adding more
and more machines to the grid as the load grows.

In this chapter, we'll learn how to incorporate asynchronous processing into
Clojure systems. We'll first talk about the landscape of messaging systems in general,
and then we'll write code to work with the RabbitMQ messaging server. We'll work our
way up to writing a Clojure abstraction that will help you write parallel-processing programs. This framework will allow your Clojure systems to span not only multiple cores
but multiple CPUs as well. You could then use the ideas in this chapter as the basis for
a large, horizontally scalable cluster of computational elements.

11.1 Messaging systems

Messaging systems come in a variety of flavors. Ultimately, they behave as middleware
systems that deliver messages from one program to another. They can usually work in
several configurations ranging from point-to-point to hub and spoke and so on.
They're a great way to achieve several things at once: decoupling between components of the application, asynchronous processing, and scalability. In this section, we'll
quickly look at the landscape of available messaging systems and at a few open source
ones in particular.

11.1.1 JMS, STOMP, AMQP

JMS stands for Java Messaging Service and is a typical message-oriented middleware
API that was introduced as part of Java Enterprise Edition. The specification is a standard (known as JSR 914) and allows programs written using the Enterprise Edition of
the JDK to communicate with each other by sending and receiving messages.

STOMP stands for Simple Text-Oriented Messaging Protocol. It's a standard that
allows clients to be written in many programming languages, and indeed, the website
lists support for most popular languages in use today. STOMP prides itself on simplicity—it uses plain text, making it easy to implement new clients.

AMQP, which stands for Advanced Message Queuing Protocol, came out of a con-
sortium of financial companies that wanted an ultra-fast messaging system that was
also extensible and yet simple. Further, they wanted to be able to fully program the
semantics of the server via the clients at runtime. Like the other protocols, several
servers support AMQP. In this chapter, we'll be using RabbitMQ, a super-fast, open
source implementation of an AMQP messaging system. Before we get started, let's take
a quick look at some of the major players in the landscape.

11.1.2 ActiveMQ, RabbitMQ, ZeroMQ

In this section, we'll glance at a few options for picking a middleware system. Most
messaging systems do the same basic job of allowing messages to be sent and received
by various producers and consumers (other programs). They might vary in the specific protocol supported for the message passing or the characteristics offered when

such messages are sent (store and forward, wait for acknowledgement, and so on). Even here, most messaging servers have adapters that can be used to bridge to other protocols and may have configuration options (or external plug-ins) that allow pretty much any server to behave in almost any desired way.

Still, other characteristics differentiate the various servers available on the market today. One important characteristic is performance and reliability, with others being how actively the project is being developed and whether there's a vibrant user community supporting it. In the following section, we'll look quickly at ActiveMQ, RabbitMQ, and ZeroMQ, all of which are open source.

ACTIVEMQ

This offering is from the Apache Software Group and is considered a stable option when it comes to messaging systems. It supports OpenWire and STOMP and has clients in most languages.

Many consider ActiveMQ somewhat heavy, and the Java technology stack that it's built upon is older than some of the other messaging systems available.

RABBITMQ

RabbitMQ is a messaging server that supports AMQP. It's built using Erlang and Erlang/OTP, which are extremely reliable and scalable platforms that Ericson developed for its telephone switching software. It's fast, promising latency in the single-digit milliseconds range.

RabbitMQ is a general messaging server that can be configured to behave in a variety of ways in order to implement the various patterns in the messaging world: point-to-point, publish-subscribe, store and forward, and so on. You'll learn more about AMQP in the following section, and you'll be using RabbitMQ later on when you build messaging support into your Clojure programs.

ZEROMQ

ZeroMQ is another open source messaging option, built to be extremely fast. It isn't quite a messaging system as much as it is a low-level socket-oriented library that can be used to build messaging systems. It advertises latencies as low as 13 microseconds and the flexibility to implement different configurations of components: publish/subscribe, request/reply, streaming, and so on. This option is also a viable one when you're deciding on a messaging system for your application.

11.2 *Clojure and RabbitMQ*

In this section, we're going to write code to perform some basic communication tasks between Clojure processes over RabbitMQ. RabbitMQ uses AMQP, so having a basic understanding of it is useful in getting the most out of the system. Our first stop, then, will be to go over the essential elements of AMQP. We'll then use the Java client library to send messages, following which we'll write code to receive messages over RabbitMQ. Our last stop in this section will be to create a convenient abstraction over incoming RabbitMQ messages for our programs that need to process messages asynchronously.

> **Which version to use?**
> The RabbitMQ project is evolving at a steady pace. The project was recently acquired by SpringSource, which is part of VMware. The version of RabbitMQ we're going to be working with is 1.8.1, and you can download it from http://www.rabbitmq.com.

11.2.1 AMQP basics

Let's look at a few key RabbitMQ concepts that are reflective of the AMQP underneath. Specifically, it's important to understand the basic concepts of the message queue, the exchange, and the routing key. Once you understand these topics, it becomes quite easy to reason about message flow and how message passing should be configured in a given application. As you'll see later on in this chapter, we'll set up point-to-point messaging, fan-out or multicast messaging, and so on by using these concepts in various ways.

THE MESSAGE QUEUE

A message queue stores messages in memory or on a disk and delivers them to various consumers (usually) in the order they come in. Message queues can be created to have a varying set of properties: private or shared, durable or not, permanent or temporary. The right combination of these properties can result in the various commonly used patterns of message queues: store and forward, temporary reply queue, and the classic publish-subscribe model. Message queues can be named, so that clients can refer to specific ones they created during the routing configuration process.

THE EXCHANGE

The exchange is a sort of clearinghouse that accepts the incoming messages and then, based on certain specified criteria, routes them to specific message queues. The criteria are called bindings and are specified by the clients themselves.

AMQP defines a few exchange types, such as direct and fan-out exchanges. By naming both exchanges and queues, clients can configure them to work with each other.

THE ROUTING KEY

An exchange can route messages to message queues based on a variety of properties of the message. The most common way depends on a single property called the routing key. You can think of it as a virtual address that the exchange can use to route messages to consumers.

Now that you've seen the fundamental constructs of AMQP, you're ready to start playing with a server that implements it. In the next section, you'll do so using RabbitMQ.

11.2.2 Connecting to RabbitMQ

In this section, you'll see how to connect to a RabbitMQ server. Further, you'll abstract away the idea of a connection to the server by creating a var to hold an open connection. First, here's the code to create a new connection:

```
(ns chapter14-rabbitmq
  (:import (com.rabbitmq.client ConnectionFactory QueueingConsumer)))
```

```
(defn new-connection [host username password]
 (.newConnection
   (doto (ConnectionFactory.)
     (.setVirtualHost "/")
     (.setUsername username)
     (.setPassword password)
     (.setHost host)))))
```

Now for the var: let's create one called *rabbit-connection* as follows:

```
(def *rabbit-connection*)
```

You can bind this to a call to new-connection whenever you need to do something with RabbitMQ. To make this easy, create a macro to do it for you. You might call such a macro with-rabbit, and it might look like this:

```
(defmacro with-rabbit [[mq-host mq-username mq-password] & exprs]
  `(with-open [connection# (new-connection ~mq-host
                                          ~mq-username ~mq-password)]
     (binding [*rabbit-connection* connection#]
       (do ~@exprs))))
```

Note that by using the with-open macro, the connection held in *rabbit-connection* is closed when you exit the with-rabbit form. Now, with the with-rabbit macro in hand, you're ready to write more code to do things like sending messages to the server and receiving messages from it. The next couple of sections show how to do this.

11.2.3   *Sending messages over RabbitMQ*

As described in the section on AMQP, the physical manifestation of a connection to RabbitMQ is the channel. Therefore, the first thing you'll need to do is get hold of a channel. Here's the function that sends a message to the server, given a specific routing key:

```
(defn send-message [routing-key message-object]
  (with-open [channel (.createChannel *rabbit-connection*)]
    (.basicPublish channel "" routing-key nil
                                (.getBytes (str message-object)))))
```

In order to send a message through the RabbitMQ server, you can now call your newly defined send-message function, like so:

```
(with-rabbit ["localhost" "guest" "guest"]
      (send-message "chapter14-test" "chapter 14 test method"))
```

Your next task is to receive such messages from the server. You'll do this in the next section.

11.2.4   *Receiving messages from RabbitMQ*

We're going to take a stab at writing a simple function that accepts a queue name (which in this case must match the routing key used to send messages out) and listens for messages addressed to it. Once you have this function, you'll put the send-message function to use in testing your capability to receive messages by printing it to the console. Once you have this working, you'll see how to write a longer-lived process that handles a stream of incoming messages.

Let's begin with a function to fetch a message from the RabbitMQ server. Consider this implementation where `next-message-from` is your final, outward-facing function:

```
(defn delivery-from [channel consumer]     ⟵— Acknowledge after processing in production
  (let [delivery (.nextDelivery consumer)]
    (.basicAck channel (.. delivery getEnvelope getDeliveryTag) false)
    (String. (.getBody delivery))))

(defn consumer-for [channel queue-name
  (let [consumer (QueueingConsumer. channel)]          ⟍  Declare queue
    (.queueDeclare channel queue-name)             ⟵—  even if exists
    (.basicConsume channel queue-name consumer)
    consumer))
                                                          ⟍  Declare vars
(defn next-message-from [queue-name]                         without root
  (with-open [channel (.createChannel *rabbit-connection*)]   ⟵—  binding
    (let [consumer (consumer-for channel queue-name)]
      (delivery-from channel consumer))))
```

Here, you create an instance of `QueueingConsumer`, which is a class provided by the RabbitMQ client library. You then declare the queue name that was passed in, and then you attach the `consumer` to the queue name via the call to `basicConsume`. The `delivery-from` function calls the `nextDelivery` method on the `consumer` object, which is a blocking call. The execution proceeds only when the consumer receives something from RabbitMQ, and then all you do is acknowledge the message by calling `basicAck` and return the contents of the message as a string.

You can confirm that this works by starting up the following program as a Clojure script:

```
(ns chapter14-receiver
  (:use chapter14-rabbitmq))

(println "Waiting...")
(with-rabbit ["localhost" "guest" "guest"]
  (println (next-message-from "chapter14-test")))
```

This will cause the program to block (because `next-message-from` blocks until a message is delivered to it from the RabbitMQ server), and in order to unblock it and see that it prints the message to the console, you have to send it a message. The following program, which can also be run as a script, does that:

```
(ns chapter14-sender
  (:use chapter14-rabbitmq))

(println "Sending...")
(with-rabbit ["localhost" "guest" "guest"]
  (send-message "chapter14-test" "chapter 14 test method"))
(println "done!")
```

If you run these two programs in two separate shells (run the receiver first!), you'll see your two functions, `send-message` and `next-message-from`, in action. Figure 11.1 shows the basics of this communication at a conceptual level.

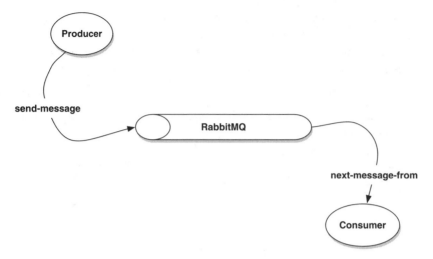

Figure 11.1 After establishing a connection with RabbitMQ via a call to `new-connection`, a message producer can send messages with a routing key using the `send-message` function. Similarly, a message consumer can accept messages sent with a particular routing key via a call to `next-message-from`.

Now that you have basic communication going over RabbitMQ, let's write a version of the receiver program that can handle multiple messages from the queue.

RECEIVING MULTIPLE MESSAGES

We wrote a program that received a single message from the RabbitMQ server, printed it, and exited. In typical projects involving messaging, a program like that might be useful for quick tests and debugging. Most production services that are meant to handle messages asynchronously, wait for such messages in a loop. These long-running processes can form the basis of a compute cluster that can offload work from services that must respond to the end user quickly. Let's rewrite the earlier program to do its job in a loop:

```
(ns chapter14-receiver-multiple1
  (:use chapter14-rabbitmq))

(defn print-multiple-messages []
  (loop [message (next-message-from "chapter14-test")]
    (println "Message: " message)
    (recur (next-message-from "chapter14-test"))))

(with-rabbit ["localhost" "guest" "guest"]
  (println "Waiting for messages...")
  (print-multiple-messages))
```

You can test this program in a similar fashion to our previous example. When you run this program, it will block, waiting for the first message to be delivered to it by the server. You can use the message sender program from the previous section to send it a few messages. The output might look like this:

```
Waiting for messages...
Message:   chapter 14 test method
Message:   chapter 14 test method
Message:   chapter 14 test method
```

Press Ctrl-C to exit this program.

This program works but isn't particularly reusable, because it mixes up the work of printing the incoming messages with the logic of waiting for messages in a loop. Let's fix that problem by creating a higher-order function that will accept a function that knows how to handle a single message. Here's the code:

```
(ns chapter14-receiver-multiple2
  (:use chapter14-rabbitmq))

(defn handle-multiple-messages [handler]
  (loop [message (next-message-from "chapter14-test")]
    (handler message)
    (recur (next-message-from "chapter14-test"))))

(with-rabbit ["localhost" "guest" "guest"]
  (println "Waiting for messages...")
  (handle-multiple-messages println))
```

With this higher-order function called `handle-multiple-messages`, you can now do whatever you please with an incoming stream of messages. Indeed, if you run several instances of this program in parallel and send messages using the same sender program, you'll see RabbitMQ deliver messages to each in a roughly round-robin manner. As we said earlier, this can form the basis of a compute cluster of some kind.

One thing to note, is that our `next-message-from` function is quite inefficient. It creates a new channel each time it's called. If you know you're going to process multiple messages, you should improve this inadequacy. Indeed, while you're at it, you should recognize the fact that an incoming sequence of messages can be modeled as a Clojure sequence. You'll do this in the next section.

MESSAGE-SEQ: A SEQUENCE ABSTRACTION FOR RECEIVING MESSAGES

We looked briefly at lazy sequences in chapter 2. If you consider the job of `next-message-from`, you can think of it producing an element of a lazy sequence each time a message is delivered to it. Using that as a foundation, you can create a new abstraction to deal with messages from the RabbitMQ server. Let's call it `message-seq`, and it might be implemented as follows:

```
(defn- lazy-message-seq [channel consumer]          ←┐ Creating infinite sequence
  (lazy-seq                                           │ of messages off RabbitMQ
    (let [message (delivery-from channel consumer)]
      (cons message (lazy-message-seq channel consumer)))))

(defn message-seq [queue-name]
  (let [channel (.createChannel *rabbit-connection*)
        consumer (consumer-for channel queue-name)]
    (lazy-message-seq channel consumer)))
```

Note that `lazy-message-seq` is a helper function that's private to this namespace. The `message-seq` function is the one that you'll use in your programs. Let's write a version of `handle-multiple-messages` that does this:

```
(ns chapter14-receiver-multiple3
  (:use chapter14-rabbitmq))

(defn handle-multiple-messages [handler]
  (doseq [message (message-seq "chapter14-test")]
    (handler message)))

(with-rabbit ["localhost" "guest" "guest"]
  (println "Waiting for messages...")
  (handle-multiple-messages println))
```

There are several advantages of this approach. The first is that it's more efficient because you're no longer creating a new channel (and consumer) for each message. Perhaps more important, because `message-seq` is a real Clojure sequence, you can use the full Clojure sequence library to work with it. The previous example shows the usage of `doseq`, but you can now map across it, `filter` out only those messages that you like, and so on. Here's an example where we only print the messages in pairs:

```
(ns chapter14-receiver-multiple4
  (:use chapter14-rabbitmq clojure.contrib.str-utils))

(defn print-two-messages [messages]
  (println (str-join "::" messages)))

(with-rabbit ["localhost" "guest" "guest"]
  (println "Waiting for messages...")
  (let [message-pairs (partition 2 (message-seq "chapter14-test"))]
    (doseq [message-pair message-pairs]
      (print-two-messages message-pair))))
```

You can test this by sending it messages using your sender program, as usual. The output of a test run might look like the following:

```
Waiting for messages...
chapter 14 test method::chapter 14 test method
chapter 14 test method::chapter 14 test method
```

The fact that you can now bring the full power of the Clojure sequence library to bear on a series of messages from RabbitMQ allows you to write idiomatic Clojure programs. No function outside the scope of `message-seq` needs to know that the sequence is lazily being fed by a RabbitMQ server somewhere on the network.

In this section, you've seen how to send messages to the RabbitMQ server and also how to process messages that are delivered to your programs by a RabbitMQ server. You can use the code we wrote as a basis for real applications to handle events in an asynchronous manner. Further, you can expand your event-processing capacity by starting up more instances of your handlers. This idea forms the basis of using messaging to scale up applications. In the next section, we'll create another abstraction on top of what we've done so far, in order to make it easy to write programs that make use of such architecture.

11.3   *Distributed parallel programming*

In the previous section, we created an abstraction called `message-seq` that was a series of messages from RabbitMQ represented as a Clojure sequence. Having this abstraction allows you to write handler programs easily. Further, by starting up more and more message-handler processes, you have the ability to horizontally scale up your application.

If you have such a cluster of processes waiting to process incoming messages, you could write programs that dispatch messages off to this cluster, in effect resulting in computations executing in parallel on different machines. It would be like using multiple threads to do something faster, only you'd no longer be limited to a single JVM. You could spread your processing load across a cloud of machines, one that could be scaled by adding more CPUs.

In this section, we'll write a small, distributed computing framework, which can make it easy to write programs that use such a cloud of message-processing services.

11.3.1 *Creating remote workers*

In the previous section, we wrote a higher-order function called `handle-multiple-messages` that accepted another function that did the work of processing the message. Now, we'll create an abstraction that makes it easy to create functions that must run on such a message-processing cluster. Next, we'll make it easy to send off requests to such a cluster of workers.

We're going to indulge in some wishful program design now. Imagine that you had a construct called `defworker` whose job it is to create a function that instead of running locally caused its computation to occur on a remote server (on one of our message-processing services). You could use it to define a worker in the following manner:

```
(ns chapter14-worker-example
  (:use chapter14-rabbitmq chapter14-worker))

(defworker long-computation-one [x y]
  (Thread/sleep 3000)
  (* x y))

(defworker long-computation-two [a b c]
  (Thread/sleep 2000)
  (+ a b c))

(defworker expensive-audit-log [z]
  (println "expensive audit log:" z)
  (Thread/sleep 4000))
```

These are contrived examples, but they serve to illustrate the idea of both expensive computations and the use of the imaginary `defworker` macro. Note also that although the `chapter14-worker` namespace doesn't exist yet, we'll build it over the next few pages.

For now, the question that presents itself is what should the `defworker` macro do?

DEFWORKER: DEFINE NEW WORKERS

We first need to think about realizing our imaginary `defworker`. Let's start with a skeleton:

```
(defmacro defworker [service-name args & exprs]
  ;;some magic here
)
```

Now we have something concrete to talk about. The `defworker` macro will need to do two things. The first is to create a function named `service-name` that can be used like regular functions. This function, when called, won't perform the work embodied in `exprs` but will send a message to RabbitMQ requesting the associated computation to be performed on a receiver process.

The other job of `defworker` is to somehow store the computation embodied in `exprs`, which can then be run on the message-processing side when someone requests it. So, the magic from the skeleton becomes the following:

```
(defmacro defworker [service-name args & exprs]
  ;; STEP 1 - store exprs somewhere for later
  ;; STEP 2 - return function that when called, sends message to RabbitMQ
)
```

Before we do anything further, we must ask ourselves a couple more questions. First, after dropping a request over RabbitMQ, is there a way to be notified when the computation completes? We can use messaging for that as well, by waiting for a reply message after dropping the request message. When the message handler picks up the request message and processes it, it will then send the result of the computation in the reply message.

The second issue to consider is the return value of the function created by `defworker`. Imagine that someone calls `long-computation-one`, which we defined earlier. What should the return value be? Clearly, the response will only be available at some point in the future, after the message that was dropped off is processed and the reply comes back. In the meantime, the callers of `long-computation-one` need something to hang onto. What should it be? We'll revisit this question shortly.

In the meantime, let's take another shot at defining `defworker`, based on our discussion so far. First, we'll represent computations (as embodied by `exprs`) as anonymous functions and store them inside a hash map. We'll put this map inside a ref, which we'll declare as follows:

```
(def workers (ref {}))
```

We'll index the map by the names of the workers being defined, so that the message-processing side can then find the appropriate function when it's requested. Our `defworker` now looks like this:

```
(defmacro defworker [service-name args & exprs]
  `(let [worker-name# (keyword '~service-name)]
     (dosync
       (alter workers assoc worker-name# (fn ~args (do ~@exprs)))
       (def ~service-name (worker-runner worker-name# ~args)))))
```

The first part does what we just talked about; it grabs the name of the worker being defined (as a keyword) and then stores the exprs (bound inside an anonymous function of the same signature) inside the workers map indexed by the worker name.

The last line creates a var by the value of service-name, which, when called, runs the function returned by an as-yet-undefined worker-runner. So we've employed imaginary design again and postponed worrying about the implementation details of worker-runner. Unfortunately, we can't ignore it for very long, and it's the focus of the next section.

WORKER-RUNNER: HANDLING WORK REQUESTS

The job of worker-runner is to create a function that, when called, runs the worker. This involves sending a message to the waiting processes, requesting that the named worker be executed given particular arguments. It also must establish a listener for the incoming response message. Finally, it should immediately return to the caller, with some sort of an object that represents this whole asynchronous process of dispatching the request and waiting for the response.

This returned object, in a sense, is a proxy of the computation being requested and performed on a different machine. This proxy object should have the ability to be queried. It should be able to answer questions like whether the computation completed, what the return value is, whether there was an error, what the error was, and so on.

Let's start with the first requirement, that of returning a function. Consider the following code:

```
(defmacro worker-runner [worker-name worker-args]
  `(fn ~worker-args
     (on-swarm ~worker-name ~worker-args)))
```

A function is returned, which when called calls another function named on-swarm, passing along the worker-name and the worker-args. The job of on-swarm, as discussed, is to send the request for the computation over RabbitMQ, establish a listener for the answer, and immediately return a proxy object that can be queried for the status of the remote computation. It's called on-swarm because the computation runs on a remote swarm of processes. Here's the implementation:

```
(defn on-swarm [worker-service args]                              ◁─┐
  (let [worker-data (ref worker-init-value)
        worker-transport (dispatch-work worker-service args worker-data)]
    (fn [accessor]
      (condp = accessor
        :complete? (not (= worker-init-value @worker-data))        Return a
        :value (attribute-from-response @worker-data :value)    closure in the
        :status (@worker-data :status)                          let-over-lambda
        :disconnect (disconnect-worker worker-transport)))))        approach
```

Here, you establish a locally created ref named worker-data that's initialized to worker-init-value. You need to define that as follows:

```
(def worker-init-value :__worker_init__)
```

This ref will store the result of the computation once the response comes back from the swarm. The work of making the request and waiting for the response is done by dispatch-work, which we'll examine next. Let's look at what is returned by this function. It returns another function, which implements the same sort of command-word pattern you've seen before.

Here, the return value can be queried using command words like :complete?, :value, :status, and :disconnect. You'll see examples of this in action before the end of this chapter. Our immediate attention, though, is on the dispatch-work function.

DISPATCH-WORK: SENDING WORK REQUESTS

The job of dispatch-work is to send a message via RabbitMQ to a waiting cluster of processes, requesting a particular computation. What we have available is the name of the computation and the arguments that the computation should be run with. We'll send all that information over as part of the request message, encoded as strings. Finally, dispatch-work also needs to set up a listener that will wait for the response. When it comes back it will set the returned value of the worker-data ref we talked about. Consider the following implementation:

```
(defn dispatch-work [worker-name args worker-ref]
  (let [return-q-name (str (UUID/randomUUID))
        request-object (request-envelope worker-name args return-q-name)
        worker-transport (update-on-response worker-ref return-q-name)]
    (send-message WORKER-QUEUE request-object)
    worker-transport))
```

dispatch-work does its job by first constructing a request message that contains the name of the service being requested, the arguments it will need, and the name of the RabbitMQ queue that the response should be sent on. Then, it calls update-on-response, a function that sets up the listener that waits for the response message from the swarm. Finally, dispatch-worker sends the request to the RabbitMQ server by calling our previously defined send-message function. WORKER-QUEUE is a well-defined name, and it's also the one your message-handling processes will be listening on. You might define it as follows:

```
(def WORKER-QUEUE "chapter14_workers_job_queue")
```

Further, you'd construct the request-object itself via a call to the request-envelope function that returns a simple Clojure map. Here's the code:

```
(defn request-envelope
  ([worker-name args]
    {:worker-name worker-name :worker-args args})
  ([worker-name args return-q-name]
    (assoc (request-envelope worker-name args) :return-q return-q-name)))
```

There are two signatures, one that accepts no return-queue-name, to allow you to call workers without waiting for a response. You'll see this in action when we add a fire-and-forget feature to our little framework. All that remains is the inner workings of update-on-response. Let's discuss that in terms of the following implementation:

```
(defn update-on-response [worker-ref return-q-name]
  (let [channel (.createChannel *rabbit-connection*)
        consumer (consumer-for channel return-q-name)
        on-response (fn [response-message]
                        (dosync
                          (ref-set worker-ref (read-string response-message))
                          (.queueDelete channel return-q-name)
                          (.close channel)))]
    (future (on-response (delivery-from channel consumer)))
    [channel return-q-name]))
```

All of this code should look familiar. A channel and consumer objects are created, which will be used for interfacing with RabbitMQ. on-response is a local function that behaves as a callback. It accepts a message and sets it as the value of the worker-ref, after which it closes the channel.

More specifically, before setting it as the value of the ref, it calls read-string on the message. Remember that the message is a string; read-string unleashes the Clojure reader on that string, resulting in the string of text being converted into a Clojure data structure. This is the job of the reader; it converts a character stream (typically source code) into Clojure data structures: lists, vectors, maps, and so on. You use the same process here as a simple form of deserialization.

Finally, on-response is called with the blocking function delivery-from. Because it's called inside a future, it runs at a later point, on a different thread. update-on-response is free to continue execution, which it does by returning a vector containing the channel and the return queue name.

We're finished with the complex part of our little distributed computing framework. The next piece will be to create a program that can handle the requests that you'll send over the RabbitMQ server.

11.3.2 Servicing worker requests

In this section, we'll write code for the other side of the picture. In the previous section, we implemented creating new workers. We wrote code that can send off requests to a waiting swarm of processes and set up a listener that waits for a response. In this section, we'll write code to do two things: the first is to handle these requests as they come off RabbitMQ, and the second is to make life easier for the code that uses your workers. Let's begin by implementing the request-handling part of the system.

HANDLING WORKER REQUESTS

Request handling code is a loop that waits for messages and processing them as they come in. Let's begin by writing a function that can process a single message:

```
(defn handle-request-message [req-str]
  (try
    (let [req (read-string req-str)
          worker-name (req :worker-name)
          worker-args (req :worker-args)
          return-q (req :return-q)
          worker-handler (@workers worker-name)]
```

```
    (if (not (nil? worker-handler))
      (do
        (println "Processing:" worker-name "with args:" worker-args)
        (process-request worker-handler worker-args return-q)))))
  (catch Exception e)))
```

First, it catches all exceptions and ignores them, to ensure that an error parsing the request message doesn't crash your entire request-processing service. In a real-world scenario, you'd probably log it or do something else useful with it.

The main thing `handle-request-message` does is to parse the request, find out if a worker is defined with the requested name (from the `workers` ref created in the previous section), and call `process-request`, if it exists. Our focus of inquiry must shift to `process-request`, which is what the next section is about.

PROCESS-REQUEST

If you recall, the worker handler is an anonymous function stored in the `workers` ref. You have the arguments needed to execute it, which `handle-request-message`, helpfully parsed for you. In order to get the result of the computation, you need to call the function. The return value can then be sent back to the caller using the queue name that came along with the request itself. You'll do this on a separate thread, so that you don't block the main one. The code for all this is quite simple:

```
(defn process-request [worker-handler worker-args return-q]
  (future
    (with-rabbit ["localhost" "guest" "guest"]
      (let [response-envelope (response-for worker-handler worker-args)]
        (if return-q (send-message return-q response-envelope))))))
```

The call to `future` takes care of the threading. The reason you check for `return-q` is that by not specifying it, you can implement the fire-and-forget feature we mentioned earlier. Lastly, in order to handle any exceptions that might be thrown while running the handler itself, you need one more level of indirection. That indirection is the function `response-for`, which is also the last part of this puzzle. The `response-for` function not only evaluates the handler with the provided `worker-args` but also constructs a suitable message that you can send back to the waiting caller on the other side. Here is `response-for`:

```
(defn response-for [worker-handler worker-args]
  (try
    (let [value (apply worker-handler worker-args)]
      {:value value :status :success})
    (catch Exception e
      {:status :error})))
```

The `try-catch` block, as explained, ensures that you don't crash if the handler crashes. You do create different response messages in the case of successful (and failed) handler executions.

We're almost finished. The final thing on this end of the picture is to set up the loop.

THE REQUEST-HANDLER LOOP

We wrote `message-seq` in the previous section, which gave you the ability to apply Clojure functions to a series of RabbitMQ messages. You're going to use that, along with `handle-request-message`, to implement your message-handling loop. Here it is:

```
(defn start-handler-process []
  (doseq [request-message (message-seq WORKER-QUEUE)]
    (handle-request-message request-message)))
```

`WORKER-QUEUE` is the same well-defined name with which the worker requests were being dispatched. So that's it; you can now start message-handling processes via something similar to the following:

```
(with-rabbit ["localhost" "guest" "guest"]
  (println "Starting worker handler...")
  (start-handler-process))
```

You can add load-sharing capacity to your swarm of message-handling processes by starting more such processes, typically on more machines. This is a simple way to scale up the computation engine for a large application. Before moving on, let's revisit the idea of the fire-and-forget feature we've mentioned a couple of times.

FIRE AND FORGET

Most use cases of remote computations will eventually use the return value. Sometimes, it may be useful to run a remote computation only for a side effect. An example might be the previously defined `expensive-audit-log`, which doesn't return anything useful and is clearly useful only for a side effect. Here, we repeat it for your convenience:

```
(defworker expensive-audit-log [z]
  (println "expensive audit log:" z)
  (Thread/sleep 4000))
```

What we'd like is a way to call this, without having to wait for a response. The way we implemented our request-handling loop gives you a natural way to add this feature. Consider the following function:

```
(defn run-worker-without-return [worker-name-keyword args]
  (let [request-object (request-envelope worker-name-keyword args)]
    (send-message WORKER-QUEUE request-object)))
```

This sends a message to your waiting cluster of worker process handlers that contains only the worker name being requested and the arguments. Your handler loop won't return anything unless a return queue name is also provided, so you're finished. Calling it might look like this:

```
(run-worker-without-return :expensive-audit-log 100)
```

This works, but it's a somewhat awkward way of calling a worker. Caller convenience is another perfect excuse for a macro, so that calls might look like this instead:

```
(fire-and-forget expensive-audit-log 100)
```

The implementation of this macro, as you can imagine, is trivial:

```
(defmacro fire-and-forget [worker-symbol & args]
  `(run-worker-without-return (keyword '~worker-symbol) '~args))
```

So, we're now at a point where we can put together all the code we wrote so far. You'll do that in the following section, and you'll also run a few tests to see if everything works as expected.

11.3.3 *Putting it all together*

Listing 11.1 shows all the code we've written so far, in one place. It also includes some you haven't seen yet, but we'll discuss that portion when you test our little remote worker framework. This listing contains all the code related to defining and using workers. We'll put the code that handles worker requests in another listing.

Listing 11.1   A simple messaging-based distributed-computing framework for Clojure

```
(ns chapter14-worker
  (:use chapter14-rabbitmq)
  (:import (java.util UUID)))

(def workers (ref {}))
(def worker-init-value :__worker_init__)
(def WORKER-QUEUE "chapter14_workers_job_queue")

(defn all-complete? [swarm-requests]
  (every? #(% :complete?) swarm-requests))

(defn disconnect-worker [[channel q-name]]
  (.queueDelete channel q-name))

(defn disconnect-all [swarm-requests]
  (doseq [req swarm-requests]
    (req :disconnect)))

(defn wait-until-completion [swarm-requests allowed-time]
  (loop [all-complete (all-complete? swarm-requests)
         elapsed-time 0]
    (if (> elapsed-time allowed-time)
      (do
        (disconnect-all swarm-requests)
        (throw (RuntimeException.
            (str "Remote worker timeout exceeded "
                    allowed-time " milliseconds!"))))
      (if (not all-complete)
        (do
          (Thread/sleep 100)
          (recur (all-complete? swarm-requests) (+ elapsed-time 100)))))))

(defmacro from-swarm [swarm-requests & expr]                    ◁─┐ from-swarm for
  `(do                                                              │ caller convenience
     (wait-until-completion ~swarm-requests 5000)
     ~@expr))

(defn update-on-response [worker-ref return-q-name]
  (let [channel (.createChannel *rabbit-connection*)
```

```
          consumer (consumer-for channel return-q-name)
          on-response (fn [response-message]
                          (dosync
                           (ref-set worker-ref (read-string response-message))
                           (.queueDelete channel return-q-name)
                           (.close channel)))]
      (future (on-response (delivery-from channel consumer)))   ◁─┐ Avoids blocking
      [channel return-q-name]))                                    │ main thread

(defn request-envelope                                        ◁─┐ Request map for
  ([worker-name args]                                            │ either worker type
    {:worker-name worker-name :worker-args args})
  ([worker-name args return-q-name]
    (assoc (request-envelope worker-name args) :return-q return-q-name)))

(defn dispatch-work [worker-name args worker-ref]
  (let [return-q-name (str (UUID/randomUUID))
        request-object (request-envelope worker-name args return-q-name)
        worker-transport (update-on-response worker-ref return-q-name)]
    (send-message WORKER-QUEUE request-object)
    worker-transport))                  ◁─ Vector of channel object and return-queue name

(defn attribute-from-response [worker-internal-data attrib-name]
  (if (= worker-init-value worker-internal-data)
    (throw (RuntimeException. "Worker not complete!")))
  (if (not (= :success (keyword (worker-internal-data :status))))
    (throw (RuntimeException. "Worker has errors!")))
  (worker-internal-data attrib-name))

(defn on-swarm [worker-name args]
  (let [worker-data (ref worker-init-value)
        worker-transport (dispatch-work worker-name args worker-data)]
    (fn [accessor]
      (condp = accessor
        :complete? (not (= worker-init-value @worker-data))
        :value (attribute-from-response @worker-data :value)
        :status (@worker-data :status)
        :disconnect (disconnect-worker worker-transport)))))

(defmacro worker-runner [worker-name should-return worker-args]
  `(fn ~worker-args
     (if ~should-return
       (on-swarm ~worker-name ~worker-args))))

(defmacro defworker [service-name args & exprs]
  `(let [worker-name# (keyword '~service-name)]
     (dosync
      (alter workers assoc worker-name# (fn ~args (do ~@exprs))))
     (def ~service-name (worker-runner worker-name# true ~args))))

(defn run-worker-without-return [worker-name-keyword args]
  (let [request-object (request-envelope worker-name-keyword args)]
    (send-message WORKER-QUEUE request-object)))

(defmacro fire-and-forget [worker-symbol args]
  `(run-worker-without-return (keyword '~worker-symbol) ~args))
```

There are a few things in listing 11.1 that you've not seen yet. Specifically, the from-swarm macro and related functions such as wait-until-completion are new and we'll discuss these shortly. Meanwhile, consider the following listing, which should be familiar, because we discussed all of it in the previous section.

Listing 11.2   Distributed worker processes to handle worker requests

```
(ns chapter14-worker-process
    (:use chapter14-rabbitmq chapter14-worker))

  (defn response-for [worker-handler worker-args]
    (try
      (let [value (apply worker-handler worker-args)]       ◁─┐ Send exceptions
        {:value value :status :success})                       │ back as error
      (catch Exception e                                    ◁─┘ status
        {:status :error})))

(defn process-request [worker-handler worker-args return-q]  ┐ Perform worker
  (future                                                  ◁─┤ requests in a
    (with-rabbit ["localhost" "guest" "guest"]                │ future
      (let [response-envelope (response-for worker-handler worker-args)]
        (if return-q (send-message return-q response-envelope))))))

(defn handle-request-message [req-str]
  (try
    (let [req (read-string req-str)
          worker-name (req :worker-name)
          worker-args (req :worker-args)
          return-q (req :return-q)
          worker-handler (@workers worker-name)]            ┐ Ignore requests for
      (if (not (nil? worker-handler))                     ◁─┘ unknown workers
        (do
          (println "Processing:" worker-name "with args:" worker-args)
          (process-request worker-handler worker-args return-q))))
    (catch Exception e)))                                   ◁─┐ Catch exceptions so
(defn start-handler-process []                                │ server isn't killed
  (println "Serving up" (count @workers) "workers.")
  (doseq [request-message (message-seq WORKER-QUEUE)]
    (handle-request-message request-message)))
```

Figure 11.2 shows the various pieces of our remote worker framework.

Now that we've put all our code together, let's test our little framework.

TESTING THE FRAMEWORK

In order to test our little parallel, distributed-computing framework, you first have to run the code shown in listing 11.2 as a process. It will leave the program waiting in a loop for incoming RabbitMQ messages, each representing a request for a particular worker. The code might look like this:

```
(ns chapter14-worker-example
  (:use chapter14-worker-example))

(with-rabbit ["localhost" "guest" "guest"]
  (println "Starting worker handler...")
  (start-handler-process))
```

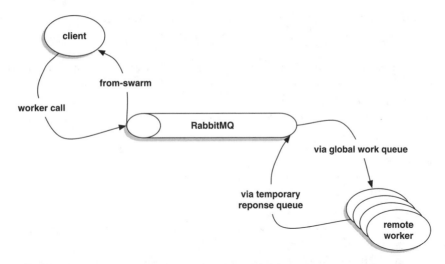

Figure 11.2   Message flow between a client and a bank of remote worker processes. A client makes a request by calling a worker function, which sends a message over RabbitMQ via a global, well-known work queue. One of several workers picks it up and services the request. When finished, it sends the response back via a temporary routing key that was specified by the calling client.

Remember that you saw the chapter14-worker-example namespace before, when we defined the long-computation-one and long-computation-two functions. Now that you have that going, you can write a little program that exercises the workers, like the one shown here:

```
(ns chapter14-worker-usage
  (:use chapter14-rabbitmq chapter14-worker chapter14-worker-example))

(println "Dispatching...")
(with-rabbit ["localhost" "guest" "guest"]
  (let [one (long-computation-one 10 20)
        two (long-computation-two 3 5 7)]
    (fire-and-forget expensive-audit-log 100)
    (from-swarm [one two]
                (println "one:" (one :value))
                (println "two:" (two :value)))))
(println "done!")
```

When this program runs, you'll see output such as the following:

```
Dispatching...
one: 200
two: 15
done!
```

And as this example runs, your worker service will show output something like the following:

```
Starting worker handler...
Serving up 3 workers.
```

```
Processing: :long-computation-one with args: [10 20]
Processing: :long-computation-two with args: [3 5 7]
Processing: :expensive-audit-log with args: 100
```

If you were to start multiple worker services, the requests would be distributed across them in a roughly round-robin manner. This way, you could add capacity as the load increases.

This example used something we haven't discussed before: the call to `from-swarm`. Let's talk about that now.

FROM-SWARM

This framework is asynchronous in nature. When a worker is called, a request is fired off over RabbitMQ to a waiting bank of processes. The worker call itself is nonblocking. The object returned by the call to the worker is a proxy to the computation that happens on the cluster of processes, and the return value of the computation eventually gets set inside it.

This allows the main program to make calls to as many workers as it needs, without blocking. At some point, the program will need the return values in order to proceed, and this is where `from-swarm` comes in. It introduces the idea of a sync point, where execution will block until the responses for the specified worker (proxy) objects come in from the remote swarm. The implementation is shown in listing 11.1, but the macro itself is reproduced here for convenience:

```
(defmacro from-swarm [swarm-requests & expr]
  `(do
    (wait-until-completion ~swarm-requests 5000)
    ~@expr))
```

This way, you can wait for any number of worker proxies. The macro calls a helper function `wait-until-completion`, which loops with a short sleep until either all the results return from the swarm or the timer expires. The timeout is hard-coded to five seconds, but that can easily be parameterized. This is a simple spin-lock, and while this works for the most part, there are better ways to implement this sync point. This is left as an exercise to the reader.

Note that in order for the worker service to handle requests for a particular worker, it needs to know about it. This is done in our example by including it in the namespace via the `:use` option. For instance, our earlier example had the following namespace declaration:

```
(ns chapter14-worker-process
  (:use chapter14-rabbitmq chapter14-worker))
```

The reason it needs to include the `chapter14-worker` namespace is so that the definitions for the workers (`long-computation-one` and `long-computation-two`) get loaded up. Then, when the message-processing loop starts, it has the workers' computations available in the `workers` ref.

This covers the essential parts of our little framework. You can now easily define new functions that will run on remote machines by calling `defworker` (instead of `defn`).

Calling these functions is no different than calling regular functions, and the only difference in semantics is in using the return values. Because the object returned by a worker function is a proxy to the computation being performed on a remote machine, it needs to be handled slightly differently than if the computation was performed locally. The from-swarm construct provides a convenient sync point for this purpose.

Our last extension to this framework will be to add a feature to broadcast a call to all worker processes. This multicast can be used for a variety of purposes, such as a health-check service where return values imply that the server is up and running, or as a way to live update code on all workers (something we'll do in chapter 15), and so on.

11.3.4 *Multicasting messages to multiple receivers*

In order to implement this feature, we're going to take advantage of RabbitMQ's exchange types. The fan-out exchange delivers messages to all message queues that have set up bindings for the exchange. We'll begin by extending our send-message function to handle exchange types. This will allow you to use a fan-out exchange to deliver a message to all subscribers. We'll later build on this function to create a mechanism to call a worker on all worker services. Next, we'll extend next-message-from to handle listening to such broadcasts. Finally, we'll modify message-seq to enable it to subscribe to a sequence of broadcast messages.

For clarity, we'll create a new version of the chapter14-rabbitmq namespace that we saw in the previous section. We'll call it chapter14-rabbitmq-multicast, and the complete implementation is shown later on in listing 11.3. The next few sections explain individual functions of interest that build up the code.

SEND-MESSAGE

Our first order of business will be to modify send-message in order to handle sending messages to a specific named exchange. This will allow you to later set up listeners on the same named exchange but bound using a fan-out exchange type. Let's first define a couple of useful vars to represent the default exchange and the (default) direct exchange type.

```
(def DEFAULT-EXCHANGE-NAME "default-ex")
(def DEFAULT-EXCHANGE-TYPE "direct")
(def FANOUT-EXCHANGE-TYPE "fanout")
```

Here's the new definition:

```
(defn send-message
  ([routing-key message-object]
    (send-message DEFAULT-EXCHANGE-NAME routing-key message-object))
  ([exchange-name routing-key message-object]
    (with-open [channel (.createChannel *rabbit-connection*)]
      (.exchangeDeclare channel exchange-name "fanout")
      (.queueDeclare channel routing-key)
      (.basicPublish channel exchange-name routing-key nil
                              (.getBytes (str message-object))))))
```

After this change, our old code from the previous section should continue to work, because it uses the first variant of send-message that accepts the two parameters routing-key and message-object. The second version accepts an extra parameter, exchange-name, which allows you to now use send-message to target messages at a specific exchange. We've now changed what we needed to on the send side of the equation. Our next stop will be to make a few modifications to the other side of the picture, beginning with next-message-from and moving on to message-seq.

NEXT-MESSAGE-FROM

Our modifications to the next-message-from function will reflect the same notion we introduced in send-message, that of addressing a specific exchange in a specific manner. First, let's create a helper function called random-queue-name that will help you create listeners for specific routing keys, where the name of the queue itself isn't important. Here's the function:

```
(defn random-queue-name []
  (str (java.util.UUID/randomUUID)))
```

Our original next-message-from function accepted only a queue name, and it internally depended on the fact that RabbitMQ defaults to using the default (direct exchange) and a routing key that's the same as the queue name. In this new implementation, we'll allow all the parameters to be specified. Here's the code:

```
(defn next-message-from                   Define this function with three signatures  ❶
  ([queue-name]
    (next-message-from DEFAULT-EXCHANGE-NAME DEFAULT-EXCHANGE-TYPE
                              queue-name queue-name))
  ([exchange-name exchange-type routing-key]
    (next-message-from exchange-name exchange-type
                            (random-queue-name) routing-key))
  ([exchange-name exchange-type queue-name routing-key]
    (with-open [channel (.createChannel *rabbit-connection*)]
      (let [consumer (consumer-for channel exchange-name exchange-type
                              queue-name routing-key)]
        (delivery-from channel consumer)))))
```

There are three signatures of the next-message-from function. Notice that the first signature allows all existing code to continue to function as before. It does this by explicitly passing the default exchange name and exchange type, as well as the value of the queue name for the routing key. This satisfies the defaults as discussed previously.

The third signature of the function accepts all the important parameters: exchange-name, exchange-type, queue-name, and routing-key ❶. The second signature is a helper version; it passes along a random queue name when we're only interested in the routing key.

This change requires us to also change the definition of consumer-for to handle these new parameters. Here's the updated implementation:

```
(defn consumer-for [channel exchange-name exchange-type
                                  queue-name routing-key]
  (let [consumer (QueueingConsumer. channel)]
    (.exchangeDeclare channel exchange-name exchange-type)
    (.queueDeclare channel queue-name)
```

```
    (.queueBind channel queue-name exchange-name routing-key)
    (.basicConsume channel queue-name consumer)
    consumer))
```

And with that, you're all set to try out our new multicast version of senders and receivers. Here's a program that uses the new send-message to multicast message to all interested listeners:

```
(ns chapter14-sender-multicast
  (:use chapter14-rabbitmq-multicast))

(println "Multicasting...")
(with-rabbit ["localhost" "guest" "guest"]
  (send-message "fanex" FANOUT-EXCHANGE-TYPE
              "chapter-14-ghz" "Broadcast! Chapter 14 multicast!"))
(println "done!")
```

We're sending a message to a fan-out exchange named "fanex", with a routing key of "chapter-14-ghz". Now we need corresponding receivers on the other side, which listen to incoming messages using our new next-message-from. The following will do quite well:

```
(ns chapter14-receiver-multicast
  (:use chapter14-rabbitmq-multicast))

(println "Waiting for broadcast...")
(with-rabbit ["localhost" "guest" "guest"]
  (println (next-message-from "fanex"
                              FANOUT-EXCHANGE-TYPE "chapter-14-ghz")))
```

This creates a process that will wait until a message is delivered on an exchange named "fanex", set up as a fan-out. The routing key used is also "chapter-14-ghz", so it matches the previous sender. If you now start up several instances of this receiver and use our sender program to drop messages, you'll see the following output on all the receiver processes:

```
Waiting for broadcast...
Broadcast! Chapter 14 multicast!
```

Now that you know how to wait for individual broadcast messages, let's modify message-seq to complete the picture we built in the previous section.

BROADCASTS AND MESSAGE-SEQ

The final piece of the puzzle is the ability of a process to handle a stream of broadcast messages. By modifying message-seq, we can continue to write code the way we did in the last section. All of Clojure's sequence libraries can be used to handle broadcast messages as well. Here's the modified version:

```
(defn message-seq
  ([queue-name]
    (message-seq DEFAULT-EXCHANGE-NAME DEFAULT-EXCHANGE-TYPE
                                       queue-name queue-name))
  ([exchange-name exchange-type routing-key]
    (message-seq exchange-name exchange-type
```

```
        (random-queue-name) routing-key))
  ([exchange-name exchange-type queue-name routing-key]
     (let [channel (.createChannel *rabbit-connection*)
           consumer (consumer-for channel exchange-name exchange-type
                     queue-name routing-key)]
       (lazy-message-seq channel consumer)))))
```

As usual, the first signature is to support our older code that doesn't care about any of this multicast stuff. It passes along the default exchange name and type, as well as the same value of the queue name as the routing key.

The third signature handles all the important parameters, as we did with next-message-from function. Finally, the second signature is for caller convenience for the case where we only care about the routing key, as you'll see shortly. We've now completed the required changes to support multicasting. The following listing shows the new version of the chapter-14-rabbitmq namespace (renamed to chapter14-rabbitmq-multicast).

Listing 11.3   The new multicast-capable messaging code

```
(ns chapter14-rabbitmq-multicast
  (:import (com.rabbitmq.client ConnectionFactory QueueingConsumer)))

(def *rabbit-connection*)
(def DEFAULT-EXCHANGE-NAME "default-ex")
(def DEFAULT-EXCHANGE-TYPE "direct")
(def FANOUT-EXCHANGE-TYPE "fanout")

(defn new-connection [host username password]
  (.newConnection
    (doto (ConnectionFactory.)
      (.setVirtualHost "/")
      (.setUsername username)
      (.setPassword password)
      (.setHost host))))

(defmacro with-rabbit [[mq-host mq-username mq-password] & exprs]
  `(with-open [connection# (new-connection ~mq-host
                             ~mq-username ~mq-password)]
     (binding [*rabbit-connection* connection#]
       (do ~@exprs))))

(defn send-message
  ([routing-key message-object]
     (send-message DEFAULT-EXCHANGE-NAME routing-key message-object))
  ([exchange-name exchange-type routing-key message-object]
     (with-open [channel (.createChannel *rabbit-connection*)]
       (.exchangeDeclare channel exchange-name exchange-type)
       (.queueDeclare channel routing-key)
       (.basicPublish channel exchange-name routing-key nil
                       (.getBytes (str message-object)))))))

(defn delivery-from [channel consumer]
  (let [delivery (.nextDelivery consumer)]
    (.basicAck channel (.. delivery getEnvelope getDeliveryTag) false)
    (String. (.getBody delivery))))
```

```
(defn consumer-for [channel exchange-name exchange-type
                                        queue-name routing-key]
  (let [consumer (QueueingConsumer. channel)]
    (.exchangeDeclare channel exchange-name exchange-type)
    (.queueDeclare channel queue-name)
    (.queueBind channel queue-name exchange-name routing-key)
    (.basicConsume channel queue-name consumer)
    consumer))

(defn random-queue-name []
  (str (java.util.UUID/randomUUID)))

(defn next-message-from
  ([queue-name]
    (next-message-from DEFAULT-EXCHANGE-NAME DEFAULT-EXCHANGE-TYPE
                                        queue-name queue-name))
  ([exchange-name exchange-type routing-key]
    (next-message-from exchange-name exchange-type
                                (random-queue-name) routing-key))
  ([exchange-name exchange-type queue-name routing-key]
    (with-open [channel (.createChannel *rabbit-connection*)]
      (let [consumer (consumer-for channel exchange-name exchange-type
                                        queue-name routing-key)]
        (delivery-from channel consumer)))))

(defn- lazy-message-seq [channel consumer]
  (lazy-seq
   (let [message (delivery-from channel consumer)]
     (cons message (lazy-message-seq channel consumer)))))

(defn message-seq
  ([queue-name]
    (message-seq DEFAULT-EXCHANGE-NAME DEFAULT-EXCHANGE-TYPE
                                queue-name queue-name))
  ([exchange-name exchange-type routing-key]
    (message-seq exchange-name exchange-type
                            (random-queue-name) routing-key))
  ([exchange-name exchange-type queue-name routing-key]
    (let [channel (.createChannel *rabbit-connection*)
          consumer (consumer-for channel exchange-name
                                exchange-type queue-name routing-key)]
      (lazy-message-seq channel consumer))))
```

You're now ready to see this in action.

PUTTING IT TOGETHER

In order to test our new message-seq, you can use the same multicast sender program we created earlier. You only need to write a new listener that will process the message sequence. Here's a simple program that does that:

```
(ns chapter14-receiver-multicast-multiple
  (:use chapter14-rabbitmq-multicast))

(println "Waiting for broadcast...")
(with-rabbit ["localhost" "guest" "guest"]
  (doseq [message (message-seq "fanex"
          FANOUT-EXCHANGE-TYPE "chapter-14-ghz")]
    (println message)))
```

If you run a few instance of this program and use the multicast sender from before, you'll see the following output on all the listeners:

```
Waiting for broadcast...
Broadcast! Chapter 14 multicast!
Broadcast! Chapter 14 multicast!
Broadcast! Chapter 14 multicast!
```

Now that you have all the plumbing in place, you're ready to implement the final feature for this mini distributed computing framework: a way to request a computation on all workers at once. As alluded to earlier, this is useful for a number of things, such as making it easy to run diagnostics/health checks on all worker processes or possibly updating code on all remote machines.

11.3.5 *Calling all workers*

The way we implemented making a call to a remote worker is via sending a message over RabbitMQ. The caller then (behind the scenes) creates a proxy object that holds a listener for the response that the remote worker will eventually send. We then implemented a way to call workers via fire-and-forget semantics. We did this by sending a request message over RabbitMQ and not setting up any proxy to wait for the response. We'll use this latter approach, combined with the multicast feature we wrote in the last section, to implement this new feature.

RUN-WORKER-EVERYWHERE

We'll make some modifications to our worker code. For starters, let's add code to create the communication channel for broadcasting. We'll do this in a way that's similar to what you saw in the previous section. Here are some useful vars:

```
(def BROADCAST-QUEUE "chapter14_workers_broadcast_queue")
(def BROADCAST-EXCHANGE "chapter14_workers_fanex")
```

Our new construct will use this queue and exchange to send the request over. The following function will suffice:

```
(defn run-worker-on-all-servers [worker-name-keyword args]
  (let [request-object (request-envelope worker-name-keyword args)]
    (send-message BROADCAST-EXCHANGE FANOUT-EXCHANGE-TYPE
                                     BROADCAST-QUEUE request-object)))
```

This will let you run a particular worker on all worker-servicing processes, by making a call such as the following:

```
(run-worker-on-all-servers :expensive-audit-log 777)
```

Similarly to the earlier case where we implemented the fire and forget feature, this is a rather awkward way of making this call. The following macro makes it easier:

```
(defmacro run-worker-everywhere [worker-symbol & args]
  `(run-worker-on-all-servers (keyword '~worker-symbol) '~args))
```

With this in place, you can now call workers on all remote servers using code such as this:

```
(run-worker-everywhere expensive-audit-log 777)
```

Now that you know what the calling side looks like, let's shift our attention to the receiving end. In this next section, we'll write code to handle such worker-request broadcasts.

HANDLING WORKER-REQUEST BROADCASTS

There are two parts to the worker-handling loop. The first is a function that will process a message-seq of broadcast requests. The other is a way to ensure that the worker-handling process continues to listen to the regular work queue. Let's do the first:

```
(defn start-broadcast-listener []
  (println "Listening to broadcasts.")
  (doseq [request-message (message-seq BROADCAST-EXCHANGE
                                       FANOUT-EXCHANGE-TYPE BROADCAST-QUEUE)]
    (handle-request-message request-message)))
```

Nothing new here—you've seen similar code before. For the second requirement, we'll have to write the program that starts the worker-handling loop in a slightly different way:

```
(ns chapter14-worker-process-multicast-example
  (:use chapter14-worker-process-multicast
        chapter14-worker-multicast-example
        chapter14-rabbitmq-multicast))

(future
  (with-rabbit ["localhost" "guest" "guest"]
    (start-broadcast-listener)))

(future
  (with-rabbit ["localhost" "guest" "guest"]
    (start-handler-process)))
```

By starting each message-handling loop inside a future, you can ensure that both the loops run concurrently. The following listing shows the updated code to support this program and all the features we've added so far.

> **Listing 11.4 A new implementation of the framework for fire and forget and multicasting**

```
(ns chapter14-worker-multicast
  (:use chapter14-rabbitmq-multicast)
  (:import (java.util UUID)))

(def workers (ref {}))
(def worker-init-value :__worker_init__)
(def WORKER-QUEUE "chapter14_workers_job_queue")
(def BROADCAST-QUEUE "chapter14_workers_broadcast_queue")
(def BROADCAST-EXCHANGE "chapter14_workers_fanex")

(defn all-complete? [swarm-requests]
  (every? #(% :complete?) swarm-requests))
```

```clojure
(defn disconnect-worker [[channel q-name]]
  (.queueDelete channel q-name))

(defn disconnect-all [swarm-requests]
  (doseq [req swarm-requests]
    (req :disconnect)))

(defn wait-until-completion [swarm-requests allowed-time]
  (loop [all-complete (all-complete? swarm-requests)
         elapsed-time 0]
    (if (> elapsed-time allowed-time)
      (do
        (disconnect-all swarm-requests)
        (throw (RuntimeException. (str "Remote worker timeout exceeded "
                                       allowed-time " milliseconds!"))))
      (if (not all-complete)
        (do
          (Thread/sleep 100)
          (recur (all-complete? swarm-requests) (+ elapsed-time 100)))))))

(defmacro from-swarm [swarm-requests & expr]
  `(do
     (wait-until-completion ~swarm-requests 5000)
     ~@expr))

(defn update-on-response [worker-ref return-q-name]
  (let [channel (.createChannel *rabbit-connection*)
        consumer (consumer-for channel DEFAULT-EXCHANGE-NAME
                               DEFAULT-EXCHANGE-TYPE return-q-name return-q-name)
        on-response (fn [response-message]
                      (dosync
                       (ref-set worker-ref (read-string response-message))
                       (.queueDelete channel return-q-name)
                       (.close channel)))]
    (future (on-response (delivery-from channel consumer)))
    [channel return-q-name]))

(defn request-envelope
  ([worker-name args]
     {:worker-name worker-name :worker-args args})
  ([worker-name args return-q-name]
     (assoc (request-envelope worker-name args) :return-q return-q-name)))

(defn dispatch-work [worker-name args worker-ref]
  (let [return-q-name (str (UUID/randomUUID))
        request-object (request-envelope worker-name args return-q-name)
        worker-transport (update-on-response worker-ref return-q-name)]
    (send-message WORKER-QUEUE request-object)
    worker-transport))

(defn attribute-from-response [worker-internal-data attrib-name]
  (if (= worker-init-value worker-internal-data)
    (throw (RuntimeException. "Worker not complete!")))
  (if (not (= :success (keyword (worker-internal-data :status))))
    (throw (RuntimeException. "Worker has errors!")))
  (worker-internal-data attrib-name))

(defn on-swarm [worker-name args]
  (let [worker-data (ref worker-init-value)
```

```
          worker-transport (dispatch-work worker-name args worker-data)]
    (fn [accessor]
      (condp = accessor
        :complete? (not (= worker-init-value @worker-data))
        :value (attribute-from-response @worker-data :value)
        :status (@worker-data :status)
        :disconnect (disconnect-worker worker-transport)))))

(defmacro worker-runner [worker-name should-return worker-args]
  `(fn ~worker-args
     (if ~should-return
       (on-swarm ~worker-name ~worker-args))))

(defmacro defworker [service-name args & exprs]
  `(let [worker-name# (keyword '~service-name)]
     (dosync
      (alter workers assoc worker-name# (fn ~args (do ~@exprs))))
     (def ~service-name (worker-runner worker-name# true ~args))))

(defn run-worker-without-return [worker-name-keyword args]
  (let [request-object (request-envelope worker-name-keyword args)]
    (send-message WORKER-QUEUE request-object)))

(defmacro fire-and-forget [worker-symbol & args]
  `(run-worker-without-return (keyword '~worker-symbol) '~args))

(defn run-worker-on-all-servers [worker-name-keyword args]
  (let [request-object (request-envelope worker-name-keyword args)]
    (send-message BROADCAST-EXCHANGE FANOUT-EXCHANGE-TYPE BROADCAST-QUEUE
      request-object)))

(defmacro run-worker-everywhere [worker-symbol & args]
  `(run-worker-on-all-servers (keyword '~worker-symbol) '~args))

(ns chapter14-worker-process-multicast
  (:use chapter14-rabbitmq-multicast chapter14-worker-multicast))

(defn response-for [worker-handler worker-args]
  (try
   (let [value (apply worker-handler worker-args)]
     {:value value :status :success})
   (catch Exception e
     {:status :error})))

(defn process-request [worker-handler worker-args return-q]
  (future
    (with-rabbit ["localhost" "guest" "guest"]
      (let [response-envelope (response-for worker-handler worker-args)]
        (if return-q (send-message return-q response-envelope))))))

(defn handle-request-message [req-str]
  (try
   (let [req (read-string req-str)
         worker-name (req :worker-name) worker-args
                              (req :worker-args) return-q (req :return-q)
         worker-handler (@workers worker-name)]
     (if (not (nil? worker-handler))
       (do
         (println "Processing:" worker-name "with args:" worker-args)
```

```
            (process-request worker-handler worker-args return-q)))))
    (catch Exception e)))

(defn start-handler-process []
  (println "Serving up" (count @workers) "workers.")
  (doseq [request-message (message-seq WORKER-QUEUE)]
    (handle-request-message request-message)))

(defn start-broadcast-listener []
  (println "Listening to broadcasts.")
  (doseq [request-message (message-seq BROADCAST-EXCHANGE
                                       FANOUT-EXCHANGE-TYPE BROADCAST-QUEUE)]
    (handle-request-message request-message)))
```

That covers everything you've seen so far. You can run several instances of the worker-handling processes. By changing the localhost setting for RabbitMQ to something more specific, you can run multiple such processes on any number of computers. Our last order of business will be to test it, and for this, we'll write a tiny program to exercise the latest code.

TESTING RUN-WORKER-EVERYWHERE

The following program is a short test of the new features. It looks similar to the example you saw with the fire-and forget-section, but it serves our purpose nicely. Here it is:

```
(ns chapter14-worker-multicast-usage
  (:use chapter14-worker-multicast chapter14-rabbitmq-multicast chapter14-
    worker-multicast-example))

(println "Dispatching...")
(with-rabbit ["localhost" "guest" "guest"]
  (let [one (long-computation-one 10 20)
        two (long-computation-two 3 5 7)]
    (run-worker-everywhere expensive-audit-log 777)
    (from-swarm [one two]
      (println "one:" (one :value))
      (println "two:" (two :value)))))
(println "done!")
```

Running this on the console looks no different from the previous case:

```
Dispatching...
one: 200
two: 15
done!
```

Our worker processes (if there are two running) might look something like this:

Console output for the first worker process:

```
Listening to broadcasts.
Serving up 3 workers.
Processing: :long-computation-one with args: [10 20]
Processing: :expensive-audit-log with args: (777)
expensive audit log: 777
```

And here's the output for the second one:

```
Listening to broadcasts.
Serving up 3 workers.
Processing: :long-computation-two with args: [3 5 7]
Processing: :expensive-audit-log with args: (777)
expensive audit log: 777
```

The specific output may look slightly different on your computer. The key is that work is being distributed across multiple processes and that the call made via run-worker-everywhere does run on both.

We're finished for now! You've seen a lot of things so far. We first looked at basic communication using RabbitMQ, and then we built on that to write a simple distributed computing framework. Obviously, weighing in at around a couple of hundred lines of Clojure, it doesn't support all the functionality you'd expect from a production version. This could form a nice base for such a system. In the next section, we'll discuss a few additional things you might add to such a framework.

11.3.6 Additional features

We've managed to build a fairly reasonable distributed computing framework over the last few sections. In a production environment, though, you might want it to sport a few more features. Examples might be better information when exceptions happen, logging, making it more unit-testing friendly, and so on. We'll discuss a few of these now.

DISTRIBUTED MODE

Writing unit tests for code that calls a remote worker is a little difficult. This is because the tests end up requiring that the worker-handling processes (at least one) be running. That in turn means that RabbitMQ needs to be running. All of these external dependencies make unit testing hard and tedious. If unit tests are difficult to run, they will be run less often, and that's a bad situation to be in. Adding a configuration parameter that can make all code written using this framework run in a nondistributed mode would be a useful thing.

EXCEPTION INFO

When an exception occurs inside a worker running on a remote machine, our framework sends back an error status. It would be easy to send information about the exception along with the return message. Examples of such data would be the name of the exception class and even the stack trace itself. This information would make it easier for the callers to debug things when they go wrong.

REQUEST PRIORITIES

Our framework treats all request messages with the same level of importance. In the real world, you might have several levels of priority. It would be useful for the framework to expand in order to offer multiple levels of importance; it would be great if the caller could specify a level when the call is being made. Perhaps the default would be "medium," but the caller could specify "low" or "high" when making the call.

PARAMETERIZE WAIT TIME

In our `from-swarm` macro, we wait for 10 seconds to see if the requests we made return their responses. In many production use cases, this would be too long. And indeed, in some it would be too short. It would be a good idea to parameterize this wait duration and to provide a nonintrusive macro, which could make it easy to provide and use.

BINDINGS AND REBINDINGS

This little framework uses futures to run each request on a different thread. It allows the main program to continue listening for incoming requests and also to handle more requests concurrently (especially if the nature of the work being done mostly isn't CPU bound). Unfortunately, because Clojure bindings are thread local, the code that runs inside a future can't see any specially set-up bindings. A useful feature to add to this distributed-computing framework would be a way to easily rebind specific dynamic vars inside the future where the request is being processed.

With these features added, and more that might be useful to specific domains, this framework could find use in a real-world application. Because RabbitMQ itself is horizontally scalable, this framework could be useful in writing applications that can also scale by adding machines.

11.4   *Summary*

This was another fairly long chapter! We started off using RabbitMQ to send and receive messages between Clojure applications. We then wrote a convenient abstraction (`message-seq`) to deal with the fact that most receiving programs process incoming messages in a loop. This made it ideal to treat the stream of messages being delivered by RabbitMQ as a sequence, thereby allowing programs to unleash the full power of the Clojure sequence library on such a message stream.

After we got the basics out of the way, we implemented a little framework to write distributed Clojure applications in an easy and intuitive manner. This framework made it simple to write applications that made use of multiple JVM processes running across machines. Over the course of the chapter, we added features to this framework, and we brought it to a point where it could form the basis of something useable in the real world. And the whole thing clocked in at fewer than 200 lines of code.

Adding a distributed computing story to Clojure opens up a whole new world of possibilities. It adds a dimension of scalability that allows truly web-scale applications to be written in the language. This is definitely useful in the large, whereas all of Clojure's other features—macros, functional programming, lazy sequences, and so on—can be brought to bear in the small. This is a great combination.

Data processing
with Clojure

This chapter covers

- The map/reduce pattern of data processing
- Analyzing log files using map/reduce
- Distributing the data processing
- Master/slave parallelization

A computer program accepts data that is given, manipulates it in some way, and provides some output. The growing volume of data collected every minute of every day is evidence that data processing is alive in most software today. This chapter is about writing such programs. Naturally, you'll want to do this in as functional and as Clojure-esque a way as possible.

We're going to examine two approaches to processing large volumes of data. The first is the approach known as map/reduce. We'll show what it is, use it to parse log data, and discuss a few open source projects that provide distributed versions of map/reduce.

Next, we'll look at a different approach, one that uses a master to dispatch works to multiple workers. Master/slave parallelization schemes inspire this traditional approach. We'll use our lessons from the chapter on messaging in order to implement a simple master/slave data processing framework.

12.1   *The map/reduce paradigm*

Google popularized the map/reduce approach to distributed computing where large volumes of data can be processed using a large number of computers. The data processing problem is broken into pieces, and each piece runs on an individual machine. The software then combines the output from each computer to produce a final answer. The breaking up of the problem into smaller problems and assigning them to computers happens in the map stage, whereas the output from individual computers is taken and combined into a single entity in the reduce stage.

Google's map/reduce is based on the functional concepts of map and reduce, functions that you've seen repeatedly in this book so far. In this section, we'll explore this combination of map and reduce to see how it can be useful in processing data. We'll use the basic ideas of mapping and reducing, and over the course of this section we'll process data that we read from files. We'll build abstractions on top of simple file input so that we eventually end up processing Ruby on Rails server log files.

12.1.1   *Getting started with map/reduce—counting words*

We're going to use a traditional example in order to understand the idea of map/reduce. The problem is to count the number of times each word appears in a corpus of text. The total volume of text is usually large, but we'll use a small amount in order to illustrate the idea. The following is the first stanza of a poem by Lewis Carroll, called "The Jabberwocky":

> *Twas brillig and the slithy toves*
> *Did gyre and gimble in the wabe*
> *All mimsy were the borogoves*
> *And the mome raths outgrabe*

It's easy to find this poem on the internet, because it's from the famous book *Through the Looking Glass*. Note that for convenience, we've removed all punctuation from the text. We put the text in a file called jabberwocky.txt in a convenient folder. Let's write some code to count the number of times each word appears in the poem.

Consider the following function that operates on only a single line of the poem:

```
(defn parse-line [line]
  (let [tokens (.split (.toLowerCase line) " ")]
    (map #(vector % 1) tokens)))
```

This will convert a given line of text into a sequence of vectors, where each entry contains a single word and the number 1 (which can be thought of as a tally mark that the word appeared once), for instance:

```
user> (parse-line "Twas brillig and the slithy toves")
(["twas" 1] ["brillig" 1] ["and" 1] ["the" 1] ["slithy" 1] ["toves" 1])
```

Next, we'll combine the tally marks, so to speak, to get an idea of how many times each word appears. Consider this:

```
(defn combine [mapped]
  (->> (apply concat mapped)
       (group-by first)
       (map (fn [[k v]]
              {k (map second v)}))
       (apply merge-with conj)))
```

This works by creating a map, where the keys are the words found by parse-line, and the values are the sequences of tally marks. The only thing of curiosity here should be the group-by function. As you can see, it takes two arguments: a function and a sequence. The return value is a map where the keys are the results of applying the function on each element of the sequence, and the values are a vector of corresponding elements. The elements in each vector are also, conveniently, in the same order in which they appear in the original sequence.

Here's the combine operation in action:

```
user> (use 'clojure.contrib.io)
nil

user> (combine (map parse-line
                 (read-lines "/Users/amit/tmp/jabberwocky.txt")))
{"were" (1), "all" (1), "in" (1), "gyre" (1), "toves" (1), "outgrabe" (1),
"wabe" (1), "gimble" (1), "raths" (1), "the" (1 1 1 1), "borogoves" (1),
"slithy" (1), "twas" (1), "brillig" (1), "mimsy" (1), "and" (1 1 1),
"mome" (1), "did" (1)}
```

The read-lines function reads in the content of a file into a sequence of lines. Consider the output. For example, notice the word *the*. It appears multiple times, and the associated value is a list of 1s, each representing a single occurrence.

The final step is to sum the tally marks. This is the reduce step, and it's quite straightforward. Consider the following code:

```
(defn sum [[k v]]
  {k (apply + v)})

(defn reduce-parsed-lines [collected-values]
  (apply merge (map sum collected-values)))
```

And that's all there is to it. Let's create a nice wrapper function that you can call with a filename:

```
(defn word-frequency [filename]
  (->> (read-lines filename)
       (map parse-line)
       (combine)
       (reduce-parsed-lines)))
```

Let's try it at the REPL:

```
user> (word-frequency "/Users/amit/tmp/jabberwocky.txt")
{"were" 1, "all" 1, "in" 1, "gyre" 1, "toves" 1, "outgrabe" 1, "wabe" 1,
"gimble" 1, "raths" 1, "the" 4, "borogoves" 1, "slithy" 1, "twas" 1,
"brillig" 1, "mimsy" 1, "and" 3, "mome" 1, "did" 1}
```

So there you have it. It might seem a somewhat convoluted way to count the number of times words appear in text, but you'll see why this is a good approach for generalized computations of this sort.

12.1.2 Generalizing the map/reduce

In the previous section, we wrote a fair bit of code to compute the frequency of words in a given piece of text. The following listing shows the complete code.

Listing 12.1   Computing the frequency of words in given text

```
(ns chapter-data.word-count-1
  (:use clojure.contrib.io
        clojure.contrib.seq-utils))

(defn parse-line [line]
  (let [tokens (.split (.toLowerCase line) " ")]
    (map #(vector % 1) tokens)))

(defn combine [mapped]
  (->> (apply concat mapped)
       (group-by first)
       (map (fn [[k v]]
              {k (map second v)}))
       (apply merge-with conj)))

(defn sum [[k v]]
  {k (apply + v)})

(defn reduce-parsed-lines [collected-values]
  (apply merge (map sum collected-values)))

(defn word-frequency [filename]
  (->> (read-lines filename)
       (map parse-line)
       (combine)
       (reduce-parsed-lines)))
```

As pointed out earlier, there are probably more direct ways to do the job. We said that we did this so we could generalize the code to compute other kinds of things. We'll do that in this section.

Consider the `word-frequency` function in listing 12.1. Clearly, the first thing to pull out is how the input lines of text are provided. By decoupling the rest of the code from the call to `read-lines`, you can pass in any other lines of text you might have to process. So your new top-level function will accept the input as a parameter.

Next, you'll decouple the code from the `parse-line` function. That way, the user of your map/reduce code can decide how to map each piece of input into the intermediate form. Your new top-level function will accept the mapper function. Figure 12.1 shows the conceptual phase of the mapping part of the map/reduce approach.

Finally, you'll also decouple the map/reduce code from the way in which the reduce happens, so that the user of your code can decide how to do this part of the computation. You'll also accept the `reducer` function as a parameter.

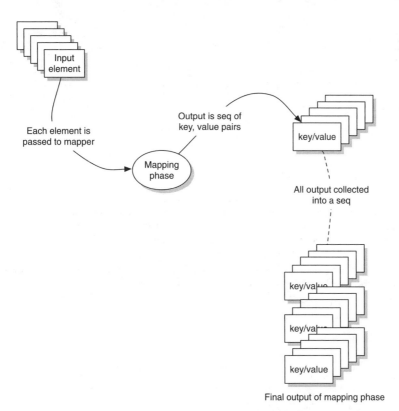

Figure 12.1 The mapping phase of the map/reduce approach applies a function to each input value, producing a list of key/value pairs for each input. All these lists (each containing several key/value pairs) are gathered into another list to constitute the final output of the mapping phase.

Given these considerations, your top-level `map-reduce` function may look like this:

```
(defn map-reduce [mapper reducer args-seq]
  (->> (map mapper args-seq)
       (combine)
       (reducer)))
```

The first line of this function is simple, and the `combine` function from our previous word count example is sufficient. Finally, `reducer` will accept the combined set of processed input to produce the result.

So with this `map-reduce` function and the `combine` function from the previous example, you have enough to try the word count example again. Recall that the idea of the combine phase is to group together common keys in order to prepare for the final reduce phase. Figure 12.2 shows the conceptual view, and listing 12.2 shows the extracted bits, followed by the word count example.

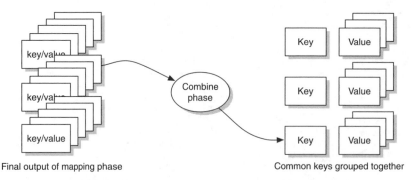

Figure 12.2   **The combine phase takes the output of the mapping phase and collects each key and associated values from the collection of lists of key/value pairs. The combined output is then a map with unique keys created during the mapping process, with each associated value being a list of values from the mapping phase.**

Listing 12.2   General map/reduce extracted out of the word-count example

```
(ns chapter-data.map-reduce
  (:use clojure.contrib.seq-utils))

(defn combine [mapped]
  (->> (apply concat mapped)
       (group-by first)
       (map (fn [[k v]]
              {k (map second v)}))
       (apply merge-with conj)))

(defn map-reduce [mapper reducer args-seq]
  (->> (map mapper args-seq)
       (combine)
       (reducer)))
```

It's time to see it in action. Consider the rewritten word-frequency function:

```
(defn word-frequency [filename]
  (map-reduce parse-line reduce-parsed-lines (read-lines filename)))
```

And here it is on the REPL:

```
user> (word-frequency "/Users/amit/tmp/jabberwocky.txt")
{"were" 1, "all" 1, "in" 1, "gyre" 1, "toves" 1, "outgrabe" 1, "wabe" 1,
"gimble" 1, "raths" 1, "the" 4, "borogoves" 1, "slithy" 1, "twas" 1,
"brillig" 1, "mimsy" 1, "and" 3, "mome" 1, "did" 1}
```

Note that in this case, the final output is a map of words to total counts. The map/reduce algorithm is general in the sense that the reduce phase can result in any arbitrary value. For instance, it can be a constant, or a list, or a map, as in the previous example, or any other value. The generic process is conceptualized in figure 12.3.

   The obvious question is, how general is this map/reduce code? Let's find the average number of words per line in the text. The code to do that's shown in the following listing.

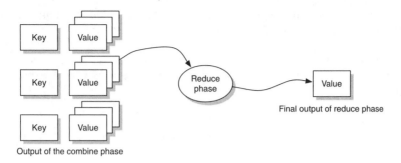

Output of the combine phase

Figure 12.3 The input to the reduce phase is the output of the combiner, which is a map, with keys being all the unique keys found in the mapping operation and the values being the collected values for each key from the mapping process. The output of the reduce phase can be any arbitrary value.

Listing 12.3 Using map/reduce to calculate average number of words in each line

```
(ns chapter-data.average-line-length
  (:use chapter-data.map-reduce
        clojure.contrib.io))

(def IGNORE "_")

(defn parse-line [line]
  (let [tokens (.split (.toLowerCase line) " ")]
    [[IGNORE (count tokens)]]))

(defn average [numbers]
  (/ (apply + numbers)
     (count numbers)))

(defn reducer [combined]
  (average (val (first combined))))

(defn average-line-length [filename]
  (map-reduce parse-line reducer (read-lines filename)))
```

Let's look at it in action:

```
user> (average-line-length "/Users/amit/tmp/jabberwocky.txt")
23/4

user> (float (average-line-length "/Users/amit/tmp/jabberwocky.txt"))
5.75
```

In this version of parse-line, you don't care about what line has what length, and you use a placeholder string "_" (named IGNORE because you don't use it later). Now, in the next section, you'll use our map/reduce code to parse some log files.

12.1.3 Parsing logs

Most nontrivial applications generate log data. Often, the logs contain information that's particularly useful in debugging or in learning how certain aspects of the application are used. In this section, you'll parse some Ruby on Rails log files to demonstrate the map/reduce approach a bit more.

THE LOG-FILE FORMAT

Let's start by looking at what we're dealing with. Here are a few lines from a typical Rails log file:

```
# Logfile created on Wed Apr 28 05:49:46 +0000 2010

Processing LoginController#show (for 10.245.114.15 at 2010-04-28 05:50:31)
[GET]
   Session ID: f1a7b029e4f8845d67cca2157785d646
   Parameters: {"action"=>"show", "controller"=>"login"}
Cookie set: cinch=cd36cdb5c80313c5b0114facd82b24db666c62ec79d7916f; path=/;
expires=Thu, 28 Apr 2011 05:50:34 GMT
Rendering login/login
Completed in 2237ms (View: 1, DB: 567) | 200 OK
[http://10.195.218.143/login]

Processing LoginController#show (for 10.245.114.15 at 2010-04-28 05:50:35)
[GET]
   Session ID: 9c985b243b385a86255487d11f693af4
   Parameters: {"action"=>"show", "controller"=>"login"}
Cookie set: cinch=97601bd094e608e1079c4c178e37bfb51f0c021c790c346c; path=/;
expires=Thu, 28 Apr 2011 05:50:35 GMT
Rendering login/login
Completed in 654ms (View: 1, DB: 567) | 200 OK
[http://10.195.218.143/login]

Processing LoginController#show (for 10.245.114.15 at 2010-04-28 05:50:51)
[GET]
   Session ID: 5d1bab09ffeadb336ea0a5387be8eaf3
   Parameters: {"action"=>"show", "controller"=>"login"}
Cookie set: cinch=e1dc75b5747750e952b75f9d5ab264a13aaa135fd10f3240; path=/;
expires=Thu, 28 Apr 2011 05:50:54 GMT
Rendering login/login
Completed in 1771ms (View: 1, DB: 685) | 200 OK
[http://10.195.218.143/login]
```

Notice that the first line is a header line noting when the logging started. A blank line follows this header. Further, a few lines of text represent each web request, and each such set is separated by two blank lines. You'll start by creating a way to operate at the level of individual web requests, as opposed to at individual lines of text. We'll call this abstraction `request-seq`.

A SEQUENCE OF REQUESTS

In order to create `request-seq`, you'll need to first read the log file. The `read-lines` function from `clojure.contrib.io` is perfect for this job. Consider the following top-level function:

```
(defn request-seq [filename]
  (->> (read-lines filename)
       (drop 2)
       (lazy-request-seq)))
```

It reads the text from the specified file and then drops the first two lines (consisting of the header and the following blank line). The resulting lines are passed to the `lazy-request-seq`, which parses and builds the sequence of web requests. Here's an implementation:

```
(defn lazy-request-seq [log-lines]
  (lazy-seq
    (let [record (next-log-record log-lines)]
      (if (empty? record)
        nil
        (cons (remove empty? record)
              (lazy-request-seq (drop (count record) log-lines)))))))
```

As you can see, the `lazy-request-seq` uses `lazy-seq` to create a lazy sequence of requests. Each request is represented by a sequence of lines from the log file, pertaining to the request. The bulk of the work, then, is in `next-log-record`, which is shown here:

```
(defn next-log-record [log-lines]
  (let [head (first log-lines)
        body (take-while (complement record-start?) (rest log-lines))]
    (remove nil? (conj body head))))
```

The only function remaining is the support function `record-start?`, which is defined here:

```
(defn record-start? [log-line]
  (.startsWith log-line "Processing"))
```

The basic approach is that you look for lines that begin with `"Processing"`, in order to identify requests. The rest is cleaning up the blank lines, terminating when the text lines run out. You can now create a `request-seq` by using the top-level function:

```
user> (def rl (request-seq "/Users/amit/tmp/logs/rails.log"))
#'user/rl
```

You can begin your exploration of this abstraction with a simple call to `count`:

```
user> (count rl)
145
```

Clearly, this is a small log file. To compare, you can check how many raw lines are in the underlying log file:

```
user> (count (read-lines "/Users/amit/tmp/logs/rails.log"))
1004
```

Yes, it's a small file containing 1004 lines that represent a total of 145 requests. Let's also see what a request record looks like:

```
user> (first rl)
("Processing LoginController#show (for 10.245.114.15 at 2010-04-28
05:50:31) [GET]" "  Session ID: f1a7b029e4f8845d67cca2157785d646" "
Parameters: {\"action\"=>\"show\", \"controller\"=>\"login\"}" "Cookie set:
cinch=cd36cdb5c80313c5b0114facd82b24db666c62ec79d7916f; path=/;
```

```
expires=Thu, 28 Apr 2011 05:50:34 GMT" "Rendering login/login" "Completed
in 2237ms (View: 1, DB: 567) | 200 OK [http://10.195.218.143/login]")
```

As we described earlier, each request record is a list of the individual lines from the log file. Now that you have `request-seq`, you can build a few useful functions that operate at the level of an individual request record (which, as a reminder, is a sequence of individual lines), for instance:

```
(defn controller-name [log-record]
  (second (.split (first log-record) " ")))
```

Let's see it working:

```
user> (controller-name (first rl))
"LoginController#show"
```

This (in Rails terminology) is saying that a request was made to a controller named `LoginController` and to an action named `show`. Here's another useful function:

```
(defn execution-time [log-record]
  (let [numbers (re-seq #"\d+" (last log-record))]
    (if (empty? numbers)
      0
      (read-string (first numbers)))))
```

It parses out the total execution time of each request, also handling the case where the time isn't present because of some error. Here it is on the REPL:

```
user> (execution-time (first rl))
2237
```

Notice that this is in milliseconds and that you used `read-string` to convert it into a number. Finally, here's a function that tells you the date the request was made:

```
(defn day-of-request-str [log-record]
  (->> (first log-record)
       (re-seq #"\d+-\d+-\d+")
       (first)))
```

And here it is on the REPL:

```
user> (day-of-request-str (first rl))
"2010-04-28"
```

These few functions are sufficient for our purposes here, but you can certainly imagine expanding this set to include other useful tasks. For instance, you might define a function to tell when a request was made:

```
(defn time-of-request [log-record]
  (->> (first log-record)
       (re-seq #"\d+-\d+-\d+ \d+:\d+:\d+")
       (first)
       (.parseDateTime GMT-FORMAT)))
```

Note that we're using the Joda time library to handle dates and times. You'll need to download it and ensure that the JAR file is on your classpath. `GMT-FORMAT` may be defined as the following:

```
(def DT-FORMAT (DateTimeFormat/forPattern "yyyy-MM-dd HH:mm:ss"))
(def GMT-FORMAT (.withZone DT-FORMAT (DateTimeZone/forID "GMT")))
```

You might also define a function to get the `session-id` of a request:

```
(defn session-id [log-record]
  (second (.split (second log-record) ": ")))
```

The complete code for our `request-seq` abstraction is shown in the following listing.

Listing 12.4   The `request-seq` abstraction for Ruby on Rails log files

```
(ns chapter-data.rails-log
  (:use clojure.contrib.io)
  (:import (org.joda.time DateTimeZone)
           (org.joda.time.format DateTimeFormat)))

(def DT-FORMAT (DateTimeFormat/forPattern "yyyy-MM-dd HH:mm:ss"))
(def GMT-FORMAT (.withZone DT-FORMAT (DateTimeZone/forID "GMT")))

(defn record-start? [log-line]
  (.startsWith log-line "Processing"))

(defn next-log-record [log-lines]
  (let [head (first log-lines)
        body (take-while (complement record-start?) (rest log-lines))]
    (remove nil? (conj body head))))

(defn lazy-request-seq [log-lines]
  (lazy-seq
    (let [record (next-log-record log-lines)]
      (if (empty? record)
        nil
        (cons (remove empty? record)
              (lazy-request-seq (drop (count record) log-lines)))))))

(defn request-seq [filename]
  (->> (read-lines filename)
       (drop 2)
       (lazy-request-seq)))

(defn controller-name [log-record]
  (second (.split (first log-record) " ")))

(defn execution-time [log-record]
  (let [numbers (re-seq #"\d+" (last log-record))]
    (if (empty? numbers)
      0
      (read-string (first numbers)))))

(defn day-of-request-str [log-record]
  (->> (first log-record)
       (re-seq #"\d+-\d+-\d+")
       (first)))

(defn time-of-request [log-record]
  (->> (first log-record)
       (re-seq #"\d+-\d+-\d+ \d+:\d+:\d+")
       (first)
       (.parseDateTime GMT-FORMAT)))
```

```
(defn session-id [log-record]
  (second (.split (second log-record) ": ")))
```

Now you're ready to try some map/reduce on this `request-seq`. The next section does that.

RAILS REQUESTS AND MAP/REDUCE

You'll now write some code to count the number of times each controller was called. This will look similar to the earlier word count example. Consider the mapper function shown here:

```
(defn parse-record [log-record]
  (let [data {:total 1}
        data (assoc data (controller-name log-record) 1)]
    [[(day-of-request-str log-record) data]]))
```

You're going to count the total number of requests (denoted by the `:total` key in our datum) and also the number of times an individual controller was called (denoted by the presence of the controller name as a key, along with a 1 as a tally mark). Next up is the reducer code:

```
(defn reduce-days [[date date-vals]]
  {date (apply merge-with + date-vals)})

(defn rails-reducer [collected-values]
  (apply merge (map reduce-days collected-values)))
```

This should remind you of the word-count example. All that remains now is the top-level function:

```
(defn investigate-log [log-file]
  (map-reduce parse-record rails-reducer (request-seq log-file)))
```

Let's see it in action!

```
user> (investigate-log "/Users/amit/tmp/logs/rails.log")
{"2010-04-28"
  {"JsonfetchController#campaign_message_templates_json" 17,
   "JsClientFileNamesController#index" 23,
   "InsertsController#index" 35,
   "PageLogsController#create" 8,
   :total 145,
   "ConsumersController#update_merchant_session" 25,
   "CartsController#create" 1,
   "CartsController#show" 16,
   "LoginController#show" 4,
   "LoginController#consumer_status" 16}}
```

We said earlier that it's similar to the word-count example but not quite the same. The difference here is that you're grouping the results by day. You didn't have this extra level of grouping when you were counting words. As you can see from the following listing, which contains the complete code for this Rails log analysis, you can do this rather easily.

Listing 12.5   Analyzing Rails log to compute frequencies of controller calls

```
ns chapter-data.rails-analyzer
  (:use chapter-data.rails-log
      chapter-data.map-reduce))

(defn parse-record [log-record]
  (let [data {:total 1}
       data (assoc data (controller-name log-record) 1)]
    [[(day-of-request-str log-record) data]]))

(defn reduce-days [[date date-vals]]
  {date (apply merge-with + date-vals)})

(defn rails-reducer [collected-values]
  (apply merge (map reduce-days collected-values)))

(defn investigate-log [log-file]
  (map-reduce parse-record rails-reducer (request-seq log-file)))
```

It's easy to gather other kinds of metrics from the Rails log files. All you have to do is add the appropriate code to the mapper function (in this case, parse-record) and make the respective change (if any) to the reducer code.

Notice how you started out reading the log file with read-lines. This returns a sequence of each line of text in the file. Then you built up the request-seq abstraction on top of it, which allows you to operate at the level of requests. In the next section, we'll show how to build one more abstraction on top this, so you can deal with data at the level of sessions.

12.1.4 Analyzing Rails sessions

In the last section, you analyzed web requests from a Rails log file. You determined how many times each controller was called on a daily basis. In this section, you'll calculate how long a web session is (in terms of the number of requests) and how long it lasts (in terms of time). In order to do this, we'd like to raise our level of abstraction beyond request-seq, so you can avoid dealing with requests directly.

Our new abstraction will be session-seq, which is a grouping of requests by their session-id. Luckily we already wrote a function to determine the session id of a request (we called it session-id and it's in the chapter-data.rails-log namespace, shown in listing 12.4). You can use it to do your grouping.

SESSION-SEQ

Let's get started on our new abstraction. Consider the following function:

```
(defn session-seq [requests]
  (group-by session-id requests))
```

The familiar group-by function makes this trivial to do. Next, you'll write some code to support the analysis of your sessions. The first thing we said we wanted was the length in terms of the number of requests. You can use count to do that. The other thing we wanted was a way to determine how long a session lasted in, say, milliseconds. Here's a function that does it:

```
(defn duration [requests]
  (let [begin (time-of-request (first requests))
        end (time-of-request (last requests))]
    (- (.getMillis end) (.getMillis begin))))
```

Here's an example:

```
user> (def rl (request-seq "/Users/amit/tmp/logs/rails.log"))
#'user/rl

user> (def ss (session-seq rl))
#'user/ss

user> (duration (val (first ss)))
18000
```

So that works, and it seems that the first session lasted 18 seconds even. The complete code for our `session-seq` namespace is shown in the following listing.

> **Listing 12.6   `session-seq` built on top of `request-seq`**

```
(ns chapter-data.session-seq
  (:use chapter-data.rails-log
        clojure.contrib.seq-utils))

(defn session-seq [requests]
  (group-by session-id requests))

(defn duration [requests]
  (let [begin (time-of-request (first requests))
        end (time-of-request (last requests))]
    (- (.getMillis end) (.getMillis begin))))
```

Now that you have the basics down, you need to decide how you're going to implement the functions needed to do the analysis. That's the focus of the next section.

SESSIONS ANALYSIS

We wanted to determine what the average length of a session is, both in terms of the number of requests in each session and in how long a session lasts in milliseconds. Because we're using our map/reduce approach, the first thing you'll need is the mapper function. Consider the following:

```
(defn parse-session [[session-id requests]]
  (let [metrics {:length (count requests)
                 :duration (duration requests)}]
    [[session-id metrics]]))
```

This gathers the metrics you want for a single session. You can test it at the REPL, like so:

```
user=> (parse-session (first ss))
[["03c008692b0a79cd99aa011c32305885" {:length 4, :duration 18000}]]
```

So all you need now is a way to reduce a collection of such data. Consider this:

```
(defn averages [collected-values]
  (let [num-sessions (count collected-values)
        all-metrics (apply concat (vals collected-values))
        total-length (apply + (map :length all-metrics))
        total-duration (apply + (map :duration all-metrics))]
    {:average-length (/ total-length num-sessions)
     :average-duration (/ total-duration num-sessions)}))
```

The final step is to pass these mapper and reducer functions to our map-reduce function. Here's a function called investigate-sessions that does this and also prints the results in a nice, readable format:

```
(defn investigate-sessions [filename]
  (let [results (map-reduce parse-session averages
                            (session-seq (request-seq filename)))]
    (println "Avg length:" (* 1.0 (:average-length results)))
    (println "Avg duration:" (* 1.0 (:average-duration results)))))
```

Now you're ready to try this at the REPL:

```
user=> (investigate-sessions "/Users/amit/tmp/logs/rails.log")
Avg length: 1.746987951807229
Avg duration: 3024.096385542169
nil
```

Done; that gives you the required averages. The complete code for the analysis work is provided in the following listing.

> **Listing 12.7 Computing the average length of sessions from a Rails log file**

```
(ns chapter-data.session-analyzer
  (:use chapter-data.map-reduce
        chapter-data.rails-log
        chapter-data.session-seq))

(defn parse-session [[session-id requests]]
  (let [metrics {:length (count requests)
                 :duration (duration requests)}]
    [[session-id metrics]]))

(defn averages [collected-values]
  (let [num-sessions (count collected-values)
        all-metrics (apply concat (vals collected-values))
        total-length (apply + (map :length all-metrics))
        total-duration (apply + (map :duration all-metrics))]
    {:average-length (/ total-length num-sessions)
     :average-duration (/ total-duration num-sessions)}))

(defn investigate-sessions [filename]
  (let [results (map-reduce parse-session averages
                            (session-seq (request-seq filename)))]
    (println "Avg length:" (* 1.0 (:average-length results)))
    (println "Avg duration:" (* 1.0 (:average-duration results)))))
```

What you've accomplished here is the ability to take a Rails log file and in a few lines of code run computations at the level of web sessions. You did this by building layers of abstractions, both on the data side and also on the map/reduce side. You can easily compute more metrics about sessions by adding to our mapper and reducer code.

In the next section, we'll go over a few examples of how this pattern of data processing is used for large-scale computations.

12.1.5 *Large-scale data processing*

The last section looked at using Clojure's map and reduce functions to operate on sequences of data in order to produce a desired output. The same basic principles have also been applied to large-scale computing. As you can imagine, as the volume of data that needs to be processed grows, more computers need to participate in the processing. Although distributed computing and multiprocessor parallelism aren't new concepts by any means, Google has popularized the distributed map/reduce approach in the industry. In 2006, they released a white paper that described their approach to large-scale data processing (http:/labs.google.com/papers/mapreduce.html), and there have been several open source projects that implemented their ideas since then.

One of the more popular ones is a project called Hadoop, which is part of the Apache family of projects. Because it's written in Java, you can imagine using it from Clojure. In this section, we'll discuss a few related open source projects in this area. Note that detailed discussions and examples of using these from Clojure are beyond the scope of this book. The concepts from the previous sections should serve to get you started, and the documentation for most of these tools is quite good.

HADOOP MAP/REDUCE, CLOJURE-HADOOP

Hadoop's map/reduce framework is built on the Google map/reduce white paper. It's a framework for writing data processing applications that can handle terabytes of input, on clusters consisting of thousands of machines. Jobs consist of map tasks and reduce tasks, and these roughly correspond to the concepts from the previous section. These tasks run in parallel on the cluster, and the framework takes care of scheduling them, monitoring them, and rescheduling them in the case of failures.

The Hadoop map/reduce framework and associated HDFS (which stands for Hadoop Distributed File System, similar in nature to the Google File System) serve as the basis for several other projects. For instance, we looked at HBase in the chapter on data storage. Although it's true that Clojure's Java Interop facilities make it easy to use Java libraries, using Hadoop map/reduce from Clojure can be less than straightforward. There are several open source projects that make this easier; in particular, clojure-hadoop (written by Stuart Sierra) is a usable wrapper.

Although simple wrappers are sufficient in many situations, some folks like to build higher abstractions on top of existing ones. We'll discuss a couple of them in the next section.

CASCADING, CASCADING-CLOJURE

Cascading is a Java library that sits on top of Hadoop map/reduce. It offers up a way to avoid thinking in map/reduce terms; instead it provides an alternative way to construct distributed data processing workflows. The way to write applications using Cascading is to think about data processing as "pipe assemblies" where data flows through processor stages (or pipes) from a "source" to a "sink." An assembly can have multiple stages that can transform data in ways that advance the computation.

Again, because it's a Java library, it's easy to use Cascading from within your Clojure programs. There are wrappers for Cascading that make programming with it closer to the Clojure style. One such library is `cascading-clojure`, written by Bradford Cross.

Whether you decide to directly use Cascading or use it via a wrapper, it may make sense to consider raw Hadoop map/reduce as low-level constructs that your application should stay above. Our last visit will be to a new but quite interesting project that sits even higher than Cascading.

CASCALOG

Cascalog is a Clojure-based query language for Hadoop. It's inspired by Datalog and shares some similarities with it, not the least is the syntax used to name variables in queries. Like Datalog, it's a declarative language, letting users type out their queries almost from a SQL-like frame of mind. Under the covers, it figures out what data needs to be looked up, how it must be joined, and what map/reduce jobs are required.

It's a relatively new project, but it's worth considering for projects that require this sort of declarative (or interactive) querying of large data sets.

This part of the chapter was about map/reduce. We first looked at what it was, from a functional language point of view, and wrote simple code to understand it. We then wrote some log-parsing code on top of it in order to understand some simple use cases. We then touched on a few industry-grade distributed map/reduce projects out there that you can incorporate into your Clojure applications. In the next chapter, we'll look at a different approach to processing data.

12.2 *Master/slave parallelization*

In this section, we'll create our own little framework to handle batch-processing requirements. We'll leverage our work from previous chapters in order to build it; specifically, we'll use our remote workers from chapter 11. Our tool will allow us to specify the individual computation as a function and then to apply the function to a sequence of parameters. Because each worker is a remote server, we'll then be able to start multiple instances (on multiple machines) in order to process large batches of input.

By itself, this isn't too complicated, because we've already written all the code for it. We'll add check pointing into the mix, so that if our program crashes, we'll be able to recover. We'll use Redis to store the status of the various jobs, and you already know how to talk to Redis. We'll first create a construct that will describe the job and then some code to manage its status. We'll then look at executing a job. Finally, we'll look at handling errors and recovering from them.

Let's get started writing this framework. The first thing you'll need to do is to specify the parameters of the batch-processing run.

12.2.1   Defining the job

We'll call a complete batch-processing run a job. A job may consist of multiple tasks, and the purpose of this little tool is to run large jobs. The benefit of using such a framework is that you can run large jobs on a cluster of machines where each machine could run one or more worker servers. As we mentioned earlier, we'll be using Redis to store the status of a job run. We'll want to give each job an identifier so you can distinguish between multiple running jobs. We'll also want to identify each child task that will run as part of the job. We could use a random, unique identifier for this, but we'll let the choice of such an id be influenced by the user of our framework.

Here's a function that will serve to define a new job:

```
(defn new-job [job-id worker batch-size batch-wait-time id-generator]
  {:tasks-atom (atom {})
   :job-id job-id
   :worker worker
   :batch-size batch-size
   :batch-wait-time batch-wait-time
   :id-gen id-generator})
```

It creates a map containing a few self-explanatory keys. The value of :tasks-atom is an atom containing an empty map. We'll use it to store tasks as they're run. The value of :id-gen is the function used to create the identifier of each task. You'll see all of these in action shortly.

12.2.2   Maintaining status

Now that we can create the representation of new tasks, we can think about running them. We know that in order to run, we'll need a list of the arguments that need to be processed. Eventually, we'll dispatch each argument (which could in turn be another list), and it will be processed by one of our remote workers. As part of the dispatch (and also execution on the worker side), we'll also track the status of each task. We'll create a key in Redis for each dispatched task, and we'll make it a compound key containing both the job id and the task id. Here's some code to create the key:

```
(def KEY-SEPARATOR "___")

(defn managed-key [job-id task-id]
  (str job-id KEY-SEPARATOR task-id))
```

Now that you have a key for each task being dispatched, you can write a function to mark the status of a task. We'll use the latest version of Redis (which at the time of this writing is 2.0.0 Release Candidate 2). This version of Redis supports the hash data type (similar to the lists and sets you saw in the chapter on data storage). Here's how you can mark the status of a task:

```
(def STATUS-FIELD "status")

(defn update-status-as [job-id task-id status]
  (redis/hset (managed-key job-id task-id) STATUS-FIELD status))
```

Note that we're using the same `redis-clojure` library you used earlier. Because it's advisable to group related code into a separate namespace, you could put all the status-related code into a new namespace. Further, instead of having to pass a value for `status` each time you call `update-status-as`, you can build a function on top of it that will more clearly express what you intend to do, for instance:

```
(def DISPATCHED "dispatched")

(defn mark-dispatched [job-id task-id]
  (update-status-as job-id task-id DISPATCHED))
```

Now you have enough to get started with dispatching a job and a few functions for maintaining status of various tasks. Before writing them, let's think through the transitions of statuses as tasks are dispatched and run. Clearly, you'll start by dispatching a task; `mark-dispatched` can handle that situation. What happens next?

Let's imagine that the worker will first mark the status as "initial processing started" or something like that. When it completes the processing, it will mark the task as "complete." You also need to handle the situation where an error occurs, so you could have the worker mark the task as "being in an error state." Finally, you'll want to retry tasks that haven't completed, so you might have a status called "recovery being attempted" and another called "second attempt in progress." You'll also create an "unknown" status in case something unexpected happens and you want to mark it explicitly (useful for debugging). So let's first define the various statuses:

```
(def INITIAL "initial")
(def COMPLETE "complete")
(def ERROR "error")
(def RECOVERY "recovery")
(def SECONDARY "secondary")
(def UNKNOWN "unknown")
```

These are in addition to the `DISPATCHED` status you already defined earlier. The next step is to write a few convenience functions to mark tasks appropriately:

```
(defn mark-error [job-id task-id]
  (update-status-as job-id task-id ERROR))

(defn mark-recovery [job-id task-id]
  (update-status-as job-id task-id RECOVERY))
```

Further, instead of defining functions to mark each status, you can define a sort of progression of status, as a sort of a status transition chain. Consider this:

```
(def next-status {
    DISPATCHED INITIAL
    INITIAL    COMPLETE
    RECOVERY   SECONDARY
    SECONDARY  COMPLETE
```

```
    " "           UNKNOWN
    nil           UNKNOWN
    UNKNOWN       UNKNOWN
})
```

With this map, given the current status of a task, you can easily look up what the next status ought to be. You'll use this to change statuses of the tasks as they run. The first thing you'll need to do is to find the current status of a particular task. Here's that function:

```
(defn status-of [job-id task-id]
  (redis/hget (managed-key job-id task-id) STATUS-FIELD))
```

With this function in hand, you can write a function to increment the status of a task based on our next-status map. Here it is:

```
(defn increment-status [job-id task-id]
  (->> (status-of job-id task-id)
       (next-status)
       (update-status-as job-id task-id)))
```

Most of the status management functions are in place. Our next stop will be to write the code that will dispatch a job.

12.2.3 Dispatching a job

As we discussed, the first step of dispatching a task is to mark its status as dispatched. We wrote the code for that in the preceding section, so you're now ready to jump right into making the call to your remote worker. You'll break up your job run into batches of tasks, so you can avoid dispatching all the tasks immediately and flooding our workers with requests. Start with your top-level function to kick off the job:

```
(defn start-job [{:keys [batch-size] :as job} args-seq]
  (let [args-batches (partition-all batch-size args-seq)]
    (doseq [args-batch args-batches]
      (run-batch job args-batch))))
```

It accepts a job map as constructed by our new-job function from earlier in the chapter. The only thing of interest at this level is batch-size, so you destructure that out of the job map while also retaining the complete map as job. You also accept an args-seq parameter that's a sequence of sequences, each inner sequence being a set of arguments to the worker.

You break the args-seq into batches by calling partition-all, a function from clojure.contrib.seq-utils. partition-all that behaves in a manner similar to partition, but it gathers remaining elements of the sequence being partitioned into a final sequence. You then call run-batch over each partitioned batch of arguments. Here's the definition of run-batch:

```
(defn run-batch [{:keys [id-gen tasks-atom batch-wait-time] :as job}
                 args-batch]
  (doseq [args args-batch]
    (run-task job (apply id-gen args) args mark-dispatched))
  (wait-until-completion (map :proxy (vals @tasks-atom)) batch-wait-time))
```

This time you destructure id-generator and tasks-atom (along with batch-wait-time) out of the job map. You then iterate over args-batch (containing one batch-size worth of the args-seq) and fire off calls to run-task, one per set of arguments. Note also that you pass to run-task the function mark-dispatched that we wrote a while back. This marks the status of a task as having been dispatched. Before proceeding, you wait for the batch to complete for the duration as specified by batch-wait-time. The final piece, then, is run-task:

```
(defn run-task [{:keys [job-id worker tasks-atom]}
                task-id args mark-status]
  (mark-status job-id task-id)
  (let [task-info {:args args
                   :proxy (apply worker [job-id task-id args])}]
    (swap! tasks-atom assoc task-id task-info)))
```

run-task does the work of making the call to the worker. Note that the arguments passed to the worker aren't args but a vector containing the job-id, the task-id, and the args. You do this so the worker also knows what task is being run. It will use this information to update the status of the task, and you'll soon write a convenient macro that will help you write task-aware worker functions.

Note that you're keeping track of the dispatched worker proxies inside our tasks-atom. Specifically, you don't maintain only the tasks but also the arguments used to call the worker. You do this so you can retry the worker in case it doesn't succeed. You'll see this in action very shortly.

Now that you have the basics of dispatching jobs, let's look at the worker side of the picture.

12.2.4 *Defining the slave*

So far, you've written code to track the status of tasks and to dispatch jobs. Our goal in this section is to create workers that can process tasks. Because we're using the remote worker framework we created in the previous chapter, you can build on that. We'll use a simple example to illustrate the point; keep in mind that worker functions are usually computationally intensive. Consider the following code:

```
(defn fact [n acc]
  (if (= n 0)
    acc
    (recur (dec n) (* n acc))))
```

It's a trivial way to compute the factorial of a given number, for instance:

```
user> (fact 5 1)
120

user> (fact 6 1)
720
```

Consider the situation where you have to calculate the factorial of each number in a large list of numbers. Using our framework, you can write a worker function similar to fact shown here and then use that to do the work in a distributed fashion. A task-processing function, as you saw, needs to be able to keep track of the status of the task executing in it. To facilitate this, this function needs to accept parameters for the job-id and the task-id.

This calls for a wrapper function, one that accepts a job-id, a task-id, and the parameters that will be used to delegate to the underlying function beneath. Here's an implementation:

```
(defn slave-wrapper [worker-function]
  (fn [job-id task-id worker-args]
    (redis/with-server (redis-config)
      (increment-status job-id task-id)
      (try
        (let [return (apply worker-function worker-args)]
          (increment-status job-id task-id)
          return)
        (catch Exception e
          (mark-error job-id task-id))))))
```

slave-wrapper accepts a regular function and returns a new function with the interface you need. Specifically, the new function accepts the job-id, task-id, and the original worker's arguments (denoted here by worker-args). Remember that you were dispatching calls to the remote workers using this set of arguments in our run-task function earlier. The first thing this new wrapped function does is increment the status of the task it's about to run. Then, it attempts to carry out the computation by calling the underlying function and passing it the worker-args. If that succeeds, it will increment the status of the task again and return the computed value. If the computation fails, it will mark the status of the task as "having encountered an error."

The only other thing of interest here is the call to redis/with-server and the function redis-config. You saw this being used in the chapter on data storage, so this should be familiar to you. As you can imagine, redis-config returns a map containing the connection parameters for the redis server. For now, you can have it return the simple map as follows:

```
(defn redis-config []
  {:host "localhost"})
```

In the real world, redis-config might return something read from a configuration file or something similar.

So you're nearly there as far as defining your remote slaves is concerned. You have a function that can be used to create a task status–aware version of a regular function. You need to now convert functions created by slave-wrapper into a remote worker. Here's a macro that makes it convenient:

```
(defmacro slave-worker [name args & body]
  `(let [simple-function# (fn ~args (do ~@body))
         slave-function# (slave-wrapper simple-function#)]
     (defworker ~name [~'job-id ~'task-id ~'worker-args]
       (slave-function# ~'job-id ~'task-id ~'worker-args))))
```

You've already seen `defworker` in the chapter on using messaging to scale out our Clojure programs. The `slave-worker` macro is a simple way to write our task status–aware remote workers. Here's our `factorial` function from before:

```
(slave-worker factorial [n]
  (let [f (fact n 1)]
    (println "Calculated factorial of" n "value:" f)
    f))
```

We've added some extra logging here so that you can see this in action on the console. All it does is call our `fact` function with the parameter n and the initial value of the accumulator set to 1. When called, it will calculate the factorial and then print the value to the standard and then return the computed result. We're now ready to give it a shot.

12.2.5 *Using the master-slave framework*

We've written most of the happy path code. Let's test it all out, so that you can be sure that things work so far. First, we'll put together the worker side of things. Here's the code:

```
(ns chapter-data.dist-fact
  (:use chapter-data.master-core))

(defn fact [n acc]
  (if (= n 0)
    acc
    (recur (dec n) (* n acc))))

(slave-worker factorial [n]
  (let [f (fact n 1)]
    (println "Calculated factorial of" n "value:" f)
    f))
```

You've seen these two functions before; we've now put them in a single namespace called `chapter-data.dist-fact`, inside a file called `dist_fact.clj`. You'll now load this in a sort of boot file, which you'll use to kick-start your remote worker process. Here it is:

```
(ns chapter-data.boot-task-processor
  (:use chapter14-rabbitmq-multicast
        chapter14-worker-process-multicast
        chapter-data.dist-fact))

(with-rabbit ["localhost" "guest" "guest"]
  (start-handler-process))
```

This is straightforward and should be familiar from the previous chapter on messaging. When you run this script via the usual Clojure incantation, you get the following output:

```
Serving up 1 workers.
```

Remember that when your worker process starts up, it informs the user about the number of workers that it has available. At that point, it's ready to begin accepting requests for remote worker computations.

Now, let's try to run the factorial program. Consider the following code:

```
(ns chapter-data.dist-fact-client
  (:use chapter-data.dist-fact
        chapter-data.status
        chapter14-worker-multicast
        chapter14-rabbitmq-multicast))

(defn dispatch-factorial [job-id task-id n]
  (redis/with-server (redis-config)
    (mark-dispatched job-id task-id)
    (factorial job-id task-id [n])))

(with-rabbit ["localhost" "guest" "guest"]
  (let [f (dispatch-factorial "test-job" "test-task" 5)]
    (from-swarm [f]
      (println "Got the answer:" (f :value)))))
```

When you run this program, you get a simple confirmation that things have worked:

```
Got the answer: 120
```

Similarly, the remote worker server has some relevant output:

```
Processing: :factorial with args: [test-job test-task [5]]
Calculated factorial of 5 value: 120
```

Finally, let's see if the status of the task is as you expect it to be:

```
user=> (redis/with-server (redis-config)
          (status-of "test-job" "test-task"))
"complete"
```

So far, so good. You're now ready to test if a larger sequence of such calls can be made, say to calculate the factorials of a series of numbers. It's exactly the reason we wrote this little framework, so let's get to it!

12.2.6 Running a job

You're ready to run our factorial function against a larger sequence of arguments. Remember that the sequence of arguments should be a nested one, because a function may take multiple arguments. In keeping with this, you'll generate your arguments thusly:

```
user=> (map list (take 10 (iterate inc 1)))
((1) (2) (3) (4) (5) (6) (7) (8) (9) (10))
```

You'll also add another functionality to the status namespace, which will let you check on the results of the job run. The following code does that:

```
(defn from-proxies [job proxy-command]
  (->> @(:tasks-atom job)
       (vals)
       (map :proxy)
       (map #(% proxy-command))))

(defn values-from [job]
  (from-proxies job :value))
```

You're now ready to define the job you want to execute. We've already written a function to do this, so you can use it:

```
(def fact-job (new-job "fact-job" factorial 5 10000 identity))
```

We've also written a function start-job to execute your jobs. The following program exercises it with our factorial function:

```
(ns chapter-data.dist-fact-client
  (:use chapter-data.dist-fact
        chapter-data.master-core
        chapter-data.status
        chapter14-worker-multicast
        chapter14-rabbitmq-multicast))

(defn dispatch-factorial [job-id task-id n]
  (redis/with-server (redis-config)
    (mark-dispatched job-id task-id)
    (factorial job-id task-id [n])))

 (def fact-job (new-job "fact-job" factorial 5 10000 identity))

(with-rabbit ["localhost" "guest" "guest"]
  (start-job fact-job (map list (take 10 (iterate inc 1))))
  (println "Values:" (values-from fact-job)))
```

Let's also start up two (or more!) worker processes, so that you can see the work distributed across more than one worker server. The output of this program is, again, easy to follow:

```
Values: (1 2 6 24 120 720 5040 40320 362880 3628800)
```

The output of our worker servers is as follows. First, the one:

```
Serving up 1 workers.
Processing: :factorial with args: [fact-job 1 (1)]
Processing: :factorial with args: [fact-job 3 (3)]
Processing: :factorial with args: [fact-job 5 (5)]
Calculated factorial of 5 value: 120
Calculated factorial of 1 value: 1
Calculated factorial of 3 value: 6
Processing: :factorial with args: [fact-job 7 (7)]
Calculated factorial of 7 value: 5040
Processing: :factorial with args: [fact-job 9 (9)]
Calculated factorial of 9 value: 362880
```

And now, the second:

```
Serving up 1 workers.
Processing: :factorial with args: [fact-job 2 (2)]
Processing: :factorial with args: [fact-job 4 (4)]
Calculated factorial of 4 value: 24
Calculated factorial of 2 value: 2
Processing: :factorial with args: [fact-job 6 (6)]
Calculated factorial of 6 value: 720
Processing: :factorial with args: [fact-job 8 (8)]
Calculated factorial of 8 value: 40320
Processing: :factorial with args: [fact-job 10 (10)]
Calculated factorial of 10 value: 3628800
```

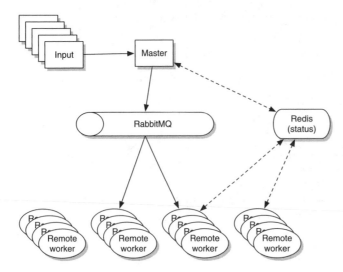

Figure 12.4   The master/slave work framework builds on the remote worker code written in the chapter on scaling out Clojure programs with RabbitMQ. A master accepts a sequence of input elements and farms out the processing of each to a bank of remote worker processes. Each task sent off this way is tracked in the Redis key/value store, and this status is updated by the master as well as by the workers.

Your output may vary depending on how many worker processes you have and on the speed of your computer. Try it with a larger sequence of arguments and more worker servers. Figure 12.4 shows the high-level conceptual view of this master/slave worker framework.

Now that the basics all work, we're going to see about handling errors during job runs.

12.2.7   *Seeing task errors*

You're now able to define and run jobs as shown in the previous section. So far, you haven't taken any advantage of the status of the tasks that are created as the job runs. You'll now see what happens when there's an error, and then you'll write some code to recover.

Before you get to that, let's add to our status namespace by creating a couple of functions to check on our jobs. The first will be a function to let us check if all tasks belonging to a job are complete. You can build on top of the `from-proxies` function we wrote earlier to support `values-from`. Consider the following definition of `job-complete?`:

```
(defn job-complete? [job]
  (every? true? (from-proxies job :complete?)))
```

This function merely tells you if a task has completed running; you'll also need a function to see if the tasks all completed successfully. Here's the code:

```
(defn task-successful? [job-id task-id]
  (= COMPLETE (status-of job-id task-id)))

(defn job-successful? [job]
  (->> @(:tasks-atom job)
       (keys)
```

```
(map (partial task-successful? (:job-id job)))
(every? true?)))
```

Remember that `task-successful?` (as with all other Redis-backed functions) needs to run inside Redis connection bindings. Next, in order to see how errors may manifest themselves in your job runs, let's add some random errors to our `factorial` function. Here's one way to do it:

```
(defn throw-exception-randomly []
  (if (> 3 (rand-int 10))
    (throw (RuntimeException. "Some error occured in fibonacci!"))))

(slave-worker factorial [n]
  (throw-exception-randomly)
  (let [f (fact n 1)]
    (println "Calculated factorial of" n "value:" f)
    f))
```

What we've done is made our `factorial` function throw an exception at random. The idea is that if you run it enough times, it will eventually succeed. You can use this to test your error-management code. Ensure that this code is in the `dist-fact` namespace as before.

Let's add a convenience macro to our master-core namespace that will help you run your jobs:

```
(defmacro with-rabbit-redis [& body]
  `(with-rabbit ["localhost" "guest" "guest"]
     (redis/with-server (redis-config)
       ~@(do body))))
```

Let's start by seeing how all this behaves. You'll modify our `chapter-data.dist-fact-client` namespace to use our new code:

```
(ns chapter-data.dist-fact-client
  (:use chapter-data.dist-fact
        chapter-data.master-core
        chapter-data.status
        chapter14-worker-multicast
        chapter14-rabbitmq-multicast))

(defn dispatch-factorial [job-id task-id n]
  (redis/with-server (redis-config)
    (mark-dispatched job-id task-id)
    (factorial job-id task-id [n])))

(def fact-job (new-job "fact-job" factorial 5 10000 identity))

(with-rabbit-redis
  (start-job fact-job (map list (take 10 (iterate inc 1))))
  (println "Status:" (job-successful? fact-job))
  (println "Values:" (values-from fact-job)))
```

Running this results in the following output:

```
Status: false
Values: (false 2 6 24 120 720 5040 40320 362880 false)
```

This indicates that the success of the job was false, and that of the expected return values, the first and the last happened to throw the random exception. Let's explore this some more, and to do that, you'll run a job from the REPL. Consider this code:

```
user=> (with-rabbit-redis
          (start-job fact-job (map list (take 10 (iterate inc 1)))))
          (println "Job success:" (job-successful? fact-job))
          (println "Values:" (values-from fact-job))
          (println "Tasks:" (task-statuses fact-job)))
```

The output, of which we're particularly interested in the statuses of all our tasks, looks like this:

```
Job success: false
Values: (false 2 false false 120 720 5040 40320 362880 3628800)
Tasks: (error complete error error complete complete complete complete
     complete complete)
```

As you can see, there are three tasks that have errors (you will probably see different results, thanks to the fact that our `factorial` function throws an exception at random). Your next job is to try to rerun those tasks that have errors. That's the focus of the next section.

12.2.8 *Rerunning the job*

So we ran our job, and a few tasks failed. We simulated this with our random exception throwing `factorial` function. In the real world, for heavy tasks, this might signify things like a broken connection, an unavailable service, or something else. Either way, it may make sense to retry the failed tasks at least once.

In order to do this, you need to be able to rerun the job. There's one more situation where you may want to do this, and that's if for some reason your job run itself crashes, the program crashes while it's dispatching tasks. It should be smart enough to not run tasks that have already been run before.

So let's begin by writing a `should-run?` function whose job it is to figure out whether it should dispatch a task to your remote servers. You can put this in your `chapter-data.status` namespace:

```
(defn should-run? [job-id task-id]
  (let [status (status-of job-id task-id)]
    (or (nil? status)
        (some #{status} [DISPATCHED RECOVERY INITIAL SECONDARY ERROR]))))
```

Now, in order to change the way tasks are dispatched, you only have to change the `run-task` function so that it uses our new `should-run?` function. Consider the changed version:

```
(defn run-task [{:keys [job-id worker tasks-atom]}
                task-id args mark-status]
  (println "Running task [" job-id task-id "]")
  (when (should-run? job-id task-id)
    (mark-status job-id task-id)
```

```
(let [task-info {:args args
                 :proxy (apply worker [job-id task-id args])}]
  (swap! tasks-atom assoc task-id task-info))))
```

We've also added a `println` so that you can see the progress at the console. We'll clear Redis and start a new job run:

```
user=> (with-rabbit-redis (redis/flushall))
"OK"
```

Let's now create a new job that you'll use to test job recovery:

```
user=> (def fact-job (new-job "fact-job" factorial 5 3000 identity))
#'user/fact-job
```

Let's run it with a sample set of 10 arguments, as we've done so far:

```
user=> (with-rabbit-redis
         (start-job fact-job (map list (take 10 (iterate inc 1)))))
Running task [ fact-job 1 ]
Running task [ fact-job 2 ]
Running task [ fact-job 3 ]
Running task [ fact-job 4 ]
Running task [ fact-job 5 ]
Running task [ fact-job 6 ]
Running task [ fact-job 7 ]
Running task [ fact-job 8 ]
Running task [ fact-job 9 ]
Running task [ fact-job 10 ]
nil
```

Now let's check on the statuses of the tasks:

```
user=> (with-rabbit-redis
         (doall (task-statuses fact-job)))
("error" "complete" "complete" "complete" "complete" "complete" "complete"
   "error" "error" "complete")
```

It appears that three tasks have failed. By the way, if you got a "Not connected to Redis" error, you must remember to wrap your call to `task-statuses` in a `doall`, or else the lazy sequence of statuses will be realized outside the Redis connection binding.

Let's now try this same job again, in order to see if the failed tasks complete this time:

```
user=> (with-rabbit-redis
         (start-job fact-job (map list (take 10 (iterate inc 1)))))
Running task [ fact-job 1 ]
Running task [ fact-job 8 ]
Running task [ fact-job 9 ]
nil
```

Notice how it ran only the tasks that hadn't been run before? Let's see if they succeeded:

```
user=> (with-rabbit-redis (doall (task-statuses fact-job)))
  ("error" "complete" "complete" "complete" "complete" "complete" "complete"
     "error" "complete" "complete")
```

One more task completed successfully, but there are still a couple in an error state. You can try this repeatedly until they all succeed:

```
user=> (with-rabbit-redis
          (start-job fact-job (map list (take 10 (iterate inc 1)))))
Running task [ fact-job 1 ]
Running task [ fact-job 8 ]
nil

user=> (with-rabbit-redis (job-successful? fact-job))
true
```

This time, both tasks completed successfully, resulting in job-successful? returning true.

Notice that in order to rerun the job, you passed it the same sequence of arguments each time. You don't have to do this; you could have found out what arguments needed to be rerun and passed only a sequence of those. Rerunning the entire job this way is useful when the program crashes and you want to start over. You could write another function that looks inside tasks-atom to see what to rerun. Here it is, suitable for the chapter-data.status namespace:

```
(defn incomplete-task-ids [{:keys [job-id tasks-atom]}]
  (remove (partial task-successful? job-id) (keys @tasks-atom)))
```

This function, given a job that has been run already, will tell you what tasks need to be run again in order for the job to complete. You can use this in a function that will attempt this recovery:

```
(defn recover-job [{:keys [tasks-atom] :as job}]
  (doseq [incomplete-id (incomplete-task-ids job)]
    (let [args (get-in @tasks-atom [incomplete-id :args])]
      (run-task job incomplete-id args mark-recovery))))
```

All this function does is iterate over each incomplete task id, get the arguments used from the previously attempted dispatch, and redispatch it. Note that this time, you pass the run-task function a different status-marker function, mark-recovery. Let's look at it in action:

First, you define a new job:

```
user=> (def fact-job (new-job "fact-job" factorial 5 3000 identity))
#'user/fact-job
```

Here's our first attempt:

```
user=> (with-rabbit-redis (start-job fact-job (map list (take 10 (iterate inc
    1)))))
Running task [ fact-job 1 ]
Running task [ fact-job 2 ]
Running task [ fact-job 3 ]
Running task [ fact-job 4 ]
Running task [ fact-job 5 ]
Running task [ fact-job 6 ]
Running task [ fact-job 7 ]
```

```
Running task [ fact-job 8 ]
Running task [ fact-job 9 ]
Running task [ fact-job 10 ]
nil
```

You've seen this before; here's the current set of statuses:

```
user=> (with-rabbit-redis (doall (task-statuses fact-job)))
("complete" "complete" "complete" "complete" "error" "complete" "complete"
    "error" "complete" "error")
```

Here are the tasks that are still incomplete:

```
user=> (with-rabbit-redis (doall (incomplete-task-ids fact-job)))
 (5 8 10)
```

Attempting to recover:

```
user=> (with-rabbit-redis (recover-job fact-job))
Running task [ fact-job 5 ]
Running task [ fact-job 8 ]
Running task [ fact-job 10 ]
nil
```

As you can see, only incomplete tasks were fired off. If you check the statuses of the tasks now, you can hope to see some progress:

```
user=> (with-rabbit-redis (doall (task-statuses fact-job)))
 ("complete" "complete" "complete" "complete" "error" "complete" "complete"
    "complete" "complete" "complete")
```

Only one task remains incomplete. You can try it again:

```
user=> (with-rabbit-redis (recover-job fact-job))
Running task [ fact-job 5 ]
```

And finally:

```
user=> (with-rabbit-redis (doall (task-statuses fact-job)))
 ("complete" "complete" "complete" "complete" "complete" "complete"
    "complete" "complete" "complete" "complete")
```

You ran `recover-job` multiple times because you could be certain our `factorial` function would eventually succeed. This may not be the case in a real-world application, so you'd need to make a decision on how many retries are worth doing and what to do after the final failure.

Note also that the main advantage of using `recover-job` is that it doesn't need to be supplied the arguments sequence again, because it already has the arguments for each task. This may be useful if it's expensive to obtain the arguments. It may also be a memory problem if the arguments sequence is extremely large, so it may make sense to have such argument caching as an optional operation.

Listing 12.8 shows the complete code that handles the definition and dispatch of batch jobs. It's followed by listing 12.9, which shows the complete code that handles the status of a job.

```
ns chapter-data.master-core
  (:use chapter14-rabbitmq-multicast
        chapter14-worker-multicast
        chapter-data.status
        clojure.contrib.seq-utils)
  (:require redis))

(defn new-job [job-id worker batch-size batch-wait-time id-generator]
  {:tasks-atom (atom {})
   :job-id job-id
   :worker worker
   :batch-size batch-size
   :batch-wait-time batch-wait-time
   :id-gen id-generator})

(defn run-task [{:keys [job-id worker tasks-atom]}
                task-id args mark-status]
  (when (should-run? job-id task-id)
    (println "Running task [" job-id task-id "]")
    (mark-status job-id task-id)
    (let [task-info {:args args
                     :proxy (apply worker [job-id task-id args])}]
      (swap! tasks-atom assoc task-id task-info))))

(defn run-batch [{:keys [id-gen tasks-atom batch-wait-time] :as job}
                 args-batch]
  (doseq [args args-batch]
    (run-task job (apply id-gen args) args mark-dispatched))
  (wait-until-completion (map :proxy (vals @tasks-atom)) batch-wait-time))

(defn start-job [{:keys [batch-size] :as job} args-seq]
  (redis/with-server (redis-config)
    (let [args-batches (partition-all batch-size args-seq)]
      (doseq [args-batch args-batches]
        (run-batch job args-batch)))))

(defn recover-job [{:keys [tasks-atom] :as job}]
  (doseq [incomplete-id (incomplete-task-ids job)]
    (let [args (get-in @tasks-atom [incomplete-id :args])]
      (run-task job incomplete-id args mark-recovery))))

(defn slave-wrapper [worker-function]
  (fn [job-id task-id worker-args]
    (redis/with-server (redis-config)
      (increment-status job-id task-id)
      (try
       (let [return (apply worker-function worker-args)]
         (increment-status job-id task-id)
         return)
       (catch Exception e
         (mark-error job-id task-id))))))

(defmacro slave-worker [name args & body]
  `(let [simple-function# (fn ~args (do ~@body))
         slave-function# (slave-wrapper simple-function#)]
```

```
      (defworker ~name [~'job-id ~'task-id ~'worker-args]
        (slave-function# ~'job-id ~'task-id ~'worker-args))))

(defmacro with-rabbit-redis [& body]
  `(with-rabbit ["localhost" "guest" "guest"]
     (redis/with-server (redis-config)
       ~@(do body))))
```

Listing 12.9   The status namespace for our master/slave batch-processing framework

```
(ns chapter-data.status
  (:require redis))

(def KEY-SEPARATOR "___")

(def STATUS-FIELD "status")

(def DISPATCHED "dispatched")
(def INITIAL "initial")
(def COMPLETE "complete")
(def ERROR "error")
(def RECOVERY "recovery")
(def SECONDARY "secondary")
(def UNKNOWN "unknown")

(def next-status {
   DISPATCHED INITIAL
   INITIAL    COMPLETE
   RECOVERY   SECONDARY
   SECONDARY  COMPLETE
   ""         UNKNOWN
   nil        UNKNOWN
   UNKNOWN    UNKNOWN
})

(defn redis-config []
  {:host "localhost"})

(defn managed-key [job-id task-id]
  (str job-id KEY-SEPARATOR task-id))

(defn status-of [job-id task-id]
  (redis/hget (managed-key job-id task-id) STATUS-FIELD))

(defn update-status-as [job-id task-id status]
  (redis/hset (managed-key job-id task-id) STATUS-FIELD status))

(defn mark-dispatched [job-id task-id]
  (update-status-as job-id task-id DISPATCHED))

(defn mark-error [job-id task-id]
  (update-status-as job-id task-id ERROR))

(defn mark-recovery [job-id task-id]
  (update-status-as job-id task-id RECOVERY))

(defn increment-status [job-id task-id]
  (->> (status-of job-id task-id)
       (next-status)
       (update-status-as job-id task-id)))
```

```clojure
(defn task-successful? [job-id task-id]
  (= COMPLETE (status-of job-id task-id)))

(defn job-successful? [job]
  (->> @(:tasks-atom job)
       (keys)
       (map (partial task-successful? (:job-id job)))
       (every? true?)))

(defn from-proxies [job proxy-command]
  (->> @(:tasks-atom job)
       (vals)
       (map :proxy)
       (map #(% proxy-command))))

(defn values-from [job]
  (from-proxies job :value))

(defn job-complete? [job]
  (every? true? (from-proxies job :complete?)))

(defn task-statuses [{:keys [job-id tasks-atom]}]
  (->> @tasks-atom
       (keys)
       (map #(status-of job-id %))))

(defn should-run? [job-id task-id]
  (let [status (status-of job-id task-id)]
    (or (nil? status)
        (some #{status} [DISPATCHED RECOVERY INITIAL SECONDARY ERROR]))))

(defn incomplete-task-ids [{:keys [job-id tasks-atom]}]
  (remove (partial task-successful? job-id) (keys @tasks-atom)))
```

You've implemented a fair bit of functionality for our little master/slave worker framework. The complete code is shown in listings 12.1 and 12.2, which shows the code for the core and status namespaces respectively. The code doesn't do everything that a robust, production-ready framework might do, but it shows a possible approach.

12.3 *Summary*

In this chapter, we've looked at a few different ways to process data. Each application that you'll end up writing will need a different model based on the specifics of the domain. Clojure is flexible enough to solve the most demanding problems, and the functional style helps by reducing the amount of code needed while also increasing the readability of the code. And in the case where rolling your own data-processing framework isn't the best course, there are plenty of Java solutions that can be wrapped with a thin layer of Clojure.

More on functional programming

So far, you've seen a lot of the Clojure programming language, and you've used it to write programs that can access data stores, communicate on message queues, consume and provide you services, crunch large amounts of data, and more. In this chapter, we'll revisit a fundamental concept of Clojure—that of functional programming.

Instead of approaching this from, say, a mathematical (or plain theoretical) standpoint, we'll write code to explore some of the main ideas. We'll start by implementing a few common higher-order functions used in functional programs, to help you become comfortable with recursion, lazy sequences, and functional abstraction and reuse in general.

Next, we'll visit the land of currying and partial application. This exposure will give you further insight into functional programming and what you can do with it.

Although partial application (and certainly currying) isn't particularly widespread in Clojure code, sometimes it's the perfect fit for the job.

The final stop will be to explore closures. The last section puts everything together to write a little object system that illustrates the ideas of OOP vis-à-vis functional programming.

13.1 *Using higher-order functions*

We talked about higher-order functions in chapter 3. A *higher-order function* is one that either accepts another function or returns a function. Higher-order functions allow the programmer to abstract out patterns of computation that would otherwise result in duplication in code. In this section, we'll look at a few simple examples of higher-order functions that can greatly simplify code. You've seen several of these functions before, in other forms, and we'll point these out as you implement them.

Overall, this section will give you a sense of how higher-order functions can be used to implement a variety of solutions in Clojure, indeed, how it's an integral part of doing so.

13.1.1 *Collecting results of functions*

Let's begin our look at higher-order functions by considering the idea of a function named `square-all` that accepts a list of numbers and returns a list of the squares of each element:

```
(defn square [x]
  (* x x))

(defn square-all [numbers]
  (if (empty? numbers)
    ()
    (cons (square (first numbers))
          (square-all (rest numbers)))))
```

This works as expected, and you can test this at the REPL as follows:

```
user=> (square-all [1 2 3 4 5 6])
(1 4 9 16 25 36)
```

Now let's look at another function, `cube-all`, which also accepts a list of numbers but returns a list of cubes of each element:

```
(defn cube [x]
  (* x x x))

(defn cube-all [numbers]
  (if (empty? numbers)
    ()
    (cons (cube (first numbers))
          (cube-all (rest numbers)))))
```

Again, this is easy to test:

```
user=> (cube-all [1 2 3 4 5 6])
(1 8 27 64 125 216)
```

They both work as expected. The trouble is that there's a significant amount of duplication in the definitions of square-all and cube-all. You can easily see this commonality by considering the fact that both functions were applying a function to each element and were collecting the results before returning the list of return values.

You've already seen that such functions can be captured as higher-order functions in languages such as Clojure:

```
(defn do-to-all [f numbers]
  (if (empty? numbers)
    ()
    (cons (f (first numbers))
          (do-to-all f (rest numbers)))))
```

With this, you can perform the same operations easily:

```
user> (do-to-all square [1 2 3 4 5 6])
(1 4 9 16 25 36)
user> (do-to-all cube [1 2 3 4 5 6])
(1 8 27 64 125 216)
```

You can imagine that the do-to-all implementation is similar to that of the map function that's included in Clojure's core library. The map function is an abstraction that allows you to apply any function across sequences of arguments and collect results into another sequence. Our implementation suffers from a rather fatal flaw. The issue is that without tail-call optimization, it will blow the call stack if a long enough list of elements is passed in. Here's what it will look like:

```
user=> (do-to-all square (range 11000))
No message.
  [Thrown class java.lang.StackOverflowError]
```

This is because Clojure doesn't provide tail-call optimization (thanks to limitations of the JVM), but it does provide a way to fix this problem. Consider the following revised implementation:

```
(defn do-to-all [f numbers]
  (lazy-seq
    (if (empty? numbers)
      ()
      (cons (f (first numbers))
            (do-to-all f (rest numbers))))))
```

Tail calls

A *tail call* is a call to a function from the last expression of another function body. When such a tail call returns, the calling function returns the value of the tail call. In most functional languages, tail calls are eliminated, so that using such calls doesn't consume the stack. This is possible because function calls from the tail position can be rewritten as jumps by the compiler or interpreter.

Clojure doesn't do this because of a related limitation on the JVM.

Now, because we made this return a lazy sequence, it no longer attempts to recursively compute all the elements to return. It now works as expected:

```
user=> (take 10 (drop 10000 (do-to-all square (range 11000))))
(100000000 100020001 100040004 100060009 100080016 100100025 100120036
    100140049 100160064 100180081)
```

This is similar to the map function that comes with Clojure (the Clojure version does a lot more). The map function is an extremely useful higher-order function, and as you've seen over the last few chapters, it sees heavy usage. Let's now look at another important operation, which can be implemented using another higher-order function.

13.1.2 *Reducing lists of things*

It's often useful to take a list of things and compute a value based on all of them. An example might be a total of a list of numbers or the largest number. Let's implement the total first:

```
(defn total-of [numbers]
  (loop [l numbers sum 0]
    (if (empty? l)
      sum
      (recur (rest l) (+ sum (first l))))))
```

This works as expected, as you can see in the following test at the REPL:

```
user> (total-of [5 7 9 3 4 1 2 8])
39
```

Now let's write a function to return the greatest from a list of numbers. First, let's write a simple function that returns the greater of two numbers:

```
(defn larger-of [x y]
  (if (> x y) x y))
```

This is a simple enough function, but now we can use it to search for the largest number in a series of numbers:

```
(defn greatest-of [numbers]
  (loop [l numbers candidate (first numbers)]
    (if (empty? l)
      candidate
      (recur (rest l) (larger-of candidate (first l))))))
```

Let's see if this works:

```
user> (greatest-of [5 7 9 3 4 1 2 8])
9
user> (greatest-of [])
nil
```

We have it working, but there's clearly some duplication in total-of and greatest-of. Specifically, the only difference between them is that one adds an element to an accumulator, whereas the other compares an element with a candidate. Let's extract out the commonality into a function:

```
(defn compute-across [func elements value]
  (if (empty? elements)
    value
    (recur func (rest elements) (func value (first elements)))))
```

Now, we can easily use `compute-across` in order to implement `total-of` and `largest-of`:

```
(defn total-of [numbers]
  (compute-across + numbers 0))

(defn greatest-of [numbers]
  (compute-across larger-of numbers (first numbers)))
```

To ensure that things still work as expected, you can test these two functions at the REPL again:

```
user> (total-of [5 7 9 3 4 1 2 8])
39

user> (greatest-of [5 7 9 3 4 1 2 8])
9
```

`compute-across` is generic enough that it can operate on any sequence. For instance, here's a function that collects all numbers greater than some specified threshold:

```
(defn all-greater-than [threshold numbers]
  (compute-across #(if (> %2 threshold) (conj %1 %2) %1) numbers []))
```

Before getting into how this works, let's see if it works:

```
user> (all-greater-than 5 [5 7 9 3 4 1 2 8])
[7 9 8]
```

It does work as expected. The implementation is simple: you've already seen how `compute-across` works. Our initial value (which behaves as an accumulator) is an empty vector. We need to conjoin numbers to this when it's greater than the threshold. The anonymous function does this.

Our `compute-across` function is similar to something you've already seen: the `reduce` function that's part of Clojure's core functions. It allows you to process sequences of data and compute some final result. Let's now look at another related example of using our `compute-across`.

13.1.3 *Filtering lists of things*

We wrote a function in the previous section that allows us to collect all numbers greater than a particular threshold. Let's now write another one that collects those numbers that are less than a threshold:

```
(defn all-lesser-than [threshold numbers]
  (compute-across #(if (< %2 threshold) (conj %1 %2) %1) numbers []))
```

Here it is in action:

```
user> (all-lesser-than 5 [5 7 9 3 4 1 2 8])
[3 4 1 2]
```

Notice how easy it is, now that we have our convenient little `compute-across` function (or the equivalent `reduce`). Also, notice that there's duplication in our `all-greater-than` and `all-lesser-than` functions. The only difference between them is in the criteria used in selecting which elements should be returned. Let's extract the common part into a higher-order `select-if` function:

```
(defn select-if [pred elements]
  (compute-across #(if (pred %2) (conj %1 %2) %1) elements []))
```

You can now use this to select all sorts of elements from a larger sequence. For instance, here's an example of selecting all odd numbers from a vector:

```
user> (select-if odd? [5 7 9 3 4 1 2 8])
[5 7 9 3 1]
```

To reimplement our previously defined `all-lesser-than` function, you could write it in the following manner:

```
(defn all-lesser-than [threshold numbers]
  (select-if #(< % threshold) numbers))
```

This implementation is far more readable, because it expresses the intent with simplicity and clarity. Our `select-if` function is another useful, low-level function that we can use with any sequence. In fact, Clojure comes with such a function, one that you've seen before: `filter`.

Over the last few pages, we've created the functions `do-to-all`, `compute-across`, and `select-if`, which implement the essence of the built-in `map`, `reduce`, and `filter` functions. The reason we did this was two-fold: to demonstrate common use cases of higher-order functions and to show that the basic form of these functions is rather simple to implement. Our `select-if` isn't lazy, for instance, but with all the knowledge you've gained so far, you can implement one that is. With this background in place, let's explore a few other topics of interest of functional programs.

13.2   *Partial application and currying*

We wrote several higher-order functions in the last section. Specifically, our functions accepted a function as one argument and applied it to other arguments. Now we're going to look at another kind of higher-order functions, those that create and return new functions. The ability to create functions dynamically is a crucial aspect of functional programming. In this section, we'll focus on a functional programming technique where we'll write functions that return new functions of less arity than the ones they accept as an argument. We'll do this by partially applying the function, the meaning of which will become clear shortly.

13.2.1   *Adapting functions*

Let's imagine you have a function that accepts a tax percentage (such as 8.0 or 9.75) and a price. It returns the price by adding the appropriate tax. You can easily implement this with a threading macro:

```
(defn price-with-tax [tax-rate amount]
  (->> (/ tax-rate 100)
       (+ 1)
       (* amount)))
```

Now you can find out what something truly costs, because you can calculate its price including the sales tax, as follows:

```
user> (price-with-tax 9.5 100)
109.5
```

If you had a list of prices that you wanted to convert into a list of tax-inclusive prices, you could write the following function:

```
(defn with-california-taxes [prices]
  (map #(price-with-tax 9.25 %) prices))
```

And you could then batch-calculate pricing with taxes:

```
user> (def prices [100 200 300 400 500])

user> (with-california-taxes prices)
(109.25 218.5 327.75 437.0 546.25)
```

Notice that in the definition of `with-california-taxes`, we created an anonymous function that accepted a single argument (a price) and applied `price-with-tax` to 9.25 and the price. Creating this anonymous function is convenient; otherwise, we might have had to define a separate function that we may never have used anywhere else, such as this:

```
(defn price-with-ca-tax [price]
  (price-with-tax 9.25 price))
```

And if we had to handle New York, it would look like this:

```
(defn price-with-ny-tax [price]
  (price-with-tax 8.0 price))
```

If we had to handle any more, the duplication would certainly get to us. Luckily, a functional language such as Clojure can make short work of it:

```
(defn price-calculator-for-tax [state-tax]
  (fn [price]
    (price-with-tax state-tax price)))
```

This function accepts a tax rate, presumably for a given state, and then returns a new function that accepts a single argument. When this new function is called with a price, it returns the result of applying `price-with-tax` to the originally supplied tax rate and the price. In this manner, the newly defined (and returned) function behaves like a closure around the supplied tax rate. Now that we have this meta function, we can remove the duplication you saw earlier, by defining state-specific functions as follows:

```
(def price-with-ca-tax (price-calculator-for-tax 9.25))
```

```
(def price-with-ny-tax (price-calculator-for-tax 8.0))
```

Notice again that we're creating new vars (and that we're directly using def here, not defn) that are bound to the anonymous functions returned by the price-calculator-for-tax function.

These new functions accept a single argument and are perfect for functions such as with-california-taxes that accept a list of prices, and call map across them. A single argument function serves well in such a case, and you can use any of the previous functions for this purpose. This is a simple case where we started out with a function of a certain arity (in this case, price-with-tax accepts two arguments), and we needed a new function that accepted a lesser number of arguments (in this case, a single-argument function that could map across a sequence of prices).

This approach of taking a function of n arguments and creating a new function of k arguments (where $n > k$) is a form of adaptation (you may be familiar with the adapter pattern from OO literature). You don't need special ceremony to do this in Clojure, thanks to functions being first class. Let's see how Clojure makes this easy.

PARTIAL APPLICATION

Let's say you have a function of n arguments and you need to fix $(n - k)$ arguments, in order to create a new function of k arguments. Let's create a function to illustrate this:

```
(defn of-n-args [a b c d e]
  (str a b c d e ))
```

Now, in order to fix, say, the first three arguments to 1, 2, and 3, you could do the following:

```
(defn of-k-args [d e]
  (of-n-args 1 2 3 d e))
```

Let's ensure that this function works as expected:

```
user> (of-k-args \a \b)
"123ab"
```

OK, so that works. If you needed to create a function that fixed, say, two or four arguments, you'd have to write similar code again. As you can imagine, if you had to do this a lot, it would get rather repetitive and tedious.

You could improve things by writing a function that generalizes the idea. Here's a function that does this:

```
(defn partially-applied [of-n-args & n-minus-k-args]
  (fn [& k-args]
    (apply of-n-args (concat n-minus-k-args k-args))))
```

Now, you could create any number of functions that fixed a particular set of arguments of a particular function, for example:

```
user> (def of-2-args (partially-applied of-n-args \a \b \c))
#'user/of-2-args
```

```
user> (def of-3-args (partially-applied of-n-args \a \b))
#'user/of-3-args
```

And you can see if these work as expected:

```
user> (of-2-args 4 5)
"abc45"

user> (of-3-args 3 4 5)
"ab345"
```

We called our new function `partially-applied` because it returns a function that's a partially applied version of the function we passed into it. For example, `of-3-args` is a partially applied version of `of-n-args`. This is such a common technique in functional programming that Clojure comes with a function that does this, and it's called `partial`.

It's used the same way:

```
user> (def of-2-args (partial of-n-args \a \b \c))
#'user/of-2-args
user> (def of-3-args (partial of-n-args \a \b))
#'user/of-3-args
```

And here it is in action:

```
user> (of-2-args 4 5)
"abc45"

user> (of-3-args 3 4 5)
"ab345"
```

You now understand what it means to partially apply a function. Although the examples showed this technique where you needed to adapt a function of a given arity to a function of a lower arity, there are other uses as well. You'll see one such usage in the next section.

13.2.2 Defining functions

In this section, we'll use the technique of partial application to define new functions. Recall the `select-if` function from the previous section:

```
(defn select-if [pred elements]
  (compute-across #(if (pred %2) (conj %1 %2) %1) elements []))
```

Note that we pass the `compute-across` function an empty vector as the last argument. We'll write a modified version of `select-if` called `select-into-if`, which will accept an initial container:

```
(defn select-into-if [container pred elements]
  (compute-across #(if (pred %2) (conj %1 %2) %1) elements container))
```

Again, as you saw in the previous section, if you had a list of numbers such as

```
(def numbers [4 9 5 7 6 3 8])
```

then you could use our new function as follows:

```
user> (select-into-if [] #(< % 7) numbers)
[4 5 6 3]
```

Similarly, you could also pass in an empty list instead of an empty vector, as shown here:

```
user> (select-into-if () #(< % 7) numbers)
(3 6 5 4)
```

Note that depending on whether you want to filter results up or down (in the same order as the elements appear or in the reverse), you can use either the empty vector as your container or the empty list. Let's now further abstract this idea of filtering results up or down as follows:

```
(def select-up (partial select-into-if []))
```

Here, we've created a new function using `partial`. We fixed the first argument of the `select-into-if` function to the empty vector. Similarly, you could define the concept of selecting down a sequence of elements as follows:

```
(def select-down (partial select-into-if ()))
```

Let's test these two functions to ensure that they work:

```
user> (select-up  #(< % 9) [5 3 9 6 8])
[5 3 6 8]

user> (select-down  #(< % 9) [5 3 9 6 8])
(8 6 3 5)
```

Obviously, there are specific implications that arise from using a vector versus a list, and depending on the situation, these may be a convenient way to filter elements of a sequence.

As you've seen, partial application of functions can be a useful tool. This section showed two situations where this technique might come in handy. The first is to adapt functions to a suitable arity by fixing one or more arguments of a given function. The second is to define functions by partially applying a more general function to get specific functions that have one or more arguments fixed. In the next section, we'll discuss a related functional programming concept called currying.

13.2.3 *Currying*

Currying is the process by which a function that takes multiple arguments is transformed into another that takes a single argument and returns a partially applied function. As you can imagine, the concepts of currying and of partial application are closely related. To understand this better, consider the following function:

```
(defn add-pair [a b]
  (+ a b))
```

Imagine that the `add-pair` function was curried. If you were to call it with only a single argument, you'd get back a new function of one argument, for example:

```
(def inc-by-two (add-pair 2))
;; this won't actually work, since Clojure functions are not curried
```

This new function would add 2 to any argument it was passed, for instance:

```
user> (inc-by-two 3)
5
```

Curried functions are particularly central to certain functional programming languages such as Haskell that have functions of only one argument. In such languages, a function such as add-pair would work the following way:

```
user> (add-pair 2 3)
=> ((anonymous-function-that-adds-two) 3)
=> 5
```

The programmer wouldn't have to do anything explicit in order to invoke such behavior; all functions are curried by default in such languages. Okay, back to Clojure. Trying the previous example on the REPL will fail because add-pair isn't curried and it needs two arguments when called. You could accomplish what we're describing here using partial, but the semantics would be different:

```
user> (def inc-by-two (partial add-pair 2))
#'user/inc-by-two
```

This would then work as expected:

```
user> (inc-by-two 3)
5
```

This difference (having to be explicit about partially applying arguments) is because Clojure functions aren't automatically curried. You might be able to write a function as follows in order to remedy this situation:

```
(defn curry-1 [f]
  (fn [x]
    (fn [y]
      (f x y))))
```

Now you could try our previous example again by first creating a curried version of add-pair as shown here:

```
user> (def add-pair-curried (curry-1 add-pair))
#'user/add-pair-curried
```

This creates a curried version of add-pair that will work as desired when applied to a single argument:

```
user> (def inc-by-two (add-pair-curried 2))
#'user/inc-by-two
```

Now inc-by-two will also work as you saw before:

```
user> (inc-by-two 3)
5
```

curry-1 worked for us because add-pair takes two arguments. What if you had more arguments, such as the following function?

```
(defn add-quadruple [a b c d]
  (+ a b c d))
```

curry-1 won't suffice to convert this into a curried function. Because Clojure functions can accept a variable number of arguments, you can write a slightly more generalized version of curry. Strictly speaking, currying returns single-argument functions because the concept applies more to languages that have only single-argument functions. Still, our function here is more applicable to languages such as Clojure that do support more than one argument. Here it is:

```
(defn curry-2 [f]
  (fn [& args]
    (fn [& more-args]
      (apply f (concat args more-args)))))
```

With this version of curry, you can create curried versions of functions that take more than two arguments as well, for instance:

```
user> (def add-quadruple-curried (curry-2 add-quadruple))
#'user/add-quadruple-curried
```

Now, you can use our curried version of the function to get new functions when applied to fewer than four arguments:

```
user> (def add-2-to-triple (add-quadruple-curried 2))
#'user/add-2-to-triple
```

And here's how you can use it:

```
user> (add-2-to-triple 3 4 5)
14
```

add-quadruple-curried will also work when passed more than one argument, as shown here:

```
user> (def add-5-to-pair (add-quadruple-curried 2 3))
#'user/add-5-to-pair

user> (add-5-to-pair 4 5)
14
```

So far, we haven't done anything too major that couldn't be accomplished with partial. If all functions were automatically curried, you'd be able to do something like the following:

```
(def inc-by-9 (add-5-to-pair 4))
;; won't work since add-5-to-pair isn't curried
```

So even though we created add-5-to-pair by calling a curried function with less than complete arguments, the returned function itself isn't curried. add-5-to-pair behaves like all regular Clojure functions in that it needs to be called with all its arguments (or passed to partial explicitly).

Let's now try to write a version of curry that returns curried functions if required. We'll have to keep track of how many parameters such a function takes so we can decide whether all arguments have been passed. The function `curried-fn` shown here does this:

```
(defn curried-fn [func args-len]
  (fn [& args]
    (let [remaining (- args-len (count args))]
      (if (zero? remaining)
        (apply func args)
        (curried-fn (apply partial func args) remaining)))))
```

Before using this function, we'll also create a wrapper around it so that we have a syntactically clear way to create curried functions. The following macro, `defcurried`, does the job:

```
(defmacro defcurried [fname args & body]
  `(let [fun# (fn ~args (do ~@body))]
     (def ~fname (curried-fn fun# ~(count args)))))
```

Now we're ready to try this out. Let's try our `add-quadruple` function again:

```
(defcurried add-quadruple [a b c d]
  (+ a b c d))
```

Now we have a curried function that returns either the result of the computation as specified in its body or another function that's the result of partially applying the supplied arguments but also curried. Here's an example:

```
user> (def add-5-to-triple (add-quadruple 5))
#'user/add-5-to-triple
```

You've seen this before, when we used the `add-quadruple-curried` version of this function. The difference that time was that the resulting `add-5-to-triple` wasn't curried but was a regular Clojure function. This time around, we can do the following:

```
user> (def add-9-to-pair (add-5-to-triple 4))
#'user/add-9-to-pair
```

And it doesn't end there. We can go further:

```
user> (def inc-by-12 (add-9-to-pair 3))
#'user/inc-by-12
```

And finally, we can use the `inc-by-12` function:

```
user> (inc-by-12 3)
15
```

So, we've added the ability to automatically curry our functions. Figure 13.1 shows the difference between Clojure's `partial` function and our new `curry` function.

This functionality is limited, to be sure. For instance, it can't handle a variable number of arguments. Even so, why would we need such a feature? Clojure has two things that reduce the necessity of such automatic currying: `partial` and anonymous functions. Between these two and the fact that Clojure functions aren't restricted to being of a single arity, automatic currying is less of a requirement. Figure 13.1 shows

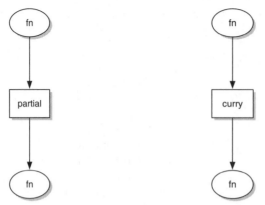

When applied, the return value will be   Returns another curried function when applied,
whatever the new version computes.   until all arguments to the original function are available.

Figure 13.1 Although both `partial` and `curry` return functions, a partially applied function is always ready to run when it's applied to the remaining arguments. If given insufficient arguments, a partially applied function will throw an exception complaining about that. Curried functions return functions that are further curried if they're applied to insufficient arguments.

the difference between partial and currying in a pictorial way. Our next stop will be to look at using anonymous functions to similar effect.

ANONYMOUS FUNCTIONS

The reader macro for anonymous functions is convenient shorthand for creating functions that are partially applied. Let's recall our regular function add-pair, whose job is to add the two numbers passed to it. Consider the following:

```
(def inc-by-3 #(add-pair 3 %1))
```

You know what this does; inc-by-3 is now a single-argument function that will add 3 to its argument. Note that this is equivalent to the following use of the partial function:

```
(def inc-by-3 (partial add-pair 3))
```

It's also similar to the use of the curried add-pair-curried:

```
(def inc-by-3 (add-pair-curried 3))
```

The anonymous function requires a little more typing, but it's more expressive. Not only can it handle variable args (via %&), but it can also handle arguments in specific places, for instance:

```
user> (def half-of #(/ %1 2))
#'user/half-of

user> (half-of 10)
5
```

You couldn't use partial (or curried functions) to do this, as shown here

```
user> ((partial / 2) 10)
1/5
```

because `partial` associates arguments in order (left to right). The same is true with curried functions. The anonymous function reader macro, on the other hand, is explicit about the order in which functions are applied. We mentioned that you could handle functions with variable arguments; let's look at an example. Consider the following function of variable arity:

```
(defn add-numbers [& numbers]
  (apply + numbers))
```

Now, you could create partially applied versions of this function using anonymous functions:

```
user> (def add-5-to-remaining #(apply add-numbers 2 3 %&))
#'user/add-5-to-remaining
```

Here it is in action:

```
user> (add-5-to-remaining 1 4 5)
15
```

As noted earlier, you couldn't have done this with our `defcurried` macro or using any related technique. A final point for Clojure's anonymous functions is that the reader macro syntax makes it abundantly clear that a function object is being constructed, whereas it isn't as clear with curried functions. Having said all that, there may well be cases where having the behavior of curried functions is what you need.

You've already seen closures, in previous chapters of this book as well as in this section. In the next section, we're going to explore them in more detail.

13.3 Closures

In this section, we're going to explore the lexical closure, which is a central concept of functional programming. How central it is can be seen from the fact that the name *Clojure* itself is a play on the term *closure*. We'll begin by reviewing what closures are and what they close over. Then we'll look at a couple of closure use cases in functional programming. Specifically, we'll look at how closures can be used to delay computation and how they can be used as objects (in the object-oriented sense of the word). At the end, we'll create a little object-oriented layer for Clojure in order to demonstrate that Clojure (and Lisps in general) go beyond traditional ideas of object-oriented programming.

13.3.1 Free variables and closures

Before we jump into what closures are, let's look at the concept of free variables. A free variable is a placeholder for a value that will be substituted in at some later point. More specifically, given a lexically scoped block of code, a free variable is one that's neither an argument nor a local variable, for instance:

```
(defn adder [num1 num2]
  (let [x (+ num1 num2)]
    (fn [y]
      (+ x y))))
```

Here, num1 and num2 are arguments of the adder function and so aren't free variables. The let form creates a lexically scoped block of code, and within that block, num1 and num2 are free variables. Further, the let form creates a locally named value called x. Therefore, within the let block, x is not a free variable. Finally, an anonymous function is created that accepts an argument called y. Within this anonymous function, y is not a free variable, but x is.

Now that you understand what a free variable is, let's examine this function a little more. Consider the following code:

```
user> (def add-5 (adder 2 3))
#'user/add-5
```

add-5 is a var that's bound to the return value of the call to adder, which is the anonymous function returned by the adder function. The function object contains within it a reference to x, which exists for only as long as the let block inside adder lives. Consider that the following works as expected:

```
user> (add-5 10)
15
```

Given the fact that the life of a locally named value such as x lasts only until the enclosing lexical block lasts, how can add-5 do its work? You might imagine that the x referenced inside add-5 ceased to be the moment add-5 was created.

The reason this works, though, is that the anonymous function returned by adder is a closure, in this case closing over the free variable x. The extent (life) of such closed-over free variables is that of the closure itself. This is why add-5 is able to use the value of x, and it adds 10 to 5 to return 15 in the example. Now let's look at what closures can do for our Clojure programs.

13.3.2 *Delayed computation and closures*

One aspect of closures is that they can be executed at any time, any number of times, or not at all. This property of delayed execution can be useful. Consider the following code:

```
(let [x 1
      y 0]
  (/ x y))
```

You know what this code will do: a nice divide-by-zero exception will be thrown. Let's wrap the code with a try-catch block so as to control the situation programmatically:

```
(let [x 1
      y 0]
  (try
    (/ x y)
    (catch Exception e
      (println (.getMessage e)))))
```

This pattern is common enough that you might want to extract it out into a higher-order control structure:

```
(defn try-catch [the-try the-catch]
  (try
   (the-try)
   (catch Exception e
     (the-catch e))))
```

Now that you have this, you could write

```
(let [x 1
      y 0]
  (try-catch #(/ x y)
             #(println (.getMessage %))))
```

Notice here that you're passing in an anonymous function that closes around x and y. You could have written a macro to do this same thing, but this shows that you don't need macros for something like this, even though the macro solution would be nicer (syntactically more convenient to use, resulting in code that's easier to read).

When we compared macros to functions, we said that Clojure evaluates function arguments in an eager manner. This behavior is an advantage of macros in that macros don't evaluate arguments, allowing us as programmers to be in control. But the function try-catch here, achieves the same intended effect by accepting functions that will be evaluated later. This is the reason we created anonymous functions that we then passed in as arguments. Because the function enclosed free variables x and y, the try-catch function was able to work correctly.

You can imagine creating other control structures in a similar manner. In the next section, you'll see another extremely useful aspect of closures.

13.3.3 *Closures and objects*

In this section, we're going to examine another benefit of the closure. As you've seen over the past few paragraphs, a closure captures the bindings of any free variables visible at the point of creation. These bindings are then hidden from view to the rest of the world, making the closure a candidate for private data. (Data hiding is somewhat of an overrated concept, especially in a language such as Clojure. You'll see more on this in the next section).

For the moment, let's continue exploring the captured bindings inside closures. Imagine that you needed to handle the concept of users in your application and that you wanted to store their login information, along with their email address. Consider the following function:

```
(defn new-user [login password email]
  (fn [a]
    (condp = a
      :login login
      :password password
      :email email)))
```

There's nothing particularly new here; you saw such code in the previous section. Here it is in action:

```
user> (def anya (new-user "anya" "secret" "anya@currylogic.com"))
#'user/anya

user> (anya :login)
"anya"

user> (anya :password)
"secret"

user> (anya :email)
"anya@currylogic.com"
```

First, we created a new function object by calling the new-user function with "anya", "secret", and "anya@currylogic.com" as arguments. Then, we were able to query it for the login, password, and email address. anya appears to behave something like a map, or at least a data object of some kind. You can query the internal state of the object using the keywords :login, :password, and :email, as shown previously.

It's also worth noting that this is the only way to access the internals of anya. This is a form of message passing: the keywords are messages that we're sending to a receiver object, which in this case is the function object anya. You can implement fewer of these should you choose to. For instance, you might deem the password to be a hidden detail. The modified function might look as follows:

```
(defn new-user [login password email]
  (fn [a]
    (condp = a
      :login login
      :email email)))
```

With this constructor of new users, there's no way to directly access the password a user was created with. Having come this far, we'll take a short break to compare functions such as anya with objects from other languages.

DATA OR FUNCTION?

Already, the line between what's clearly a function and what might be construed to be data in languages such as Java and Ruby should have started to blur. Is anya a function or is it a kind of data object? It certainly behaves similarly to a hash map, where one can query the value associated with a particular key. In this case, we wrote code to expose only those keys that we considered public information, while hiding the private pieces. Because anya is a closure, the free variables (the arguments passed to new-user) are captured inside it and hang around until the closure itself is alive. Technically, although anya is a function, semantically it looks and behaves like data.

Although data objects such as hash maps are fairly static (in that they do little more than hold information), traditional objects also have behavior associated with them. Let's blur the line some more by adding behavior to our user objects. We'll add a way to see if a given password is the correct one. Consider this code:

```
(defn new-user [login password email]
  (fn [a & args]
    (condp = a
      :login login
```

```
            :email email
            :authenticate (= password (first args)))))
```

Now let's try it out:

```
user> (def adi (new-user "adi" "secret" "adi@currylogic.com"))
#'user/adi

user> (adi :authenticate "blah")
false

user> (adi :authenticate "secret")
true
```

Our little closure-based users can now authenticate themselves when asked to do so. As mentioned earlier, this form of message passing resembles calling methods on objects in languages such as Java and Ruby. The format for doing so could be written like so:

```
(object message-name & arguments)
```

Objects in object-oriented programming are usually defined as entities that have state, behavior, and equality. Most languages also allow them to be defined in a manner that allows inheritance of functionality. So far, we've handled state (information such as login, password, and email) and behavior (such as :authenticate). Equality depends on the domain of usage of these objects, but you could conceivably create a generic form of equality testing based on, say, a hash function. In the next section, we'll consolidate the ideas we talked about in this section and add inheritance and a nicer syntax to define such objects.

13.3.4 *An object system for Clojure*

In the previous section, we created a function named new-user that behaves as a sort of factory for new user objects. You could call new-user using the data elements that a user comprises (login, password, and email address), and you'd get a new user object. You could then query it for certain data or have it perform certain behaviors. We made this possible by implementing a simple message passing scheme, with messages such as :login and :authenticate.

In this section, we'll generalize the idea of creating objects that have certain data and behavior into what traditional object-oriented languages call classes. We'll allow a simple class hierarchy, and we'll let objects refer to themselves by providing a special symbol, traditionally named, this. Finally, we'll wrap this functionality in a syntactic skin in order to make it appear more familiar.

DEFINING CLASSES

We'll start simple. We'll create the ability to define classes that have no state or behavior. We'll lay the foundations of our object system starting with the ability to define a class that's empty. For instance, we'd like to be able to say

```
(defclass Person)
```

This would define a class that would behave as a blueprint for future instances of people. We could then ask for the name of such a class:

```
(Person :name)
;"Person"
```

That would return the string "Person", which is the name of the class we're defining. Once we implement this, we can start adding more functionality to our little object system. Consider the following implementation:

```
(defn new-class [class-name]
  (fn [command & args]
    (condp = command
      :name (name class-name))))

(defmacro defclass [class-name]
  `(def ~class-name (new-class '~class-name)))
```

So our little Person class is a function that closes over the class-name, passed in along with a call to defclass. Our classes support a single message right now, which is :name. When passed :name, our Person function returns the string "Person". This allows us to do the following:

```
user> (def some-class Person)
#'user/some-class

user> (some-class :name)
"Person"
```

This is to show that the name of the class isn't associated with the var (in this case Person) but with the class object itself. Now that you can define classes, we'll make it so you can instantiate them.

CREATING INSTANCES

Because our classes are closures, our instantiated classes will also be closures. We'll create this with a function called new-object that will accept the class that we'd like to instantiate. Here's the implementation:

```
(defn new-object [klass]
  (fn [command & args]
    (condp = command
      :class klass)))
```

Here it is in action:

```
(def cindy (new-object Person))
```

As you can tell, the only message you can send this new object is one that queries its class. You can say

```
user> (cindy :class)
#<user$new_class__4224$fn__4226 user$new_class__4224$fn__4226@26ced1a8>
```

That isn't terribly informative, because it's returning the class as the function object. You can instead further ask its name:

```
user> ((cindy :class) :name)
```
"Person"

You could add this functionality as a convenience message that an instantiated object itself could handle:

```
(defn new-object [klass]
  (fn [command & args]
    (condp = command
      :class klass
      :class-name (klass :name))))
```

You can test this now, but you'll need to create the object again, because we redefined the class. Here it is:

```
user> (def cindy (new-object Person))
```
#'user/cindy

```
user> (cindy :class-name)
```
"Person"

Finally, you're going to be instantiating classes a lot, so you can add a more convenient way to do so. You'd like something like a new operator that's common to several languages such as Java and Ruby. Luckily, we've already set up our class as a function that can handle incoming messages, so we'll add to the vocabulary with a :new message. Here's the new implementation of new-class:

```
(defn new-class [class-name]
  (fn klass [command & args]
    (condp = command
      :name (name class-name)
      :new (new-object klass))))
```

Notice that new-object accepts a class, and we need to refer to the class object from within it. We were able to do this by giving the anonymous function a name (klass) and then refer to it by that name in the :new clause. With this, creating new objects is easier and more familiar:

```
user> (def nancy (Person :new))
```
#'user/nancy

```
user> (nancy :class-name)
```
"Person"

So here you are: you're able to define new classes as well as instantiate them. Our next stop will be to allow our objects to maintain state.

OBJECTS AND STATE

In chapter 6, we explored Clojure's support for managing state. In this section, we'll use one of those available mechanisms to allow objects in our object system to also become stateful. We'll use a ref so that our objects will be able to participate in coordinated transactions. We'll also expand the vocabulary of messages that our objects can understand by supporting :set! and :get. They'll allow us to set and fetch values from our objects, respectively.

Consider the following updated definition of our `new-object` function:

```
(defn new-object [klass]
  (let [state (ref {})]
    (fn [command & args]
      (condp = command
        :class klass
        :class-name (klass :name)
        :set! (let [[k v] args]
                (dosync (alter state assoc k v))
                nil)
        :get (let [[key] args]
               (key @state))))))
```

So now the messages that you can pass to your objects include :class, :class-name, :set!, and :get. Let's see our new stateful objects in action:

```
user> (def nancy (Person :new))
#'user/nancy

user> (nancy :set! :name "Nancy Warhol")
nil

user> (nancy :get :name)
"Nancy Warhol"
```

You can also update your objects using the same :set! message, as follows:

```
user> (nancy :set! :name "Nancy Drew")
nil

user> (nancy :get :name)
"Nancy Drew"
```

We're coming along in our journey to create a simple object-system. You now have the infrastructure to define classes, instantiate them, and manage state. Our next stop will be to add support for method definitions.

DEFINING METHODS

So far, we've dealt with the state side of objects. In this section, we'll start working on behavior by adding support for method definitions. The syntax we'd like to support is to include the methods along with the class definition so as to keep it together. This is another common pattern with languages such as Java and C++. The following is the syntax we'd like to be able to use:

```
(defclass Person
  (method age []
    (* 2 10))
  (method greet [visitor]
    (str "Hello there, " visitor)))
```

We've started with simple methods. The age method, for instance, doesn't take any arguments and returns the result of a simple computation. Similarly, the greet method accepts a single argument and returns a simple computation involving it.

Now that we've laid out the expected syntax, we can go about the implementation. First, we'll work on defclass, in order to make the previous notation valid. Consider the following function, which operates on a single method definition s-expression:

```
(defn method-spec [sexpr]
  (let [name (keyword (second sexpr))
    body (next sexpr)]
    [name (conj body 'fn)]))
```

This creates a vector containing the name of the method definition (as a keyword) and another s-expression, which can later be evaluated to create an anonymous function. Here's an example:

```
user> (method-spec '(method age [] (* 2 10)))
[:age (fn age [] (* 2 10))]
```

Because you're going to specify more than one method inside your class definition, you'll need to call method-spec for each of them. The following method-specs function will accept the complete specification of your class, pick out the method definitions by filtering on the first symbol (it should be method), and then call method-spec on each. Here it is:

```
(defn method-specs [sexprs]
  (->> sexprs
       (filter #(= 'method (first %)))
       (mapcat method-spec)
       (apply hash-map)))
```

The easiest way to see what's going on is to examine a sample output:

```
user> (method-specs '((method age []
                        (* 2 10))
                      (method greet [visitor]
                        (str "Hello there, " visitor))))
{:age (fn age []
        (* 2 10)),
 :greet (fn greet [visitor]
          (str "Hello there, " visitor))}
```

We now have a literal map that can be evaluated to return one containing keywords as keys for each method definition and an associated anonymous function. This map could then be passed to our new-class function for later use. Here's the associated revision of new-class:

```
(defn new-class [class-name methods]
  (fn klass [command & args]
    (condp = command
      :name (name class-name)
      :new (new-object klass))))
```

Now that all the supporting pieces are in place, we can make the final change to defclass, which will allow us to accept method definitions:

```
(defmacro defclass [class-name & specs]
  (let [fns (or (method-specs specs) {})]
    `(def ~class-name (new-class '~class-name ~fns))))
```

Now, our desired syntax from before will work:

```
user> (defclass Person
        (method age []
          (* 2 10))
        (method greet [visitor]
          (str "Hello there, " visitor)))
#'user/Person
```

So we've successfully made it possible to specify methods along with our class definitions. Now, all you have to do is to extend our objects so that you can invoke these methods. We'll do this in the next section.

INVOKING METHODS

In order to be able to invoke a method on one of our objects, such as nancy, you'll need some way to look up the definition from the associated class. You'll need to be able to query the class of a given object for a particular method. Let's add the :method message to our classes, which would accept the name of the method you're looking for. Consider the following revision to our new-class function:

```
(defn new-class [class-name methods]
  (fn klass [command & args]
    (condp = command
      :name (name class-name)
      :new (new-object klass)
      :method (let [[method-name] args]
                (find-method method-name methods)))))
```

We haven't defined find-method yet, so this code isn't quite ready to be compiled. In order to find a method from our previously created map of methods, you can do a simple hash map lookup. Therefore, the implementation of find-method is simple:

```
(defn find-method [method-name instance-methods]
  (instance-methods method-name))
```

With this addition, you can look up a method in a class, using the same keyword notation you've been using for our all other messages. Here's an example:

```
(Person :method :age)
#<user$age__3921 user$age__3921@1b4865b1>
```

Now that you can get a handle on the function object that represents a method, you're ready to call it. Indeed, you can call the previous function on the REPL, and it will do what we laid out in the class definition:

```
user> ((Person :method :age))
20
```

That works, but it's far from pretty. You should be able to support the same familiar interface of calling methods on objects that they belong to. Let's expand the capability of the message-passing system we've built so far in order to handle such methods also. Here's an updated version of `new-object` that does this:

```
(defn new-object [klass]
  (let [state (ref {})]
    (fn [command & args]
      (condp = command
        :class klass
        :class-name (klass :name)
        :set! (let [[k v] args]
                (dosync (alter state assoc k v))
                nil)
        :get (let [[key] args]
               (key @state))
        (let [method (klass :method command)]
          (if-not method
            (throw (RuntimeException.
              (str "Unable to respond to " command))))
          (apply method args))))))
```

What we added was a default clause to `condp`. If the message passed in isn't one of `:class`, `:class-name`, `:set!`, or `:get`, then we assume it's a method call on the object. We ask the class for the function by passing along the received command as the method name, and if we get back a function, we execute it. Here it is in action:

```
user> (def shelly (Person :new))
#'user/shelly

user> (shelly :age)
20

user> (shelly :greet "Nancy")
"Hello there, Nancy"
```

Remember, in order for this to work, the definition of `Person` would need to be reevaluated after these changes. Once you're satisfied that your implementation does what you want so far, you'll be ready to move on. Our next little feature is the ability of our objects to refer to themselves.

REFERRING TO THIS

So far, our method definitions have been simple. But there's often a need for methods within a class definition to call each other. Most programming languages that support this feature do so via a special keyword (usually named `this` or `self`), which refers to the object itself. We'll support the same functionality by providing a special name, which we'll also call `this`.

Once we're finished, we'd like to be able to say the following:

```
(defclass Person
  (method age []
    (* 2 10))
  (method about [diff]
    (str "I was born about " (+ diff (this :age)) " years ago")))
```

Notice how the about method calls the age method via the this construct. In order to implement this, we'll first create a var named this, so that our class definitions continue to work (without complaining about unresolved symbols).

```
(declare this)
```

This var will need a binding when any method executes so that its bound value refers to the object itself. A simple binding form will do, as long as we have something to bind to. We will employ the same trick we did when we named the anonymous class function klass earlier, by naming the anonymous object function thiz. Here's the updated code for the new-object function:

```
(defn new-object [klass]
  (let [state (ref {})]
    (fn thiz [command & args]
      (condp = command
        :class klass
        :class-name (klass :name)
        :set! (let [[k v] args]
                (dosync (alter state assoc k v))
                nil)
        :get (let [[key] args]
               (key @state))
        (let [method (klass :method command)]
          (if-not method
            (throw (RuntimeException.
              (str "Unable to respond to " command))))
          (binding [this thiz]
            (apply method args)))))))
```

And that's all there is to it. You can confirm that it works on the REPL:

```
user>  (def shelly (Person :new))
#'user/shelly

user> (shelly :about 2)
"I was born about 22 years ago"
```

Remember to evaluate the new, revised definition of new-object before trying it out. We've added almost all the features we wanted to when we started this section. The last thing we'll add is the ability of a class to inherit from another.

CLASS INHERITANCE

We're about to add a final feature to our little object system. Traditional OO programming languages such as Java and Ruby allow modeling of objects using inheritance, so that problems can be decomposed into hierarchies of functionality. The lower in a hierarchy you go, the more specific you get. For instance, Animal might be a parent class of Dog. In this section, we'll add the ability to do that.

The first thing we'll do is allow our class definition to specify the parent class. Imagine that our syntax will look like this:

```
(defclass Woman
    (extends Person)
```

```
(method greet [v]
  (str "Hello, " v))
(method age []
  (* 2 9))))
```

Here, our new Woman class inherits from a previously defined Person class. We've used the term extends to signify this relationship, as is common to other OO languages. Okay, now that we have our notation, let's implement it. The first step is to write a function that can extract the parent class information from the class definition. Before we can do so, we have to decide what to do if one isn't provided.

Again, we'll look at other languages for the answer. Our class hierarchies will all be singly rooted, and the top-level class (highest parent class) will be OBJECT. We'll define this shortly. For now, we're ready to write parent-class-spec, the function that will parse the specification of the parent class from a given class definition:

```
(defn parent-class-spec [sexprs]
  (let [extends-spec (filter #(= 'extends (first %)) sexprs)
        extends (first extends-spec)]
    (if (empty? extends)
      'OBJECT
      (last extends))))
```

To confirm that this works, try it at the REPL. You'll pass it the specification part of a class definition:

```
user> (parent-class-spec '((extends Person)
                           (method age []
                             (* 2 9))))
Person
```

Now that we have the parent class, we'll pass it to our new-class function. We don't want to pass a symbol as the parent class but rather the var named by that symbol. For instance, the value returned by the call to parent-class-spec is a Clojure symbol. If you have a symbol, you can find the var of that name by using the var special form:

```
user> (var map)
#'clojure.core/map
```

There's a reader macro for the var special form, #' (the hash followed by a tick). With this information in hand, we can make the needed modification to defclass:

```
(defmacro defclass [class-name & specs]
  (let [parent-class (parent-class-spec specs)
        fns (or (method-specs specs) {})]
    `(def ~class-name (new-class '~class-name #'~parent-class ~fns))))
```

Note that we're now passing an extra parameter (the parent class) to the new-class function, so we'll have to change that to accommodate it:

```
(defn new-class [class-name parent methods]
  (fn klass [command & args]
    (condp = command
      :name (name class-name)
```

```
:parent parent
:new (new-object klass)
:method (let [[method-name] args]
          (find-method method-name methods)))))
```

There's one more thing to handle before we can use our new defclass. We're looking up the parent class using var, so we'll need OBJECT to resolve to something. It's now time to define it:

```
(def OBJECT (new-class :OBJECT nil {}))
```

With these changes, the definition of the Woman class from earlier in this section should work. Let's check this on the REPL:

```
user>(defclass Person
       (method age []
         (* 2 10))
       (method about [diff]
         (str "I was born about " (+ diff (this :age)) " years ago")))
#'user/Person
```

This is our parent class; now we'll inherit from it to create the Woman class:

```
user>(defclass Woman
       (extends Person)
       (method greet [v]
         (str "Hello, " v))
       (method age []
         (* 2 9)))
#'user/Woman
```

We've only half finished the job we started out to do. Although we can specify the parent class in our calls to defclass, method calls on our objects won't work right with respect to parent classes. The following illustrates the problem:

```
user>(def donna (Woman :new))
#'user/donna

user>(donna :greet "Shelly")
"Hello, Shelly"

user>(donna :age)
18

user>(donna :about 3)
; Evaluation aborted.
Unable to respond to :about
  [Thrown class java.lang.RuntimeException]
```

In order to fix this last error, we'll have to improve our method lookup in order to find the method in the parent class. Indeed, we'll have to search up the hierarchy of classes (parent of the parent of the parent...) until we hit OBJECT. We'll implement this new method lookup by modifying the find-method function as follows:

```
(defn find-method [method-name klass]
  (or ((klass :methods) method-name)
```

```
(if-not (= #'OBJECT klass)
  (find-method method-name (klass :parent)))))
```

In order for this to work, we'll need to have our classes handle another message, namely, :methods. Also, our classes will use this new version of find-method in order to perform method lookup. Here's the updated code:

```
(defn new-class [class-name parent methods]
  (fn klass [command & args]
    (condp = command
      :name (name class-name)
      :parent parent
      :new (new-object klass)
      :methods methods
      :method (let [[method-name] args]
                (find-method method-name klass)))))
```

With this final change, our object system will work as planned. Figure 13.2 shows the conceptual model of the class system we've built.

Here's the call to the :about method that wasn't working a few paragraphs back:

```
user>   (donna :about 3)
"I was born about 21 years ago"
```

Again, remember to reevaluate everything after the last change, including the definition of donna itself. Notice that the :about method is being called from the parent class Person. Further notice that the body of the :about method calls :age on the

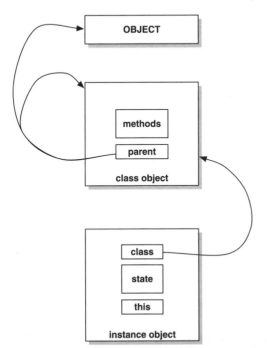

Figure 13.2 The minimal object system we've built implements a major portion of features that are supported by most common OO systems. Everything ultimately derives from a common entity called OBJECT. Instances look up the class they derive from and look up methods there. Methods can also be looked up in the chain of hierarchy.

this reference, which is defined in both `Person` and `Woman`. Our object system correctly calls the one on donna, because we overrode the definition in the `Woman` class.

We've completed what we set out to do. We've written a simple object system that does most of what other languages provide. We can define classes, inherit from others, create instances, and call methods that follow the inheritance hierarchy. Objects can even refer to themselves using the `this` keyword. The following listing shows the complete code.

Listing 13.1 A simple object system for Clojure

```clojure
(declare this find-method)

(defn new-object [klass]
  (let [state (ref {})]
    (fn thiz [command & args]
      (condp = command
        :class klass
        :class-name (klass :name)
        :set! (let [[k v] args]
                (dosync (alter state assoc k v))
                nil)
        :get (let [[key] args]
               (key @state))
        (let [method (klass :method command)]
          (if-not method
            (throw (RuntimeException.
                     (str "Unable to respond to " command))))
          (binding [this thiz]
            (apply method args)))))))

(defn new-class [class-name parent methods]
  (fn klass [command & args]
    (condp = command
      :name (name class-name)
      :parent parent
      :new (new-object klass)
      :methods methods
      :method (let [[method-name] args]
                (find-method method-name klass)))))

(def OBJECT (new-class :OBJECT nil {}))

(defn find-method [method-name klass]
  (or ((klass :methods) method-name)
      (if-not (= #'OBJECT klass)
        (find-method method-name (klass :parent)))))

(defn method-spec [sexpr]
  (let [name (keyword (second sexpr))
        body (next sexpr)]
    [name (conj body 'fn)]))

(defn method-specs [sexprs]
  (->> sexprs
       (filter #(= 'method (first %)))
```

```
      (mapcat method-spec)
      (apply hash-map)))
(defn parent-class-spec [sexprs]
  (let [extends-spec (filter #(= 'extends (first %)) sexprs)
        extends (first extends-spec)]
    (if (empty? extends)
      'OBJECT
      (last extends))))
(defmacro defclass [class-name & specs]
  (let [parent-class (parent-class-spec specs)
        fns (or (method-specs specs) {})]
    `(def ~class-name (new-class '~class-name  #'~parent-class ~fns))))
```

So that's it, clocking in at a little over 50 lines of code. We haven't added several features that are provided by more robust object systems, but you can certainly do so. For instance, this function doesn't perform a lot of error checking. The key to this implementation is the lexical closure. It's left up to you to take a stand on the old debate: are objects a poor man's closures, or is it the other way around?

More than anything else, though, it's important to remember this: although this little example showed some of the power of functional programming (and that traditional object-oriented programming features aren't particularly special), in most cases, such artificial constructs are unnecessary in languages such as Clojure. We'll talk about this briefly next.

DATA ABSTRACTION

We said that constructs such as our object system aren't particularly useful in a language such as Clojure. There are two reasons for this.

The first relates to abstraction. Despite popular belief, you don't need objects to create data abstraction. There's a real alternative in Clojure in its core data structures: each implementation of the sequence abstraction (the hash map, the vector, and so on) is a suitable candidate to represent data in an application. Given that these are immutable and therefore thread safe, there's no strict need for procedural abstractions that wrap their mutation.

The second reason is a bit more subjective. Alan Perlis once said that it's better to have a 100 functions that operate on a single data structure instead of 10 functions that operate on 10 data structures. Having a common data structure (in Clojure's case, the sequence abstraction) allows for more code reuse, because code that works on sequences can be used no matter what specific data it contains. An example is the large sequence library, which works no matter what the specific implementation is.

Using the let-over-lambda technique shown previously has its value, as you saw in the earlier part of the chapter. But creating an object system like the one we created in the second half raises a barrier of inoperability with other libraries that don't know about it. In conclusion, although the object system serves to illustrate the usage of closures and some traditional OOP concepts, using the built-in core data structures is a much better choice in your own programs.

FINAL NOTES

It's worth recalling that the implementation of this little object system was done using functions. Fewer than half of the total lines of code were for manipulating the functions, and the rest were to make the syntax look a certain way. The macro `defclass` and the supporting functions (`parent-class-spec`, `method-specs`, and `method-spec`) account for over half the code. This syntactic layer sports an arbitrarily chosen syntax. The semantics of the object system wouldn't change if we decided to use a different syntax. The syntax isn't important (in this case certainly, and also in general); instead, it's the underlying mechanisms and features that make a piece of code useful. Having said that, a nice syntax certainly helps! The first reason is that it makes for convenient, intuitive usage. The second is that you can write error checkers by analyzing the code as data and give meaningful errors that are easier to understand and correct. You could certainly do more at the syntactic level to make this library easier to use.

Similarly, there are many features that you could add at a semantic level. For instance, there's no reason for a class hierarchy to be static. Instead of it being cast in stone when `defclass` is called, you could add messages that support modifying the hierarchy at runtime. As an example, our classes could respond to `:set-class!` and `:set-parent!`. Adding such features might be an interesting exercise for a spare afternoon.

13.4 *Summary*

This chapter was about functional programming, the understanding of which is crucial to programming in Clojure. If you're coming from an imperative background, this transition can take some effort. But the results are sweet, because functional code is more expressive, more reusable, and usually shorter.

We started out creating our own implementations of `map`, `reduce`, and `filter`—the workhorses of functional programming languages. Thinking recursively and in terms of lazy sequences is another important skill that will have a big impact on your Clojure programs. We then looked at partial application of functions and the associated concept of currying. Although these aren't used that often in Clojure, the insight you gleaned from these concepts can help when they do fit.

Our final stop was to explore closures, another fundamental tool in the functional programmer's tool belt. Once we presented a basic explanation of them, we gathered everything from this chapter (and from the ones so far!) to create our own little object system. This exercise was meant to demonstrate the power of closures and to also shed light on the fact that functional programming transcends traditional object-oriented programming.

Protocols, records, and types

This chapter covers

- An overview of the expression problem
- A custom solution to the expression problem
- Clojure's solution to the expression problem
- A look at `deftype`, `defrecord`, `reify`

Abstraction is an important tenet of software development because it allows code that's maintainable and extensible. Clojure itself is built on abstractions. For instance, most things in Clojure are coded to interfaces rather than being direct concrete implementations. This allows for reuse of code that expects those interfaces and allows the addition of more implementations to the mix.

Sooner or later, during your time on most projects, you'll run into an abstraction-oriented issue known as the *expression problem*. It has to do with how to cleanly extend or use existing code—either something you wrote yourself or, more important, something you don't own. Clojure's approach to handling this issue is protocols. In order to get to this topic, though, we'll first explore the problem in some depth. Then, we'll come up with our own solution. Finally, we'll explore protocols, data types, and the `reify` macro.

14.1   *The expression problem*

In this section, we'll explore the expression problem. Instead of going at it from a definitional point of view, we'll dive into some code. Specifically, we'll examine a situation that comes up quite often: we need to take two or more classes or sets of classes (or any other abstractions) and make them work together in a seamless way. Further, whatever solution we come up with to do this, there's usually the need to support further extensibility, perhaps to support even more operations or data types.

Our example code is based on the Clojure programming language and some Java code. It will serve to illustrate the expression problem, as well as lead to ways of solving it.

14.1.1   *The Clojure world*

Let's imagine that we've been writing an application to manage employee expenses, one that will eventually replace an existing Java application that does a similar job. Naturally, we're writing it in Clojure. Here's a part of the expense namespace, with a function to create a simple map containing expense information:

```
(ns chapter-protocols.expense
  (:import [java.text SimpleDateFormat]))

(defn new-expense [date-string dollars cents category merchant-name]
  {:date (.parse (SimpleDateFormat. "yyyy-MM-dd") date-string)
   :amount-dollars dollars
   :amount-cents cents
   :category category
   :merchant-name merchant-name})
```

As you've seen several times already, using a map is straightforward and is the idiomatic way in Clojure to hold data of any kind. Now, for the purposes of illustration, here's a function called total-cents that computes the expense amount in cents:

```
(defn total-cents [e]
  (-> (:amount-dollars e)
      (* 100)
      (+ (:amount-cents e))))
```

Nothing in this function ought to be unfamiliar, including the threading macro, which you saw in chapter 2.

Let's also add a function to calculate the total amount, given a list of expenses, and possibly a criteria function by which to select expenses from a list:

```
(defn total-amount
  ([expenses-list]
    (total-amount (constantly true) expenses-list))
  ([pred expenses-list]
    (->> expenses-list
         (filter pred)
         (map total-cents)
         (apply +))))
```

Let's finally add a couple of functions to help us create the predicate functions that can be used with `total-amount`, specifically to select a particular category of expenses:

```
(defn is-category? [e some-category]
  (= (:category e) some-category))

(defn category-is [category]
  #(is-category? % category))
```

The second function is syntactic sugar to help create single argument predicates so our code reads easier. Let's see how it looks by writing some code that tests these functions. Consider a new namespace, such as `expense-test`, which we'll start by creating a few sample expenses to play with:

```
(ns chapter-protocols.expense-test
  (:use [chapter-protocols.expense]
        [clojure.test]))

(def clj-expenses [(new-expense "2009-8-20" 21 95 "books" "amazon.com")
                   (new-expense "2009-8-21" 72 43 "food" "mollie-stones")
                   (new-expense "2009-8-22" 315 71 "car-rental" "avis")
                   (new-expense "2009-8-23" 15 68 "books" "borders")])
```

Here's a test that uses this set of data to compute the total amounts:

```
(deftest test-clj-expenses-total
  (is (= 42577 (total-amount clj-expenses)))
  (is (=  3763 (total-amount (category-is "books") clj-expenses))))
```

If you run these tests, you'll see that they pass (if you'd like a refresher on using the `clojure.test` library or on how to run tests, refer to chapter 8). So now, we have some basic code that shows the intent of our application. You can imagine a lot more functionality that helps an organization track expenses, but we've written sufficient code to demonstrate the issues we set out to face, so let's move on.

14.1.2 *The Java world*

It's now time to face a kind of reality we often face when working on application rewrites: business reasons compel us to deal with the old codebase alongside our new one. For the purposes of this example, this means that we're going to have to deal with instances of the Java-based `Expense` class. You could imagine such a class being similar to the one shown in the following listing.

Listing 14.1 Skeleton Java class implementing the concept of the expense item

```java
package com.curry.expenses;

import java.util.Calendar;
import java.text.SimpleDateFormat;
import java.text.ParseException;

public class Expense {
    private Calendar date;
    private int amountDollars;
```

```
    private int amountCents;
    private String merchantName;
    private String category;

    public Expense(String dateString, int amountDollars, int amountCents,
            String category, String merchantName) throws ParseException {
        this.date = Calendar.getInstance();
        this.date.setTime(new SimpleDateFormat(
                            "yyyy-MM-dd").parse(dateString));
        this.amountDollars = amountDollars;
        this.amountCents = amountCents;
        this.merchantName = merchantName;
        this.category = category;
    }

    public Calendar getDate() {
        return date;
    }

    public int getAmountDollars() {
        return amountDollars;
    }

    public int getAmountCents() {
        return amountCents;
    }

    public String getMerchantName() {
        return merchantName;
    }

    public String getCategory() {
        return category;
    }

    public int amountInCents() {
        return this.amountDollars*100 + this.amountCents;
    }

}
```

To begin working with this class, we'll write a sanity test to ensure everything is in order. Consider the following:

```
(def java-expenses [(Expense. "2009-8-24" 44 95 "books" "amazon.com")
                    (Expense. "2009-8-25" 29 11 "gas" "shell")])

(deftest test-java-expenses-total
  (let [total-cents (map #(.amountInCents %) java-expenses)]
    (is (= 7406 (apply + total-cents)))))
```

Again, running this test will result in it passing. Now that we're able to access the Java class, we need to tackle the situation where we have both kinds of expenses together. For instance, we have to deal with a list of Clojure expense maps constructed via the new-expense function, as well as instances of the com.curry.expenses .Expense class.

We'll capture this requirement in another test. Consider the following:

```
(def mixed-expenses (concat clj-expenses java-expenses))

(deftest test-mixed-expenses-total
  (is (= 49983 (total-amount mixed-expenses)))
  (is (= 8258 (total-amount (category-is "books") mixed-expenses)))))
```

Now, running these tests won't pass. Indeed, the first assertion will print a long exception stack trace, because total-amount (and the underlying total-cents and is-category?) function only knows to deal with Clojure map versions of expenses. To fix this, we're going to have to deal with a design issue.

14.1.3 *The expression problem*

Philip Wadler is an ACM fellow and a computer science professor at the University of Edinburgh. He has made several important contributions to the field of functional programming, including to the theory behind the Haskell programming language. He also coined the term "expression problem:":

> *The Expression Problem is a new name for an old problem. The goal is to define a data-type by cases, where one can add new cases to the data-type and new functions over the data-type, without recompiling existing code, and while retaining static type safety (e.g., no casts).*

How can we add functionality to our code (our data type) so it plays well with code (data types) written by someone else (or any other code that we have no control over)? With the previous test we wrote to handle the case of mixed expenses, we're faced with the expression problem. Specifically, we need the total-amount function to accept and work with an entirely new data type that has its own set of operations (functions) defined for it. We'd also like the category-is function to create functions that can operate on this new data type, even though the new data type has no notion of such a category selector function right now.

The expression problem is common in our industry. There are several approaches to handle the issue, and we'll briefly look at a few.

WRAPPERS

Because we have no control over the new data type (the Expense class), this approach creates a new wrapper class around it with the right methods that we can call from our program. The trouble with this approach is that it increases incidental complexity because we've added a new class to our system.

First of all, we've confused identity: is an object that wraps an instance of Expense identical to it? How should code written elsewhere treat this new wrapper class if it's passed in? Such an identity crisis is an example of the kind of nonlocal trouble that can arise when an instance of the wrapper is passed to unsuspecting code elsewhere in the system. We'd have to create a wrapper class each time a new data type such as this comes along, leading to an explosion of such wrappers.

When all is said and done, languages such as Java often have no other choice than to go this route.

344 CHAPTER 14 *Protocols, records, and types*

MONKEY PATCHING

Languages such as Ruby are more dynamic and support open classes. This is in contrast with Java's classes, where once they've been written and compiled, they can't be modified (without manipulating byte code). Open classes, on the other hand, can be changed by anyone using the class, even after the original programmer has moved on. Often, the syntax looks the same as writing the class the first time around, and any new methods defined (or redefined) become part of the original class.

The problem with this approach is that it's a dangerous one, almost even more so than the wrapper approach. Because all changes to a class happen in a global manner (the class itself being the namespace), it has the potential for collisions. If you open a class and monkey patch it with a new method named total-cents, and someone else comes along and does the same, they'll overwrite your patch. Such collisions can cause insidious side effects, because they aren't immediately obvious.

IF-THEN-ELSE

Finally, there's the approach of not using any well-structured tactic at all and checking for types inline with the code as needed. Client code such as the total-amount function will need to do different things depending on whether it was passed a Clojure map or an instance of the Java Expense class, using good old if-then-else constructs.

This quickly gets complex, depending on how many data types need to be handled. Moreover, if support for a new data type needs to be added at a later point, it isn't possible without modifying the code in all the places where this type checking is done. The incidental complexity of this approach is too great given that the solution is both rigid and inelegant.

What's needed is an approach that doesn't suffer from these problems. The Clojure programming language has the feature for this, and you saw it earlier, in chapter 4. We're talking about multimethods, and in the next section, we'll write an implementation that works as desired.

14.1.4 *Clojure's multimethods solution*

Multimethods allow us to decouple data types and operations on the data types in an elegant manner. We demonstrated this in chapter 4, where we used multimethods to handle a situation that would've required the visitor pattern in a language such as Java. In this section, we'll use multimethods to get our latest test to pass without modifying the Java code for the Expense class and without creating wrappers or monkey patches.

Let's refresh our memory by looking at the test that won't pass right now:

```
(deftest test-mixed-expenses-total
  (is (= 49983 (total-amount mixed-expenses)))
  (is (= 8258 (total-amount (category-is "books") mixed-expenses)))))
```

As we said before, the trouble is that our total-amount, is-category?, and total-cents functions only know how to work with Clojure maps. Our first step, then, will be to address this issue by changing the implementation of the total-cents and is-category? functions. We won't touch total-amount, because it's an example of client code (perhaps written by someone using our expense library). We'll assume that we don't control it, and indeed, that it's a requirement of solving the expression problem and we can't change the alien data type or the client code.

Consider the following code, which is a replacement of the total-cents function:

```
(defmulti total-cents class)

(defmethod total-cents clojure.lang.IPersistentMap [e]
  (-> (:amount-dollars e)
      (* 100)
      (+ (:amount-cents e))))
```

Similarly, the following code will serve as the replacement of the is-category? function:

```
(defmulti is-category? (fn [e category] (class e)))

(defmethod is-category? clojure.lang.IPersistentMap [e some-category]
  (= (:category e) some-category))
```

We haven't changed a lot of code; the bodies of the functions are the same as before. All we did was convert the functions to multimethods and redefine the old functions as methods, focusing on the fact that the expense object will be an instance of clojure.lang.IPersistentMap (which all Clojure maps are). Refer to chapter 5 in order to get a refresher on how this works with respect to dispatch functions and dispatch values.

At this point, if we run our tests, the old tests should still pass. Also, the new test will still fail because we haven't written any code to deal with the Java Expense class. Let's do that now, starting with the total-cents function:

```
(defmethod total-cents com.curry.expenses.Expense [e]
  (.amountInCents e))
```

And similarly, here's the is-category? function:

```
(defmethod is-category? com.curry.expenses.Expense [e some-category]
  (= (.getCategory e) some-category))
```

With this, our new test will pass. Note, once again, that we didn't change the Java Expense class in any way: we didn't write a wrapper class for it, and we didn't change the calling code (the total-amount function). We also kept all of our code in our own namespace, allowing others to create their own functions named total-cents and is-category?, without the fear of collisions.

Using multimethods has allowed us to solve this problem of handling new data types in an easy and elegant manner. We're even set up to deal with more data types now, for example, if we need to ever deal with a third-party expense library.

There are a couple of downsides to this approach, though. The first is that even though multimethods allow us to dispatch via arbitrary functions, we're using only the class of the first argument, which is either the Clojure map containing expense information or the Java Expense class. We don't need the full power of multimethods here, and it would be nice if we didn't have to explicitly write our dispatch functions the way we did previously.

The second issue is that even though the two multimethods we wrote are related to the task of computing totals, it isn't obvious in the code. If someone were to read this code later, the fact that the two belong together wouldn't jump out at them. This is even more apparent when you have multiple multimethods that should ideally show some kind of logical grouping. We'll try to solve these issues next.

14.2   *Modus operandi*

In this section, we'll try to solve the two issues we mentioned in the previous section, the first being that we don't need the conceptual or syntactic complexity of full multi-methods when we only want to dispatch on the class of the first argument. The second is that we want to group related multimethods together so they read better.

We'll call our solution to this modus operandi, which is a Latin phrase that means "method of operating." The name reflects our intention here, which is to describe a set of operating procedures for something.

14.2.1   *def-modus-operandi*

Let's start with the code we'd like to be able to write:

```
(def-modus-operandi ExpenseCalculations
  (total-cents [e])
  (is-category? [e category]))
```

What we're saying here is that we're defining a modus operandi called Expense-Calculations that will consist of two methods, namely total-cents and is-category?. We won't specify the dispatch function as we did before, because we always want it to be the class of the first argument of each method. In this case, both the methods will dispatch based on the class of the expense object, be it a Clojure map or the Java Expense class or any other data type we end up supporting.

Now, let's look at implementing it. As you can imagine, def-modus-operandi is a macro. Here's the code along with a couple of associated helper functions:

```
(defn dispatch-fn-for [method-args]
  `(fn ~method-args (class ~(first method-args))))

(defn expand-spec [[method-name method-args]]
  `(defmulti ~method-name ~(dispatch-fn-for method-args)))

(defmacro def-modus-operandi [mo-name & specs]
  `(do
     ~@(map expand-spec specs)))
```

So all we're doing is generating code that creates multimethods. Here's what the expanded version looks like:

```
(do
  (clojure.core/defmulti total-cents (clojure.core/fn [e]
                                       (clojure.core/class e)))
  (clojure.core/defmulti is-category? (clojure.core/fn [e category]
                                        (clojure.core/class e))))
```

Notice that the expanded form of is-category? is the same as when we wrote it by hand earlier. The expansion for total-cents is slightly different, only because we can generate the same dispatch function no matter how many arguments the function takes.

Now that we have a way to specify the methods in our modus operandi, we need a way to detail it for the types we'd like to support. We'll do that next.

14.2.2 *detail-modus-operandi*

After defining the *what* of a modus operandi, we need to define the *how*. We'll create a new macro called detail-modus-operandi that we'll use in the following manner:

```
(detail-modus-operandi ExpenseCalculations
  clojure.lang.IPersistentMap
  (total-cents [e]
    (-> (:amount-dollars e)
        (* 100)
        (+ (:amount-cents e))))

  (is-category? [e some-category]
    (= (:category e) some-category)))
```

Most of the code should be familiar to you, because it's nearly identical to the code from the previous section. Because all the methods are being defined for the same dispatch value, we've made it so that we only have to specify it once. Here's the implementation of the macro, along with an associated helper function:

```
(defn expand-method [data-type [name & body]]
  `(defmethod ~name ~data-type ~@body))

(defmacro detail-modus-operandi [mo-name data-type & fns]
  `(do
     ~@(map #(expand-method data-type %) fns)))
```

The expansion of this call to detail-modus-operandi is as follows:

```
(do
  (clojure.core/defmethod total-cents clojure.lang.IPersistentMap [e]
    (-> (:amount-dollars e)
        (* 100)
        (+ (:amount-cents e))))
  (clojure.core/defmethod is-category? clojure.lang.IPersistentMap
                                                 [e some-category]
    (= (:category e) some-category)))
```

So we've done what we set out to do. We have a new abstraction that sits atop multimethods that behave like subtype polymorphism. Our methods dispatch on the type of the first argument.

Notice that even though we specified the name of our modus operandi here (we called it ExpenseCalculations), we haven't used it for anything. We can make our modus operandi more useful if we use the named objects to track such things as what it contains and who implements it. Let's do that next.

14.2.3 *Tracking our modus operandi*

So far, we've allowed declarations of a modus operandi that's a set of related multi-methods that dispatches on the type of the first argument. In this section, we'll collect some meta information about these methods that we can use to programmatically query things about the modus operandi.

DURING DEF-MODUS-OPERANDI

The first thing we'll do is to define a var with the name of the modus operandi. Doing that by itself is easy enough: we add a call to def in our def-modus-operandi macro. The question is, what should the var be bound to? A simple option is to create a map containing information about the modus operandi. Let's try that approach:

```
(defmacro def-modus-operandi [mo-name & specs]
  `(do
     (def ~mo-name ~(mo-methods-registration specs))
     ~@(map expand-spec specs)))
```

We've delegated to a helper function called mo-methods-registration, so let's implement that next:

```
(defn mo-method-info [[name args]]
  {(keyword name) {:args `(quote ~args)}})

(defn mo-methods-registration [specs]
  (apply merge (map mo-method-info specs)))
```

We're collecting the name and arguments of each method into a map. This map, with all the information about the methods being specified as part of the modus operandi, will become the root binding of a var by the same name as the modus operandi. Let's try it. First, we'll redefine the modus operandi:

```
user> (def-modus-operandi ExpenseCalculations
        (total-cents [e])
        (is-category? [e category]))
#'user/is-category?
```

Next, let's see what the ExpenseCalculation var is bound to:

```
user> ExpenseCalculations
{:is-category? {:args [e category]}, :total-cents {:args [e]}}
```

So we have the basic information. Next, we'll collect some more information every time detail-modus-operandi is called.

DURING DETAIL-MODUS-OPERANDI

To collect information of the implementer of a modus operandi, we'll first need to pass the modus operandi into the expand-method function:

```
(defmacro detail-modus-operandi [mo-name data-type & fns]
  `(do
     ~@(map #(expand-method mo-name data-type %) fns)))
```

Now that our `expand-method` knows what modus operandi it's going to create a method for, we can collect information about it:

```
(defn expand-method [mo-name data-type [method-name & body]]
  `(do
     (alter-var-root (var ~mo-name) update-in
                 [(keyword '~method-name) :implementors] conj ~data-type)
     (defmethod ~method-name ~data-type ~@body)))
```

To better understand this addition to the `expand-method` function, let's talk about the data we're collecting. Recall that the modus operandi `var` is bound to a map that contains a key for each method. The value for each such key is another map. The only key in the inner map so far is `:args`, and to collect the data types of the implementors to this map, we'll introduce another key called `:implementors`. So here we're going to `conj` the data type onto the list of implementors (if any) each time a method of a modus operandi is implemented. Finally, let's look at the function `alter-var-root`. Here's the doc string:

```
user> (doc alter-var-root)
clojure.core/alter-var-root
([v f & args])
Atomically alters the root binding of var v by applying f to its current
    value plus any args
```

So we're passing it the `var` for the modus operandi and the function `update-in`. The argument to `update-in` is a sequence of keys that locates a nested value and a function that will be applied to the existing value along with any other arguments. In this case, `update-in` is passed the function `conj` along with the data type we'd like recorded.

Phew, that's a lot of work for a single line of code. The following listing shows the complete implementation of modus operandi in a single namespace.

Listing 14.2 Implementing modus operandi on top of multimethods

```
(ns chapter-protocols.modus-operandi)

(defn dispatch-fn-for [method-args]
  `(fn ~method-args (class ~(first method-args))))

(defn expand-spec [[method-name method-args]]
  `(defmulti ~method-name ~(dispatch-fn-for method-args)))

(defn mo-method-info [[name args]]
  {(keyword name) {:args `(quote ~args)}})

(defn mo-methods-registration [specs]
  (apply merge (map mo-method-info specs)))

(defmacro def-modus-operandi [mo-name & specs]
  `(do
     (def ~mo-name ~(mo-methods-registration specs))
     ~@(map expand-spec specs)))
```

```
(defn expand-method [mo-name data-type [method-name & body]]
  `(do
     (alter-var-root (var ~mo-name) update-in [(keyword '~method-name)
     :implementors] conj ~data-type)
     (defmethod ~method-name ~data-type ~@body)))

(defmacro detail-modus-operandi [mo-name data-type & fns]
  `(do
     ~@(map #(expand-method mo-name data-type %) fns)))
```

Let's look at it in action. First, let's make a call to `detail-modus-operandi`:

```
user> (detail-modus-operandi ExpenseCalculations
         clojure.lang.IPersistentMap
       (total-cents [e]
         (-> (:amount-dollars e)
             (* 100)
             (+ (:amount-cents e))))

       (is-category? [e some-category]
         (= (:category e) some-category)))
#<MultiFn clojure.lang.MultiFn@4aad8dbc>
```

Now let's look at our `ExpenseCalculations` var:

```
user> ExpenseCalculations
{:is-category? {:implementors (clojure.lang.IPersistentMap),
                :args [e category]},
 :total-cents {:implementors (clojure.lang.IPersistentMap),
               :args [e]}}
```

As you can see, we've added the new `:implementors` key to the inner maps, and they have a value that's a sequence of the implementors so far. Let's implement the modus operandi for the Java `Expense` class now:

```
user> (detail-modus-operandi ExpenseCalculations
  com.curry.expenses.Expense
  (total-cents [e]
    (.amountInCents e))

  (is-category? [e some-category]
    (= (.getCategory e) some-category)))
#<MultiFn clojure.lang.MultiFn@4aad8dbc>
```

Let's now see what our `ExpenseCalculations` var is bound to:

```
user> ExpenseCalculations
{:is-category? {:implementors (com.curry.expenses.Expense
                               clojure.lang.IPersistentMap),
                :args [e category]},
 :total-cents {:implementors (com.curry.expenses.Expense
                              clojure.lang.IPersistentMap),
               :args [e]}}
```

And there you have it: we're collecting a sequence of all implementing classes inside the map bound to the `modus-operandi` var. Let's now ensure that everything still works with our original code. Figure 14.1 shows a conceptual view of the process of

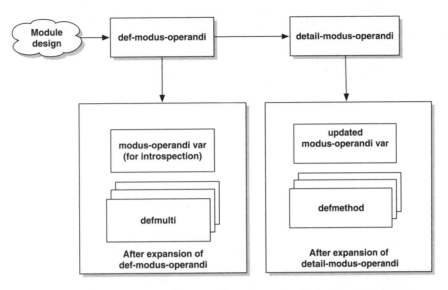

Figure 14.1 Calling `def-modus-operandi` creates a `var` that will hold information about the modus operandi, which can later be used to introspect it. The macro itself makes as many calls to `defmulti` as needed. The `detail-modus-operandi` macro is the other side of the modus operandi concept: it fills out the implementation details by expanding to as many `defmethod` calls as specified. It also updates the `modus-operandi` `var` to reflect the implementor information.

defining a modus operandi and then detailing it out. Listing 14.3 shows the complete code for our expense namespace.

Listing 14.3   The expense namespace using the modus operandi multimethod syntax

```
(ns chapter-protocols.expense-modus-operandi
  (:use chapter-protocols.modus-operandi)
  (:import [java.text SimpleDateFormat]
           [java.util Calendar]))

(defn new-expense [date-string dollars cents category merchant-name]
  (let [calendar-date (Calendar/getInstance)]
    (.setTime calendar-date
         (.parse (SimpleDateFormat. "yyyy-MM-dd") date-string))
    {:date calendar-date
     :amount-dollars dollars
     :amount-cents cents
     :category category
     :merchant-name merchant-name}))

(def-modus-operandi ExpenseCalculations
  (total-cents [e])
  (is-category? [e category]))

(detail-modus-operandi ExpenseCalculations
  clojure.lang.IPersistentMap
  (total-cents [e]
```

```
      (-> (:amount-dollars e)
          (* 100)
          (+ (:amount-cents e))))

  (is-category? [e some-category]
    (= (:category e) some-category)))

(detail-modus-operandi ExpenseCalculations
  com.curry.expenses.Expense
  (total-cents [e]
    (.amountInCents e))

  (is-category? [e some-category]
    (= (.getCategory e) some-category)))

(defn category-is [category]
  #(is-category? % category))

(defn total-amount
  ([expenses-list]
     (total-amount (constantly true) expenses-list))
  ([pred expenses-list]
     (->> expenses-list
          (filter pred)
   .      (map total-cents)
          (apply +))))
```

Similarly, the following listing shows the tests we wrote so far, all in one place. We'll run the tests next.

Listing 14.4   Testing the implementation of modus operandi calculating expense totals

```
(ns chapter-protocols.expense-test
  (:import [com.curry.expenses Expense])
  (:use [chapter-protocols.expense-modus-operandi]
        [clojure.test]))

(def clj-expenses [(new-expense "2009-8-20" 21 95 "books" "amazon.com")
                   (new-expense "2009-8-21" 72 43 "food" "mollie-stones")
                   (new-expense "2009-8-22" 315 71 "car-rental" "avis")
                   (new-expense "2009-8-23" 15 68 "books" "borders")])

(deftest test-clj-expenses-total
  (is (= 42577 (total-amount clj-expenses)))
  (is (=  3763 (total-amount (category-is "books") clj-expenses))))

(def java-expenses [(Expense. "2009-8-24" 44 95 "books" "amazon.com")
                    (Expense. "2009-8-25" 29 11 "gas" "shell")])

(deftest test-java-expenses-total
  (let [total-cents (map #(.amountInCents %) java-expenses)]
    (is (= 7406 (apply + total-cents)))))

(def mixed-expenses (concat clj-expenses java-expenses))

(deftest test-mixed-expenses-total
  (is (= 49983 (total-amount mixed-expenses)))
  (is (= 8258 (total-amount (category-is "books") mixed-expenses))))
```

These tests should all pass:

```
user> (use 'clojure.test) (run-tests 'chapter-protocols.expense-test)

Testing chapter-protocols.expense-test

Ran 3 tests containing 5 assertions.
0 failures, 0 errors.
{:type :summary, :test 3, :pass 5, :fail 0, :error 0}
```

Finally, before wrapping up this section, let's write a couple of functions that will make it easy to query data about our modus operandi, like ExpenseCalculations.

QUERYING MODUS OPERANDI

The first function we'll write discerns what data types implement a particular modus operandi. Consider this code:

```
(defn implementors [modus-operandi method]
  (get-in modus-operandi [method :implementors]))
```

And this allows us to do things like this:

```
user> (implementors ExpenseCalculations :is-category?)
(com.curry.expenses.Expense clojure.lang.IPersistentMap)
```

Let's write another function that when given a class of a particular data type can tell us if it implements a particular method of a modus operandi. Here's the code:

```
(defn implements? [implementor modus-operandi method]
  (some #{implementor} (implementors modus-operandi method)))
```

Let's test it at the REPL:

```
user> (implements? com.curry.expenses.Expense ExpenseCalculations
                                               :is-category?)

com.curry.expenses.Expense
```

Note that implements? returns the class itself, which is truthy. Here's a negative scenario:

```
user> (implements? java.util.Date ExpenseCalculations :is-category?)
nil
```

Now that we have a function such as implements?, we can also write a broader function to see if a class implements a modus operandi completely:

```
(defn full-implementor? [implementor modus-operandi]
  (->> (keys modus-operandi)
       (map #(implements? implementor modus-operandi %))
       (not-any? nil?)))
```

Here it is in action:

```
user> (full-implementor? com.curry.expenses.Expense ExpenseCalculations)
true
```

To test the negative side, let's partially implement the modus operandi:

```
user> (detail-modus-operandi ExpenseCalculations
        java.util.Date
```

```
        (total-cents [e]
          (rand-int 1000))))
#<MultiFn clojure.lang.MultiFn@746ac18c>
```

And now we can test what we were after:

```
user> (full-implementor? java.util.Date ExpenseCalculations)
false
```

We can implement other functions such as these, because the value bound to the modus-operandi var is a regular map that can be inspected like any other. We're nearly at the end of this section. Before moving on though, let's examine the downsides to our modus operandi approach to the expression problem.

14.2.4   *The next step*

In this section, we took multimethods and wrote a little DSL on top of them that allows us to write simpler, clearer code when we want to dispatch on the class of the first argument. We were also able to group related multimethods together via this new syntax, and this allowed the code to be self-documenting by communicating that certain multimethods are related to each other.

What we haven't touched on at all is error handling. For instance, if you eval the same detail-modus-operandi calls multiple times, our data-collection functions would add the class to our modus operandi metadata map multiple times. It's an easy fix, but this isn't the most robust code in the world, because we wrote it to demonstrate the abstraction.

There are other trouble spots as well. For instance, because we built this on top of multimethods, and multimethods support hierarchies (and Java inheritance hierarchies by default), our implements? and related functions won't give accurate answers as they stand now.

Further, because this is such a barebones implementation, many other features might be desirable in a more production-ready version. The other downside is that there's a small performance hit when using multimethods because they have to call the dispatch function and then match the dispatch value against available multimethods. After all, our approach is syntactic sugar on top of multimethods.

In the next section, you'll see Clojure's version of the solution.

14.3   *Protocols and data types*

You've already seen what the expression problem is and a variety of ways to solve it. Clojure's multimethods are perfectly suited to writing code that allows independent extension of the supported data types and operations. We also created an abstraction called modus operandi that supports the most common use of multimethods, that of single dispatch (the first argument) based on the type (or class).

Because Clojure is written in Java, and the multimethod mechanism is implemented in Clojure itself, there's a performance penalty to be paid every time a multimethod is called. In most cases, this is negligible, and the increased expressiveness of code more than makes up for it. But as Clojure matures and moves more of its implementation into Clojure itself, there needs to be a way to support its abstraction and data-definition facilities without this performance hit. Protocols and data types are that solution, and they also offer a high-performance solution to the commonly encountered version of the expression problem.

In this section, we'll examine what protocols and data types are and how they can be used. Keep in mind our design of modus operandi as we work through this.

14.3.1 *defprotocol and extend-protocol*

The word *protocol* means the way something is done, often predefined and followed by all participating parties. Clojure protocols are analogous to our modi operandi, and `defprotocol` is to protocols what `def-modus-operandi` is to modi operandi. Similarly, `extend-protocol` is to protocols what `detail-modus-operandi` is to modi operandi. Listing 14.3 showed the implementation of the expense calculation, and the next listing shows the same logic implemented using Clojure protocols.

Listing 14.5 The expense namespace using a Clojure protocol

```
(ns chapter-protocols.expense-protocol
  (:import [java.text SimpleDateFormat]
           [java.util Calendar]))

(defn new-expense [date-string dollars cents category merchant-name]
  (let [calendar-date (Calendar/getInstance)]
    (.setTime calendar-date (.parse (SimpleDateFormat. "yyyy-MM-dd")
                                                        date-string))

    {:date calendar-date
     :amount-dollars dollars
     :amount-cents cents
     :category category
     :merchant-name merchant-name}))

(defprotocol ExpenseCalculations
  (total-cents [e])
  (is-category? [e category]))

(extend-protocol ExpenseCalculations
  clojure.lang.IPersistentMap
  (total-cents [e]
    (-> (:amount-dollars e)
        (* 100)
        (+ (:amount-cents e))))

  (is-category? [e some-category]
    (= (:category e) some-category)))

(extend-protocol ExpenseCalculations
  com.curry.expenses.Expense
  (total-cents [e]
    (.amountInCents e))

  (is-category? [e some-category]
    (= (.getCategory e) some-category)))
```

```
(defn category-is [category]
  #(is-category? % category))

(defn total-amount
  ([expenses-list]
     (total-amount (constantly true) expenses-list))
  ([pred expenses-list]
     (->> expenses-list
          (filter pred)
          (map total-cents)
          (apply +))))
```

The only thing that's different from the implementation based on modus operandi is that we've removed the dependence on the `chapter-protocols.modus-operandi` namespace, and we've replaced the calls to `def-modus-operandi` and `detail-modus-operandi` with calls to `defprotocol` and `extend-protocol`. At a conceptual level, the code in listing 14.5 should make sense. We'll get into the specifics now.

DEFINING NEW PROTOCOLS

As you might have guessed, new protocols are defined using the `defprotocol` macro. It defines a set of named methods, along with their signatures. Here's the official syntax:

```
(defprotocol AProtocolName

    ;optional doc string
    "A doc string for AProtocol abstraction"

  ;method signatures
    (bar [this a b] "bar docs")
    (baz [this a] [this a b] [this a b c] "baz docs"))
```

The protocol as well as the methods that form it can accept doc strings. A call to `defprotocol` results in a bunch of vars being created: one for the protocol itself and one for each polymorphic function (or method) that's a part of the protocol. These functions dispatch on the type of the first argument (and therefore must have at least one argument), and by convention, the first argument is called `this`. So from listing 14.5, the following snippet defines a protocol named `ExpenseCalculations`:

```
(defprotocol ExpenseCalculations
    (total-cents [e])
    (is-category? [e category]))
```

We're defining a set of related methods (`total-cents` and `is-category?`) that can be implemented any number of times by any data type. A call to `defprotocol` also generates an underlying Java interface. So, because the previous code exists in the namespace `chapter-protocols.expense-protocol`, it will result in a Java interface called `chapter_protocols.expense_protocol.ExpenseCalculations`. The methods in this interface will be the ones specified in the definition of the protocol, `total_cents` and `is_category_QMARK_`, the latter of which is the translated name of a Clojure function (one that ends with a question mark) into Java. The fact that `defprotocol` generates a Java interface also means that if some other Java code wants to participate in a protocol, it can implement the generated interface and proceed as usual.

Now that we've defined a protocol, any data type can participate in it.

PARTICIPATING IN PROTOCOLS

Having defined a protocol, let's see how you can use it. As an example, consider the call to extend-protocol, also from listing 14.5:

```
(extend-protocol ExpenseCalculations
  com.curry.expenses.Expense
  (total-cents [e]
    (.amountInCents e))

  (is-category? [e some-category]
    (= (.getCategory e) some-category)))
```

This means that the com.curry.expenses.Expense data type will participate in the ExpenseCalculations protocol, and when either total-cents or is-category? is called with an instance of this class as the first argument, it will be correctly dispatched to the previous implementation.

You can also specify more than one participant at a time; you can define the implementations of the protocol methods for more than a single data type. Here's an example:

```
(extend-protocol ExpenseCalculations

  clojure.lang.IPersistentMap
  (total-cents [e]
    (-> (:amount-dollars e)
        (* 100)
        (+ (:amount-cents e))))

  (is-category? [e some-category]
    (= (:category e) some-category))

  com.curry.expenses.Expense
  (total-cents [e]
    (.amountInCents e))

  (is-category? [e some-category]
    (= (.getCategory e) some-category)))
```

We'll now look at another way to specify how data types can participate in protocols.

THE EXTEND-TYPE MACRO

extend-protocol is a helper macro, defined on top of another convenient macro named extend-type. It's sort of the other way of specifying a participant of a protocol, in that it focuses on the data type. Here's an example of extend-type in use:

```
(extend-type com.curry.expenses.Expense
  ExpenseCalculations
  (total-cents [e]
    (.amountInCents e))

  (is-category? [e some-category]
    (= (.getCategory e) some-category)))
```

Again, because a single data type can participate in multiple protocols, extend-type lets you specify any number of protocols. Although extend-protocol and extend-type make it quite easy to use protocols, they both ultimately resolve to calls to the extend function.

THE EXTEND FUNCTION

The extend function lives in Clojure's core namespace, and it's the one that does the work of registering protocol participants and associating the methods with the right data types. Here's an example of the extend function in action:

```
(extend com.curry.expenses.Expense
  ExpenseCalculations {
    :total-cents (fn [e]
                    (.amountInCents e))
    :is-category? (fn [e some-category]
                    (= (.getCategory e) some-category))}})
```

This might look similar to the code we generated in our implementation of modus operandi. For each protocol and data type pair, extend accepts a map that describes participation of that data type in the protocol. The keys of the map are keyword versions of the names of the methods, and the values are the function bodies that contain the implementation for each. The extend function is the most flexible in terms of building an implementation of a protocol.

Figure 14.2 shows the conceptual flow of defining and using protocols, in a manner analogous to figure 14.1.

We've covered protocols and how they're defined and used. We'll say another couple of things about them before moving on to the remaining topics of this chapter.

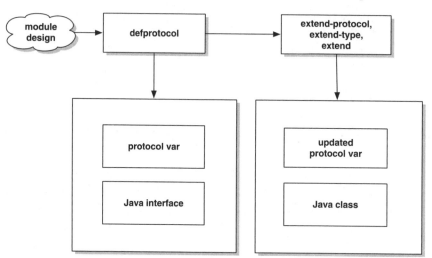

Figure 14.2 Calling defprotocol **performs an analogous operation where a** var **is created to hold information about the protocol and its implementors. The underlying implementation will also result in a Java interface that pertains to the protocol being defined. Calls to** extend, extend-type, **and** extend-protocol **will update the** var **with implementor details and generate Java classes that implement the protocol.**

PROTOCOLS AND NIL

You've seen that protocol methods are dispatched based on the class of the first argument. A natural question arises: what will happen if the first argument to a protocol method is nil? What is the class of nil?

```
user> (class nil)
nil
```

If you call a protocol method, say total-cents from our expense example with nil, you'll get an error complaining that no implementation was found. Luckily, protocols can be extended on nil:

```
(extend-protocol ExpenseCalculations nil
  (total-cents [e] 0))
```

After this, calling total-cents with nil will return zero. Our last stop in this section will be to explore a few functions that help us reflect on defined protocols.

REFLECTING ON PROTOCOLS

Sometimes it's useful to programmatically reflect on specific protocols and their extenders. When we wrote modus operandi, we also wrote some helper functions that let us reflect on implements?, implementors, and full-implementor. Clojure protocols also have functions that work in a similar fashion. Let's take a look at them.

```
user> (extends? ExpenseCalculations com.curry.expenses.Expense)
true

user> (extends? ExpenseCalculations clojure.lang.IPersistentMap)
true

user> (extends? ExpenseCalculations java.util.Date)
false
```

Needless to say, the function extends? can be used to check if a particular data type participates in a given protocol. The next function that's useful around such querying is extenders:

```
user> (extenders ExpenseCalculations)
(nil com.curry.expenses.Expense clojure.lang.IPersistentMap)
```

Again, the extenders function lists all the data types that participate in a particular protocol. The final function of interest is called satisfies? and it works like this:

```
user> (satisfies? ExpenseCalculations (com.curry.expenses.Expense. "10-10-
    2010" 20 95 "books" "amzn"))
true

user> (satisfies? ExpenseCalculations (new-expense "10-10-2010" 20 95 "books"
    "amzn"))
true

user> (satisfies? ExpenseCalculations (java.util.Random.))
false
```

Note that the satisfies? function works on instances of extenders, not extender data types themselves. You'll find this function even more useful once you've seen the reify macro in action, which we'll explore in the next section. We've now covered all the topics about protocols that we set out to cover. The next section is about the other side of this picture; we'll review a couple of ways to define data types.

14.3.2 *deftype, defrecord, and reify*

We started this chapter by considering the expression problem, and as you might recall, there are two sides to it, namely, data types and the operations on them. So far, we've been looking primarily at the operations side of the situation; in this section we'll look at a couple of ways to define data types.

The mechanisms we're going to talk about create underlying classes on the host platform (namely Java today, but it could be others tomorrow). This means that they share the same performance as the native version of such data types, as well as the same polymorphic capabilities supported by the host. We'll first look at `defrecord`, followed by `deftype`. We'll close the section with a look at `reify`.

DEFRECORD

Let's start with an example of using `defrecord`:

```
(defrecord NewExpense [date amount-dollars amount-cents
                                    category merchant-name])
```

As we mentioned, this call defines a named class (`chapter-protocols.expense-record.NewExpense`) that has the specified set of fields with names as specified in the call to `defrecord`. Because this is a proper class on the host environment, the type of class is fully specified and known, allowing for a high-performance dispatch of fields and methods. Similarly, it has a named constructor, similar to other Java classes. Here's how you'd create an instance of the `NewExpense` data type:

```
user> (import chapter-protocols.expense-record.NewExpense)
chapter-protocols.expense-record.NewExpense

user> (NewExpense. "2010-04-01" 29 95 "gift" "1-800-flowers")
#:chapter-protocols.expense-record.NewExpense{:date "2010-04-01",
                                    :amount-dollars 29,
                                    :amount-cents 95,
                                    :category "gift",
                                    :merchant-name "1-800-flowers"}
```

Notice that the printer shows this object as being an instance of the generated class, as expected. The only downside to this is that the reader can't reconstruct this if asked to read a string containing this text. This support may be added in a future version.

Now that we've come this far, let's go ahead and change the implementation of our expense namespace to use this. The following listing shows the new implementation.

> **Listing 14.6 The expense namespace using a Clojure protocol and `defrecord`**

```
(ns chapter-protocols.expense-record
  (:import [java.text SimpleDateFormat]
           [java.util Calendar]))
```

```
(defrecord NewExpense [date amount-dollars amount-cents
                       category merchant-name])

(defn new-expense [date-string dollars cents category merchant-name]
  (let [calendar-date (Calendar/getInstance)]
    (.setTime calendar-date (.parse (SimpleDateFormat. "yyyy-MM-dd")
                                                       date-string))
    (NewExpense. calendar-date dollars cents category merchant-name)))

(defprotocol ExpenseCalculations
  (total-cents [e])
  (is-category? [e category]))

(extend-type NewExpense
  ExpenseCalculations
  (total-cents [e]
    (-> (:amount-dollars e)
        (* 100)
        (+ (:amount-cents e))))

  (is-category? [e some-category]
    (= (:category e) some-category)))

(extend com.curry.expenses.Expense
  ExpenseCalculations {
    :total-cents (fn [e] (.amountInCents e))
    :is-category? (fn [e some-category] (= (.getCategory e)
                                           some-category))})

(extend-protocol ExpenseCalculations nil
  (total-cents [e] 0))

(defn category-is [category]
  #(is-category? % category))

(defn total-amount
  ([expenses-list]
    (total-amount (constantly true) expenses-list))
  ([pred expenses-list]
    (->> expenses-list
         (filter pred)
         (map total-cents)
         (apply +))))
```

Notice the call to `extend-type` and how we use the name of our newly defined record `NewExpense` instead of the previously used, more generic `IPersistentMap`. This shows that records can participate fully in protocols and indeed can participate in as many as needed. By the way, for completeness, it's worth modifying the `test` namespace to depend on the new `chapter-protocols.expense-record` namespace and checking to see if all tests pass. They should.

Notice how you can access the fields of the `NewExpense` instances using keywords. This is because `defrecord` creates a class that already implements several interfaces, including `IPersistentMap`, `IKeywordLookup`, and `ILookup`. In this manner, they work in the same way as regular Clojure maps, including with respect to destructuring, metadata, and the use of functions such as `assoc` and `dissoc`. A useful point to note is that records are extensible in that they can accept values for keys that weren't originally specified as part of the `defrecord` call. The only penalty to this is that such keys have the same performance as Clojure maps. Records also implement the `hashCode` and `equals` methods, in order to support value-based equality out of the box. A final note is that the field specification supports type hints.

In listing 14.6, you've already seen how records can participate in protocols. We made nearly no change to our code from the previous implementation from listing 14.5, but records have more direct support for protocols. They can supply the implementations of protocols inline with their definition. The following listing shows this version.

Listing 14.7 **The expense namespace with `defrecord` and inline protocol**

```clojure
(ns chapter-protocols.expense-record-2
  (:import [java.text SimpleDateFormat]
           [java.util Calendar]))

(defprotocol ExpenseCalculations
  (total-cents [e])
  (is-category? [e category]))

(defrecord NewExpense [date amount-dollars amount-cents
                                        category merchant-name]
  ExpenseCalculations
  (total-cents [this]
    (-> amount-dollars
        (* 100)
        (+ amount-cents)))

  (is-category? [this some-category]
    (= category some-category)))

(defn new-expense [date-string dollars cents category merchant-name]
  (let [calendar-date (Calendar/getInstance)]
    (.setTime calendar-date (.parse (SimpleDateFormat. "yyyy-MM-dd")
                                                 date-string))
    (NewExpense. calendar-date dollars cents category merchant-name)))

(extend com.curry.expenses.Expense
  ExpenseCalculations {
    :total-cents (fn [e] (.amountInCents e))
    :is-category? (fn [e some-category] (= (.getCategory e)
                                           some-category))})

(extend-protocol ExpenseCalculations nil
  (total-cents [e] 0))

(defn category-is [category]
  #(is-category? % category))

(defn total-amount
  ([expenses-list]
    (total-amount (constantly true) expenses-list))
  ([pred expenses-list]
    (->> expenses-list
        (filter pred)
```

```
(map total-cents)
(apply +))))
```

The main change is in the following snippet:

```
(defrecord NewExpense [date amount-dollars amount-cents
                                     category merchant-name]
  ExpenseCalculations
  (total-cents [this]
    (-> amount-dollars
        (* 100)
        (+ amount-cents)))

  (is-category? [this some-category]
    (= category some-category)))
```

Notice that we followed the field names with the protocol name that we wish to implement. The protocol name is followed by the implementations of the protocol methods. You can similarly follow that with more protocol specifications (the protocol name followed by the implementation).

JAVA SUPPORT

What's more, this isn't restricted to protocols; you can also specify and implement Java interfaces. The code would look similar to the previous protocol specification: you'd specify the interface name followed by the implementation of the interface methods. Instead of a protocol or an interface, you can also specify object and override methods from the `Object` class. Recall that the first parameter of all protocol methods is the implementor instance itself, so you must pass the conventionally named `this` parameter as before. This means that there will be one more parameter for each interface or object method when compared to the corresponding definition. Finally, if the method implementation needs to call `recur`, the `this` parameter shouldn't be passed, because it will be passed automatically.

With this discussion, we've covered records. They can be used in all places where maps might have been used because they're faster and also support protocols. Note that our implementation of protocol methods didn't result in closures, and when this functionality is needed, you can use the `reify` macro. You'll see that shortly, but our next stop is the `deftype` macro.

DEFTYPE

When you use `defrecord`, you get a whole bunch of functionality for free. You get map-like behavior of using keywords to look stuff up, you get value-based equality behavior, you get metadata support, and you get serialization. This is usually exactly what you need when developing application domain data types, such as our `expense` data type from the previous few sections.

But there are times when you don't need any of this; indeed, at times you want to specify your own implementations for some of these interfaces. It's for these times that Clojure also provides the `deftype` macro:

```
(deftype Mytype [a b])
```

This generates an underlying Java class that looks like this:

```
public final class Mytype {
    public final Object a;
    public final Object b;

    public Mytype(Object obj, Object obj1) {
        a = obj;
        b = obj1;
    }
}
```

As you can see, the fundamental difference between `defrecord` and `deftype` is that the latter produces a bare-metal class that you can do whatever you want with. The most common use case of `deftype` is to build infrastructure abstractions. Examples of such an abstraction might be a special collection to hold your domain-specific objects or a custom transaction manager. When you do need such a data type, with the performance characteristics of the native host, you can use `deftype`. In most other cases, `defrecord` should suffice.

We're nearly finished! In the previous section, we briefly mentioned closures. In the next section, we'll show how to create anonymous data types and instances of them using the `reify` macro.

REIFY

Reification means to bring something into being or to turn something into a concrete form. The `reify` macro takes a protocol, which by itself is an abstract set of methods, and creates a concrete instance of an anonymous data type that implements that protocol. It does so with the full power of Clojure's lexical closures. For example, you might implement the `new-expense` function as follows:

```
(defn new-expense [date-string dollars cents category merchant-name]
  (let [calendar-date (Calendar/getInstance)]
    (.setTime calendar-date
              (.parse (SimpleDateFormat. "yyyy-MM-dd") date-string))
    (reify ExpenseCalculations
      (total-cents [this]
        (-> dollars
          (* 100)
          (+ cents)))
      (is-category? [this some-category]
        (= category some-category)))))
```

In a pattern that's similar to one you've seen before, `reify` accepts one or more protocols and their implementation. In this example, `reify` was passed the `ExpenseCalculations` protocol along with the implementations of the `total-cents` and `is-category?` methods. The object returned by `reify` is a closure; in the case of `new-expense`, the lexically bound closure includes the parameters passed to `new-expense`, along with the names created in the `let` form.

Here's another example from the chapter on messaging using RabbitMQ. The following snippet is taken from listing 11.4:

```
(defn on-swarm [worker-name args]
  (let [worker-data (ref worker-init-value)
        worker-transport (dispatch-work worker-name args worker-data)]
    (fn [accessor]
      (condp = accessor
        :complete? (not (= worker-init-value @worker-data))
        :value (attribute-from-response @worker-data :value)
        :status (@worker-data :status)
        :disconnect (disconnect-worker worker-transport)))))
```

This on-swarm function returns a closure that accepts command keywords such as
:value and :status. An example of using this closure is the all-complete? function,
also taken from the same listing:

```
(defn all-complete? [swarm-requests]
  (every? #(% :complete?) swarm-requests))
```

The parameter swarm-requests is a sequence of closures returned by the on-swarm
function. We'll rewrite this using a protocol. First, we'll define one:

```
(defprotocol RemoteWorker
  (complete? [rw])
  (value [rw])
  (status [rw])
  (disconnect [rw]))
```

Next, we'll redefine on-swarm:

```
(defn on-swarm [worker-name args]
  (let [worker-data (ref worker-init-value)
        worker-transport (dispatch-work worker-name args worker-data)]
    (reify RemoteWorker
      (complete? [rw]
        (not (= worker-init-value @worker-data)))
      (value [rw]
        (attribute-from-response @worker-data :value))
      (status [rw]
        (@worker-data :status))
      (disconnect [rw]
        (disconnect-worker worker-transport)))))
```

We'll also fix places where the closure was being used in the old way, such as the all-
complete? function:

```
(defn all-complete? [swarm-requests]
  (every? complete? swarm-requests))
```

This is a far more natural way to write this function. The reify macro is useful whenever you have a situation such as the one here, where it makes sense to create and
return a closure.

The benefit of using protocols here is that you can create new versions of objects
that implement this protocol, such as one that doesn't delegate the computation to a
remote worker process but executes it locally (useful for testing) or one that uses an
entirely different transport mechanism (instead of RabbitMQ). As far as the client

code is concerned, it will keep working as long as an extender of `RemoteWorker` is passed in.

You've now learned enough about protocols and data types to use them in your own programs. In order to round off this chapter, we'll make a few observations about protocols and compare them to multimethods.

14.4 Summary

Protocols were originally introduced to satisfy the need for low-level implementation techniques that would be fast enough to implement the language itself in, a la Clojure in Clojure. They also serve to solve 90% of the expression problem cases, where class-based single dispatch is acceptable. In this way, they're less powerful than multimethods.

Even with that, protocols have several advantages. Similar to multimethods, they don't tie polymorphism to inheritance. They allow grouping of related methods into a conceptual unit, which makes for clearer, self-documenting code. Because protocols generate interfaces from the underlying host, they're able to provide performance that's on par with the host itself. Similar to multimethods, they're an open way of solving the expression problem. This means that new data types and operations can be added while making minimum changes to existing code. Similarly, openness is maintained with respect to who is allowed to participate in protocols. Any number of data types can implement a single protocol, and a data type can implement any number of protocols. Finally, because protocols belong to the namespace they're defined in, there's no danger of name collisions if someone defines a protocol with the same name that you chose.

As a parting note, it's worth mentioning that even before the introduction of `defrecord`, using maps to store information was the idiomatic way to implement things. Hiding information behind non-generic interfaces (such as getters/setters or even more custom methods) makes such information less reusable by code that wasn't designed to access such an API. Maps provide far more generic manipulability, and records take that one step further by making it perform as fast as the host platform can make it.

When coupled with protocols, your Clojure code will be built on abstractions. This will ensure that it's more flexible and easier to maintain, as well as being easy for other people to work with. In this manner, protocols give a huge benefit even beyond solving the most common case of the expression problem.

15

More macros and DSLs

This chapter covers

- A review of Clojure macros
- Anaphoric macros
- Shifting computation to compile time
- Macro generating macros
- Domain-specific languages in Clojure

This final chapter is about what many consider the most powerful feature of Clojure. John McCarthy, the inventor of the Lisp programming language, once said that Lisp is a local maximum in the space of programming languages. Clojure macros make Clojure a programmable programming language because it can do arbitrary code transformations of Clojure code, using Clojure itself. No programming language outside the Lisp family can do this in such a simple way. To reiterate the obvious, this is possible because code is data.

You've seen a lot of macros through the course of this book, including in chapter 7, which served as an introduction to the topic. In this section, you're going to see a lot more but with two new points of focus. The first will be advanced uses of macros, and the second will be the conscious design of a simple domain-specific language.

15.1 *Macros*

This section is about the things you can do with macros. You've already used macros quite a bit, so you should be familiar with the basics. As a refresher, we'll write a little macro in order to remind you what macros make possible. You've used Clojure's `let` macro several times so far. Although `let` itself is a macro, it's implemented in terms of the `let*` special form, which sets up lexical scope for the symbols named in the binding form. We'll now implement a subset of the functionality of `let` via a macro that generates function calls. This is what we'd like to do:

```
(my-let [x 10
         y x
         z (+ x y)]
  (* x y z))
```

This should return 2000, because `x` is 10, `y` is also 10, and `z` is 20. Here's the implementation:

```
(defmacro single-arg-fn [binding-form & body]
  `((fn [~(first binding-form)] ~@body) ~(second binding-form)))

(defmacro my-let [lettings & body]
  (if (empty? lettings)
    `(do ~@body)
    `(single-arg-fn ~(take 2 lettings)
       (my-let ~(drop 2 lettings) ~@body))))
```

Although this is a limited implementation, you still get all the advantages that arise from using functions underneath the covers. For instance, you can do the following:

```
user> (my-let [[a b] [2 5]
               {:keys [x y]} {:x (* a b) :y 20}
               z (+ x y)]
        (println "a,b,x,y,z:" a b x y z)
        (* x y z))
a,b,x,y,z: 2 5 10 20 30
6000
```

We're not doing any error checking, but hopefully this example has reminded you how macros work, as well as shown you how to seemingly add features to the Clojure language itself. Use `macroexpand-1` and `macroexpand` to get a hint as to how the `my-let` does its thing. We're now ready to look beyond the basics.

Broadly speaking, in this section, we're going to explore three new concepts. The first is that of *anaphora*, an approach of writing macros that utilize intentional variable capture to their advantage. You'll see why they're called anaphoric and what they might be used for.

The second concept we'll explore is the idea of moving some of the computation from a program's runtime into its compile time. Some computation that would otherwise be done when the program is already running will now be done while the code is being compiled. You'll see not only where this might be useful but also an example.

Finally, we'll look at writing macros that generate other macros. This can be tricky, and we'll look at a simple example of such a macro. Understanding macro-generating macros is a sign of being on the path to macro zen.

Without further ado, our first stop is Clojure anaphora.

15.1.1 *Anaphoric macros*

In the chapter on the basics of macros, we talked about the issue of variable capture. You saw that Clojure solves this issue in an elegant manner through two processes: the first is that names inside a macro template get namespace qualified to the namespace that the macro is defined in, and the second is by providing a convenient auto-gensym reader macro.

Macros that do their work based on intentional variable capture are called anaphoric macros. The chapter on web services introduced the use of anaphoric macros in the section on Compojure. In this section, we'll do more variable capture but in a slightly more complex manner. To get things started, we'll visit a commonly cited example that illustrates this concept. We'll then build on it to write a useful utility macro.

15.1.2 *The anaphoric if*

Writing the anaphoric version of the if construct is the "Hello, world!" of anaphora. The anaphoric if is probably one of the simplest of its ilk, but it illustrates the point well, while also being a useful utility macro.

Consider the following example, where we first do a computation, check if it is truthy, and then proceed to use it in another computation. Imagine that we had the following function:

```
(defn some-computation [x]
  (if (even? x) false (inc x)))
```

It's a placeholder to illustrate the point we're about to make. Now consider a use case as follows:

```
(if (some-computation 11)
  (* 2 (some-computation 11)))
```

Naturally, you wouldn't stand for such duplication, and you'd use the let form to remove it:

```
(let [computation (some-computation 11)]
  (if computation
    (* 2 computation)))
```

You also know that you don't need to stop here, because you can use the handy if-let macro:

```
(if-let [computation (some-computation 11)]
  (* 2 computation))
```

Although this is clear enough, it would be nice if you could write something like the following, for it to read more clearly:

```
(anaphoric-if (some-computation 11)
  (* 2 it))
```

Here, it is a symbol that represents the value of the condition clause. Most anaphoric macros use pronouns such as it to refer to some value that was computed. The word *anaphor* means a word or phrase that refers to an earlier word or phrase.

IMPLEMENTING ANAPHORIC-IF

Now that you've seen what you'd like to express in the code, let's set about implementing it. You could imagine writing it as follows:

```
(defmacro anaphoric-if [test-form then-form]
  `(if-let [~'it ~test-form]
     ~then-form))
```

Here's the macro expansion of the example from earlier:

```
user> (macroexpand-1 '(anaphoric-if (some-computation 11)
         (* 2 it)))
(clojure.core/if-let [it (some-computation 11)] (* 2 it))
```

That expansion looks exactly like what you need because it creates a local name it and binds the value of the test-form to it. It then evaluates the then-form inside the let block created by the if-let form, which ensures that it happens only if the value of it is truthy. Here it is in action:

```
user> (anaphoric-if (some-computation 12)
         (* 2 it))
nil

user> (anaphoric-if (some-computation 11)
         (* 2 it))
24
```

Notice how we had to force Clojure to not namespace qualify the name it. We did this by unquoting a quoted symbol (that's what the strange notation ~'it is). This forces the variable capture. We'll use this technique (and the unquote splice version of it) again in the following sections.

There you have it, a simple macro that adds some convenience. It's important to remember that when using anaphora, you're using variable capture. So although it may be OK that the symbol it is captured in this case, it may not be in other cases. You have to be watchful for situations where intentional variable capture can cause subtle bugs.

Now that we have an anaphoric version of if, we're ready to move on to a more complex example. Before we do, let's write a macro that generalizes our anaphoric if a little.

GENERALIZING THE ANAPHORIC IF

Let's recall our implementation of the anaphoric if macro:

```
(defmacro anaphoric-if [test-form then-form]
  `(if-let [~'it ~test-form]
     ~then-form))
```

Note that we built this on the `if-let` macro, which in turn is built on the `if` special form. If you were to remove the hard dependency on the `if` special form and instead specify it at call time, you could have a more general version of this code on your hands. Let's take a look:

```
(defmacro with-it [operator test-form & exprs]
  `(let [~'it ~test-form]
     (~operator ~'it ~@exprs)))
```

So, we take the idea from `anaphoric-if` and create a new version of it where we need to pass in the thing we're trying to accomplish. For instance, the example from before would now read like this:

```
user> (with-it if (some-computation 12)
        (* 2 it))
nil

user> (with-it if (some-computation 11)
        (* 2 it))
24
```

Why would you want to do this? Because now you can have an anaphoric version of more than the `if` form. For example, you could do the following:

```
user> (with-it and (some-computation 11) (> it 10) (* 2 it))
24
```

Or you could do this:

```
user> (with-it when (some-computation 11)
        (println "Got it:" it)
        (* 2 it))
Got it: 12
24
```

Try these out at the REPL, and also try versions that use `if-not`, `or`, `when-not`, and so on. You could even go back and define macros like `anaphoric-if` in terms of `with-it`, for instance:

```
(defmacro anaphoric-if [test-form then-form]
  `(with-it if ~test-form ~then-form))
```

You could define all such variants (using `if`, `and`, `or`, and so on) in one swoop. This wraps up our introduction to anaphoric macros. As we mentioned at the start of this section, these examples are quite simple. The next one will be slightly more involved.

15.1.3 *The thread-it macro*

A couple of the most useful macros in Clojure's core namespace are the threading macros. This refers to the thread-first and the thread-last macros, which we covered in chapter 2. As a refresher, we'll write a function to calculate the surface area of a cylinder with a radius r and height h. The formula is

```
2 * PI * r (r + h)
```

Using the thread-first macro, you can write this as

```
(defn surface-area-cylinder [r h]
  (-> r
      (+ h)
      (* 2 Math/PI r)))
```

You saw a similar example when we first encountered this macro. Instead of writing something like a let form with intermediate results of a larger computation, the result of the first form is fed into the next form as the first argument, the result of that's then fed into the next form as *its* first argument in turn, and so on. It's a significant improvement in code readability.

The thread-last macro is the same, but instead of placing consecutive results in the first argument position of the following form, it places them in the position of the last argument. It's useful in code that's similar to the following hypothetical example:

```
(defn some-calculation [a-collection]
  (->> (seq a-collection)
       (filter some-pred?)
       (map a-transform)
       (reduce another-function)))
```

Now, although both the thread-first and thread-last macros are extremely useful, they do have a possible shortcoming: they both fix the position of where each step of the computation is placed into the next form. The thread-first places it as the first argument of the next call, whereas the thread-last macro places it in the position of the last argument.

Occasionally, this can be limiting. Consider our previous snippet of code. Imagine if you wanted to use a function written by someone else called compute-averages-from that accepts two arguments: a sequence of data and a predicate *in that order.* As it stands, you couldn't plug that function into the threaded code shown previously, because the order of arguments was reversed. You'd have to adapt the function, perhaps as follows:

```
(defn another-calculation [a-collection]
  (->> (seq a-collection)
       (filter some-pred?)
       (map a-transform)
       (#(compute-averages-from % another-pred?))))
```

You've seen the use of anonymous functions to create adapter functions such as this before, but it isn't pretty. It spoils the overall elegance by adding some noise to the code. What if, instead of being limited to threading forms as the first and last arguments of subsequent forms, you could choose where to thread them?

IMPLEMENTING THREAD-IT

As you can guess from the fact that we're in the middle of a section on anaphoric macros, we're going to choose a symbol, which will be the placeholder for where we'd like our new threading macro to thread forms into. We'll use the it symbol and call the macro thread-it. With our new macro, we'd be able to do something like this:

```
(defn yet-another-calculation [a-collection]
  (thread-it (seq a-collection)
             (filter some-pred? it)
             (map a-transform it)
             (compute-averages-from it another-pred?))))
```

Before we jump into the implementation, let's add another change to the way Clojure's built-in threading macros work, in that they expect at least one argument. We'd like to be able to call our `thread-it` macro without any arguments. This may be useful when you're using it inside another macro. Although the following doesn't work

```
user> (->> )
Wrong number of args (2) passed to: core$--GT
  [Thrown class java.lang.IllegalArgumentException]
```

we'd like our macro to do this:

```
user> (thread-it)
nil
```

Now we're ready to look at the implementation. Consider the following:

```
(defmacro thread-it [& [first-expr & rest-expr]]
  (if (empty? rest-expr)
    first-expr
    `(let [~'it ~first-expr]
       (thread-it ~@rest-expr)))))
```

As you can see, the macro accepts any number of arguments. The list of arguments is destructured into the first (named `first-expr`) and the rest (named `rest-expr`). The first task is to check to see if `rest-expr` is empty (which happens when either no arguments were passed in or a single argument was passed in). If this is so, the macro will return `first-expr`, which will be `nil` if there were no arguments passed into `thread-it` or the single argument if only one was passed in.

If there are arguments remaining inside `rest-expr`, the macro expands to another call to itself, with the symbol `it` bound to the value of `first-expr`, nested inside a `let` block. This recursive macro definition expands until it has consumed all the forms it was passed in. Here's an example of it in action:

```
user> (thread-it (* 10 20) (inc it) (- it 8) (* 10 it) (/ it 5))
386
```

Also, the way we've implemented it, the following behavior is expected:

```
user> (thread-it it)
; Evaluation aborted.
Unable to resolve symbol: it in this context
  [Thrown class java.lang.Exception]
```

This happens because we don't start by binding anything to `it`. You could change this behavior by initially binding `it` to a default value of some kind. That's all there is to the implementation. It can be a useful macro in situations where the functions (or macros) in a threading form take arguments in an irregular order. Further, as a refinement, or perhaps as another version of this macro, you could replace the let with an if-let. This will short-circuit the computation if any step results in a logically false value. The implementation of that is straightforward and is left as an exercise to the reader.

This leads us to the end of the discussion on anaphora. It's a useful technique at times, even though it breaks hygiene because it involves variable capture. As we mentioned, you have to be careful while using it, but when you do, it can result in code that's more readable than it would be otherwise.

Our next stop is to examine another use case of macros. We're going to make the Clojure compiler work harder by doing some work that would otherwise have to be done by our program at runtime.

15.1.4   *Shifting computation to compile time*

So far in this book, you've seen several uses of macros and have written several macros yourself. In this section, you're going to see another use of macros, and it has to do with performance. In order to illustrate the concept, we'll examine a simple code cipher called ROT13. It stands for "rotate by 13 places" and is a simple cipher that can be broken quite easily. But its purpose is to hide text in a way that isn't immediately obvious, not to communicate spy secrets. It's commonly used as the online equivalent of text printed upside down (for example, in magazines and newspapers), to give out puzzle solutions, answers to riddles, and the like.

ABOUT THE ROT13 CIPHER

Table 15.1 shows what each letter of the alphabet corresponds to.

Table 15.1   The alphabet rotated by 13 places

1	2	3	4	5	6	7	8	9	10	11	12	13	14	15	16	17	18	19	20	21	22	23	24	25	26
a	b	c	d	e	f	g	h	i	j	k	l	m	n	o	p	q	r	s	t	u	v	w	x	y	z
n	o	p	q	r	s	t	u	v	w	x	y	z	a	b	c	d	e	f	g	h	i	j	k	l	m

The first row is the index for each letter of the alphabet, starting at 1. The second row is the alphabet itself. The last row is the alphabet shifted by 13. Each letter on this last row corresponds to the letter that will be used in place of the letter above it in a message encrypted using this cipher system. For example, the word *abracadabra* becomes *noenpnqnoen*.

Decrypting a rotation cipher is usually done by rotating each letter back the same number of times. ROT13 has the additional property of being a reciprocal cipher. A message encrypted using a reciprocal cipher can be decrypted by running it through the cipher system itself. The encryption process also works to decrypt encrypted messages. In this section, we'll implement a generalized rotation cipher by allowing the rotation length to be passed in as a parameter.

GENERALIZED ROTATION CIPHERS

Let's begin our implementation with the letters of the alphabet. Recall that Clojure has a convenient reader macro to represent literal characters:

```
(def ALPHABETS [\a \b \c \d \e \f \g \h \i \j \k \l \m \n \o \p \q \r \s \t
    \u \v \w \x \y \z])
```

Let's also define a few convenience values based on the alphabet shown:

```
(def NUM-ALPHABETS (count ALPHABETS))
```

```
(def INDICES (range 1 (inc NUM-ALPHABETS)))
```

```
(def lookup (zipmap INDICES ALPHABETS))
```

Now, let's talk about our approach. Because we want to implement a generic rotation mechanism, we'll need to know at which numbered slot a letter falls when it's rotated a specific number of times. We'd like to take a slot number such as 14, rotate it by a configurable number, and see where it ends up. For example, in the case of ROT13, the letter in slot number 10 (which is the letter *j*) ends up in slot 23. We'll write a function called `shift`, which will compute this new slot number. We can't add the shift-by number to the slot number, because we'll have to take care of overflow. Here's the implementation of `shift`:

```
(defn shift [shift-by index]
  (let [shifted (+ (mod shift-by NUM-ALPHABETS) index)]
    (cond
      (<= shifted 0) (+ shifted NUM-ALPHABETS)
      (> shifted NUM-ALPHABETS) (- shifted NUM-ALPHABETS)
      :default shifted)))
```

There are a couple of points to note here. The first is that we calculated `shifted` by adding `(mod shift-by NUM-ALPHABETS)` to the given `index` (and not `shift-by`) so that we can handle the cases where `shift-by` is more than `NUM-ALPHABETS`. Because we handle overflow by wrapping to the beginning, this approach works, for example:

```
user> (shift 10 13)
23
```

```
user> (shift 20 13)
7
```

Now that you have this function, you can use it to create a simple cryptographic tableau, a table of rows and columns with which you can decrypt or encrypt information. In our case, for ROT13, the tableau would be the second and third rows from table 15.1. Here's a function that computes this:

```
(defn shifted-tableau [shift-by]
  (->> (map #(shift shift-by %) INDICES)
       (map lookup)
       (zipmap ALPHABETS)))
```

This creates a map where the keys are alphabets that need to be encrypted, and values are the cipher versions of the same. Here's an example:

```
user> (shifted-tableau 13)
{\a \n, \b \o, \c \p, \d \q, \e \r, \f \s, \g \t, \h \u, \i \v, \j \w, \k \x,
    \l \y, \m \z, \n \a, \o \b, \p \c, \q \d, \r \e, \s \f, \t \g, \u \h, \v
    \i, \w \j, \x \k, \y \l, \z \m}
```

Because our cipher is quite simple, a simple map such as this suffices. Now that you have our tableau, encrypting messages is as simple as looking up each letter. Here's the encrypt function:

```
(defn encrypt [shift-by plaintext]
  (let [shifted (shifted-tableau shift-by)]
    (apply str (map shifted plaintext))))
```

Try it at the REPL:

```
user> (encrypt 13 "abracadabra")
"noenpnqnoen"
```

That works as expected. Recall that ROT13 is a reciprocal cipher. Let's see if it works:

```
user> (encrypt 13 "noenpnqnoen")
"abracadabra"
```

It does! If you rotate by anything other than 13, you'll need a real decrypt function. All you need to do to decrypt a message is to reverse the process. Let's express that as follows:

```
(defn decrypt [shift-by encrypted]
  (encrypt (- shift-by) encrypted))
```

decrypt works by rotating an encrypted message the other way by the same rotation. Let's see it work at the REPL:

```
user> (decrypt 13 "noenpnqnoen")
"abracadabra"
```

Great, so we have all the bare necessities in place. In order to implement a particular cipher, such as ROT13, you can define a pair of functions as follows:

```
(def encrypt-with-rot13 (partial encrypt 13))
```

```
(def decrypt-with-rot13 (partial decrypt 13))
```

Now try it at the REPL:

```
user> (decrypt-with-rot13 (encrypt-with-rot13 "abracadabra"))
"abracadabra"
```

So there you have it; we've implemented the simple cipher system. The complete code is shown in the following listing.

Listing 15.1   A general rotation cipher system to implement things like ROT13

```
(ns chapter-macros.shifting)
```

```
(def ALPHABETS [\a \b \c \d \e \f \g \h \i \j \k \l \m \n \o \p \q \r \s \t
    \u \v \w \x \y \z])
```

```clojure
(def NUM-ALPHABETS (count ALPHABETS))

(def INDICES (range 1 (inc NUM-ALPHABETS)))

(def lookup (zipmap INDICES ALPHABETS))

(defn shift [shift-by index]
  (let [shifted (+ (mod shift-by NUM-ALPHABETS) index)]
    (cond
      (<= shifted 0) (+ shifted NUM-ALPHABETS)
      (> shifted NUM-ALPHABETS) (- shifted NUM-ALPHABETS)
      :default shifted)))

(defn shifted-tableau [shift-by]
  (->> (map #(shift shift-by %) INDICES)
       (map lookup)
       (zipmap ALPHABETS )))

(defn encrypt [shift-by plaintext]
  (let [shifted (shifted-tableau shift-by)]
    (apply str (map shifted plaintext))))

(defn decrypt [shift-by encrypted]
  (encrypt (- shift-by) encrypted))

(def encrypt-with-rot13 (partial encrypt 13))

(def decrypt-with-rot13 (partial decrypt 13))
```

The issue with this implementation is that you compute the tableau each time you encrypt or decrypt a message. This is easily fixed by memoizing the shifted-tableau function. This will take care of this problem, but in the next section, we'll go one step further.

MAKING THE COMPILER WORK HARDER

So far, we've implemented functions to encrypt and decrypt messages for any rotation cipher. Our basic approach has been to create a map that can help us code (or decode) each letter in a message to its cipher version. As discussed at the end of the previous section, we can speed up our implementation by memoizing the tableau calculation.

Even with memoize, the computation still happens at least once (the first time the function is called). Imagine, instead, if you created an inline literal map containing the appropriate tableau data. You could then look it up in the map each time, without having to compute it. Such a definition of encrypt-with-rot13 might look like this:

```clojure
(defn encrypt-with-rot13 [plaintext]
  (apply str (map {\a \n \b \o \c \p} plaintext)))
```

In an implementation, the tableau would be complete for all the letters of the alphabet, not only for \a, \b, and \c. In any case, if you did have such a literal map in the code itself, it would obviate the need to compute it at runtime. Luckily, we're coding in Clojure, and you can bend it to your will. Consider the following:

```clojure
(defmacro def-rot-encrypter [name shift-by]
  (let [tableau (shifted-tableau shift-by)]
    `(defn ~name [~'message]
       (apply str (map ~tableau ~'message)))))
```

This macro first computes the tableau for `shifted-by` as needed and then defines a function by the specified name. The function body includes the computed table, in the right place, as we illustrated in the code sample a moment ago. Look at its expansion:

```
user> (macroexpand-1 '(def-rot-encrypter encrypt13 13))
(clojure.core/defn encrypt13 [message] (clojure.core/apply clojure.core/str
    (clojure.core/map {\a \n, \b \o, \c \p, \d \q, \e \r, \f \s, \g \t, \h
    \u, \i \v, \j \w, \k \x, \l \y, \m \z, \n \a, \o \b, \p \c, \q \d, \r
    \e, \s \f, \t \g, \u \h, \v \i, \w \j, \x \k, \y \l, \z \m} message)))
```

This looks almost exactly like our desired function, with an inline literal tableau map. Figure 15.1 shows the flow of the code.

Let's check to see if it works:

```
user> (def-rot-encrypter encrypt13 13)
#'user/encrypt13

user> (encrypt13 "abracadabra")
"noenpnqnoen"
```

And there you have it. Our new `encrypt13` function at runtime doesn't do any tableau computation at all. If you were to, for instance, ship this code off to someone as a Java library, they wouldn't even know that `shifted-tableau` was ever called.

As a final item, we'll create a convenience way to define a pair of functions, which can be used to encrypt or decrypt functions in a rotation cipher:

```
(defmacro define-rot-encryption [shift-by]
  `(do
      (def-rot-encrypter ~(symbol (str "encrypt"
      shift-by)) ~shift-by)
      (def-rot-encrypter ~(symbol (str "decrypt"
      shift-by)) ~(- shift-by))))
```

And finally, here it is in action:

```
user> (define-rot-encryption 15)
#'user/decrypt15
```

Here, it prints the decrypt function var, because it was the last thing the macro expansion did. Let's use our new pair of functions:

```
user> (encrypt15 "abracadabra")
"pqgprpspqgp"

user> (decrypt15 "pqgprpspqgp")
"abracadabra"
```

Shifting computation to the compile cycle can be a useful trick when parts of the computation needed are known in advance. Clojure macros make it easy to run arbitrary

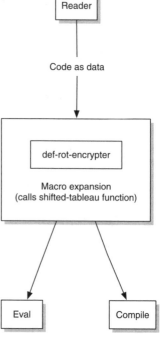

Figure 15.1   As usual, the Clojure reader first converts the text of our programs into data structures. During this process, macros are expanded, including our `def-rot-encrypter` macro, which generates a tableau. This tableau is a Clojure map and is included in the final form of the source code as an inline lookup table.

code during the expansion phase and to give the programmer the power of the full Clojure language itself. In this example, for instance, we wrote the `shifted-tableau` function with no prior intention of using it in this manner. Moving computation into macros this way can be quite handy at times, despite how simple it is to do.

15.1.5 *Macro-generating macros*

Now that you understand what it is to move computation to the compile phase of program execution, you're ready for a new adventure. We'll expand your mind a little as we try to write code that writes code that writes code—we're going to write a macro that writes a macro.

We'll take an example that's most often used to illustrate this, and it's probably the simplest example of such a macro. But it will serve well to illustrate this topic. The macro will create a synonym for an existing function or macro. Imagine you have two vars as follows:

```
user> (declare x y)
#'user/y
```

And if you use our new macro `make-synonym`

```
user> (make-synonym b binding)
#'user/b
```

then the following should work:

```
user> (b [x 10 y 20] (println "X,Y:" x y))
X,Y: 10 20
```

We'll implement the `make-synonym` macro in this section.

AN EXAMPLE TEMPLATE

When writing a macro, it's usually easier to start with an example of the desired expansion. In this case, we can use the previous example:

```
(b [x 10 y 20] (println "X,Y:" x y))
```

And in order for it to do so, b should be replaced with `binding`, resulting in the expansion:

```
(binding [x 10 y 20] (println "X,Y:" x y))
```

You could easily solve this if you wrote a custom macro defining b in terms of `binding`, as follows:

```
(defmacro b [& stuff]
  `(binding ~@stuff))
```

This replaces the symbol b with the symbol `binding`, keeping everything else the same. We aren't interested in the vars being bound, or the body itself, which is why we lump everything into `stuff`.

Now that we have a version of b that works as expected, we need to generalize it into `make-synonym`. The previous code is an example of what our `make-synonym` macro ought to produce.

IMPLEMENTING MAKE-SYNONYM

You know `make-synonym` is a macro and that it accepts two parameters. The first parameter is a new symbol that will be the synonym of the existing macro or function, whereas the second parameter is the name of the existing macro or function. We can begin implementing our new macro by starting with an empty definition:

```
(defmacro synonym [new-name old-name])
```

The next question is, what should go in the body? We can start by putting in the sample expansion from the previous section. Here's what it looks like:

```
(defmacro make-synonym [new-name old-name]
  (defmacro b [& stuff]
    `(binding ~@stuff)))
```

Obviously, this won't work as desired, because no matter what's passed in as arguments to this version of `make-synonym`, it will always create a macro named b (that expands to binding).

What we want, instead, is for `make-synonym` to produce the inner form containing the call to `defmacro`, instead of calling it. We know we can do this using the back quote. In this case, we'll have two back quotes. While we're at it, instead of the hard-coded symbols b and `binding`, we'll use the names passed in as parameters. Consider the following increment of our `make-synonym` macro:

```
(defmacro make-synonym [new-name old-name]
  `(defmacro ~new-name [& stuff]
     `(~old-name ~@stuff)))
```

This is a little confusing, because we have two back quotes in play here, one nested inside the other. The easiest way to understand what's happening is to look at an expansion. We'll try it at the REPL:

```
user> (macroexpand-1 '(make-synonym b binding))
(clojure.core/defmacro b [& user/stuff]
  (clojure.core/seq (clojure.core/concat (clojure.core/list user/old-name)
                                         user/stuff)))
```

In order to understand this expansion, let's first look at what happens to a back quote when it's expanded:

```
user> (defmacro back-quote-test []
        `(something))
#'user/back-quote-test

user> (macroexpand '(back-quote-test))
(user/something)
```

This isn't surprising, because the Clojure namespace qualifies any names unless explicitly asked not to. Now, let's add a back quote:

```
user> (defmacro back-quote-test []
        ``(something))
#'user/back-quote-test
```

We've added another back quote to the one already present. What we're saying is instead of expanding the back-quoted form and using its return value as the expansion of the `back-quote-test` macro, we want the back-quoting mechanism itself. Here it is at the REPL:

```
user> (macroexpand '(back-quote-test))
(clojure.core/seq (clojure.core/concat (clojure.core/list
                                          (quote user/something))))
```

Because we're using the symbol `something` as is, Clojure is namespace qualifying, as you'd expect. Now that you know what the back-quote mechanism itself is, we can return to the expansion of `make-synonym`:

```
user> (macroexpand-1 '(make-synonym b binding))
(clojure.core/defmacro b [& user/stuff]
  (clojure.core/seq (clojure.core/concat (clojure.core/list user/old-name)
                                          user/stuff)))
```

Here, the symbol `b` gets substituted as part of the expansion of the outer back-quote expansion. Because we don't explicitly quote the symbol `stuff`, it gets namespace qualified (we'll need to fix that soon). To understand what's happening to `old-name` inside the nested back quote, let's look at the following:

```
user> (defmacro back-quote-test []
        ``(~something))
#'user/back-quote-test
```

```
user> (macroexpand '(back-quote-test))
(clojure.core/seq (clojure.core/concat (clojure.core/list user/something)))
```

If you compare this to the previous version of `back-quote-test` and the expansion it generated, you'll notice that `user/something` is no longer wrapped in a `quote` form. This is again as expected, because we're unquoting it using the `~` reader macro. This explains why the nested back-quote form of the `make-synonym` macro expands with `user/old-name` as it does. Again, we'll need to fix this problem because we don't want the symbol `old-name` but the argument passed in.

Finally, in order to see what's going on with the unquote splicing and the `stuff` symbol, let's look at the following simpler example:

```
user> (defmacro back-quote-test []
        ``(~@something))
#'user/back-quote-test
```

```
user> (macroexpand '(back-quote-test))
(clojure.core/seq (clojure.core/concat user/something))
```

If you now compare this version of the expansion with the previous one, you'll note that `user/something` is no longer wrapped in a call to `list`. This is in line with our expected behavior of `unquote-slice` in that it doesn't add an extra set of parentheses.

At this point, we've walked through the complete expansion of our `make-synonym` macro. The only problem is that it still doesn't do what we intended it to do. The two problems we identified were that both `stuff` and `old-name` weren't being expanded correctly. Let's fix `stuff` first. Consider the following change to `make-synonym`:

```
(defmacro make-synonym [new-name old-name]
  `(defmacro ~new-name [& ~'stuff]
     `(~old-name ~@~'stuff)))
```

Here's the expansion:

```
user> (macroexpand-1 '(make-synonym b binding))
(clojure.core/defmacro b [& stuff]
  (clojure.core/seq (clojure.core/concat
                       (clojure.core/list user/old-name) stuff)))
```

Finally, we'll fix the issue with `user/old-name`:

```
(defmacro make-synonym [new-name old-name]
  `(defmacro ~new-name [& ~'stuff]
     `(~'~old-name ~@~'stuff)))
```

And here's the expansion:

```
user> (macroexpand-1 '(make-synonym b binding))
(clojure.core/defmacro b [& stuff]
  (clojure.core/seq (clojure.core/concat
    (clojure.core/list (quote binding)) stuff)))
```

To check to see if this is what we expect, let's compare it with our original template:

```
(defmacro b [& stuff]
  `(binding ~@stuff))
```

This is indeed what we set out to do, and you can test it as follows:

```
user> (declare x y)
#'user/y

user> (make-synonym b binding)
#'user/b

user> (b [x 10 y 20] (println "X,Y:" x y))
X,Y: 10 20
nil
```

Phew, we're finished. That was a lot of calisthenics for three lines of code. We'll wrap up this section with why we even bothered with this somewhat esoteric code.

WHY MACRO-GENERATING MACROS

There are at least two reasons why it's useful to know how to write macros that generate macros. The first is the same reason you'd write any other kind of macro: to create abstractions that remove the duplication that arises from patterns in the code. This is important when these duplications are structural and are difficult to eliminate without some form of code generation. Clojure macros are an excellent tool to do this job, because they give the programmer the full power of Clojure to do it. The fact that code generation is a language-level feature does pull its weight.

Having said this, although writing macros is a common thing to do in a Clojure program, it isn't often the case that a macro generates another macro. You'll probably do it only a handful of times in your career. Combined with the other usages you've seen, such as moving computation to compile time and intentional symbol capture—the few times when you do need macros to abstract patterns out of macros themselves—writing macros to generate macros can lead to a solution that would be difficult without the technique.

The second reason, and the more commonly useful one, for knowing this concept is to drive home the process of macro expansion, quoting, and unquoting. If you can understand and write macros that generate macros, then you'll have no trouble writing simpler ones.

With these topics about macro writing out of the way, we're ready to move on to a couple of examples. In the next section, we'll look at using macros to create domain-specific languages (DSLs).

15.2 Domain-specific languages

We're now going to look at explicitly doing something we've been doing implicitly so far. In several chapters, we've written macros that appear to add features to the Clojure language itself. An example is def-worker, which allowed us to create functions that can run on multiple worker machines in a cluster. We also created a simple object system with most of the semantics of regular object-oriented languages. We created def-modus-operandi, which allowed multimethods to be used in a manner similar to Clojure protocols. We won't list all the other examples here, because it should be clear that macros have helped us in presenting our abstractions as a convenient feature of the language.

In this section, we're going to further explore the idea of wrapping our abstractions in a layer of language. Taking this idea to its logical end brings us to the concept of metalinguistic abstraction—the approach of creating a domain-specific language that's then used to solve the problem at hand. It allows us to solve not only the problem we started out with but a whole class of problems in that domain. It leaves us with a system that's highly flexible and maintainable, while staying small and easier to understand and debug. Let's begin by examining the design philosophy that leads to such systems.

15.2.1 DSL-driven design

When given the requirements of a software program, the first step usually involves thinking about what approach to take. This might end with a big design session that produces a detailed breakdown of the various components and pieces that will compose the final solution. This often goes hand in hand with the traditional top-down decomposition technique of taking something large and complex and breaking it into pieces that are smaller, independent, and easier to understand.

By itself, this approach has been known to not work particularly well in most cases. This is because the requirements for most systems are never specified perfectly, which causes the system to be redesigned in ways big and small. Many times, the requirements explicitly change over time as the reality of the business itself changes. This is why most agile teams prefer an evolutionary design, one that arises from incrementally building the system to satisfy more and more of the requirements over time.

When such an approach is desirable (and few systems can do without it these days), it makes sense to think not only in a top-down manner but also in a bottom-up way. Decomposing a problem in a bottom-up manner is different from the top-down version. With the bottom-up approach, you create small abstractions on top of the core programming language to handle tiny elements of the problem domain. These domain-specific primitives are created without explicit thought to exactly how they'll eventually be used to solve the original problem. Indeed, at this stage, the idea is to create primitives that model all the low-level details of the problem domain.

The other area of focus is combinability. The various domain primitives should be combinable into more-complex entities as desired. This can be done using either the combinability features of the programming language itself (for instance, Clojure's functions) or by creating new domain-specific constructs on top of existing ones. Macros can help with such extensions, because they can manipulate code forms with ease.

Functional programming aids in the pursuit of such a design. In addition to recursive and conditional constructs, being able to treat functions as first-class objects allows higher levels of complexity and abstraction to be managed in a more natural manner. Being able to create lexical closures adds another powerful piece to our toolset. When higher-order functions, closures, and macros are used together, the domain primitives can be combined to solve more than the original problem specified in the requirements document. It can solve a whole class of problems in that domain, because what gets created at the end of such a bottom-up process is a rich set of primitives, operators, and forms for combination that closely models the business domain itself.

The final layers of such a system consist of two pieces. The topmost is literally the respecification of the requirements in an executable, domain-specific language. This is metalinguistic abstraction, manifested in the fact that the final piece of the system that seems to solve the problem is written not in a general-purpose programming language but in a language that has been grown organically from a lower-level programming language. It's often understandable by nonprogrammers and indeed is sometimes suitable for them to use directly. The next piece is a sort of runtime adapter, which either executes the domain-specific code by interpreting it or by compiling it down to the language's own primitives. An example may be a set of macros that translate the syntactically friendly code into other forms, and code that sets up the right evaluation context for it. Figure 15.2 shows a block diagram of the various layers described.

It's useful to point out that a domain-specific language isn't about using macros, even though they're often a big part of the final linguistics. Macros help with fluency of the language, especially as used by the end users but also at lower levels to help create

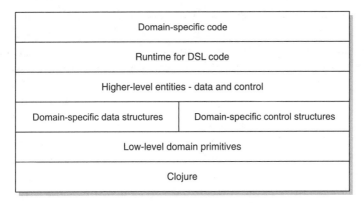

Figure 15.2 The typical layers in a DSL-driven system are shown here. Such systems benefit from a bottom-up design where the lowest levels are the primitive concepts of the domain modeled on top of the basic Clojure language. Higher layers are compositions of these primitives into more complex domain concepts. Finally, a runtime layer sits on top of these, which can execute code specified in a domain-specific language. This final layer often represents the core solution of the problem that the software was meant to solve.

the abstractions themselves. In this way, they're no different from other available features of the language such as higher-order functions and conditionals. The point to remember is that the core of the DSL approach is the resulting bottom-up design and the set of easily combinable domain primitives.

In the next section, we'll explore the creation of a simple domain-specific language.

15.2.2 User classification

Most websites today personalize the experience for individual users. Many go beyond simple preferences and use the users' own usage statistics to improve their experience. Amazon, for example, does a great job of this by showing users things they might like to buy based on their own purchase history and browsing patterns. Other web services use similarly collected usage statistics to show more relevant ads to users as they browse. In this section, we'll explore this business domain.

The goal here is to use data about the user to do something special for them. It could be showing ads or making the site more specific to their tastes. The first step in any such task is to know what kind of user it is. Usually, the system can recognize several classes of users and is able to personalize the experience for each class in some way. The user has to be classified into the known segments before anything can be done. The business folks would like to be able to change the specification of the various segments as they're discovered, so the system shouldn't hardcode this aspect. Further, they'd like to make such changes quickly, potentially without requiring development effort and without requiring a restart of the system after making such changes. In an ideal world, they'd even like to specify the segment descriptions in a nice little GUI application.

This example is well suited to our earlier discussion, but aspects of this apply to most nontrivial systems being built today. For this example in particular, we'll build a domain-specific language to specify the rules that classify users into various segments. To get started, we'll describe the lay of the land, which in our case will be a small part of the overall system design, as well as a few functions available to find information about our users.

THE DATA ELEMENT

We'll model a few primitive domain-specific data elements. We'll focus our example on things that can be gleaned from the data that users' browsers send to the server along with every request. There's nothing to stop you from extending this approach to things that are looked up from elsewhere, such as a database of the users' past behavior, or indeed anything else, such as stock quotes or the weather in Hawaii. We'll model the session data as a simple Clojure map containing the data elements we care about, and we'll store it in Redis. We'll not focus on how we create the session map, because this example isn't about parsing strings or loading data from various data stores.

Here's an example of a user session:

```
{:consumer-id "abc"
 :url-referrer "http://www.google.com/search?q=clojure+programmers"
 :search-terms ["clojure" "programmers"]
 :ip-address "192.168.0.10"
 :tz-offset 420
 :user-agent :safari}
```

Again, sessions can contain a lot more than what comes in via the web request. You can imagine loads of precomputed information being stored in such a session to enable more useful targeting as well as a caching technique so that things don't have to be loaded or computed more than once in a user's session.

USER SESSION PERSISTENCE

We'll need a key to store such sessions in Redis, and for this example `:consumer-id` will serve us well. We'll add a level of indirection so the code will read better as well as let us change this decision later if we desire:

```
(def redis-key-for :consumer-id)
```

Let's now define a way to save sessions into Redis and also to load them back out. Here's a pair of functions that do that:

```
(defn save-session [session]
  (redis/set (redis-key-for session) (pr-str session)))

(defn find-session [consumer-id]
  (read-string (redis/get consumer-id)))
```

Now that we have the essential capability of storing and loading sessions, we have a design decision to make. If we consider the user session to be the central concept in our behavioral targeting domain, then we can write it such that the DSL always executes in context of a session. We could define a var called `*session*` that we'll then bind to the specific one during a computation:

```
(declare *session*)
```

And we could define a convenience macro that sets up the binding:

```
(defmacro in-session [consumer-id & body]
  `(binding [*session* (find-session ~consumer-id)]
     (do ~@body)))
```

The following listing shows the complete session namespace that we've defined so far.

Listing 15.2   Basic functions to handle session persistence in Redis

```
(ns chapter-macros.session
  (:require redis))

(def redis-key-for :consumer-id)

(declare *session*)

(defn save-session [session]
  (redis/set (redis-key-for session) (pr-str session)))

(defn find-session [consumer-id]
  (read-string (redis/get consumer-id)))

(defmacro in-session [consumer-id & body]
  `(binding [*session* (find-session ~consumer-id)]
     (do ~@body)))
```

Now that we've dealt with persisting user sessions, we'll focus on the segmentation itself.

SEGMENTING USERS

We're going to now talk about the process of describing user segmentation. In our application, we'd like to satisfy two qualitative requirements of this segmentation process. The first is that these rules shouldn't be hardcoded into our application and that it should be possible to dynamically update the rules. The second is that these rules should be expressed in a format that's somewhat analyst friendly. It should be in a domain-specific language that's somewhat simpler for nonprogrammers to express ideas in. Here's an example of something we might allow:

```
(defsegment googling-clojurians
    (and
      (> (count $search-terms) 0)
      (matches? $url-referrer "google")))
```

Here's another example of the desired language:

```
(defsegment loyal-safari
    (and
      (empty? $url-referrer)
      (= :safari $user-agent)))
```

Notice the symbols prefixed with $. These are meant to have special significance in our DSL, because they're the elements that will be looked up and substituted from the user's session. Our job now is to implement def-segment so that the previous definition is compiled into something meaningful.

> ### Syntax of Clojure DSLs
>
> In many programming languages, especially dynamic ones such as Ruby and Python, domain-specific languages have become all the rage. There are two kinds of DSLs: internal and external. Internal DSLs are hosted on top of a language such as Ruby and use the underlying language to execute the DSL code. External DSLs are limited forms of regular programming languages in the sense that they have a lexer and parser that convert DSL code that conforms to a grammar into executable code. Internal DSLs are often simpler and serve most requirements that a DSL might need to satisfy.
>
> Such DSLs are often focused on providing English-like readability, and a lot of text-parsing code is dedicated to converting the easy-to-read text into constructs of the underlying language. Clojure, on the other hand, has its magical reader. It can read an entire character stream and convert it into a form that can be executed. The programmer doesn't have to do anything to support the lexical analysis, tokenizing, and parsing. Clojure even provides a macro system to further enhance the capabilities of textual expression.
>
> This is the reason why many Clojure DSLs look much like Clojure. Clojure DSLs are often based on s-expressions because using the reader to do the heavy lifting of creating a little language is the most straightforward thing to do. The book *DSLs in Action* by Debasish Ghosh (Manning Publications) is a great resource if you're interested in DSLs in a variety of languages.

We can start with a macro skeleton that looks like this:

```
(defmacro defsegment [segment-name & body])
```

Let's begin by handling the $ prefixes. We'll transform the body expressions such that all symbols prefixed by the $ will be transformed into a session lookup of an attribute with the same name. Something like $user-agent will become (:user-agent *sessions*). To perform this transformation, we'll need to recursively walk the body expression to find all the symbols that need this substitution and then rebuild a new expression with the substitutions made. Luckily, we don't have to write this code because it exists in the clojure.walk namespace. The postwalk function fits the bill:

```
user> (doc postwalk)
-----------------------
clojure.walk/postwalk
([f form])
  Performs a depth-first, post-order traversal of form.  Calls f on
  each sub-form, uses f's return value in place of the original.
  Recognizes all Clojure data structures except sorted-map-by.
  Consumes seqs as with doall.
nil
```

This is what we need, so we can transform our DSL code using the following function:

```
(defn transform-lookups [dollar-attribute]
  (let [prefixed-string (str dollar-attribute)]
    (if-not (.startsWith prefixed-string "$")
      dollar-attribute
      (session-lookup prefixed-string))))
```

We'll need a couple of support functions, namely, session-lookup and drop-first-char, which can be implemented as follows:

```
(defn drop-first-char [name]
  (apply str (rest name)))

(defn session-lookup [dollar-name]
  (->> (drop-first-char dollar-name)
       (keyword)
       (list '*session*)))
```

Let's test that the code we wrote does what's expected:

```
user> (transform-lookups '$user-agent)
(*session* :user-agent)
```

This is a simple test, but note that the resulting form can be used to look up attributes of a user session if the *session* special var is bound appropriately.

Now, let's use postwalk to test our replacement logic on a slightly more complex form:

```
user> (postwalk transform-lookups '(> (count $search-terms) 0))
(> (count (*session* :search-terms)) 0)
```

That works as expected. We now have a tool to transform the DSL body expressed using our $-prefixed symbols into usable Clojure code. As an aside, we also have a place where we can make more complex replacements if we need to.

We can now use this in our definition of defsegment as follows:

```
(defmacro defsegment [segment-name & body]
  (let [transformed (postwalk transform-lookups body)])
```

We've now transformed the body as specified by the user of our DSL, and we now need to convert it into something we can execute later. Let's look at what we're working with:

```
user> (postwalk transform-lookups '(and
                                      (> (count $search-terms) 0)
                                      (= :safari $user-agent)))
(and
  (> (count (*session* :search-terms)) 0)
  (= :safari (*session* :user-agent)))
```

The simplest way to execute this later is to convert it into a function. You can then call the function whenever you need to run this rule. We used a similar approach when we defined our remote worker framework, where we stored computations as anonymous functions that were executed on remote servers. If we're going to do this, we'll need a place to put the functions. We'll create a new namespace to keep all code related to this storing of functions for later use. It's shown in the following listing.

```
(ns chapter-macros.dsl-store)

(def RULES (ref {}))

(defn register-segment [segment-name segment-fn]
  (dosync
   (alter RULES assoc-in [:segments segment-name] segment-fn)))

(defn segment-named [segment-name]
  (get-in @RULES [:segments segment-name]))

(defn all-segments []
  (:segments @RULES))
```

Now that you know you can put functions where you can find them again later, we're ready to improve our definition of `defsegment`:

```
(defmacro defsegment [segment-name & body]
  (let [transformed (postwalk transform-lookups body)]
    `(let [segment-fn# (fn [] ~@transformed)]
       (register-segment ~(keyword segment-name) segment-fn#))))
```

We now have all the pieces together for our DSL to compile. The next listing shows the complete segment namespace.

```
(ns chapter-macros.segment
  (:use chapter-macros.dsl-store
        clojure.walk))

(defn drop-first-char [name]
  (apply str (rest name)))

(defn session-lookup [dollar-name]
  (->> (drop-first-char dollar-name)
       (keyword)
       (list '*session*)))

(defn transform-lookups [dollar-attribute]
  (let [prefixed-string (str dollar-attribute)]
    (if-not (.startsWith prefixed-string "$")
      dollar-attribute
      (session-lookup prefixed-string))))

(defmacro defsegment [segment-name & body]
  (let [transformed (postwalk transform-lookups body)]
    `(let [segment-fn# (fn [] ~@transformed)]
       (register-segment ~(keyword segment-name) segment-fn#))))
```

Here it is in action, at the REPL:

```
user> (defsegment loyal-safari
        (and
          (empty? $url-referrer)
```

```
          (= :safari $user-agent)))
{:segments
  {:loyal-safari
     #<user$eval3457$segment_fn__3232__auto____3458
       user$eval3457$segment_fn__3232__auto____3458@5054c2b8>}}
```

Our definition of googling-clojurians still won't work, because it will complain about an unknown matches? function. We're going to solve this and add more functionality in the next couple of sections.

THE POWER OF THE DSL

So far, we've put together the plumbing of the DSL. You can define some DSL code and expect it to compile and some functions to be created and stored as a result. At least three things influence how powerful our DSL can be.

The first, obviously, is the data inside a user's session. Entities such as $url-referrer and $search-terms are examples of this. These data elements are obtained either directly from the web session of the user, from historical data about the user, or from any other source that has been used to load information into the user's session.

The second factor is the number of primitives that can be used to manipulate the data elements. Examples of such primitives are empty? and count. We've leveraged Clojure's own functions here, but there's nothing to stop you from adding more. The function matches? that we'll add shortly is an example of such an addition.

The final factor is combinability, which is to say how the data elements and the language primitives can be combined to create more complex forms. Here again you can use all of Clojure's built-in facilities. For example, in our previous examples, we used and and >.

In the next section, we'll focus on creating new primitives, and then we'll write code to execute the DSL.

ADDING PRIMITIVES TO THE EXECUTION ENGINE

As you can imagine, matches? is a function. For the purposes of our example here, it can be as simple as this:

```
(defn matches? [^String superset ^String subset]
  (and
   (not (empty? superset))
   (> (.indexOf superset subset) 0)))
```

You can add more functions such as this one, and they can be as complex as needed. The user of the DSL doesn't need to know how they're implemented, because they'll be described as the primitives of the domain-specific language.

Now, let's go ahead and define the remainder of the execution engine. The first piece is a function to load up with the DSL program. Typically, this will be some text either written by a user or generated by another program such as a graphical rules editor. Given that ultimately the DSL is Clojure code, you can use load-string to load it. Consider the following code:

```
(ns chapter-macros.engine
  (:use chapter-macros.segment
```

```
          chapter-macros.session
          chapter-macros.dsl-store))

(defn load-code [code-string]
  (binding [*ns* (:ns (meta load-code))]
    (load-string code-string)))
```

Note that the load-code function first switches the namespace to its own, because all
supporting functions are available in it. This way, load-code can be called from anywhere, and all supporting functions can be found. It then calls load-string.

   Our next step is to execute a segment function and to see if it returns true or
false. A true value means that the user belongs to that segment. The following function checks this:

```
(defn segment-satisfied? [[segment-name segment-fn]]
  (if (segment-fn)
    segment-name))
```

You now have all the pieces to take a bunch of segment definitions and classify a user
into one or more of them (or none of them). Consider the classify function:

```
(defn classify []
  (->> (all-segments)
       (map segment-satisfied?)
       (remove nil?)))
```

The complete source of our engine namespace is shown in the following listing.

Listing 15.5   The simple DSL execution engine to classify users into segments
---

```
(ns chapter-macros.engine
  (:use chapter-macros.segment
        chapter-macros.session
        chapter-macros.dsl-store))

(defn load-code [code-string]
  (binding [*ns* (:ns (meta load-code))]
    (load-string code-string)))

(defn matches? [^String superset ^String subset]
  (and
   (not (empty? superset))
   (> (.indexOf superset subset) 0)))

(defn segment-satisfied? [[segment-name segment-fn]]
  (if (segment-fn)
    segment-name))

(defn classify []
  (->> (all-segments)
       (map segment-satisfied?)
       (remove nil?)))
```

Let's test it at the REPL. We'll begin by creating a string that contains our definitions
of the two segments in our new DSL:

```
user> (def dsl-code (str
  '(defsegment googling-clojurians
```

```
     (and
       (> (count $search-terms) 0)
       (matches? $url-referrer "google")))
   '(defsegment loyal-safari
       (and
         (empty? $url-referrer)
         (= :safari $user-agent)))))
#'user/dsl-code
```

Next, we'll bring in our little DSL engine:

```
user> (use 'chapter-macros.engine)
nil
```

It's now easy to load up the segment definitions:

```
user> (load-code dsl-code)
{:segments {:loyal-safari #<engine$eval3399$segment_fn__2833_
TRUNCATED OUTPUT
```

In order to test classification, we're going to need a user session and Redis running. We can set up a session for testing purposes by defining one at the REPL as follows:

```
user> (def abc-session {
      :consumer-id "abc"
      :url-referrer "http://www.google.com/search?q=clojure+programmers"
      :search-terms ["clojure" "programmers"]
      :ip-address "192.168.0.10"
      :tz-offset 480
      :user-agent :safari})
#'user/abc-session
```

And let's put it into Redis:

```
user> (require 'redis) (use 'chapter-macros.session)
nil

user> (redis/with-server {:host "localhost"}
          (save-session abc-session))
"OK"
```

Everything is set up now, and we can test segmentation:

```
user> (redis/with-server {:host "localhost"}
          (in-session "abc"
            (println "The current user is in:" (classify))))
The current user is in: (:googling-clojurians)
nil
```

It works as expected. Note that the classify function returns a lazy sequence that's realized by the call to println. If you were to omit that, you'd need a doall to see it at the REPL; otherwise, it will complain about the *session* var not being bound.

With this, we have the basics working end to end. Expanding the DSL is as easy as adding new data elements and new primitives such as the matches? function. We can also expand the $attribute syntax by doing more in the postwalk transformation.

Before addressing updating rules, we'll add a way to name the abstractions we're defining and allow for segments to be reused.

INCREASING COMBINABILITY

Imagine that you'd like to narrow the scope of the googling-clojurians crowd. You'd like to know which of these folks are also using the Chrome browser. You could create a segment as follows:

```
(defsegment googling-clojurians-chrome
    (and
     (> (count $search-terms) 0)
     (matches? $url-referrer "google")
     (= :chrome $user-agent))))
```

This will work fine, but it has the obvious problem that two out of the three conditions are duplicated in the googling-clojurians segment. In a normal programming language, creating a named entity and replacing the duplicate code in both places with that entity can remove such duplication. For example, you could create a Clojure function and call it from both places.

If you do that, you'll expose the lower-level details of the implementation of our DSL to the eventual users of the DSL. It would be ideal if you could hide that detail while letting them use named entities. Consider this revised implementation of def-segment:

```
(defmacro defsegment [segment-name & body]
  (let [transformed (postwalk transform-lookups body)]
    `(let [segment-fn#  (fn [] ~@transformed)]
       (register-segment ~(keyword segment-name) segment-fn#)
       (def ~segment-name segment-fn#))))
```

The change we made does what we talked about doing by hand. The definition of a segment now also creates a var by the same name. It can be used as follows:

```
(defsegment googling-clojurians-chrome
    (and
     (googling-clojurians)
     (= :chrome $user-agent)))
```

This is equivalent in functionality to the previous definition of this segment, with the duplication removed. This is an example of increasing the combinability of domain-specific entities, where segment definitions are built on top of the lower-level session-lookup primitives, combined with built-in logical operators. Note that because our DSL code is all executed within a single namespace, we have a single namespace going. This could cause problems with name conflicts, and this may need to be addressed, depending on the requirements.

Another example of a language-level construct is in-session, which given a customer id sets up the execution context for classification. It abstracts away the details of where the session is stored and how to access and load it.

Although this is a small example, we've explored several of the concepts we talked about in the opening discussion. The last step will be to look at how the DSL can be updated dynamically.

DYNAMIC UPDATES

With the DSL, we've exposed a linguistic layer to the code that follows. We also said we would like to add dynamic updates to the rules. You've already seen that, but we didn't focus on it. Consider again a definition such as this:

```
(defsegment googling-clojurians
    (and
     (> (count $search-terms) 0)
     (matches? $url-referrer "yahoo")))
```

You know that evaluating this code will change the definition of the segment known as googling-clojurians (not to mention that it's named incorrectly, because Yahoo search is being used). But the following code has the same effect:

```
(load-code (str '(defsegment googling-clojurians
    (and
     (> (count $search-terms) 0)
     (matches? $url-referrer "yahoo")))))
```

The point to note, if not already obvious, is that load-code accepts a string. This DSL code snippet can be created anywhere, even from outside our execution engine. It could be created, say, from a text editor and loaded in via a web service.

Let's take another example by imagining you had a set of remote worker processes that implemented our rule engine to classify users into segments. You can imagine classify being implemented using def-worker. When sent a request, it will access a commonly available Redis server, find the specified user session, and classify the user into segments. This is no different from what you've seen earlier, except for the fact that this code would run on multiple remote servers.

Now, let's imagine load-code also being implemented as a def-worker. In this scenario, not only could you remotely load DSL code, but you could also use run-worker-everywhere to broadcast DSL updates across all remote workers. You'd get the ability to update our segmentation cluster in real time, with no code to deploy. This change requires very little code, thanks to our remote workers framework from the previous chapters, and the implementation is left as an exercise to you.

We'll end this section with one last point. We haven't addressed error checking the DSL code so far, and in a production system you'd definitely need to do that. We've also built quite a minimal domain-specific language, and you could certainly make it arbitrarily powerful. Being able to use the full Clojure language inside it is a powerful feature that can be used by power users if so desired. As the capability of the DSL itself is expanded to do more than segmentation, the ability to update running code in such a simple way as described previously could prove to be useful.

15.3   Summary

We're at the end of this chapter and of this book. We left macros for the end because they're special. When most people start out with the Lisp family of programming languages, they first ask about the odd syntax. The answer to that question is the macro system. In that sense, we've come full circle. Macros are special because they make Clojure a programmable programming language. They allow the programmer to mold the core language into one that suits the problem at hand. In this way, Clojure blurs the line between the designers of the language itself and the programmer.

This chapter started with a few advanced uses of Clojure macros. Anaphoric macros aren't used a lot, and they certainly come with their gotchas, but when applied carefully, they can result in truly elegant solutions. Similarly, moving computation into the compile phase of your program seems like something that isn't done often. Certainly, the example we looked at gives only a glimpse into what's possible. It's an important technique, though, that can be effective when needed. Finally, macros that define other macros threaten to send us down the rabbit hole. Understanding such use of the macro system is the only way to true Lisp mastery.

Lisp encourages a certain style of programming. Everyone seems to be talking about domain-specific languages these days, but in Clojure, it's the normal way to build programs, and there's nothing advanced about it at all. It's my hope that our behavioral targeting DSL example didn't seem particularly complicated or new. We've written similar code throughout this book, be it our mocking framework to help us write tests, our object system utility, our library for distributed stream processing, or our faux protocols library we called modus operandi. Some people express concern about the misuse of macros, but I believe that the real concern should be an incomplete understanding of the Lisp way.

What you've seen in this book is only the tip of the iceberg. Lisp, and thus Clojure, makes it possible to build systems that can withstand today's demanding requirements. It isn't far-fetched to think that the revival of Lisp will prompt systems that can someday do what we mean. In order to do that, we'll need more than a few language features or a macro system. We'll need more than DSLs.

We'll need a system that can adapt itself to new and changing requirements. Programmers will need to recognize that evaluators are themselves programs, and they can be built like everything else, allowing new kinds of evaluation rules and paradigms. We'll need programs that watch themselves as they run and modify themselves to improve their output. All this might seem like fantasy, but it's possible. In the words of Alan Kay, the computer revolution hasn't even started yet. And paraphrasing him some more, the way to build systems that can do all this is to play it grand. We have to build our systems grander than we think they can be. A language like Clojure gives us the tools to make this happen.

index